Scioto County, Ohio, Newspaper Index

Scioto County, Ohio, Newspaper Index

Deaths and Marriages
1818 to 1865

Barbara Keyser Gargiulo

Little Miami Publishing Co., Milford, Ohio

Little Miami Publishing Co.
P.O. Box 588
Milford, Ohio 45150-0588
Copies of this book can be obtained by contacting the publisher.

Edited by Kimberly A. Peet

Printed in the United States of America

ISBN 0-9666489-0-0

Library of Congress Catalog Card Number 98-091702

Contents

WEDDINGS AND FUNERALS—An exchange says, "it is a fact worthy of noting that since the beginning of the rebellion more marriages have taken place than during any previous period of the same duration." The same observation is true of funerals—and that's worthy of note, too.

—*Portsmouth Times*
21 Nov 1863

Preface

For the professional genealogist, or for those interested in learning more about their own family history, newspaper articles relating to deaths and marriages can be valuable resources. From these articles, you can learn about birth places, parents, siblings and their places of residence, occupations and organizational involvement, and religious affiliations. Information in newspaper notices and articles can describe events leading to a person's death that could not be found on a death certificate, or where a marriage took place that would not be indicated on a marriage certificate. However, if you do not know what dates to use for your search, and a marriage or death index is not available, this information can be difficult to find.

I have been rewarded with an abundance of information and leads on family members from articles in various newspapers, in both German and English, that I never would have found without the aid of an index to those notices. While researching my Scioto County roots, I realized that the newspapers could give me greater insight—but only if I knew where to look. Unfortunately, even though many resources are available to aid the family researcher in Scioto County, no newspaper index existed. Without an index, finding information on all family members would be a long, arduous task. Therefore, with the help of archivists, librarians, and family members, I began the task of indexing every paper that I could find that was printed in Scioto County, Ohio, beginning with the year 1818. A list of newspapers, their repositories, and call numbers is provided in Appendix A for convenience.

My indexing project began in the History and Genealogy Department of the Portsmouth Public Library. Further research was accomplished by ordering microfilm from the Ohio Historical Society Library Archives in Columbus, Ohio, and the Ohio University Library in Athens, Ohio, through interlibrary loan departments at The Public Library of Cincinnati and Hamilton County in Cincinnati, Ohio, and the Clermont County Library in Milford, Ohio. After researching all the microfilmed rolls, I then spent many days and weeks in the library of the Ohio Historical Society reading original papers that had not been microfilmed, that were stored in the stacks or vault. Every paper that was available to me for the years included in this index, whether hard copy or microfilm, was indexed. Although the first volume of this index ends in 1865, further indexing already has begun for later years.

I intended to index only the notices of marriages and deaths. However, I soon realized that deaths were not always listed under the heading "Died," but often were written within the text as a current news event. Therefore, I went through the papers again and indexed additional names from many news articles.

While indexing the notices and articles, I noticed that some of the communities mentioned were unfamiliar to me and could no longer be found on a map. Therefore, I began researching the history of the various towns and communities and found that many either no longer exist or have experienced name changes. Many of these can be found in Appendix B.

Although every effort has been made to make the contents of this book as accurate as possible, I realize that mistakes are evident in such a compilation and will readily welcome any and all corrections that the reader or researcher may find.

While working on this project, many people helped along the way and deserve my thanks. Carolyn Cottrell and Betsy DeMent, the knowledgeable and personable librarians at the Portsmouth Public Library, warmly welcomed me and my project to their History and Genealogy Department, providing me with information and helping in whatever way they could. Also, the entire staff in the library archives at the Ohio Historical Society, from reference to interlibrary loan, was always helpful, courteous, and considerate. In addition, the reference and interloan librarians at the Ohio University Library were most helpful. I am also grateful to Carl and Elizabeth Shamhart for sharing their research on Scioto County post offices, enlightening me about many community name changes that occurred within the county.

A special thanks goes to my daughter, Kimberly Peet, who juggled her time among family, graduate school, and work to edit this book and put it into a format suitable for print, not to mention providing room and board for the time that I had to spend in Columbus.

My greatest appreciation goes to my husband, Joe, whose encouragement and support I greatly needed and received, during the many days and weeks that I spent away from home.

On behalf of myself and every person who will find these materials helpful, I would like to thank the Ohio Historical Society for preserving and making available to us all, the newspapers of Scioto County, Ohio.

B. K. G.

Introduction

Society was very dynamic during the last century and Portsmouth, especially, experienced a hub of riverboat activity, being both situated on the Ohio River and the site of the terminus of the Ohio-Erie Canal. Many people stayed in one place for a while, then moved on as more territory opened to the west. They often left family in Scioto County, as well as back east. When a family moved either across the territory or only to the next county, court records of their marriages and deaths cannot be found in Scioto County. The local papers, however, often copied notices and articles from other papers in surrounding counties and states, as well as territorial reports, and printed them in their own papers. This Scioto County, Ohio, index is designed to help the professional or novice genealogist, historian, or biographer find clues to an individual's background that will lead to further research.

With this in mind, this first volume lists more than deaths and marriages that occurred within the boundaries of Scioto County. It also includes, among others, deaths resulting from Indian raids, duels, steamboat and rail accidents, cholera and yellow fever, and reports of unusual deaths and marriages as extracted from other papers. The famous and infamous are included, from Presidents to notorious criminals. The primary focus for this index is on local reports or items of local interest, and an effort was made to include them all.

When a researcher finds someone listed in this index, then proceeds to find the original article in which he or she was mentioned, additional information can be obtained from local civil or church sources, if in Scioto County. If the article or notice was extracted from another newspaper, then more research can be conducted in the county or state from which that article originated.

Some names can be found more than once for a death or marriage, if the notice was printed on more than one date in a particular newspaper or was printed in more than one newspaper. Spellings of names can differ between dates or papers; additional information may be found by researching all dates and papers listed. The following explanation of the index format describes what can be found in this volume.

Contents of Indices

Contents of Death Notice Index

Deaths are listed beginning on page 15; they contain the following information:

Name: Surname (or family name), followed by the given name and/or initial, followed by any title that may have been listed. Often, a female's given name was not mentioned, but that of her husband was. In this case, the surname is followed by the word "female." If a male's name was not listed, the word "male" follows. If both the given name and gender are unknown, the word "unknown" follows. A sexton's report seldom mentions the name of a child, but typically mentions the full name of a parent instead. *Note that the names are printed as they are found in the paper. The printer may have misspelled the name; therefore, it is beneficial to look for all spelling variations.*

Notice Date: All date(s) on which a newspaper notice or article can be found. *Note that occasionally, the printer forgot to change a date for the next publication or only changed the date on the first or second page. This may have continued for several publications. If you are unsuccessful in finding the name on the date listed in this index, try the following or preceding date.*

Death Date: The date of death reported or implied by the paper. Many notices contain the word "ultimo" or "ult.," which refers to the prior month, or "instant" or "inst.," which refers to the present month. In some cases, if the notice appeared to be incorrect or was otherwise confusing, the date was omitted in this index. In these cases, the reader may consult the source paper to try to determine the correct interpretation. *Note that the sexton's reported date also is listed here, but it may be the date of interment rather than the actual date of death. If the date came from a sexton's report, the notation (S) follows the abbreviation given for the paper. See also "Paper" on page 3.*

Age: The person's age listed in the paper. If only the number of years is indicated in the paper, a number appears in this column. If more exacting information is given, then a letter for years (y), months (m), weeks (w), and/or days (d) is indicated. If an average or range was given, one year was assigned.

Comments: Any details that do not fall into the categories previously described. Maiden names are indicated by "nee." Finding clues of African-American descent have been difficult for some researchers; therefore, if descriptive terms such as "colored," "negro," or "slave" were given, they are provided here. Also, references to Native Americans are addressed in this column. Other self-explanatory remarks also can be found here.

Paper: An abbreviation (or set of initials) for the newspaper where the complete article or notice can be found. See "Newspaper History" on page 11 for a list of Scioto County newspapers and their assigned abbreviations. The notation (S) after the abbreviation indicates a sexton's report.

Contents of Marriage Notice Index

The marriage notice index is listed twice: first by groom's name and then by bride's name. The list organized by groom's name begins on page 119. The list organized by bride's name begins on page 157.

Name (Groom): The groom's name. The names follow the format described in "Name" on page 2. In the marriage notices listed by groom's name, the names are listed in alphabetical order by groom's surname.

Name (Bride): The bride's name. The names follow the format described in "Name" on page 2. In the marriage notices listed by bride's name, the names are listed in alphabetical order by bride's surname. If the bride was previously married, and if the maiden name was listed, both are indexed.

Notice Date: The newspaper publication date. See "Notice Date" on page 2 for further information.

Marriage Date: The marriage date as reported in the paper. See "Death Date" on page 2 for further information about dates.

Paper: The abbreviation for the newspaper in which the complete article or notice can be found. See "Paper" above for further information.

Marriages

Scioto County marriages have been recorded from the early 1800s, and they typically provide the main facts: groom's name, bride's name, and date of marriage. Sometimes, however, newspaper notices provide additional information that is of interest to the researcher. In addition to naming the person who performed the ceremony, for example, the home, church, hotel, or other location of the wedding may be mentioned. Some notices provide the names of the bride's and/or groom's parents. The following excerpts are examples of such notices.

On Tuesday evening, Sept. 19th, by Rev. S.P. Cummins, Mr. JOHN HILL, of California, to Miss ELIZA A. REDDICK, eldest Daughter of Wm. Reddick Esq., of Wheelersburg. This couple start to California on the first of October next.

—The Daily Evening Dispatch
20 September 1854

January 26th, by Rev. N. P. Bailey of Painesville, Orrin B. Gould, Esq. of Franklin Furnace, Scioto Co., and Mrs. Lavinia S. Willard, daughter of Uri Seeley, Esq., of Painesville.

—Weekly Portsmouth Tribune
2 Feb 1859

If the wedding took place outside Scioto County, a newspaper notice may be the quickest way to trace the family. Also, notices may have been submitted well after the ceremony took place. The following example typifies the above-mentioned conditions, and gives a clue to this widow's maiden name.

Married. At the residence of R. P. Sow, Esq., at Bloomington, Iowa. By the Reverend Mr. Stoeker, on Thursday 28th Nov. Mr. G. W. Humphries, Sheriff of Musketeen County, Iowa Territory, to Mrs. Martha J. Aldrich, daughter of the Rev. J. R. Turner, of Portsmouth, Ohio.

—Tribune
2 Jan 1845

Some newspapers required payment for insertion of the marriage notice. At times, with or without a payment, the staff was surprised by the delivery of wedding cake. The surprise prompted the newspaper staff to send their special wishes to the newlyweds, along with their thanks for the delicious dessert. The idea for such enticements may have arisen from the following notice.

MARRIAGE NOTICESS [*sic*]—A western paper gives the following notice: all notices of marriages where no *bride cake* is sent, will be set up in small type, and poked into some outlandish corner of the paper. Where a handsome piece of cake is sent, it will be placed conspicuously in *large letters*; but when *gloves*, or other bride favors are added, a piece of illustrative poetry will be given in addition. When, however, the Editor attends the ceremony in propria personæ and kisses the bride, it will have a *special notice*: VERY LARGE TYPE, and the most appropriate poetry that can be begged, borrowed, stolen, or coined from the brain editorial.

—*Portsmouth Tribune*
14 July 1843

Poetry was very popular in those days, and newspaper editors and copywriters often could not contain themselves when it came to people they personally knew or names that seemed to beg for verse. Many humorous poems were added below the announcement, unknown, no doubt, to the happy couple until they read it the following day or week. The following excerpts provide examples of such poetry.

Married at Podunk on the 23rd ultimo, by the Rev. D. Willis, Mr. H. HOE to Miss ANN HANDLE, all of this city.

"How useless a *handle* without any *Hoe*,
And useless a *Hoe* without *Handle*;
No better a winter without any snow,
Or a candle-stick minus a candle.

But here, joined in one, the Handle and Hoe,
With life's rugged journey smooth over;
And each proove a helper in this world below,
Till death shall *hoe both* to another".

—*Portsmouth Daily Dispatch,*
April 29, 1853

On the 14th inst., by Rev. J Wheeler, Mr. JOSEPH STEPHENSON and Mrs. HARRIET BAKER, all of this county.

> If curious folks desire to know,
> What caused this man to take her;
> He thought his *cake* would soon be *dough*,
> Unless he got a **Baker**.

—*Portsmouth Daily Dispatch*
February 21, 1854

Gretna Green

If you had lived in England, particularly near the Scottish border, from 1754 to 1856, you would have been familiar with a village in Scotland called Gretna Green. It is located in Dumfriesshire, across the English border. During this time, English law allowed neither quick marriages nor marriages under the age of 21 without parental consent. However, the only requirements for marriage in Scotland were witnesses (anyone, even the village blacksmith could officiate) and that the couple had reached the age of 16. Parental consent was required for those younger than 16. The fee was usually paid before the ceremony ended to ensure payment before the ensuing parents arrived to interrupt the ceremony. Since then, any town offering hasty marriages is sometimes dubbed "Gretna Green." (By the way, the Scottish parliament ended the practice in 1856 by requiring a residency of at least twenty-one days by one of the parties before a marriage license would be issued. However, for romantic reasons, many couples continued the practice of going to Gretna Green to be married.)

Due to its proximity to Kentucky, Ohio boasted its own "Gretna Green." The age requirement, among other things, was probably a strong factor that drove many young lovers across the Ohio River to make their vows. During the years covered by this index, Ohio law permitted males aged twenty-one or older, and females aged eighteen or older, to marry without parental consent. Kentucky law, while allowing marriage at a very young age with parental consent, stated that the female, as well as the male, must be twenty-one years of age in order to marry without the consent of the father or guardian. However, Kentucky law generally accepted the marriage as valid if it was valid in the state in which the marriage occurred.

Several stories surfaced in the Portsmouth papers, in which the town of Aberdeen received comparisons to Gretna Green. Therefore, if you feel that your ancestor came from Kentucky, but are unable to locate any information about him or her, there is a good possibility that you will find the marriage listed in a Scioto County, Ohio, newspaper; the Scioto County courthouse; or other courthouses in southern Ohio.

The following are excerpts from articles found in *The Portsmouth Tribune and Clipper* that made such references.

Gretna Green

The Maysville Eagle says that 'Squire Shelton, of Aberdeen, has, within the past two weeks, united some dozen couple of runaway lovers. The old 'Squire always demands the *fee*, and as will be seen by the following, he is not easily overcome by appeals to do the job for nothing, or even for "beans after harvest:"

'A poor fellow the other day arrived at the 'Squire's door with his intended spouse. Whether from original feebleness of constitution, or from severe depletion in the exigences [*sic*] of his break-neck flight from the anger of the damsel's daddy, his purse was in a state of melancoly [*sic*] collapse. His eloquent appeal, beseeching to be made happy "any how," or on credit, moved not the heart of the 'Squire. He would have his fee—that is, the offering to Hymen—or the divinity, however ardently worshipped, should not smile propitiously upon the bridal pair. But it moved the hearts of the spectators—that is to say, it made them feel in their pockets, which is said to be the best evidence of true feeling— who contributed the amount of fee required; whereupon the 'Squire consented— that is, the divinity relented—and Hymen smiled upon and sanctioned the loves of the twain, who departed happy at least for the moment, and, we trust, happier than many others united in wedlock with consent of parents.

—*The Portsmouth Tribune and Clipper*
3 September 1851

Thomas Shelton, Esq., the Gretna Green Blacksmith of the West, has been re-elected Justice of the Pease [*sic*], at Aberdeen, Ohio, by a majority of 85 votes.

—*The Portsmouth Tribune and Clipper*
4 February 1852.

Aberdeen--The Maysville Eagle, speaking of Aberdeen, the "Gretna Green" for runaway lovers, on the Ohio side opposite Maysville, says--"We understand that more than 3000 couples have been united by 'Squire Shelton' since his advent in the capacity of 'Squire.' Wouldn't it make a big army, if he could only muster together now, the progeny of those who have stood before him as deserters from the protecting care of papas and mamas."

—*Weekly Portsmouth Tribune*
19 January 1859

Deaths

The Probate Court for Scioto County maintains death records dating from 1856. However, if the resident died outside the county, his or her record will not be found there. Therefore, newspapers are a superb source for information on those who died before 1856, those who may have been out of the county or had recently moved, or family of Scioto County residents. In addition, death notices and articles often give details of the death, such as personal facts surrounding the death, that cannot be found on a death certificate. Examples of typical death notices are given below.

Of typhoid fever, at Jackson furnace, on Wednesday, the 31st., CYRUS MARTIN STEVENS, formerly of Jericho, Vt., but latterly of this place, age 22 years. The deceased was a young man of exemplary deportment, and beloved by all who know him. His parents reside in Canada.

—*The Daily Evening Dispatch*
2 June 1854

At Capt. Wm. M'Lean's (M'Lean's Landing, 10 miles above New Richmond) on Sunday evening the 18th inst., at 8 o'clock, Mrs. SARAH THOMPSON, wife of Moses Thompson, of this place.

—*The Daily Evening Dispatch*
19 June 1854

Occasionally in the old newspapers, a list of deceased persons follows the heading of "Sexton's Report." A sexton usually was an employee of a church or municipality and maintained records of people buried in the church or municipal cemetery. Those records would be submitted to the paper, listing those who died over the course of a week or month. The date published is probably that of the interment, rather than death, but it is included in this index under the heading of "Death Date." To indicate a sexton's report, "(S)" appears in this index after the newspaper abbreviation. In the newspaper, the cause of death usually is published, as well as the age of the deceased, and father's name if it is a child.

A child's first name usually was not mentioned in a sexton's report and rarely was published in an article relating the death. However, it usually was mentioned in a death notice. For this index, if a child's given name is not listed, the word "male" or "female" is provided when the gender of a child is known, and "unknown" is used when it was not. If an age was not listed in the paper, then "infant" or "child" is provided in the "Age" column.

In sexton's reports and death notices, females receive the opposite treatment of children. Although her given name may be listed in the sexton's report, articles and death notices may refer to her only as a "consort of," or "wife of," or "Mrs.," followed by her husband's name. In such instances, "female" is used in this index. It is rare to find a maiden name in the papers. In some instances, you can find additional information by finding a marriage notice.

Not all deaths are neatly listed under the heading of "Died" or "Obituary" in the Scioto County newspapers. Often, the Masonic Lodge or an organization to which the deceased had been a member offered a "Tribute" or "Resolution" to the deceased in the paper. If the circumstances were unusual, such as an accident, unusual illness, Indian attack, duel, hanging, major disaster (tornadoes, train accident, steamship explosion, etc.) the notice is in the form of a news article and might be buried in small type anywhere the editors could squeeze it in. In this index, an attempt has been made to include these deaths. A keen eye and a little patience can unearth information that a death notice or death certificate might not mention. If you are not doing the research yourself, be sure to mention this fact to the librarian or researcher who is doing the work for you.

Obituaries were not very common during the early- to mid-1800s. It was costly to submit one, since there was a charge for each line. If you are fortunate to find one for your ancestor, you may certainly learn much about the individual and the extended family as well.

Whether you locate the person you are researching under the heading of "Died," "Obituary," "Resolution," or "Tribute," or an article outlining the events of the death, you will be fortunate to be able to add some information to your research, and possibly to find clues about where to continue looking.

Scioto County Geographical Changes

Before the present-day boundaries for Scioto County became permanent, they experienced many changes. As early as 1769, this territory was part of Botetourt in Virginia. Within twenty years, in 1787, the land became part of the Northwest Territory, followed by Washington County in 1788 and Adams County in 1797. Soon after Ohio was declared a state, in 1803, Scioto County was created. The boundaries changed only slightly after that period. Four townships were formed immediately within the county, but have since been divided into many smaller townships. A detailed history of this period can be found in many county histories written for this time and era. Some of these books are listed in the bibliography.

A number of towns experienced name changes throughout the years, and some no longer exist. Many communities became known by the name of their post office, riverboat landings, or iron furnaces. In order to help the researcher locate the area referred to in these notices, several resources were researched to provide a list of those communities and their present-day names or locations. Some of these changes are listed in Appendix B. For a complete list of post offices since 1805, please see *The History of Scioto County Post Offices, 1805-1991*, by Carl and Elizabeth Shamhart. Maps containing the names and locations of riverboat landings, as well as county evolution and former township boundaries, can be found in *Scioto, A County History*, by Roy E. Vastine and *A History of Scioto County, Ohio, together with a Pioneer Record of Southern Ohio*, by Nelson W. Evans, among other resources.

Newspaper History

This volume covers newspapers that were printed under as many as twenty different names. Not all were totally independent from another or under separate ownership. Some papers found it necessary to add the name of another county in order to increase circulation. For example, shortly after being published as the *Scioto Telegraph*, the editor found it advantageous to publish an enlarged edition in Lawrence County as well. The name was changed to reflect this expansion and was called the *Scioto Telegraph and Lawrence County Gazette*.

The *Portsmouth Gazette* was the first newspaper printed in Portsmouth, Ohio, in 1818. It lasted a little over six months. Another publishing attempt was made, using the same name, in 1824. However, in less than six months, it expanded under the new name of the *Portsmouth Gazette and Lawrence Advertiser.*

Other papers merged or carried additional editions—weekly or daily— thereby changing only part of the original name, such as the *Scioto Tribune* to the *Portsmouth Tribune* to *The Tribune and Clipper* after merging with *The Portsmouth Clipper*. The *Weekly Portsmouth Tribune* was published, as well as the *Daily Evening Tribune*. Although the actual name of the paper in which a marriage or death notice or article appears is listed in this index, the microfilm may be filed under a simpler term, such as *The Portsmouth Gazette* or *Tribune*. A history of these early publications, among others, may be found in books or papers listed in this book's bibliography. Appendix A lists the library repositories and locations or roll numbers that were used to find the original article for which an index entry is provided.

The newspapers that were published in Scioto County, Ohio, from 1818 to 1865 and that were researched for this index are listed below, with their abbreviations. The newspapers are listed in alphabetical order by abbreviation.

Abbreviation	Newspaper
CLIPPER	*The Portsmouth Clipper*
DENQ	*The Democratic Enquirer*
DET	*The Daily Evening Tribune*
OP	*The Ohio Pennant*
PC	*Portsmouth Courier*
PC&WT	*Portsmouth Courier and Western Times*
PDD	*Portsmouth Daily Dispatch*
PDEM	*Portsmouth Democrat*
PG&LA	*Portsmouth Gazette & Lawrence Advertiser*

Abbreviation	Newspaper
PGAZ	*Portsmouth Gazette*
PI	*Portsmouth Inquirer*
PSOT	*Portsmouth Spirit of the Times*
PT&C	*Portsmouth Tribune & Clipper*
PTIMES	*Portsmouth Times*
STEL	*Scioto Telegraph*
STRIB	*Scioto Tribune*
SVREP	*Scioto Valley Republican*
TRIB	*Portsmouth Tribune*
WPT	*Weekly Portsmouth Tribune*
WT	*Western Times*

* In the indices, sexton's reports are designated by "(S)" after the newspaper abbreviation.

Newspaper and Microfilm Repositories

The Ohio Historical Society has microfilmed many issues of the Scioto County newspapers. You may view microfilm of these papers in the History Department of the Portsmouth Public Library. Also, you may write the library for copies of articles. You will be charged for copies and postage. In addition, the librarians will do research for you. Contact the library for current fees.

> The Portsmouth Public Library
> 1220 Gallia Street
> Portsmouth, OH 45662
> (740) 354-5688

You may also view microfilm in the Archives/Library Department at the Ohio Historical Society in Columbus, Ohio. In addition, you may view any of the many papers that have not been microfilmed that are stored in the vault or other storage areas. You may borrow microfilm for a small fee, through a library with interlibrary loan privileges, by asking your local librarian to submit a form along with a check made out to the Ohio Historical Society. You may also purchase microfilm. Although the Ohio Historical Society Archives/Library Department librarians will do research, they will not do newspaper research or retrieval for you. Contact the Ohio Historical Society for all current fees.

The Ohio Historical Society
Archives/Library Division
1982 Velma Avenue
Columbus, OH 43221
(614) 297-2510

The Ohio University in Athens, Ohio, is a repository for these papers as well. You may view the microfilm in their library or order the microfilm through their interlibrary loan department. There is no charge, at this time, for borrowing the microfilm through certain interlibrary loan libraries with which they have reciprocal agreements. There is a fee, however, if you order the microfilm through a non-reciprocal library. Your local librarian can request microfilm for you either by submitting an American Library Association (ALA) form or online through OCLC.

The Ohio University
Alden Library
Athens, OH 45701
(740) 593-2690

If you are unable to go to the Ohio Historical Library to research these newspapers, you can obtain a list of individuals who may do the research for you by contacting the Ohio Genealogical Society.

The Ohio Genealogical Society
713 South Main
Mansfield, OH 44907
(419) 756-7294

Pride of Ancestry,—There was much sound truth in the speech of a country lad to an idler, who boasted his descent from an ancient family. 'So much the worse for you,' said the peasant, 'as we ploughmen say— the older the seed, the worse the crop.'

—*Portsmouth Times*
21 Nov 1863

Deaths

Name	Notice Date			Death Date	Age	Comment	Paper
_____, female	28	Nov	1859			nee Moore	DET
_____, female	30	Nov	1859			nee Moore	WPT
Abbot, Sarah Rebecca	28	Jul	1851	21 Jul 1851	30		PI
Abrams, Charles	15	Sep	1854	11 Sep 1854			PDD
Ackley, unknown (Dr.)	04	May	1859	01 May 1859	50		WPT
Adames, male	30	Oct	1854				DET
Adams, Charles A.	21	Feb	1854	16 Feb 1854			PDD
Adams, David L. (Esq.)	08	Jul	1854	03 Jul 1854			PDD
Adams, female	27	Jul	1855				DET
Adams, Horatio E.	20	Jan	1854	17 Jan 1854	1y7d		DET
Adams, John	04	Feb	1852				PT&C
Adams, John	27	Jul	1826	04 Jul 1826	91	ex-Pres.	WT
Adams, John B.	24	Sep	1851	18 Sep 1851			PT&C
Adams, male	02	May	1860				WPT
Adams, male	09	Jan	1851	04 Dec 1850	14		PT&C
Adams, male	27	Aug	1851	16 Aug 1851			PT&C
Adams, unknown (Dr.)	30	Oct	1854				DET
Adams, William H.	16	May	1855	11 May 1855	29		DET
Adderly, John	12	Sep	1844	10 Sep 1844	33		TRIB
Addie, Mary	14	Aug	1855	30 Jul 1855			DET
Addison, William	12	Sep	1848	03 Sep 1848	40		DENQ
Adelbert, unknown	22	Nov	1862		child		PTIMES
Agnew, Wm.	03	Oct	1860	24 Sep 1860			WPT
Ahrends, Charles	20	Mar	1854				PDD
Ainslie, unknown (Col.)	27	Oct	1854				PDD
Albaugh, Zachariah	16	Nov	1857	08 Nov 1857	109		DET
Aldrich, Asa	09	Jun	1843	02 Jun 1843	34		TRIB
Aldridge, Robert	27	Oct	1860	05 Oct 1860			PTIMES
Alexander, James	09	Dec	1853				PDD
Alford, Chauncy W.	06	Sep	1853	09 Aug 1853	40		PDD
Alford, Clara Belle	02	May	1850	26 Apr 1850	6		PT&C
Alford, R. B.	13	Mar	1855	05 Feb 1855	68		DET (S)
Alford, R.B.	08,17	Feb	1855		68		DET
Algar, male	20	Jul	1855				DET
Allen, male	06	Aug	1853				DET
Allen, male	22	Aug	1829	14 Aug 1829			WT
Allen, Manlius	31	Aug	1855	21 Aug 1855			DET

Deaths

Name	Notice Date			Death Date	Age	Comment	Paper
Allen, Martha	12	Jul	1853	25 Jun 1853			DET
Allen, Robert Hugh	09	Oct	1854		infant		DET
Allen, William C.	02	Oct	1854	23 Sep 1854			DET
Allen, Wm. R.	06	Jun	1863	16 May 1863			PTIMES
Allison, Maria A.	12	Nov	1853	7 Nov 1853	23	nee Davisson	DET
Allright, Jacob	30	Dec	1853	22 Dec 1853			PDD
Allston, Washington (Esq.)	28	Jul	1843				TRIB
Amlin, James M.	09	Apr	1864	02 Apr 1864			PTIMES
Ammon, Jane	09	May	1855	24 Apr 1855	23m		DET (S)
Amon, male	30	Oct	1854				DET
Anderson, Bill	17	Dec	1864				PTIMES
Anderson, Chas. H.	30	Jan	1855				DET
Anderson, H.D.	07	May	1851	15 Apr 1851			PT&C
Anderson, James (Corp.)	07	May	1864				PTIMES
Anderson, male	15	Dec	1853				PDD
Anderson, Sally	31	Aug	1854	25 Aug 1854	77		DET
Anderson, Wm. R. (Rev.)	12	Mar	1846				TRIB
Andrew, Charles H.	15	Jul	1853				PDD
Andrews, Catherine	09	Nov	1858	27 Oct 1858	30	nee Hayward	PTIMES
Andrews, N.W. (Dr.)	24	Feb	1843	23 Feb 1843	49		TRIB
Apley, female	13	Aug	1864	07 Aug 1864			PTIMES
Applebury, James (Private)	10	Oct	1863				PTIMES
Applegate, female	16	Nov	1854	15 Nov 1854	child		DET
Appler, Jonathan	14	Nov	1863	12 Nov 1863	77		PTIMES
Appleton, Charles A.	12	Apr	1859	04 Apr 1859			PTIMES
Applewhaite, unknown (Lieut.)	26	Oct	1854				DET
Applewhaite, unknown (Lieut.)	27	Oct	1854				PDD
Archer, male	09	May	1854		15		PDD
Areb, male	30	Jun	1854	17 Jun 1854			PDD
Argabright, Wesley F.	10	Sep	1856	26 Aug 1856	6m4d		WPT
Armstead, female	13	Aug	1855				DET
Armstead, unknown (Major)	13	Aug	1855				DET
Armstrong, John (Esq.)	20	Aug	1851	19 Aug 1851			PT&C
Armstrong, Matilda	04	Apr	1860				WPT
Armstrong, unknown (Gen.)	01	Mar	1854				PDD
Armstrong, unknown (Gen.)	21	Apr	1843	01 Apr 1843	84		TRIB
Arnold, James Robertson (Lieut.Gen.)	09	Feb	1855	26 Dec 1854			DET
Arnote, male	21	Jun	1853	16 Jun 1853			PDD

Name	Notice Date			Death Date	Age	Comment	Paper
Arp, George	09	Jun	1860	Jun 1860			PTIMES
Arthur, unknown	13	Mar	1855	06 Mar 1855	14m		DET (S)
Arthurs, Marshall	19	Dec	1863				PTIMES
Arthurs, William	10	Sep	1864				PTIMES
Ashby, male	21	Jun	1862	07 Jun 1862			PTIMES
Askeen, Joseph M.	11	Aug	1852	26 Jul 1852			PT&C
Atkinson, Merritt	12	Jun	1855	11 Jun 1855	23		DET
Atkinson, Samuel	08	Oct	1851				PT&C
Aubrey, F.X.	19	Sep	1854	20 Aug 1854			PDD
Aunt Molly	18	Jun	1851		100	Negro	PT&C
Austin, Benjamin	01	Jun	1820	04 May 1820	68		STEL
Axtel, male	30	Jul	1851	Jul 1851			PT&C
Babcock, male	30	Oct	1854				DET
Backus, Isabella Graham	01	Sep	1855	20 Aug 1855	30	nee Carrick	DET
Bacon, Sarah C.	10	Jan	1855				DET
Bacon, unknown (Capt.)	28	Sep	1854				PDD
Bacon, W.	11	May	1853				PDD
Baden, unknown (Rev.)	27	Apr	1853		98		PT&C
Badgely, Andrew P.	17	Feb	1857	05 Feb 1857	25		PSOT
Baggs, Levina	12	Apr	1854	08 Apr 1854	17		PDD
Bagot, Charles (Gov.Gen. of Canada)	02	Jun	1843				TRIB
Bailey, Gamaliel (Dr.)	05	Jun	1859				PTIMES
Bailey, George B. (Lieut.Col.)	23	Nov	1861	09 Nov 1861			PTIMES
Bailey, male	22	Dec	1860	29 Nov 1860	2		PTIMES
Baird, Emma	07	Aug	1854	22 Jul 1854			DET
Baird, James	20	Jan	1854				PDD
Baker, Charles	01	Mar	1859				PTIMES
Baker, Charles	02	Mar	1859	22 Feb 1859			WPT
Baker, Charles	26	Feb	1859				DET
Baker, Henry F.	25	Feb	1857	25 Feb 1857	58		WPT
Baker, M.	17	Aug	1854	11 Aug 1854	26		DET (S)
Baker, male	09	Sep	1865				PTIMES
Baker, male	16	Feb	1844				TRIB
Baker, male	19	Sep	1860	14 Sep 1860			WPT
Baker, Narcissa	16	May	1853	14 May 1853	30		PDD
Baker, Narcissa	18	May	1853	14 May 1853	30		PT&C
Baker, Narsisa	03	Oct	1851	30 Sep 1851	17m		PI
Baker, Samuel D.	26	Jul	1855	22 Jul 1855			DET
Baker, unknown	21	Aug	1854	16 Aug 1854	18m		DET (S)
Baldwin, Ann	12	Dec	1850	11 Dec 1850	62		PT&C
Baldwin, Roger Sherman	28	Feb	1863	26 Feb 1863	70		PTIMES
Baldwin, Samuel, Jr.	18	May	1820	01 May 1820			STEL
Baldwin, Thos.	14	Nov	1850	23 Oct 1850			PT&C

Deaths

Name	Notice Date			Death Date	Age	Comment	Paper
Baldwin, unknown (Judge)	03	May	1844	22 Apr 1844			TRIB
Bale, H.W., Jr.	14	Jan	1852	09 Jan 1852			PT&C
Ball, female	16	Aug	1853		7		DET
Ball, female	16	Aug	1853		17		DET
Ball, female	17	Aug	1853		9		PT&C
Ball, female	17	Aug	1853		17		PT&C
Ball, female	18	Aug	1853	15 Aug 1853	17		PDD
Ball, female	18	Aug	1853	15 Aug 1853	9		PDD
Ball, J.B.	23	Feb	1853				PT&C
Ball, Jane	03	Oct	1854	03 Oct 1854			DET
Ball, Jane	13	Oct	1854	03 Oct 1854	22		PDD (S)
Ball, male	28	Apr	1852	14 Apr 1852			PT&C
Ballard, James R.	26	May	1857	09 May 1857	21y4m5d		PSOT
Ballogh, Madame	29	Jun	1855				DET
Ballou, Hosea	16	Jun	1852		81		PT&C
Ballou, Ruth	06	Apr	1853	01 Apr 1853	74		PT&C
Bankin, Alfred Giles	07	Mar	1855	06 Mar 1855	5y1m9d		DET
Bannon, Edward	17	Oct	1863	02 Oct 1863	65		PTIMES
Bannon, Hugh	03	Dec	1853				PDD
Barbee, Joseph	13	Jun	1855	08 Jun 1855			DET
Barbee, Mary E.	03	Oct	1850	28 Sep 1850			PT&C
Barbee, Mary E.	30	Sep	1850	28 Sep 1850			PI
Barber, Catharine	22	Oct	1851	18 Oct 1851	18		PT&C
Barbour, male	30	Aug	1854	27 Aug 1854			DET
Bard, Margaret Ann	16	May	1853	10 May 1853	2y8m		PDD
Bard, Margaret Ann	18	May	1853	10 May 1853	2y8m		PT&C
Barker, John	12	Nov	1859	07 Nov 1859			PTIMES
Barker, Joseph (Judge)	09	Jan	1860	06 Jan 1860			DET
Barlow, unknown	21	Sep	1853	15 Sep 1853	2		PDD (S)
Barnard, Robert	31	Aug	1854				PDD
Barnard, Wm.	23	Jul	1856	Jul 1856			WPT
Barnes, female	08	Jan	1846	05 Jan 1846			TRIB
Barnes, male	12	May	1852				PT&C
Barnes, Wm. (Major General)	08	Jan	1846	05 Jan 1846			TRIB
Barnham, female	09	Jun	1860	Jun 1860			PTIMES
Barns, Gasper	30	Jan	1855				DET
Barnum, unknown	09	Jun	1860	03 Jun 1860	child		PTIMES
Barr, female	21	Oct	1865	14 Oct 1865			PTIMES
Barr, female	30	Jul	1855	30 Jul 1855	8		DET
Barr, George Griswold	23	May	1848	19 May 1848	7		DENQ
Barr, John	07	May	1864				PTIMES
Barr, Oliver	11	May	1853				PDD
Barr, William	01	Apr	1837	18 Mar 1837	60		STRIB

Name	Notice Date			Death Date	Age	Comment	Paper
Barrett, Lyman	23	Jan	1856	08 Dec 1855			WPT
Barron, Edward (Rev.)	23	Sep	1854				PDD
Barsdale, female	21	Apr	1843	19 Mar 1843			TRIB
Bartlett, Josiah (Dr.)	11	May	1853				PDD
Barton, F.	17, 18	Aug	1855				DET
Barton, female	24	Nov	1852				PT&C
Barton, John	26	Feb	1860				DET
Barton, Willim (Maj.)	14	Mar	1860	05 Mar 1860	77		DET
Basham, Augustus	10	Jun	1831	04 Apr 1831	10		PC&WT
Bass, B.	06	Jun	1863	16 May 1863			PTIMES
Bass, Wm.	06	Jun	1863	16 May 1863			PTIMES
Bassett, Thos.	28	Jun	1855	25 Jun 1855			DET
Bates, Wm. H.	29	Dec	1843				TRIB
Batlow, female	19	Jan	1854				PDD
Batterson, Addison	19	Mar	1864	14 Mar 1864	44y16d		PTIMES
Bayles, Jehn (Private)	10	Oct	1863				PTIMES
Baymiller, Mary A.	25	May	1854	25 May 1854	25		DET
Bays, Wm.	01	Dec	1853	29 Nov 1853			DET
Bays, Wm.	29	Nov	1853				PDD
Beach, D.	10	May	1853	06 May 1853			PDD
Beach, Walter H.	19	Aug	1854	11 Aug 1854	11m14d		DET
Beall, female	06	Sep	1859	02 Sep 1859			DET
Beall, Reasin (Gen.)	17	Mar	1843	20 Feb 1843	73		TRIB
Beaman, male	29	Oct	1851		80		PT&C
Bear, Jennie	15	Sep	1854	09 Sep 1854		Knight (adopted)	DET
Beasley, James	11	Jul	1855	10 Jul 1855	22		DET
Beatty, Samuel	15	Jul	1859	02 Jul 1859			DET
Beaty, unknown	16	May	1863				PTIMES
Beaver, unknown	12	Jul	1853	8 Jul 1853	2		PDD
Beck, Anna	09	Jun	1860	04 Jun 1860	64		PTIMES
Beck, L.C. (Prof.)	04	May	1853	21 Apr 1853			PT&C
Beckman, Fountain	22	Oct	1859				PTIMES
Beebe, C.F.	29	Apr	1854	27 Apr 1854			DET
Beebe, Cyrus F. (Officer)	01	May	1854	30 Apr 1854			PDD
Beecher, George (Rev.)	07	Jul	1843	01 Jul 1843			TRIB
Beecher, male (twin)	20	Jul	1853	04 Jul 1853			PT&C
Beecher, male (twin)	20	Jul	1853	04 Jul 1853			PT&C
Beery, Nicholas	08	Apr	1820				STEL
Beeson, Martha S.	01	Aug	1829	14 Jul 1829	19		WT
Beggs, James	18	Jun	1851				PT&C
Behrens, John	20	Jan	1857	10 Jan 1857	50		PSOT
Belknap, Daniel	21	Nov	1850	26 Oct 1850	86		PT&C
Belknap, female	06	Aug	1856				WPT
Bell, Isaac	22	Mar	1827	04 May 1826	104		WT

Deaths

Name	Notice Date			Death Date	Age	Comment	Paper
Bell, John L.	19	Aug	1854	13 Aug 1854	24y10m		DET
Bell, male	06	Jul	1854		15		DET
Bell, Mary Ann	07	Jul	1852	24 Jun 1852	16		PT&C
Bellam, John	05	Dec	1853				DET
Bellam, John	03, 06	Dec	1853				PDD
Belle, Clara	29	Apr	1850	26 Apr 1850	6	adopted da. of Alford	PI
Bellwood, John	21	Sep	1820	10 Sep 1820			STEL
Belote, John	20	Oct	1852	04 Oct 1852			PT&C
Bender, male	12	Aug	1854	30 Jul 1854			PDD
Benham, Wm. G.	27	Oct	1843	10 Oct 1843			TRIB
Bennett, Caleb	10, 17	May	1862	22 Apr 1862	55y7m25d		PTIMES
Bennett, David	25	Jun	1855				DET
Bennett, Ella R.	04	Mar	1865	01 Mar 1865	4		PTIMES
Bennett, George	10	Sep	1864				PTIMES
Bennett, James H.	29	Aug	1863	27 Aug 1863	35		PTIMES
Bennett, Joseph	25	Jun	1855				DET
Bennett, Lorenzo C.	08	Jan	1846	05 Jan 1846	23		TRIB
Bennett, Thomas	15	Dec	1854	05 Dec 1854	70		DET
Bennett, unknown (Lieut.)	23	Jan	1864				PTIMES
Bennett, William	06	Sep	1854		10		PDD
Benning, male	28	Mar	1829				WT
Bennington, John	19	Jul	1854	17 Jun 1854			DET
Benson, male	06	Aug	1851	01 Aug 1851			PT&C
Bentley, Corwin	16	May	1854				PDD
Bentley, Jane	09	Nov	1859		39y5m		DET
Bentley, Luther	01	Feb	1862	04 Jan 1862			PTIMES
Bentz, M. Jacob	09	Oct	1854	04 Oct 1854			DET
Berge, unknown (Pastor)	23	Jun	1852	08 Jun 1852			PT&C
Bergen, James	09	Feb	1853	05 Feb 1853			PT&C
Bergin, William	01	Jun	1853	28 May 1853	7		PT&C
Bergin, William	31	May	1853	28 May 1853	7		PDD
Berry, Amelia	10	Aug	1854	01 Aug 1854		nee Spurck	DET
Berry, David	02	Feb	1859				WPT
Bertram, Aaron	17	Nov	1852	13 Nov 1852	5m		PT&C
Bertram, Aaron	19	Nov	1852	Nov 1852	5m		PI
Bertram, Amalia	18	Aug	1857	16 Aug 1857	33y3m3d		PSOT
Bertram, James	03	Sep	1864	24 Aug 1864	14		PTIMES
Best, Mary	04	Jun	1851				PT&C
Betts, Mary E.	29	Sep	1854	24 Sep 1854		nee Wilson	DET
Betts, Morgan L.	03	Feb	1855	29 Jan 1855			DET
Beugnot, Nicholas	06	Apr	1854	02 Apr 1854			PDD
Bevington, male	11	Aug	1853				DET
Bewer, Matthew	09	Jun	1852	18 May 1852			PT&C
Beymer, Simon (Gen.)	17	Mar	1843	18 Feb 1843	65		TRIB

Name	Notice Date			Death Date	Age	Comment	Paper
Bickel, Samuel E.	01	Feb	1862	21 Dec 1861			PTIMES
Biddle, Nicholas	08	Mar	1844	Feb 1844			TRIB
Bigeby, unknown	09	Jun	1860	Jun 1860	child		PTIMES
Bigelow, unknown	24	Mar	1860	20 Mar 1860	child		DET
Bigler, Susan	23	Mar	1854	16 Mar 1854	70		PDD
Bihlman, Catharine	01	Sep	1858	24 Aug 1858	21		PSOT
Bimeler, Joseph	26	Jul	1853	20 Jul 1853			DET
Binckley, Millard Fillmore	28	Nov	1853	19 Nov 1853	6m		DET
Bingham, Harry	02	Apr	1864		41		PTIMES
Birdsall, male	03	Mar	1843	Feb 1843			TRIB
Birkhimer, Temperance	02	Mar	1860	26 Jan 1860		nee Hood	DET
Birkhimer, Temperance	25	Feb	1860			nee Hood	PTIMES
Bishop, Ann	09	Sep	1859	08 Sep 1859			DET
Bishop, Benjamin W.	06	May	1853	29 Apr 1853	3y11m21d		PDD
Bishop, female	05	Oct	1854				PDD
Bishop, male	26	Aug	1850	19 Aug 1850			PI
Black, Isaac	01	Feb	1862	26 Dec 1861			PTIMES
Black, John L. (Capt.)	20	Aug	1853		42		DET
Black, John L. (Capt.)	24	Aug	1853		42		PT&C
Black, unknown	27	Jun	1854	21 Jun 1854	2		PDD (S)
Blackburn, Anthony	11	Jul	1853	01 Jul 1853			DET
Blackburn, Anthony	13	Jul	1853	01 Jul 1853			PT&C
Blackburn, Thomas	27	Jan	1854	15 Jan 1854			PDD
Blackford, Benj.	29	Aug	1855	20 Aug 1855			DET
Blacksnake, Gov.	14	Jan	1860	29 Dec 1859	123	Indian Chief	DET
Blake, Abby Jane	26	Oct	1858		20		PTIMES
Blake, David	06	Jan	1855	22 Dec 1854	92		DET
Blake, Henry	04	Aug	1851	28 Jul 1851			PI
Blake, Henry	06	Aug	1851	28 Jul 1851			PT&C
Blake, Louisa	13	Jul	1858	01 Jul 1858	27		PSOT
Blake, William	28	May	1864	May 1864			PTIMES
Blanest, unknown	03, 06	Dec	1853				PDD
Blankemyer, male	07	Sep	1855	07 Sep 1855			DET
Blankenship, Isom	30	Apr	1864		80		PTIMES
Blennernassett, Herman	27	Sep	1854	17 Aug 1854			PDD
Blentlinger, Andrew J.	13	Apr	1858	28 Mar 1858	31		PSOT
Blessing, John R. (Maj.)	18	Apr	1863	10 Apr 1863			PTIMES
Bligger, Stephen	28	Jun	1859				PTIMES
Blinn, male	14	Mar	1854				PDD
Bliss, Esther	20	Jul	1826	8 Jul 1826	41		WT
Blocksom, William (Judge)	11	Apr	1860	05 Apr 1860			DET
Blocksom, William (Judge)	18	Apr	1860	05 Apr 1860			WPT
Blynn, female	13	Jun	1860				DET

Deaths

Name	Notice Date			Death Date	Age	Comment	Paper
Bocker, John	07	May	1864				PTIMES
Bodman, unknown	16	May	1863				PTIMES
Boggs, Andrew	12	Jul	1855				DET
Boker, John G.	10	Mar	1860				PTIMES
Bolinger, Andrew	04	May	1853	22 Apr 1853			PT&C
Bolinger, Michael	04	May	1853	22 Apr 1853			PT&C
Bond, James	24	Nov	1852				PT&C
Bond, William Key	27	Feb	1864	17 Feb 1864	72		PTIMES
Bonnear, Charles	12	Dec	1850	09 Dec 1850			PT&C
Bonnell, male	05	Sep	1860	01 Sep 1860	45		WPT
Bonnell, unknown	01	Sep	1860	01 Sep 1860	45		DET
Bonsall, Joseph	03	Mar	1843	25 Feb 1843			TRIB
Bonsall, S.N. (Capt.-A.Q.M.)	29	Jul	1865	19 Jul 1865	56		PTIMES
Bonser, Jacob	30	Mar	1853	20 Mar 1853			PT&C
Bookwalter, Henry	10	Apr	1860	04 Apr 1860	40-50		DET
Boon, Daniel	02	Sep	1818				PGAZ
Boone, Daniel	15	Jun	1855	01 May 1855	70		DET
Booth, J.B.	08, 15	Dec	1852		56		PT&C
Booth, John Wilkes	29	Apr	1865				PTIMES
Boothe, Thos. G.	28	Aug	1855	24 Aug 1855			DET
Borick, Henry	27	Jun	1855	26 Jun 1855			DET
Bossier, male	03	May	1844	25 Apr 1844			TRIB
Boston, Catharine	13	Jan	1860	05 Jan 1860	109-111		DET
Bostwick, Charles	17	Apr	1854	11 Apr 1854			DET
Bostwick, Charles	20	Apr	1854	17 Apr 1854			PDD
Boswell, John L.	02	Aug	1854	30 Jul 1854			DET
Bothel Loammi (Priv.)	12	Dec	1863	Nov 1863			PTIMES
Bourbon, James	22	Aug	1850				PT&C
Bourne, unknown	06	Oct	1853			child	DET
Boursholt, Lewis	10	Sep	1864				PTIMES
Bouts, George	03	Mar	1858				WPT
Bowden, G.F. (Rev.)	05	Sep	1853				DET
Bowen, female	08	Jan	1846	18 Dec 1845			TRIB
Bowen, male	08	Jan	1846	18 Dec 1845			TRIB
Bowen, unknown	08	Jan	1846	18 Dec 1845		child	TRIB
Bowles, male	30	Jun	1853				DET
Bowman, Geo.	09	Dec	1865				PTIMES
Bowman, George	06	Jun	1863	01 May 1863			PTIMES
Bowman, Rosan	13	Oct	1854	11 Oct 1854	52		PDD (S)
Bowman, Ruth	07	Mar	1854	28 Feb 1854	32		PDD (S)
Boyd, female	14	Mar	1859				DET
Boyd, female	16	Mar	1859				WPT
Boyd, John L.	02	Oct	1855	01 Oct 1855			DET
Boyd, Lynn	24	Dec	1859	19 Dec 1859			PTIMES

Name	Notice Date			Death Date	Age	Comment	Paper
Boyd, male	18	Feb	1852	06 Feb 1852			PT&C
Boyer, Alexander	07	Apr	1860	06 Apr 1860			PTIMES
Boyer, Alexander	11	Apr	1860	06 Apr 1860			WPT
Bradfield, Wm.	28	May	1864	04 May 1864			PTIMES
Bradford, C.W.	18	Jan	1859	10 Dec 1858	38		PTIMES
Bradly, female	03	Aug	1853				PT&C
Bradly, female	30	Jul	1853	24 Jul 1853			DET
Bradly, James	01	Mar	1854	24 Feb 1854			PDD
Brady, female	14	Jan	1852	03 Jan 1852			PT&C
Brady, James	14	Jan	1852	03 Jan 1852			PT&C
Brady, Jno.	23	Jul	1856	Jul 1856			WPT
Brady, male	14	Jan	1852	03 Jan 1852			PT&C
Brady, R.L. (Dr.)	28	Dec	1854	12 Dec 1854	22		DET
Bramble, unknown	06	Jan	1854	25 Dec 1853	5m		PDD (S)
Brammer, Catherine	14	Mar	1859	23 Feb 1859	47		DET
Brammer, Catherine	16	Mar	1859	23 Feb 1859	47		WPT
Brammer, Mahala	14	Mar	1859	16 Jan 1859	24		DET
Brammer, Mahala	16	Mar	1859	16 Jan 1859	24		WPT
Branch, A.G.	31	May	1854	29 May 1854	26		PDD
Branch, Harry	04	May	1853	27 Apr 1853	15m		PT&C
Branch, Harry	28	Apr	1853	27 Apr 1853	15		PDD
Brandbury, Edward A.	10	Dec	1851				PT&C
Brandis, S.	28	Jul	1852	22 Jul 1852	19		PT&C
Brandon, J.H.	07	Mar	1860	03 Mar 1860			WPT
Brandon, John	02	Aug	1862				PTIMES
Brandon, Thomas	01	Jun	1853	24 May 1853			PT&C
Branum, unknown	22	Nov	1862	17 Nov 1862			PTIMES
Bratt, Mary Alice	12	Dec	1857	11 Dec 1857	2y11m22d		DET
Bratt, Mary Alice	16	Dec	1857	11 Dec 1857	2y11m22d		WPT
Bratten, Susan C.	26	May	1858	10 May 1858	25		WPT
Bratten, Susan C.	21	May	1858	10 May 1858	25		DET
Brattin, Susan C.	25	May	1858	10 May 1858	25		PSOT
Brattin, Thomas A. (Esq.)	30	Dec	1865	19 Dec 1865			PTIMES
Bray, unknown (Lieut.)	26	Oct	1854				DET
Bray, unknown (Lieut.)	27	Oct	1854				PDD
Brayton, Lydia	05	Aug	1850	31 Jul 1850	1m4d		PI
Breckinridge, O.H.P.	21	Jun	1854	Jun 1854	40		PDD
Breeden (or Greeden), Betsy	09	Jan	1856	26 Dec 1855	80		WPT
Brenan, George	02	Mar	1861	24 Feb 1861			PTIMES
Brenham, Robert L.	03	Nov	1843				TRIB
Brewer, female	03	Aug	1820	25 Jul 1820			STEL
Brewer, female	03	Mar	1852	27 Feb 1852			PT&C
Brewer, Justus (or Justice)	03	Mar	1852	24 Feb 1852			PT&C

Name	Notice Date			Death Date	Age	Comment	Paper
Brewley, female	21	Nov	1854	17 Nov 1854			DET
Brewley, unknown	21	Nov	1854	17 Nov 1854	infant		DET
Brice, Frances	22	Sep	1857	13 Sep 1857	57		PSOT
Bridwell, Andrew	21	Nov	1860	12 Nov 1860	36		WPT
Brier, David	21	May	1853	16 May 1853			PDD
Briggs, female	30	Jun	1843	21 Jun 1843			TRIB
Briggs, John	03	Jul	1860	01 Jul 1860	60		DET
Briggs, John	04	Jul	1860	01 Jul 1860	60		WPT
Brigham, female	08	Jul	1857				WPT
Briles, Berry	10	Sep	1864				PTIMES
Brinkerhoff, H.J. (Hon.)	17	May	1844				TRIB
Britton, male	28	Nov	1854				DET
Britton, male	28	Nov	1854				DET
Broad, male	12	Nov	1864				PTIMES
Brocard, (Very Rev. Father)	21	Apr	1852	01 Apr 1852			PT&C
Bronson, Melissa C.	26	May	1857	15 May 1857	29		PSOT
Bronstetter, Geo.	03	Oct	1854				DET
Brooks, Ann	03	May	1859				PTIMES
Brooks, Phoeba Ann	01	Sep	1855	28 Aug 1855	2y7m		DET
Brooks, Preston	04	Feb	1857	27 Jan 1857			WPT
Broome, Julia Matilda	01	Apr	1865	29 Mar 1865	7		PTIMES
Brounstead, Mary	08	Sep	1857	29 Aug 1857	10y8m		PSOT
Browing, James W.	28	May	1864	May 1864			PTIMES
Brown, Amos	03	Apr	1854				PDD
Brown, Cager H.	11	Nov	1830	05 Nov 1830	20		WT
Brown, Charles	13	Apr	1859			Negro	WPT
Brown, D.	26	Nov	1851	14 Oct 1851			PT&C
Brown, Daniel	05	Feb	1851				PT&C
Brown, Eva	19	Aug	1859	19 Aug 1859	4y9m		DET
Brown, Eva	24	Aug	1859	19 Aug 1859			WPT
Brown, female	09	Jul	1853	04 Jul 1853			PDD
Brown, female	17	Jun	1853	03 Jun 1853			PDD
Brown, female	25	Apr	1855				DET
Brown, female	28	May	1851	16 May 1851			PT&C
Brown, George	12	Mar	1851	02 Mar 1851			PT&C
Brown, Hannah	25	Feb	1825		80		PG&LA
Brown, Henry	19	May	1852	01 May 1852			PT&C
Brown, Jacob F.	11	Jan	1855				DET
Brown, Jerusha	25	Sep	1854				DET
Brown, John	10	Dec	1859	02 Dec 1859			PTIMES
Brown, John (Rev.)	30	Mar	1859		70		WPT
Brown, John (Rev.)	24, 25	Mar	1859	23 Mar 1859	70		DET
Brown, Lewis	12	Jan	1853	07 Jan 1853			PT&C
Brown, male	14	May	1853				PDD

Name	Notice Date			Death Date	Age	Comment	Paper
Brown, Owen	21	Jun	1854	17 Jun 1854			PDD
Brown, Samuel M.	31	Oct	1844	Oct 1844			TRIB
	07	Nov	1844				
Brown, Sophia	05	Jan	1854	2 Oct 1853			DET
Brown, unknown	16	May	1863				PTIMES
Brown, unknown	28	Sep	1853	19 Sep 1853	3		PDD (S)
Brown, W.S.	30	Nov	1857	30 Nov 1857	44		DET
Brown, Walter L. (Corp.)	09	May	1863				PTIMES
Brown, William	10	Jun	1854		18		PDD
Brown, William H.	03	Aug	1859	02 Aug 1859	24y23d		WPT
Brown, William H.	02, 03	Aug	1859	02 Aug 1859	24y23d		DET
Browne, L.M.	19	Aug	1854	06 Aug 1854		nee Bell	DET
Browning, Arthur	12	Jul	1853				PDD
Browning, William	01	Feb	1862	06 Dec 1861			PTIMES
Brunel, Isambard Kingdom	04	Oct	1859		53		PTIMES
Bruner, Samuel	02	Jan	1855	02 Jan 1855	37		DET
Brunner, Anna Lucy	02	Apr	1864	27 Mar 1864	6y11m22d		PTIMES
Brunner, Frederick	04	Jan	1862	01 Jan 1862			PTIMES
Brunner, Melinda	02	Apr	1864	Mar 1864			PTIMES
Brunson, male	12	Apr	1844	28 Mar 1844			TRIB
Bryan, Henry C.	28	May	1864	May 1864			PTIMES
Bryan, John L.	09	Feb	1859	02 Feb 1859	37		WPT
Bryson, male	02	May	1850	28 Apr 1850			PT&C
Bryson, male	02	May	1850	28 Apr 1850			PT&C
Buchanan, (Dr.)	23	Sep	1854				DET
Buchanan, Alexander	26	Oct	1858		98		PTIMES
Buchanan, Elizabeth	20	Mar	1838		19	nee Belt	STRIB
Buchanan, John	16, 23	Jul	1851	12 Jul 1851			PT&C
	06	Aug	1851				
Buchanan, Margaret B.	16, 23	Jul	1851	10 Jul 1851			PT&C
	06	Aug	1851				
Buchanan, Thomas J. (Esq.)	02	Jan	1845	19 Dec 1844			TRIB
Buck, D.	09	Jun	1860	Jun 1860			PTIMES
Bucknick, male	12	Aug	1859	12 Aug 1859			DET
Bucknick, male	16	Aug	1859	16 Aug 1859	8		PTIMES
Buhoup, Sarah	15	Oct	1851				PT&C
Bulkingen, Michael	27	Jun	1854	11 Jun 1854	23		PDD (S)
Bullinger, male	07	Nov	1850	04 Nov 1850			PT&C
Bunch, F.M. (Dr.)	04	Oct	1859				PTIMES
Bundrant, male	12	Apr	1844	28 Mar 1844			TRIB
Burch, female	24	Aug	1853		10		DET
Burgess, James	17	Feb	1851	10 Feb 1851	40		PI
Burgess, James	19	Feb	1851	10 Feb 1851	40		PT&C
Burgos, Luis (Joaquin)	20	Mar	1854				PDD

Deaths

Name	Notice Date			Death Date	Age	Comment	Paper
Burk, Ann Marie	06	Oct	1843	Sep 1843			TRIB
Burke, John	08	Sep	1857	13 Aug 1857	41		PSOT
Burke, male	20	Apr	1855				DET
Burke, Robert	03	Oct	1860	24 Sep 1860			WPT
Burke, Wm.	03	Oct	1860	24 Sep 1860			WPT
Burnet, Jacob (Judge)	18	May	1853	10 May 1853	87		PT&C
Burnet, Judge	14	May	1853	10 May 1853			PDD
Burnet, Robert (Maj.)	28	Dec	1854	30 Nov 1854	98		DET
Burnett, Emily M.	22	Jul	1865		17		PTIMES
Burns, Arthur	15	Mar	1859	Mar 1859	53		PTIMES
Burns, Charles Raymond	11	Feb	1860	10 Feb 1860	6y4m26d		DET
Burns, Charles Raymond	15	Feb	1860	10 Feb 1860	6y4m26d		WPT
Burns, female	15	Mar	1859	Mar 1859			PTIMES
Burns, Robert	01	Dec	1860				PTIMES
Burns, unknown	23	Jul	1853	21 Jul 1853	3		DET
Burr, Anna Howard	24	Sep	1856	21 Sep 1856			WPT
Burt, Alice	22	Jul	1850	16 Jul 1850	13m		PI
Burt, Alice	25	Jul	1850	16 Jul 1850	13m		PT&C
Burt, Francis	10	Nov	1854	18 Oct 1854	45		PDD
Burt, Francis (Gov.)	09	Nov	1854	09 Nov 1854	45		DET
Burton, female	29	Jul	1853				PDD
Burtwell, James (Col.)	07	Oct	1818	20 Sep 1818	52		PGAZ
Busey, John P.	02	Apr	1864	28 Mar 1864	23		PTIMES
Busey, John P.	02	Apr	1864	27 Mar 1864	23		SVREP
Bush, Llewellyn	05	Apr	1859	12 Mar 1859			PTIMES
Buskirk, Charles Tracy	08	Oct	1857	07 Oct 1857	2y7m		DET
Bussey, Demsey	01	Jul	1853				DET
Bussey, Demsey	02, 04	Jul	1853				PDD
Butaff, Augustus	07	Jul	1853	01 Jul 1853			DET
Butaff, Augustus	07	Jul	1853				PDD
Butler, female	21	Oct	1865	14 Oc 1865			PTIMES
Butler, unknown	16	Aug	1859	Aug 1859			PTIMES
Butler, unknown (Lieut.)	26	Oct	1854				DET
Butler, unknown (Lieut.)	27	Oct	1854				PDD
Butler, William A. (Esq.)	10	Nov	1843	26 Oct 1843			TRIB
Butler, Wm. (Col.)	21	Oct	1865	14 Oct 1865			PTIMES
Butler, Wm. H. (Barney)	21	Oct	1865	14 Oct 1865			PTIMES
Butler, Wm. H.G. (Prof.)	10	Nov	1853	09 Nov 1853			DET
Butt, Eliza	25	Mar	1830	19 Mar 1830	21	nee White	WT
Byers, Elizabeth R.	07	Nov	1850	05 Nov 1850			PT&C
Byers, James E.	25	Aug	1852	24 Aug 1852			PT&C
Bynum, Junius A.	21	Jun	1853				DET
Bynum, Junius A.	22	Jun	1853				PT&C
Byrne, Luke	28	Apr	1853				PDD
Byrnes, Robert	08	Jan	1846	18 Dec 1845			TRIB

Name	Notice Date			Death Date	Age	Comment	Paper
Cabel, Samuel	29	Jul	1865				PTIMES
Cable, Martha	24	Apr	1860	19 Apr 1860			DET
Caflin, male	19	Sep	1860	14 Sep 1860			WPT
Cahill, Wm.	04	Aug	1853	29 Jul 1853	72		DET
Cain, Daniel	24	Dec	1853	21 Dec 1853			PDD
Calb, Madaline	02	May	1854	26 Apr 1854	32		PDD (S)
Caldwell, Charles (Prof.)	16	Jul	1853				DET
Caldwell, Charles (Prof.)	20	Jul	1853	16 Jul 1853			PT&C
Caldwell, Hugh (Capt.)	26	Oct	1857	11 Oct 1857			DET
Caldwell, Hugh (Capt.)	28	Oct	1857	20 Oct 1857	22m9d		WPT
Caldwell, Jacob (Capt.)	20	Aug	1864	Aug 1864			PTIMES
	17	Sep	1864				
Caldwell, James D.	02	Jan	1855	01 Jan 1855	60		DET
Caldwell, John	08	Oct	1851				PT&C
Calhoun, John	22	Oct	1859	13 Oct 1859			PTIMES
Calhoun, male	09	May	1850				PT&C
Calhoun, unknown	02	Mar	1859	27 Feb 1859			DET
Callaway, John W.	21	Aug	1854				DET
Callaway, male	18	Aug	1854				PDD
Calloway, female	22	Aug	1853				DET
Camden, female	19	Jan	1860	19 Jan 1860	3		DET
Camden, Margaret A.	17	Jun	1865	05 Jun 1865	43y11m1d		PTIMES
Camden, Nanny E.	21	Jan	1860	19 Jan 1860	2y7m18d		PTIMES
Camden, William P.	01	Jun	1857	30 May 1857			DET
Camden, William P.	02	Jun	1857	30 May 1857			PSOT
Camden, William P.	03	Jun	1857	30 May 1857			WPT
Camden, William P.	17	Jun	1850	12 Jun 1850	16m12d		PI
Cameon, William	09	Jul	1864	04 Jul 1864			PTIMES
Cameron, Daniel	09	Jul	1864	04 Jul 1864			PTIMES
Camerone, Robert	09	Aug	1855				DET
Camp, James M.	07	Jun	1855	01 Jun 1855	38		DET
Campbell, Emeline	14	Apr	1851	4 Apr 1851	21y9m		PI
Campbell, female	01	May	1838				STRIB
Campbell, female	01	May	1838				STRIB
Campbell, Geo.	29	Aug	1850				PT&C
Campbell, George	18	Nov	1854	04 Nov 1854	70		DET
Campbell, Hugh	23	Jul	1856	Jul 1856			WPT
Campbell, J.W. (Dr.)	08	Dec	1852	28 Nov 1852			PT&C
Campbell, James	01	Jul	1854	28 Jun 1854			PDD
Campbell, James M.	15	Sep	1859	07 Sep 1859			DET
Campbell, James M.	20	Sep	1859	07 Sep 1859			PTIMES
Campbell, Joseph	01	Jun	1854		97		DET
Campbell, Lebens	24	Mar	1852	01 Mar 1852			PT&C
Campbell, male	22	Aug	1850	18 Aug 1850			PT&C
Campbell, Robert	04	Nov	1854	30 Oct 1854			DET

Deaths

Name	Notice Date			Death Date	Age	Comment	Paper
Campbell, unknown	26	Aug	1850	17 Aug 1850			PI
Campbell, unknown (Capt.)	23	Jul	1856	17 Jul 1856			WPT
Campbill, Darius S.	01	Feb	1862	16 Oct 1861			PTIMES
Campcell, M.W.	01	Dec	1843	18 Nov 1843			TRIB
Campfield, David	04	May	1853				PT&C
Canfield, Augustus (Capt.)	26	May	1854	13 Apr 1854			PDD
Canfield, Horace	03	Jan	1854	29 Dec 1853			PDD
Canfield, unknown	03, 06	Dec	1853				PDD
Canfield, unknown (Capt.)	25	Apr	1854				PDD
Cannon, Dennis	02	Aug	1854	30 Jul 1854			DET
Cannon, Dennis	03	Aug	1854	30 Jul 1854			PDD
Canter, Levi	20	Oct	1854	13 Oct 1854			DET
Canter, Levi	23	Oct	1854	13 Oct 1854			PDD
Canter, William	30	May	1863				PTIMES
Caperton, Woods	01	Dec	1860	28 Nov 1860			PTIMES
Carawan (or Caraman), Geo. W.	14, 19	Dec	1853				PDD
Carel, Joseph	13	Sep	1858				DET
Carel, Joseph	15	Sep	1858		65		WPT
Carel, Sarah	18	Apr	1854	16 Apr 1854	46		PDD
Carel, Sarah	19	Apr	1854		59		SVREP
Carey, Archibald (Esq.)	30	Sep	1854	Sep 1854			PDD
Carmine, David C.	01	Feb	1862	01 Jan 1862			PTIMES
Carmine, Tuman M.	01	Feb	1862	07 Jan 1862			PTIMES
Carpenter, male	09	Jul	1853	05 Jul 1853			PDD
Carr, Benton	04	Jun	1864				PTIMES
Carr, E.W.	16	Nov	1859				WPT
Carre, William J.	28	Jan	1865	21 Jan 1865	16y5m		PTIMES
Carrico, Thomas	01	Jul	1865				PTIMES
Carrigan, male	11	May	1853				PDD
Carroll, male	17	Dec	1851				PT&C
Carroll, Wm. (Hon.)(ex-Gov./Tenn.)	05	Apr	1844	22 Mar 1844	56		TRIB
Carskadon, John	02	Jun	1860	21 May 1860			PTIMES
Carter, Francis M.	28	May	1864	May 1864			PTIMES
Carter, Joseph	21	Sep	1853	07 Sep 1853			DET
Carter, Richard	11	Feb	1852	16 Jan 1852			PT&C
Cartner, female	12	May	1843			nee Parke	TRIB
Cartner, John	12	May	1843				TRIB
Cartner, unknown	12	May	1843		infant		TRIB
Carty, unknown	24	May	1854				PDD
Caruthers, Alexander A.	20	Feb	1838	12 Feb 1838	27		STRIB
Cary, John	05	Aug	1859	05 Aug 1859			DET

Name	Notice Date			Death Date	Age	Comment	Paper
Cary, John	07	Jul	1843	02 Jul 1843	114		TRIB
Case, John C.	05	Apr	1859	20 Mar 1859	29		PTIMES
Case, Lucius	30	Jul	1864	23 Jul 1864			PTIMES
Casey, James	24	Feb	1855				DET
Casey, Michael	10	Sep	1864				PTIMES
Casey, Thomas	03	Oct	1854	29 Sep 1854			DET
Cass, Lewis	29	Jul	1850	24 Jul 1850	22m		PI
Cassidy, Benjamin L.	02	Apr	1858	31 Mar 1858	10m		DET
Cassidy, William Harper	08	Sep	1858	08 Sep 1858	25y1m20d		DET
Casting, Victor	26	Apr	1844	05 Apr 1844			TRIB
Castle, male	11	Jun	1851				PT&C
Catlin, A. (Dr.)	02	Feb	1856	13 Jan 1855	85		DET
Cavanaugh, unknown	25	Feb	1852	10 Feb 1852	child		PT&C
Chamberlain, J.S.	03	Mar	1843	25 Feb 1843			TRIB
Chamberlain, male	06	Sep	1859	02 Sep 1859			DET
Chambers, Anderson	11	Jun	1851				PT&C
Chambers, John S.	09	Aug	1855				DET
Chambers, male	21	Apr	1843				TRIB
Chambers, Martin V.	30	Jul	1864				PTIMES
Chambers, Tho. (or Robert)	02, 03	Jun	1854	31 May 1854			DET
Chambers, Thomas	02	Jun	1854	31 May 1854			PDD
Chandler, Deborah	20	Jul	1857	20 Jul 1857	86		DET
Chandler, Deborah	21	Jul	1857	20 Jul 1857	86		PSOT
Chandler, Deborah	22	Jul	1857	20 Jul 1857	86		WPT
Chandler, Ellis	16	May	1850	11 May 1850	79		PT&C
Chandler, Ellis	20	May	1850	11 May 1850	79		PI
Chapin, Rhoda	20	Mar	1854	03 Mar 1854			DET
Chapman, George A.	11	Feb	1854	03 Feb 1854	7		DET
Chapman, Levi	22	Sep	1853	03 Sep 1853	17		DET
Chapman, male	09	Feb	1854	08 Feb 1854			PDD
Chapman, unknown	08	Feb	1854				DET
Chapman, W.S.	21	Apr	1855				DET
Charlesworth, female	02	Jul	1851	29 Jun 1851			PT&C
Charlesworth, Lewellan B.	21	Jul	1851	15 Jul 1851			PI
Charvis, Antonio Jose David	12, 19	May	1843				TRIB
Chase, Alice J.	22	Feb	1859	17 Feb 1859	52		DET
Chase, female	04	Feb	1852				PT&C
Chase, Philander (Rev.)	06	Oct	1852				PT&C
Chase, Richard H.	09	Feb	1855	09 Feb 1855	43		DET
Chase, unknown	09	Jun	1860	Jun 1860	child		PTIMES
Chavalier, Thomas H.	28	May	1864	May 1864			PTIMES
Cheney, male	10	Oct	1854				DET
Chenoweth, Gideon	16	Feb	1847		24		CLIPPER

Name	Notice Date			Death Date	Age	Comment	Paper
Chester, John K.	15	Jan	1851				PT&C
Chester, unknown (Col.)	26	Oct	1854				DET
Chester, unknown (Col.)	27	Oct	1854				PDD
Chickering, Jonas A.	13	Dec	1853	08 Dec 1853			PDD
Childs, male	23	Jul	1855				DET
Childs, male	23	Jul	1855	22 Jul 1855			DET
Chinn, C.	25	Sep	1858	04 Sep 1858			DET
Chinn, C.C.	28	Sep	1858	14 Sep 1858			PSOT
Chinn, C.C.	28	Sep	1858	14 Sep 1858			PTIMES
Chipman, unk. (Prof.)	23	Jun	1852	08 Jun 1852			PT&C
Chowing, James	30	Dec	1853	26 Dec 1853	50		DET
Chubbuck, Lavinia R.	14	Jul	1855	02 Jul 1855	70	aka Forrester, Fanny	DET
Church, Hannah	07	Aug	1860	27 Jul 1860	105		DET
Churchhill, female	19	Jun	1854	17 Jun 1854	50-60		DET
Churchhill, female	24	Mar	1854		3		PDD
Chute, A.S. (Lieut.)	06	Jun	1863	16 May 1863			PTIMES
Clapper, Edward (Priv.)	12	Dec	1863	Nov 1863			PTIMES
Clark (or Harsham), Louisa	30	Nov	1853	26 Nov 1853	18		PDD
Clark, Clarence	21	Dec	1859		9		DET
Clark, D.C.	28	Jan	1854	12 Jan 1854			PDD
Clark, Earl	07	Jun	1859				PTIMES
Clark, Eliza	02	Jan	1854	29 Dec 1853	45		PDD
Clark, Elizabeth	06	Jan	1854	30 Dec 1853	49		PDD (S)
Clark, Ella	16	Sep	1865	11 Sep 1865	5m11d		PTIMES
Clark, Ellen	23	Jul	1856	Jul 1856			WPT
Clark, female	08	Jun	1859	04 Jun 1859			WPT
Clark, female	26	Mar	1851	Mar 1851			PT&C
Clark, George	02	Mar	1860	13 Feb 1860	59		DET
Clark, George	25	Feb	1860	13 Feb 1860			PTIMES
Clark, Jerome	18	Mar	1865	15 Mar 1865		alias Sue Mundy	PTIMES
Clark, John (Gen.)	14, 28	Jan	1854				DET
Clark, Josephine Frances	09	Jul	1864	01 Jul 1864	25y3m13d		PTIMES
Clark, male	23	Jun	1854	07 Jun 1854			PDD
Clark, Maria	01	Dec	1860	30 Nov 1860	60		PTIMES
Clark, William	14	Feb	1854	1 Feb 1854	3		DET
Clark, William	19	Aug	1857	14 Aug 1857			WPT
Clark, Wm.	16	Feb	1844	09 Feb 1844		alias Graham	TRIB
Clarke, Harriet	09	Jan	1854	28 Dec 1853	33	nee Culberson	DET
Clarke, J.W. (Dr.)	01	Aug	1863				PTIMES
Clarke, John E.	21	May	1858	18 May 1858	47		DET
Clarke, John E.	25	May	1858	18 May 1858	47		PSOT

Name	Notice Date			Death Date	Age	Comment	Paper
Clarke, John E.	26	May	1858	18 May 1858	47		WPT
Clarkson, unknown	24	Jan	1854	14 Jan 1854		slave of	PDD
Clarkson, unknown	24	Jan	1854	14 Jan 1854		slave of	PDD
Clarkson, unknown	24	Jan	1854	14 Jan 1854		slave of	PDD
Clarkston, Annie Cade	26	May	1857	14 May 1857	7m		PSOT
Clay, Henry	14	Jun	1862	05 Jun 1862			PTIMES
Clay, Henry	07, 14	Jul	1852	28 Jun 1852			PT&C
Clay, Lucretia	16	Apr	1864	06 Apr 1864	83		PTIMES
Clayton, Thomas (Hon.)	29	Aug	1854		77		DET
Clayton, Walters A.	21	Jan	1852		37		PT&C
Clem, Andrew	01	Feb	1862	25 Nov 1861			PTIMES
Clem, George	29	Oct	1859	06 Oct 1859	83y2m17d		PTIMES
Clemens, Jere. (Hon.)	27	May	1865				PTIMES
Clement, J.B. (Dr.)	08	Jul	1854				PDD
Clendinen, William	12	Mar	1846				TRIB
Clerkner, unknown	30	Aug	1853	24 Aug 1853	1		PDD
Cleveland, male	12	Jul	1860	05 Jul 1860			DET
Cleveland, male	21	Jan	1852				PT&C
Cleveland, Margaret	31	Oct	1848	26 Oct 1848		nee Waller	DENQ
	07	Nov	1848				
Clevenger, unknown	24	Nov	1843	28 Sep 1843			TRIB
Clever, John	23	Dec	1865		110		PTIMES
Clifford, L.	06	Jun	1863	16 May 1863			PTIMES
Cline, female	02	Jul	1851	29 Jun 1851			PT&C
Clingman, Charles Scarborough	02	Aug	1839	31 Jul 1839	17m		STRIB
Clingman, Jacob	25	May	1820		8m		STEL
Clingman, Jane	17	Aug	1820	16 Aug 1820	28		STEL
Clough, Charles P.	01	Oct	1844		3y2m		PDEM
Clough, Sarah	09	Oct	1854	04 Oct 1854			DET
Clugsten, female	29	Dec	1857	29 Dec 1857			DET
Cobb, Julia	01	Apr	1865				PTIMES
Coburn, unknown	16	May	1863				PTIMES
Cochlan, male	24	Mar	1860	18 Mar 1860			DET
Cochran, D.K.	17	Dec	1855	15 Dec 1855	55		DET
Cochran, D.K.	19	Dec	1855	15 Dec 1855	55		WPT
Cochran, male	01	Mar	1844	16 Feb 1844			TRIB
Cochrane, female	02	Jun	1860	21 May 1860	child		PTIMES
Cody, E.	03	Sep	1851				PT&C
Coffman, Sarah	28	Dec	1858	20 Nov 1858			PTIMES
Colamy, Perry	26	Aug	1850	21 Aug 1850			PI
Colbath, Isaac	11	May	1853				PDD
Cole, Alaniah	30	Sep	1865	23 Sep 1865	65		PTIMES
Cole, Eddie	13	May	1865	14 Apr 1865			PTIMES

Deaths

Name	Notice Date			Death Date	Age	Comment	Paper
Cole, H.N.	16, 23	Jul	1851	09 Jul 1851			PT&C
	06	Aug	1851				
Cole, Jos. H. (2d Lieut.)	10	Oct	1863				PTIMES
Cole, Leonard	31	Dec	1853	26 Dec 1853	70		DET
Cole, Lucius	30	Nov	1826	Nov 1826			WT
Cole, male	26	Jan	1853	08 Jan 1853			PT&C
Cole, Minerva	22	Aug	1850	15 Aug 1850			PT&C
Cole, Minerva	19, 26	Aug	1850	15 Aug 1850			PI
Cole, unknown	06	Dec	1853	28 Nov 1853	2y		PDD (S)
Coleman, female	11	Feb	1852	02 Feb 1852			PT&C
Coleman, George	05	Mar	1851				PT&C
Coleman, S.H.	06	May	1853	27 Apr 1853			PDD
Coles, Thomas K. (Lieut.)	10	Dec	1864	18 Nov 1864	19		PTIMES
Collings, Elijah	25	Mar	1865	10 Mar 1865	79y5d		PTIMES
Collings, John	16	Jul	1851				PT&C
Collins, John	08	Jun	1855	05 Jun 1855			DET
Collins, John	13	May	1854	May 1854			PDD
Collins, male	14	Oct	1865	30 Aug 1865			PTIMES
Collins, male	24	Jan	1854	14 Jan 1854			PDD
Collins, male	30	Jun	1852	29 Jun 1852			PT&C
Collins, Robert Bruck	21	Apr	1858	20 Apr 1858			DET
Collins, Robert Bruck	28	Apr	1858	20 Apr 1858	2y3m		WPT
Collis, Nancy	11	Oct	1855	09 Oct 1855			DET
Colson, female	29	Mar	1859	Mar 1859			PTIMES
Colt, female	08	Feb	1862	03 Feb 1862	infant		PTIMES
Colt, Samuel (Col.)	01	Mar	1862	10 Jan 1862	49		PTIMES
Compston, female	20	Jun	1863	16 Jun 1863	2y8m		PTIMES
Compston, Frank	03	Jun	1865	02 Jun 1865			PTIMES
Comstock, Caroline H.	19	Nov	1864	15 Nov 1864	40		PTIMES
Comstock, George W.	05	Apr	1854	5 Apr 1854	30		DET
Comstock, John L. (Dr.)	14	Dec	1858	21 Nov 1858			PTIMES
Condeacon, (Indian Chief)	22	Oct	1859		100	Ontonagon Tribe	PTIMES
Conklin, Edgar	27	Dec	1854		22		DET
Connell, Patrick	22	Jun	1853				PDD
Connelly, unknown	21	Aug	1854	19 Aug 1854	10		DET (S)
Conner, Thomas	30	Dec	1859	28 Dec 1859			DET
Connolly, Henry	22	Apr	1857	16 Apr 1857	19		WPT
Connolly, unk. (Capt.)	26	Oct	1854				DET
Connolly, unk. (Capt.)	27	Oct	1854				PDD
Conolly, Henry	19	May	1857	17 Apr 1857	20		PSOT
Conolly, James	18	Aug	1854	18 Aug 1854	10		DET
Conrad, George P.	07	Nov	1850	16 Oct 1850			PT&C
Conrad, male	25	Jun	1856				WPT
Converse, male	19	Dec	1863		17		PTIMES

Name	Notice Date			Death Date	Age	Comment	Paper
Cook, Alexander Jerome	16	Apr	1856	07 Apr 1856	3y4m9d		WPT
Cook, Elihu	12	Sep	1860	11 Sep 1860			DET
Cook, Elihu	12	Sep	1860	11 Sep 1860			WPT
Cook, Hannah Sophia	23	Jun	1851	17 Jun 1851			PI
Cook, J.B.	11	Mar	1865	05 Mar 1865			PTIMES
Cook, John (Capt.)	20	Jun	1863	22 May 1863	51		PTIMES
Cook, John E.	17, 24	Dec	1859	16 Dec 1859			PTIMES
Cook, Joseph	21	Nov	1855				DET
Cook, male	02	Feb	1859		18		WPT
Cook, Maria Louisa	03	Oct	1850	26 Sep 1850	8		PT&C
Cook, Marie Louisa	30	Sep	1850	26 Sep 1850	8		PI
Cooke, unknown (Lieut.)	26	Oct	1854				DET
Cooke, unknown (Lieut.)	27	Oct	1854				PDD
Cooley, William	13	Aug	1855	12 Aug 1855	1y11d		DET
Coolwine, Frederick	10	Feb	1854	31 Jan 1854			DET
Coolwine, Frederick	13	Feb	1854				PDD
Coon, unknown (Dr.)	27	Feb	1854	24 Feb 1854			PDD
Coones, Duncan McArthur	25	Jun	1864	23 Jun 1864			PTIMES
Cooper, male	11	Aug	1858	27 Jul 1858			WPT
Cooper, unknown	16	May	1860	09 May 1860			WPT
Cooper, W.	16	Aug	1855				DET
Copeland, male	17, 24	Dec	1859	16 Dec 1859			PTIMES
Coppic, Edwin	17, 24	Dec	1859	16 Dec 1859			PTIMES
Corder, Thomas Jefferson	16	Jan	1851				PT&C
Coriell, Eva	06	Aug	1859	06 Aug 1859	5y2m		DET
Cork, John	18	Jul	1850	Jul 1850			PT&C
Corlies, Chares G.	31	Mar	1843				TRIB
	07	Apr	1843				
Cormick, J.R.	31	Oct	1844	Oct 1844			TRIB
Cornell, John M.	28	Oct	1854				DET
Corns, unknown	13	Mar	1855	06 Mar 1855	2		DET (S)
Correns, Jessie	07	Jan	1865	02 Jan 1865			PTIMES
Corson, William H.	27	Feb	1852	24 Feb 1852	2y5m		PI
Corwin, Ebenezer	14	Apr	1851	9 Apr 1851	60		PI
Corwin, female	29	Oct	1824	23 Oct 1824			PG&LA
Corwin, Harriet	24	Jun	1825	19 Jun 1825	33		PG&LA
Corwin, Sarah	16	May	1853	10 May 1853	81		PDD
Corwin, Thomas (Hon.)	23	Dec	1865	18 Dec 1865	71		PTIMES
Corwine, Elizabeth	13	May	1850	10 May 1850			PI
Corwine, Elizabeth	16	May	1850	10 May 1850			PT&C
Corwine, George	02	Jun	1852	28 May 1852	72		PT&C
Corwine, George	04	Jun	1852	28 May 1852	72		PI
Cory, Stephen	22	Dec	1853	18 Dec 1853	81		DET

Deaths

Name	Notice Date			Death Date	Age	Comment	Paper
Cosgrove, male	30	Jan	1855	25 Jan 1855			DET
Cosgrove, unk. (Capt.)	30	Jan	1855	25 Jan 1855			DET
Coterman, unknown	21	Sep	1853	17 Sep 1853	2		PDD (S)
Cotton, Nellie Buckminster	26	Mar	1864	14 Mar 1864	13m27d		PTIMES
Coultrin, Mary	26	Jul	1854	15 Jul 1854	18		DET
Counie, Sallie Ann	13	May	1854	May 1854	8		PDD
Courson, Samuel	21	Apr	1858	Apr 1858			WPT
Cousins, John	07	May	1851				PT&C
Cowne, T.W.	14	Nov	1863				PTIMES
Cox, female	07	Dec	1854	06 Dec 1854	child		DET
Cox, John	23	Jan	1838		85		STRIB
Cox, male	18	Jul	1855	04 Jul 1855	8		DET
Cox, unknown (Capt.)	02	Jan	1851	Dec 1850			PT&C
Cox, Wm. H.	18	Jun	1851				PT&C
Coyle, Jos.	17	Aug	1854	09 Aug 1854	42		DET (S)
Crabb, female	13	Aug	1864				PTIMES
Crabtree, Sylvester	01	Feb	1862	23 Dec 1861			PTIMES
Cradall, Nancy A.	05	Jul	1853	28 Jun 1853	22	nee Glidden	DET
Craddock, Paschal D.	10	Sep	1856				WPT
Craddock, unknown	19	Jan	1844	04 Jan 1844	child		TRIB
Craddock, unknown	19	Jan	1844	04 Jan 1844	child		TRIB
Craddock, unknown	19	Jan	1844	04 Jan 1844	child		TRIB
Craig, C.J. (Dr.)	05	Dec	1853	Oct 1853			DET
Crain, Adanijah	08	Mar	1854	07 Mar 1854	43		SVREP
Crain, Adanijah	09	Mar	1854	07 Mar 1854	43		PDD
Crain, E.	13	Mar	1855	18 Feb 1855	16		DET (S)
Crain, Ellen	17	Feb	1855	16 Feb 1855			DET
Crain, Ellen	23	Feb	1855	15 Feb 1855	16y10m		PI
Crain, Flora	12	May	1843	07 May 1843	7		TRIB
Crain, Horace	24	Dec	1851	18 Dec 1851	38		PT&C
Crain, Roswell	04	Mar	1853	2 Mar 1853	72		PI
Craine, Roswell	09	Mar	1853	02 Mar 1853	70		PT&C
Cram, John O.	21	Nov	1860				WPT
Cramer, male	18	Feb	1865				PTIMES
Crandall, Andrew	31	May	1859		12		PTIMES
Crandall, Nancy A.	06, 13	Jul	1853	28 Jun 1853	22	nee Glidden	PT&C
Crawford, Alice Mills	13	Apr	1853	31 Mar 1853	16m		PT&C
Crawford, Frances	22	Sep	1857	14 Sep 1857	37		PSOT
Crawford, Jane	06	Aug	1851				PT&C
Crawford, Jerome	06	May	1853	01 May 1853	10y26d		PDD
Crawford, John	22	May	1854				DET
Crawford, male	16, 30	Jun	1852	09 Jun 1852			PT&C
Crawford, Samuel	03	Aug	1853	25 Jul 1853			PT&C

Name	Notice Date			Death Date	Age	Comment	Paper
Creamer, Elizabeth	23	Mar	1854	15 Mar 1854			PDD
Creed, John (Esq.)	26	May	1843	27 Apr 1843	64		TRIB
Creighton, Jas. (Capt.)	15	Mar	1854				DET
Creighton, Robert	01	Jun	1820	18 May 1820	10y9d		STEL
Creighton, Wm.	10	Oct	1851	1 Oct 1851	93		PI
Crichton, Andrew Franklin	15	Sep	1854	15 Sep 1854	infant		DET
Crichton, Andrew, Jr.	14, 15	Mar	1855	14 Mar 1855	35		DET
Crichton, Florence	03	Nov	1852	01 Nov 1852	2y2m14d		PT&C
Crichton, Ruby K.W.	31	Dec	1858	24 Dec 1858	32		DET
Crichton, unknown	27	Sep	1854	16 Sep 1854	18m		DET (S)
Crichton, unknown	27	Sep	1854	16 Sep 1854	18m		PDD (S)
Crittenden, John J.	16	Oct	1854	13 Oct 1854			DET
Croasdale, Mary Orrel	20	Jun	1850	16 Jun 1850	8m16d		PT&C
Crockett, female	31	Mar	1860		74	Mrs. Davy	PTIMES
Crockett, unknown (Col.)	22, 23	Feb	1844				TRIB
Cromlish, John	03	May	1844	23 Apr 1844	23		TRIB
Crontinger, Dougherty	27	Sep	1854	22 Sep 1854	48		DET (S)
Crontinger, Dougherty	27	Sep	1854	22 Sep 1854	48		PDD (S)
Cropp, Mary	09	Jun	1860	Jun 1860			PTIMES
Cropper, Maggie	24	Mar	1858	23 Mar 1858	16		DET
Cropper, Maggie	31	Mar	1858	23 Mar 1858	16		WPT
Cropsey, male	18	Jun	1853	11 Jun 1853	8		DET
Cropsey, male	18	Jun	1853		5		DET
Cropsey, male	22	Jun	1853		8		PDD
Cropsey, male	22	Jun	1853		5		PDD
Crosden, female	05, 19	Mar	1851	28 Feb 1851		nee	PT&C
	04	Jun	1851			Webster (?)	
Crosden, male	05, 12	Mar	1851	28 Feb 1851			PT&C
	04	Jun	1851				
Crossly, Thomas	04	Jun	1864				PTIMES
Crouse, David	22	Apr	1837	15 Apr 1837			STRIB
Crouse, John	30	Jul	1856	25 Jul 1856	64		WPT
Crufield, John	19	Jan	1854	09 Jan 1854			PDD
Crull, Ruth	22	Jul	1825	16 Jul 1825			PG&LA
Crumlish, John C.	17	May	1844	23 Apr 1844	22		TRIB
Crutchfield, unknown	05	Dec	1853				DET
Crutchfield, unknown	03, 06	Dec	1853				PDD
Cruthers, James (Sgt.)	04	Jun	1864				PTIMES
Cull, Catharine	20	Jul	1854	17 Jul 1854	89		DET
Cull, Michael	19	Aug	1854	14 Aug 1854			DET
Cull, Patrick	23	Mar	1853				PT&C
Cummings, Rebecca	25	Jul	1829		30		WT
Cummings, unknown	18	Jun	1851	07 Jun 1851	child		PT&C
Cummins, George	02	May	1850	28 Apr 1850			PT&C

Name	Notice Date			Death Date	Age	Comment	Paper
Cunningham, E.L.	10	May	1855	06 May 1855			DET
Cunningham, James	30	May	1844	19 May 1844	23y1m18d		TRIB
Curles, Wm. L.	27	Jun	1855	22 Jun 1855			DET
Curran, Hannah	09	Jun	1860	Jun 1860			PTIMES
Currie, female	28	May	1851	11 May 1851			PT&C
Currie, Samuel A. (Capt.)	19	Apr	1862				PTIMES
Curry, Otway	26	Feb	1855	22 Feb 1855			DET
Curtis, Caroline	19	Aug	1850	13 Aug 1850			PI
Curtis, W.B.	09	Aug	1855				DET
Curtiss, L.G.	05	May	1852	28 Apr 1852			PT&C
Curvis, Caroline	15	Aug	1850	13 Aug 1850			PT&C
Cushing, Luther C.	12	Jan	1854	05 Jan 1854			PDD
Cushing, William V.H.	17	Apr	1838	27 Mar 1838	35		STRIB
Cushman, Diodate	20	Mar	1838	27 Feb 1838	45		STRIB
Cutler, Ephraim (Judge)	18	May	1854				DET
Cutler, Ephram	19	Jul	1853		87		PDD
Cutler, Henry M.	11	Aug	1852	02 Aug 1852	40y1m		PT&C
Cutler, Jonathan B.	23	Feb	1853	12 Feb 1853	44		PT&C
Cutler, Laura Jane	16	Feb	1853	07 Feb 1853	3y4m		PT&C
Cutler, Lydia Ann	02	Mar	1853	01 Mar 1853	17		PT&C
Cutler, Lydia Ann	04	Mar	1853		14		PI
Cutler, Lyman	10	Dec	1851	03 Dec 1851	22		PT&C
Cutler, Rhoda B.	26	Mar	1856	09 Mar 1856	33		WPT
Cutler, Rusina D.	16	Feb	1853	08 Feb 1853	20y9m		PT&C
Cypress, Catherine	03	Nov	1854				DET
Cysley, Mary J.	14	Sep	1853	08 Sep 1853	2		PDD (S)
Dahrley, John	07	May	1855	29 Apr 1855			DET
Dailey, unknown	26	Apr	1859	25 Apr 1859	4		DET
Dallam, unknown (Major)	21	Jun	1862	15 Jun 1862			PTIMES
Dallas, Alexander J. (Commander)	28	Jul	1843				TRIB
Dallas, George M.	07	Jan	1865			ex-V.Pres.	PTIMES
Dalton, William	08	Sep	1854				PDD
Damarin, Charles A.M.	02	May	1860	25 Apr 1860	63		WPT
Damarin, Charles A.M.	26	Apr	1860	25 Apr 1860	63		DET
Damarin, Charles A.M.	28	Apr	1860	25 Apr 1860	63		PTIMES
Damarin, female	20	Oct	1843	16 Oct 1843	68		TRIB
Damarin, Louis Augustus	17	Dec	1864	14 Dec 1864	9m27d		PTIMES
Damarin, Pauline	04	Jun	1859	03 Jun 1859	4		DET
Damarin, Pauline	08	Jun	1859	03 Jun 1859	4		WPT
Damarin, Pauline Hariette M.	15	Mar	1844	08 Mar 1844			TRIB
Damarin, William Virgie	14	Jan	1860	13 Jan 1860	5m		DET
Damarin, William Virgie	18	Jan	1860	13 Jan 1860	5m		WPT
Dan, Samuel	22	Mar	1855	15 Mar 1855	101		DET

Name	Notice Date			Death Date	Age	Comment	Paper
Dana, John (Dr.)	30	Jun	1855	11 Jun 1855	28		DET
Dandridge, Nathaniel	24	Nov	1852	09 Nov 1852			PT&C
Daniels, William	13	Jun	1850	06 Jun 1850	13		PT&C
Dann (or Dunn) I.T.	01	Aug	1854				DET
Danon, Emanuel	30	Jan	1854				DET
Darbor, William D.	19	Nov	1864				PTIMES
Darby, Sanders	16	Sep	1825	13 Sep 1825	59		PG&LA
Darlington, Joseph (Gen)	13	Aug	1851	09 Aug 1851	86		PT&C
Darst, female	28	Nov	1855	21 Nov 1855		nee Curtis	WPT
Darst, Jacob	16	Apr	1856				WPT
Daugherty, John James	19	Aug	1859	28 Jun 1859	23		DET
Daugherty, John James	24	Aug	1859	28 Jun 1859	23		WPT
Daughters, James	02	Jul	1853	15 Jun 1853	92y9m9d		PDD
Davey, Alfred Ingalls	18	Jun	1851	11 Jun 1851	1y6m15d		PT&C
David, B.	10	May	1853	06 May 1853			PDD
Davidson, Morris W.	28	Oct	1854				DET
Davidson, Nancy	17	Dec	1853	5 Dec 1853	50		DET
Davies, R.	30	Aug	1854	27 Aug 1854			DET
Davies, Sam W. (Col.)	05	Jan	1844	22 Dec 1843	67		TRIB
Davies, Thomas E.	17	Nov	1854	10 Nov 1854	23y7m		DET
Davis, A.	13	Oct	1854	09 Oct 1854	60		PDD (S)
Davis, Amelia	09	Jun	1860	Jun 1860			PTIMES
Davis, Arthur C.	30	May	1863	22 May 1863	57		PTIMES
	06	Jun	1863				
Davis, Charles	16	Jan	1854				DET
Davis, Charles	16	Jan	1854				PDD
Davis, Charles H.	16	Aug	1862	10 Aug 1862	29y5m		PTIMES
Davis, David	07	Dec	1858		104		PTIMES
Davis, Elizabeth H.	20	Oct	1857	09 Oct 1857	37		PSOT
Davis, Elizabeth H.	21	Oct	1857	09 Oct 1857	37		DET
Davis, Enoch	06	Aug	1864				PTIMES
Davis, Evan J.	03	Jan	1855	05 Dec 1854	55		DET
Davis, female	19	Sep	1860	14 Sep 1860			WPT
Davis, female	20	Aug	1851				PT&C
Davis, female	29	Dec	1843	09 Dec 1843	child		TRIB
Davis, female	29	Oct	1851	19 Oct 1851			PT&C
Davis, Genevieve Hamilton	05	Nov	1859	04 Nov 1859	6y	or Hamilton	DET
Davis, Henry	15	Aug	1854	Aug 1854			PDD
Davis, J.A.D. (Lieut.)	23	Jan	1854	21 Jan 1854			PDD
Davis, James	14	Mar	1854	07 Mar 1854			PDD
Davis, Jeremiah	13	Aug	1851	24 Jul 1851			PT&C
Davis, Jno.	25	Aug	1852	09 Jul 1852	27		PT&C
Davis, John	01	May	1854				DET
Davis, John	22	Aug	1850				PT&C

Name	Notice Date			Death Date	Age	Comment	Paper
Davis, male	09	Jun	1860	Jun 1860	child		PTIMES
Davis, male	11	Mar	1854	07 Mar 1854			DET
Davis, R.D.	06	Jun	1863	16 May 1863			PTIMES
Davis, Samuel	11	Jan	1832	05 Jan 1832	infant		PC
Davis, Sarah	24	Oct	1860	24 Oct 1860	50		DET
Davis, Sarah	31	Oct	1860	24 Oct 1860	50		WPT
Davis, Sarah	31	May	1862	25 May 1862	28		PTIMES
Davis, unknown	23	Jul	1859		9		DET
Davis, Wm. Wallace (Esq.)	01	Apr	1854	20 Mar 1854			PDD
Davisson, John	18	Mar	1831				PC&WT
Davisson, John	23	Jul	1851	10 Jul 1851	2y2m		PT&C
Davisson, John	28	Jul	1851	10 Jul 1851	2y2m		PI
Davisson, Reuben	07	May	1856	24 Apr 1856	58		WPT
Day, John F.	22	Sep	1857	25 Aug 1857	45		PSOT
Day, Morgan	12	Feb	1851		22		PT&C
Day, unknown	03	Mar	1843	Feb 1843			TRIB
Dayton, Wm. L. (Hon.)	24	Dec	1864	02 Dec 1864			PTIMES
De Sangua, female	11	May	1853				PDD
Deaver, James	21, 28	Jun	1859	19 Jun 1859			DET
Deaver, male	20	Jul	1854				PDD
Dedson, John	23	Jul	1856	Jul 1856			WPT
Deever, James	22	Jun	1859	19 Jun 1859			WPT
DeGrummond, Willie	17	Sep	1856	11 Sep 1856	14m		WPT
Deitz, Conrad	08	Jul	1853	07 Jul 1853	24		PDD
Delancy, Bishop	08	Apr	1865				PTIMES
Delano, H.C. (Dr.)	26	May	1860	21 May 1860			PTIMES
Delner, male	12	Apr	1844	28 Mar 1844			TRIB
Delong, Ann Jane	29	Mar	1827	28 Mar 1827	33	nee Porter	WT
Demit, Isaac	19	Aug	1854	15 Aug 1854			DET
Dempsey, J.W.	04	Aug	1852	27 Jul 1852	35		PT&C
Deniston, female	12	Jun	1854	08 Jun 1854		nee Taylor	DET
Deniston, female	12	Jun	1854	08 Jun 1854		nee Taylor	PDD
Denning, female	11	Mar	1837				STRIB
Denning, unknown (Col.)	12	Oct	1858				PSOT
Dennis, J.W. (M.D.)	19	Sep	1863	16 Sep 1863			PTIMES
Dennis, Joanna E.	01	Jun	1858	29 May 1858	28y1m11d		DET
Dennis, Joanna E.	01	Jun	1858	29 May 1858	28y1m11d		PSOT
Dennis, John	14	Apr	1858	03 Apr 1858	28		WPT
Dennis, Mary Ann	28	Apr	1852	26 Apr 1852	40		PT&C
Dennis, Mary Ann	30	Apr	1852	26 Apr 1852	40		PI
Dennis, Mary Emma	28	Apr	1851	22 Apr 1851	10m		PI
Dennis, R.	13	Apr	1858	05 Apr 1858	28		PSOT
Dennis, Thomas	19	Jan	1853	Jan 1853			PT&C

Name	Notice Date			Death Date	Age	Comment	Paper
Densmore, Judith Elizabeth	21	Oct	1865	15 Oct 1865	1y3m13d		PTIMES
Densmore, Sydney Francis	14	Jan	1860	14 Jan 1860	15m		DET
Densmore, Sydney Francis	18	Jan	1860	14 Jan 1860	15m		WPT
Denton, Anna	01	Mar	1854	09 Feb 1854			PDD
Denton, male	22	May	1854	11 May 1854			PDD
Denton, W.B.	13	Apr	1855	13 Apr 1855			DET
DeRomas, J.C.	15	Sep	1843	21 Aug 1843			TRIB
Derr, Alex.	15	Jun	1854	12 Jun 1854			DET
Desmond, Jane	31	Aug	1854				PDD
Devacht, Jane Frances	26	Jan	1856	18 Jan 1855	81		DET
Devacht, Jane Frances	30	Jan	1856	18 Jan 1856	81		WPT
Devers, James	21	Jun	1859				PTIMES
Devight, male	12	May	1853				PDD
Devise, Phillip	08	Jun	1855	05 Jun 1855			DET
Dew, unknown (Capt.)	27	Oct	1854				PDD
Dew. unknown (Capt.)	26	Oct	1854				DET
Dewey, Amos	22	Aug	1853	21 Aug 1853			PDD
Dexter, Francis S.	24	Sep	1856	22 Sep 1856			WPT
Dickinson, Elizabeth	06	Oct	1853	19 Sep 1853	95	aka Clugsten	DET
Dickson, unk. (Major)	24	Jul	1855				DET
Digen, W.H.	05	May	1854				PDD
Dille, Lewis	04	Nov	1854				DET
Dillon, Alfred Gerard	01	Jul	1850	29 Jun 1850	15m		PI
Dillon, John	23	Jul	1856	Jul 1856			WPT
Dillon, Mary	05	Apr	1855	20 Mar 1855		nee Hamilton	DET
Dillon, Missouri Alice	20	Jul	1858	01 Jul 1858	11m15d		PSOT
Dimmock, D.W.	11	May	1853				PDD
Dinton, female	18	Aug	1854				PDD
Diver, Joseph A.	05	Nov	1851	30 Oct 1851			PT&C
Divis, B.S.	11	May	1853				PDD
Dixon, Meredith	04	Feb	1854	10 Jan 1854			DET
Doane, Catharine W.	09	Sep	1853		33		DET
Doane, Charles Edward	18	Mar	1858	14 Mar 1858			DET
Doane, female	14	Sep	1853	10 Sep 1853	28		PDD (S)
Doane, George Washington	31	May	1859	25 May 1859	60		PTIMES
Dobbins, John W.	30	Apr	1864	15 Apr 1864			PTIMES
Dobyn, male	20	Dec	1853	16 Dec 1853			DET
Dobyns, Luther	22	Dec	1853				PDD
Dobyns, Mary	09	Jan	1855	01 Jan 1855	14		DET
Doddridge, Ellen S.	04	Mar	1857	26 Feb 1857	40		WPT
Doddridge, Julian B.	01	Feb	1862	25 Dec 1862			PTIMES

Deaths

Name	Notice Date			Death Date	Age	Comment	Paper
Doddridge, Juliana	17	Aug	1859	22 Jul 1859	82		WPT
Doddridge, Phillip B. (Capt.)	19	Sep	1860	09 Sep 1860	65		WPT
Doddridge, Phillip B. (Capt.)	12, 14	Sep	1860	09 Sep 1860	65		DET
Dodds, T.B.	06	Jun	1863	16 May 1863			PTIMES
Dodge, Ellen	20	Jul	1854				DET
Dodge, male	01	Aug	1853	22 Jul 1853			DET
Dois, Fred (Lt.)	16	May	1863				PTIMES
Dole, Elizabeth Emily	15	Aug	1844	08 Aug 1844	9m9d		TRIB
Dole, Samuel	30	Apr	1856	26 Apr 1856	64		WPT
Doley, unknown	27	Jul	1853	19 Jul 1853	3		PDD (S)
Donahoe, John	01	Nov	1862	29 Oct 1862			PTIMES
Donaldson, Israel	02	Mar	1860	09 Feb 1860	95		DET
Donaldson, Israel	25	Feb	1860	09 Feb 1860	95		PTIMES
Donelly, Robert	13	Jul	1853				PDD
Donelly, Thos.	21	Apr	1855				DET
Donley, Dan	17	Nov	1852				PT&C
Donnavan, Gilbert	19	May	1852	10 May 1852			PT&C
Donne, Charles	31	Oct	1844	Oct 1844			TRIB
	07	Nov	1844				
Donohey, John	25	Jul	1854				DET
Donohoe, Samuel Wilson	15	Dec	1854	09 Dec 1854	11y7m		DET
Donovan, Timothy	07	May	1851	03 May 1851			PT&C
Door, male	17	May	1855	12 May 1855			DET
Dopp, Jacob	29	Mar	1859	Mar 1859			PTIMES
Doran, Jno.	23	Jul	1856	Jul 1856			WPT
Doras, James	07	Nov	1844	Oct 1844			TRIB
Dorer, unknown	28	Sep	1853	19 Sep 1853	1		PDD (S)
Dorman, Rufus	28	May	1851				PT&C
Dorne, unknown	24	Aug	1853		1		DET
Dorr, female	09	Jun	1860	03 Jun 1860			PTIMES
Dorr, male	09	Jun	1860	03 Jun 1860			PTIMES
Dorr, Thomas W.	30	Dec	1854	27 Dec 1854			DET
Dorries, unknown (Lieut.)	23	May	1863				PTIMES
Doty, Abner	19	Sep	1844	17 Sep 1844	42		TRIB
Doucett, male	01	Jun	1853				PT&C
Dougherty, Charles	28	Jul	1852				PT&C
Dougherty, male	29	Sep	1852	12 Sep 1852			PT&C
Douglas, John W.	21	Aug	1854				DET
Douglas, male	06	Aug	1851	01 Aug 1851			PT&C
Douglas, male	28	Oct	1854				DET
Douglas, Mary	21	Nov	1855	18 Nov 1855	1y2m29d		DET
Douglas, W. (Lieut.)	21	May	1855				DET
Douglass, Richard (Esq.)	18	Feb	1852	14 Feb 1852	67		PT&C

Name	Notice Date			Death Date	Age	Comment	Paper
Douglass, Thomas	23	Jun	1853				PDD
Dowd, Philander W.	19	Aug	1859	05 Aug 1859	21		DET
Dowd, Philander W.	24	Aug	1859	05 Aug 1859	21		WPT
Dowdal, unknown (Capt.)	26	Oct	1854				DET
Dowdal, unknown (Capt.)	27	Oct	1854				PDD
Dowling, Edward	05	Feb	1851		child		PT&C
Downey, Eliza	01	Oct	1856	25 Sep 1856	21	nee Dewey	WPT
Downey, Lake Erie	08	Mar	1854	07 Mar 1854	2y1m1d		SVREP
Downey, M. (Corporal)	06	Jun	1863	16 May 1863			PTIMES
Downing, William	25	Aug	1854	22 Aug 1854	30		DET
Downing, William	26	Aug	1854	22 Aug 1854			PDD
Downs, J.F.J.	17	Dec	1856	13 Dec 1856			WPT
Downy, Lake Erie	08	Mar	1854	07 Mar 1854	2		PDD
Drake, Thomas M. (Dr.)	17	May	1859	16 May 1859			PTIMES
Drake, Harriet	13	Jul	1858	25 Jun 1858		nee Rochester	PSOT
Drake, Paul P.	03	Nov	1860	30 Oct 1860	25		DET
Drake, Paul P. (or B.)	07	Nov	1860	30 Oct 1860	25		WPT
Drake, Ruth Francenia	06	Jun	1850	04 Jun 1850	11m1w		PT&C
Drake, unknown (Dr.)	17	Nov	1852	12 Nov 1852			PT&C
Dray, male	24	Aug	1853	09 Aug 1853			PT&C
Drayer, male	18	Aug	1853	09 Aug 1853			PDD
Dresbach, David	15	Apr	1865	04 Apr 1865	60		PTIMES
Drescher, Nancy	21	Nov	1850	19 Nov 1850	child		PT&C
Dresher, A.	13	Oct	1854	04 Oct 1854	35		PDD (S)
Dresher, Caspar	15	May	1854				PDD
Dresher, male	05	Oct	1854				DET
Drew, Albert	22	Sep	1857	15 Sep 1857	10m		PSOT
Driggs, Alice	23	Jan	1864	14 Jan 1864	18		PTIMES
Drum, Edward	13, 20	Aug	1851	04 Aug 1851			PT&C
Drummonds, Polly	30	Sep	1858	23 Sep 1858	35		DET
Duchlin, male	07	Dec	1853	03 Dec 1853			PDD
Duchlin, unknown	05	Dec	1853	03 Dec 1853			DET
Dudley, Wm. E. (Capt.)	03	Dec	1851				PT&C
Duffey, male	30	Mar	1855				DET
Dugan, Agnes	28	Nov	1859	27 Nov 1859	4y3m12d		DET
Dugan, Betty M.	14	Nov	1863	06 Nov 1863	3y6m		PTIMES
Dugan, Hannah M.	14	Nov	1863	07 Nov 1863	1y9m		PTIMES
Dugan, Taylor Mulin	30	Nov	1859	26 Nov 1859	10y8m		WPT
Dugan, Taylor Mulin	26, 28	Nov	1859	26 Nov 1859	10y8m		DET
Dumhauf, Charles	28	Jun	1862	03 May 1862	26y4m		PTIMES
Dumond, unknown	16	Aug	1859	01 Aug 1859			DET
Dumond, unknown	24	Aug	1859	01 Aug 1859	child		WPT
Dunbar, Aaron	02, 22	Jan	1855	28 Nov 1854	45		DET
Dunbar, David	31	May	1859				PTIMES

Name	Notice Date			Death Date	Age	Comment	Paper
Duncan, Alexander (Hon./Dr.)	30	Mar	1853	23 Mar 1853			PT&C
Duncan, Joseph	09	Feb	1844				TRIB
Duncan, male	18	Mar	1865		5		PTIMES
Duncan, unknown (Capt.)	26	May	1852				PT&C
Dungan, Julia Ann	21	Mar	1863	16 Mar 1863	37y1m7d		PTIMES
Dunham, Bennajah C.	15	Dec	1854	12 Dec 1854	11		DET
Dunham, Daniel H.	04	Jul	1854				PDD
Dunham, male	10	Nov	1860	09 Nov 1860	2		PTIMES
Dunlap, Robert	03	Mar	1843	27 Feb 1843	infant		TRIB
Dunn, John H.	21	Jun	1854				PDD
Dunn, Thomas	22	Mar	1855				DET
Dunn, unknown (Maj.)	31	Aug	1854				DET
Dupont, female	11	Feb	1852				PT&C
Dupont, unk. (Rear Adm.)	08	Jul	1865	23 Jun 1865	62		PTIMES
Dupuy, Jesse L.	11	Apr	1829		48		WT
Dupuy, William (Capt.)	28	Nov	1844	21 Nov 1844	74		TRIB
Durand, Ferdinand	29	Jul	1857	20 Jul 1857			WPT
Durham, Jacob	17	Nov	1854	15 Oct 1854	74		DET
Durham, James M.	21	Jan	1854	11 Jan 1854			PDD
Duvall, male	04	Oct	1854	02 Oct 1854			DET
Dwight, N.G.O. (Rev.)	08	Feb	1862	01 Feb 1862			PTIMES
Dwight, W.G.	11	May	1853				PDD
Dye, male	02	Jul	1851	14 Jun 1851	15		PT&C
Dye, William (Rev.)	02	Jul	1851	14 Jun 1851			PT&C
Eagen, Josph	04	Nov	1865				PTIMES
Earley, Patrick	15	Mar	1859	24 Feb 1859	46		PTIMES
East, Charlotte Laura	04	Nov	1850	24 Oct 1850			PI
East, Charlotte Laura	31	Oct	1850	24 Oct 1850			PT&C
East, George	22	May	1855				
East, Julia Almira	04	Nov	1850	26 Oct 1850			PI
East, Julia Almira	31	Oct	1850	26 Oct 1850			PT&C
East, Martha Louisa	31	Oct	1850	26 Oct 1850			PT&C
East, Martha Louise	04	Nov	1850	26 Oct 1850			PI
Eastly, male	28	Jul	1854	30 Jun 1854			PDD
Eaton, T.	06	Jun	1863	16 May 1863			PTIMES
Eba, Mary Francis	24	Aug	1854	11 Aug 1854	2y6m8d		DET
Eckenberger, male	02	Dec	1850				PI
Eckhart, Eleanor Ann	28	Apr	1854	17 Apr 1854	39	nee Carlisle	DET
Eddington, unk. (Capt.)	26	Oct	1854				DET
Eddington, unk. (Capt.)	27	Oct	1854				PDD
Eddington, unk. (Lieut.)	26	Oct	1854				DET
Eddington, unk. (Lieut.)	27	Oct	1854				PDD
Eddleman, female	11	Aug	1852				PT&C
Eddleman, unknown	11	Aug	1852		child		PT&C

Name	Notice Date			Death Date	Age	Comment	Paper
Edgar, Arch	25	Feb	1860				PTIMES
Edinger, male	18	Feb	1865	12 Feb 1865	3		PTIMES
Edmands, H.S.	03	Mar	1843	25 Feb 1843			TRIB
Edminston, James	04	Sep	1854	02 Sep 1854			PDD
Edmonds, unknown	13	Mar	1855	26 Feb 1855	2m		DET (S)
Edmonds, Zala	06	Dec	1854	05 Dec 1854	5 or 6		DET
Edmondson, A.V.	06	May	1854				PDD
Edson, Mary	06	Oct	1858	01 Oct 1858		Swingle (stepfather)	WPT
Edwards, A.E.	07	Nov	1844	Oct 1844			TRIB
Edwards, Clinton	10	Aug	1859				DET
Edwards, Frederick	28	Nov	1844				TRIB
Edwards, George	06	Aug	1855				DET
Edwards, Jesse	12	Nov	1856	Nov 1856	103		WPT
Edwards, Joseph (Rev.)	18	Aug	1860	17 Aug 1860	31		DET
Edwards, Joseph (Rev.)	22	Aug	1860	17 Aug 1860	31		WPT
Edwards, male	08	Sep	1852	03 Sep 1852			PT&C
Edwards, male	08	Sep	1852	03 Sep 1852			PT&C
Edwards, male	08	Sep	1852	03 Sep 1852			PT&C
Effner, E.	09	Jun	1860	Jun 1860			PTIMES
Egerton, Graham (Col.)	19	May	1855	17 May 1855			DET
Eggleston, female	30	Jul	1864	23 Jul 1864			PTIMES
Eichelstein, male	20	Sep	1862	14 Sep 1862	12		PTIMES
Elden, male	11	Feb	1857	05 Feb 1857	infant		WPT
Elden, Martha	13	Apr	1858	13 Apr 1858	2m		DET
Elden, Martha	14	Apr	1858	13 Apr 1858	2m		WPT
Elden, Martha	20	Apr	1858	13 Apr 1858	2m		PSOT
Elden, William	10	Jul	1854	10 Jul 1854	infant		DET
Elkins, male	23	Jun	1854	07 Jun 1854			PDD
Ellafield, unknown	29	Jun	1855		2		DET
Ellafield, unknown	29	Jun	1855		4		DET
Ellery, William	18	Mar	1820		94		STEL
Ellington, James	26	Apr	1860				DET
Elliott, John	25	May	1854	23 May 1854			DET
Ellis, F.M.	26	Mar	1855		35		DET
Ellis, male	02	Apr	1855				DET
Ellis, unknown	20	Apr	1853	13 Apr 1853	child		PT&C
Ellis, unknown	20	Apr	1853	13 Apr 1853	child		PT&C
Ellis, unknown (Major)	10	Oct	1863				PTIMES
Ellison, Felix	02	Mar	1860	11 Feb 1860	50		DET
Ellison, George	29	Oct	1851	26 Oct 1851			PT&C
Ellison, William	18	Nov	1865				PTIMES
Ellison, Wm. A.	04	Jun	1864				PTIMES
Ellston, Jonathan	14	Feb	1854				PDD
Ely, D.L. (Dr.)	04	Apr	1863	21 Mar 1863			PTIMES

Name	Notice Date			Death Date	Age	Comment	Paper
Ely, Sarah Wilson	11	Jun	1855	07 Jun 1855	14y16d		DET
Emery, Samuel (Rev.)	27	Jan	1860		75		DET
Emig, male	31	Aug	1855				DET
Emrich, Jacob	11	Nov	1853	9 Nov 1853	82		DET
Endicott, Daniel	28	May	1851	25 Apr 1851			PT&C
Engelbrecht, F.W.	28	May	1864	25 May 1864	42		PTIMES
Englebrecht, Charlotte Barbara	09	Sep	1850	5 Sep 1850			PI
Englison, female	22	Feb	1855		infant		DET
Englison, male	22	Feb	1855		2		DET
Ennis, Susan	05	Aug	1831			nee Clingman	PC&WT
Enochs, male	12	Apr	1844	28 Mar 1844			TRIB
Enslow, Mary	25	Sep	1858	07 Sep 1858	58		DET
Enslow, Mary	28	Sep	1858	17 Sep 1858	58		PSOT
Enslow, Mary	28	Sep	1858	17 Sep 1858	58		PTIMES
Enslow, Resin	03	Sep	1844		48		PDEM
Enslow, Rezin	05	Sep	1844		48		TRIB
Ereeman (or Freeman), James	26	Jan	1855	17 Jan 1855			DET
Estill, Eliphaz	06	Dec	1862	23 Nov 1862	28		PTIMES
Estill, unknown (Judge)	19	Jul	1853				DET
Estill, unknown (Judge)	20	Jul	1853	14 Jul 1853			PT&C
Eustis, unk. (Brig. Gen.)	14	Jul	1843	27 Jun 1843	57		TRIB
Eustis, William	18	Mar	1825	06 Feb 1825			PG&LA
Evans, David	07	Jul	1855	21 Jun 1855			DET
Evans, Elijah	12	May	1860	02 May 1860			DET
Evans, female	20	Aug	1851				PT&C
Evans, James (Corp.)	06	Jun	1863	01 May 1863			PTIMES
Evans, John	22	Mar	1855				DET
Evans, male	24	Dec	1853				PDD
Evans, Mary	09	Dec	1853	03 Dec 1853	37	nee Poage	PDD
Evans, Mary	31	Dec	1853	03 Dec 1853	37	nee Poage	DET
Evans, unknown (Capt.)	02	Jun	1860	29 May 1860			PTIMES
Evans, unknown (Capt.)	26	Oct	1854				DET
Evans, unknown (Capt.)	27	Oct	1854				PDD
Evans, William	22	Jul	1854				DET
Evans, William	24	Jul	1854	17 Jul 1854			PDD
Everett, Edward	21	Jan	1865	15 Jan 1865	71		PTIMES
Ewing, female	06	Aug	1856				WPT
Ewing, female	27	Feb	1864				PTIMES
Ewing, Presley	02	Oct	1854	27 Sep 1854			DET
Exline, Daniel	03	Sep	1851	27 Aug 1851			PT&C
Fagan, Ann	24	Aug	1854	20 Aug 1854			PDD
Falls, Bellows	11	May	1853				PDD
Fanning, male	16	Dec	1857				WPT

Name	Notice Date			Death Date	Age	Comment	Paper
Fanshaw, Daniel	03	Mar	1860	Feb 1860	72		PTIMES
Farden, Ella	21	Mar	1863	04 Mar 1863	25		PTIMES
Farenbaugh, Cephas	10, 16	May	1855	03 May 1855	23		DET
Farmer, John W.	29	Mar	1859	24 Mar 1859			PTIMES
Farney, Mary	18	Feb	1852	06 Feb 1852			PT&C
Farrar, Nancy	25	Aug	1854	17 Aug 1854			DET
Farrer, male	16	Jul	1853				PDD
Farrer, male	20	Jul	1853				PT&C
Farrer, male	20	Jul	1853				PT&C
Farril, Edward	27	Jun	1860	25 Jun 1860			WPT
Farris, William	24	Aug	1853				PDD
Farwell, O.K.	18	Feb	1854	13 Feb 1854			PDD
Fasgan, Ann	23	Aug	1854	20 Aug 1854			DET
Faulkner, Neil	12	May	1852	04 May 1852			PT&C
Fee, Nancy	27	Jun	1855				DET
Fee, William Marcus	17	Feb	1854	7 Feb 1854	3y1m12d		DET
Ferguson, unknown	05	Aug	1825		infant		PG&LA
Ferguson, Wm. I. (Hon.)	26	Oct	1858	14 Sep 1858	34		PTIMES
Ferrand, Jerod	12	Jul	1862	09 Jul 1862	105y7m7d		PTIMES
Ferree, A.H.	07	Dec	1853	30 Nov 1853			PDD
Ferree, John (Rev.)	18	Jul	1850	06 Jul 1850			PT&C
Ferrill, Horatio N.	21	May	1853	21 May 1853			PDD
Ferrill, Patrick	14	Mar	1854	02 Mar 1854	40		PDD
Fetman, male	03	Dec	1853		3		DET
Fetman, male	03	Dec	1853		1y6m		DET
Feurt, Frank B. (or Benjamin Franklin)	23	Jun	1852	15 Jun 1852	16		PT&C
Feurt, Gabriel	16	Sep	1850	9 Sep 1850	71		PI
Filley, Homer	11	Mar	1865				PTIMES
Fillmore, Charles	04	Aug	1854	27 Jul 1854			DET
Fillmore, female	06	Apr	1853	30 Mar 1853			PT&C
Fillmore, James	08	Aug	1854				PDD
Fillmore, Mary Abby	04	Aug	1854				DET
Filmore, female	28	Jul	1854	26 Jul 1854	22		DET
Findling, Valentine	01	Feb	1862	16 Dec 1861			PTIMES
Finn, Geo. H.	25	Oct	1854		21		PDD
Finney, James S.	23	Jun	1852	03 Jun 1852	12		PT&C
Finney, Samuel J.	23	Jun	1852	03 Jun 1852	20		PT&C
Fish, J.L.	19	Dec	1850	10 Dec 1850			PT&C
Fisher, Henry	08	Feb	1854	26 Jan 1854	45		PDD
Fisher, Lewis	09	May	1855	23 Apr 1855	3		DET (S)
Fisher, Margaret	06	Dec	1853				PDD
Fisher, Peter	09	Aug	1853	3 Aug 1853	47		DET
Fisher, Peter	10	Aug	1853	03 Aug 1853	47		PT&C
Fisher, unknown	27	May	1854	May 1854	child		PDD

Name	Notice Date			Death Date	Age	Comment	Paper
Fisher, unknown	27	May	1854	May 1854	child		PDD
Fisher, unknown	27	May	1854	May 1854	child		PDD
Fisk, female	16	Aug	1853				DET
Fisk, male (Dr.)	16	Aug	1853				DET
Fisk, unknown	16	Aug	1853		child		DET
Fitch, Abel (Dr.)	16	Jul	1851				PT&C
Fitzgerald, Harmeon	22	Jul	1854	14 Jul 1854	29	Mitchel/ Cisens	DET
Fitzgerald, Jane	27	Jul	1853	23 Jul 1853	25		PDD (S)
Fitzgerald, John	23	Mar	1855	23 Mar 1855	36		DET
Fitzgibbon, (Lord)	16	Dec	1854				DET
Fitzpatrick, John	10	May	1853		21		PDD (S)
Fitzpatrick, John	25	Jan	1855	22 Jan 1855			DET
Fitzsimmons, Hugh	11	Mar	1854				PDD
Fitzsimmons, Hugh	27	Feb	1854				DET
Fitzwilliams, Elisha (Lieut.)	07	May	1864	23 Apr 1864	21		PTIMES
Flanders, George Oscar	31	Aug	1859	28 Aug 1859	2		WPT
Flanders, John (Col.)	28	Apr	1843	26 Apr 1843	40		TRIB
Fleming, David	21	Oct	1854	18 Oct 1854			DET
Fleming, male	03	Dec	1851				PT&C
Flemming, John	11	Jun	1851	05 Jun 1851			PT&C
Flint, C.A.	06	Aug	1856				WPT
Fluert, female	10	May	1853	06 May 1853			PDD
Fogarty, Lawrence	02	Dec	1853	25 Nov 1853	24		PDD
Foley, John Pat	15	Nov	1862	09 Nov 1862	27		PTIMES
Folsom, Jos. L. (Col.)	25 07	Aug Sep	1855 1855	20 Jul 1855			DET
Folwell, Joshua	08	Feb	1854	04 Feb 1854			PDD
Foote, Andrew H. (Rear Adm.)	18	Jul	1863		56		PTIMES
Forbes, Agnes	18	Mar	1865	09 Mar 1865	2		PTIMES
Forbes, Alice	11	Mar	1865	04 Mar 1865	7y6m		PTIMES
Forbes, Mary Elizabeth	25	Feb	1865	20 Feb 1865	5y10m		PTIMES
Forbush, Charles Christopher	23	Sep	1865	21 Sep 1865	33		PTIMES
Ford, Bill	05	Apr	1844				TRIB
Ford, Nicholas	31 07	Oct Nov	1844 1844	Oct 1844			TRIB
Ford, Seabury (ex-Gov.)	10, 12	May	1855	08 May 1855	56-60		DET
Forrest, female	17	Dec	1851				PT&C
Forrest, male	17	Dec	1851		8		PT&C
Forrest, unknown	17	Dec	1851		child		PT&C
Forrester, B.W.	11	May	1853				PDD
Forsyth, Clara	17	Aug	1853	Aug 1853	79		WPT
Forsythe, Clara	02	Aug	1853	17 Jul 1853	69	nee Meigs	PDD

Name	Notice Date			Death Date	Age	Comment	Paper
Forsythe, Clara	10	Aug	1853	07 Aug 1853	79		DET
Forsythe, David	23	Aug	1854				PDD
Forward, Amor T. (or J.)	15	Sep	1843				TRIB
	24	Nov	1843				
Forward, Walter (Hon.)	01	Dec	1852	24 Nov 1852	65		PT&C
Foss, Margaret	09	Jun	1860	Jun 1860			PTIMES
Foss, Mary	09	Jun	1860	Jun 1860			PTIMES
Foster, female	08	Dec	1854				DET
Foster, Genoa	18	Jan	1855	20 Dec 1854	20		DET
Foster, George W.	12	May	1855				DET
Foster, Hester	16	Feb	1844	09 Feb 1844			TRIB
Foster, James Jr.	28	Oct	1854				DET
Foster, James Sr.	27	Jul	1856	13 Jul 1856	60		WPT
Foster, male	14	Jan	1852	28 Dec 1851	20		PT&C
Foster, Margaret Ann	05	Dec	1860	30 Nov 1860	29y4d		WPT
Foster, Rebecca	31	Oct	1844	Oct 1844			TRIB
Foster, unknown	07	Nov	1844	Oct 1844	child		TRIB
Foster, unknown	07	Jul	1855	04 Jul 1855			DET
Foster, unknown (Capt.)	24	Jul	1855				DET
Fournier, M. Antoine	30	Dec	1854	07 Dec 1854			DET
Fowler, Charles	11	Jul	1853	05 Jul 1853	19		DET
Fowler, John	18	Oct	1862				PTIMES
Fowler, John A.	26	Jun	1855	23 Jun 1855			DET
Fowler, Julius J.	14	May	1864				PTIMES
Fox, Newton (Dr.)	23	Jan	1854	21 Jan 1854			PDD
France, A.	06	Aug	1853	03 Aug 1853	19 or 20		DET
Frank, George	15	Jun	1854				PDD
Franklin, Burt	21	May	1857				DET
Franklin, John (Sir)	30	Oct	1854				PDD
Franklin, John (Sir)	23, 26	Oct	1854				DET
Frazier, male	14	Oct	1854				PDD
Frazier, unknown (Capt.)	01	Aug	1855				DET
Frazier, Wm.	07	May	1864				PTIMES
Fredrick, D.R.	02	Mar	1853	22 Feb 1853	35		PT&C
Freeland, M.	06	Jun	1863	16 May 1863			PTIMES
Freeman, female	07	Mar	1854	24 Feb 1854			PDD
Freeman, John W.	21	May	1853	16 May 1853			PDD
Freeman, Nelson	30	May	1853	27 May 1853	15		PDD
Freeman, unknown	01	Aug	1853		20m		DET
Frelinghuy, Theodore (Hon.)	26	Apr	1862	12 Apr 1862	75		PTIMES
French, A.C.	10	Sep	1864	04 Sep 1864		(ex-Gov.)	PTIMES
French, Charles Scott	08	Sep	1857	28 Aug 1857	17m3d		PSOT
French, Henry R.	21	May	1858	15 May 1858	89		DET
French, Henry R.	25	May	1858	15 May 1858	39		PSOT

Name	Notice Date			Death Date	Age	Comment	Paper
French, Henry R.	26	May	1858	15 May 1858	89		WPT
French, Ida D.	18	Jan	1859		35		PTIMES
French, Walter	10	May	1853	06 May 1853			PDD
French, Walter	11	May	1853	06 May 1853			PT&C
Freshel, Mathias	12	Aug	1854	10 Aug 1854	9m		PDD
Freshell, unknown	17	Aug	1854	10 Aug 1854	3m		DET (S)
Freshour, James	01	Feb	1862	15 Dec 1861			PTIMES
Fresthel, George	23	Sep	1865	21 Sep 1865			PTIMES
Friday, Henry W.	02	Aug	1853	29 Jul 1853	31		PDD
Friday, Henry W.	03	Aug	1853	29 Jul 1853	31		PT&C
Friday, Henry W.	30	Jul	1853	29 Jul 1853	31		DET
Friday, Magdaline	07	May	1856	07 May 1856	21		WPT
Friley, Wm.	06	Jun	1863	01 May 1863			PTIMES
Frippin, Lot	28	May	1864	May 1864			PTIMES
Fristoe, John H.	14	Jul	1854				PDD
Frohman, Samuel	02	Dec	1854				DET
Frost, J.W.	23	Jul	1851	10 Jul 1851			PT&C
Fry, female	20	Oct	1853				DET
Fulks, Noah	26	Mar	1851	19 Mar 1851			PT&C
Fuller, Olive	10, 23	Jun	1854	07 Jun 1854			DET
Fuller, Samuel S.	22, 29	Nov	1862	18 Nov 1862	66y10m		PTIMES
Fullerton, Wm. (Sergeant)	10	Oct	1863				PTIMES
Fulmer, Abram	03	Aug	1853				DET
Fulmer, Abram	10	Aug	1853				PT&C
Fulton, John	18	Aug	1852	03 Aug 1852			PT&C
Fulton, unk. (Senator)	12	Sep	1844	15 Aug 1844			TRIB
Fultz, Abraham	10	Nov	1860				DET
Funk, Jesse	09	Jan	1851	09 Dec 1850			PT&C
Funk, Mary Ann	21	May	1864	17 May 1864	25y8m17d		PTIMES
Furrey, Joseph	11	Feb	1865	04 Feb 1865			PTIMES
Gaffy, Charles J.	23	Aug	1862	17 Aug 1862	10m23d		PTIMES
Gaffy, Isabella	17	May	1862	11 May 1862	26y6m29d		PTIMES
Gage, female	30	Jun	1855				DET
Gahr, Frank	09	May	1855	30 Apr 1855	6		DET (S)
Gahr, Valentine	25	Jun	1851	22 Jun 1851			PT&C
Gahr, Valentine	30	Jun	1851	22 Jun 1851	41		PI
Gaines, Elizabeth	15	Oct	1851	13 Aug 1851			PT&C
Galbreath, Franklin	16	Aug	1855	13 Aug 1855			DET
Galbreath, unknown	25	Feb	1852	19 Feb 1852	5m		PT&C
Galford, John	30	Aug	1854	06 Aug 1854	1y6m		DET
Gallagher, David	03	Mar	1860		71		PTIMES
Gallagher, female	10	Aug	1855	09 Aug 1855			DET
Gallagher, James	09	Feb	1853	05 Feb 1853			PT&C

Name	Notice Date			Death Date	Age	Comment	Paper
Galloway, Samuel Buchanan	28	Jan	1857	17 Jan 1857	9y11m		WPT
Gannen, George W.	22	Nov	1862				PTIMES
Gantt, male	25	Feb	1860				PTIMES
Garber, male	11	Feb	1852	28 Jan 1852			PT&C
Garden, Alexander	22	Dec	1853				PDD
Gardener, male	07	Jan	1852				PT&C
Gardette, Sullema	08	Oct	1853	19 Sep 1853			DET
Gardiner, James B. (Col.)	22	Apr	1837	13 Apr 1837	55		STRIB
Gardiner, unknown (Dr.)	08	Mar	1854				DET
Gardner (or Gardiner) male (Dr.)	07, 08, 16	Mar	1854	03 Mar 1854			PDD
Gardner, David	08	Mar	1844	28 Feb 1844			TRIB
Gardner, male	09	Jun	1843				TRIB
Gardner, male	10	Jan	1855	25 Dec 1854	infant		DET
Gardner, Melzar (Esq.)	14	Apr	1843				TRIB
Garney, Jas.	23	Jul	1856	Jul 1856			WPT
Garraghan, Thomas	10	Sep	1851				PT&C
Garrett, Frances	14	Oct	1837			nee Suiter	STRIB
Garrett, Samuel L.	06	Aug	1856				WPT
Garrison, John H.	06	Jun	1844	05 Jun 1844	42		TRIB
Garrison, male	11	Feb	1852				PT&C
Gassaway, S.G. (Rev.)	23, 24, 27	Feb	1854				DET
Gassaway, Wm.	04	Nov	1853	01 Nov 1853			DET
Gaston, William (Judge)	09	Feb	1844				TRIB
Gates, Dolly	04	Aug	1857		infant		DET
Gates, John M.	18	Mar	1854	13 Mar 1854			PDD
Gates, male	19	Jan	1854				PDD
Gaul, Harry	10	Dec	1856	04 Dec 1856			WPT
Gaylord, Lucy S.	26	Nov	1851	13 Nov 1851			PT&C
Gaylord, Lydia Brayton	01	Aug	1850	31 Jul 1850	1m4d		PT&C
Gearhart, John	30	Jun	1843				TRIB
Gedge, Frederick	11	Nov	1854	10 Nov 1854			DET
Geiger, R.	21	Aug	1854				DET
Geis, George	13, 20	Aug	1856	11 Aug 1856			WPT
Geismer, Sophia	13	Jul	1853		20		DET
Geismer, Sophia	20	Jul	1853	14 Jul 1853	20		PT&C
Geist, John	02	Aug	1855	29 Jul 1855	19		DET
Gerlach, Matilda	11	Jul	1860	10 Jul 1860	8m10d		DET
Gerlach, Matilda	18	Jul	1860	10 Jul 1860	8m10d		WPT
Gerry, female	10	Jun	1854		19		DET
Gerry, female	10	Jun	1854		17		DET
Gerry, female	10	Jun	1854		9		DET
Gesinger, David Dallas	25	Feb	1857	18 Feb 1857	10y7m1d		WPT
Getty (or Yetta), unk.	21	Oct	1865				PTIMES

Deaths

Name	Notice Date			Death Date	Age	Comment	Paper
Gharey, David, Sr.	15	Aug	1850	09 Aug 1850	76		PT&C
Gharky, Eliza Jane	10	Aug	1826	25 Jul 1826	3		WT
Gharky, Sarah Elizabeth	11	Mar	1865	04 Mar 1865	3y6m7d		PTIMES
Gharky, William	24	Mar	1851	20 Jan 1851	40		PI
Gherkin, C.H.	10	Sep	1851	16 Aug 1851			PT&C
Gibbons, Cyrus S.	10	Sep	1864				PTIMES
Gibbs, Ashley	26	Aug	1859	28 Jul 1859	73		DET
Gibbs, Ashley	31	Aug	1859	28 Jul 1859	73		WPT
Gibbs, D.H.	11	Aug	1850	24 Aug 1850	42		PI
	02	Sep	1850				
Gibbs, D.H.	05	Sep	1850	24 Aug 1850	42		PT&C
Gibbs, male	30	Jul	1851	28 Jul 1851			PT&C
Gibson, Henry	31	Mar	1852	18 Mar 1852	101y24d		PT&C
Gibson, unknown	11	Feb	1852				PT&C
Gibson, William	17	Nov	1854	31 Oct 1854	26		DET
Giddings, Joshua R.	03	Dec	1864	15 Nov 1864			PTIMES
Giddings, Joshua R.	04	Jun	1864	27 May 1864	69		PTIMES
Giering, Henry	25	Jan	1862	19 Jan 1862	19		PTIMES
Gies, unknown	28	Sep	1853	18 Sep 1853	6y8m		PDD (S)
Gilbert, Agustus	16	Apr	1864	27 Mar 1864			SVREP
Gilbert, Augustus B.	02	Apr	1864	27 Mar 1864	21		PTIMES
Gilbert, Jennie	14	Oct	1865	09 Oct 1865	7y8m7d		PTIMES
Gilbert, Lavina	09	Apr	1856		34		WPT
Gilbert, male	19	Jul	1853				PDD
Gilbert, male	30	Jun	1853				PDD
Giles, Charles (Capt.)	24	Apr	1860	10 Apr 1860			DET
Gill, Eliza	16	Jul	1856	07 Jul 1856		nee Hull	WPT
Gillespie, male	03	Sep	1855				DET
Gillet, Percival	06	May	1853	29 Apr 1853	26		PDD
Gillett, James	01	Apr	1865	27 Mar 1865	23		PTIMES
Gillett, John	08	Sep	1857	02 Sep 1857			PSOT
Gillett, John	09	Sep	1857	02 Sep 1857			WPT
Gillette, Abigail	17	Jul	1858	16 Jul 1858			DET
Gillmore, A.	22	Jan	1851	17 Jan 1851			PT&C
Gilmer, Thos. W.	08	Mar	1844	28 Feb 1844			TRIB
Gilmore, John	06	Dec	1853				DET
Gilroy, unknown	17	Aug	1854	10 Aug 1854	13 m		DET (S)
Gilroy, unknown	21	Sep	1853	14 Sep 1853	2		PDD (S)
Gilroy, unknown	27	Sep	1854	06 Sep 1854	18m		DET (S)
Gilroy, unknown	27	Sep	1854	06 Sep 1854	18m		PDD (S)
Gilroy, unknown	28	Sep	1853	19 Sep 1853	2		PDD (S)
Gimble, Solomon	27	Jul	1853	23 Jul 1853			PDD
Given, Thomas	04	Oct	1853	03 Oct 1853			DET
Givens, male	24	Nov	1852	Nov 1852	13		PT&C
Glass, unknown (Capt.)	19	Jul	1862				PTIMES

Name	Notice Date			Death Date	Age	Comment	Paper
Glidden, Catharine W.	25	May	1858	25 May 1858	45		DET
Glidden, Catharine W.	26	May	1858	25 May 1858	45		WPT
Glidden, Cora Belle	09	Apr	1855	08 Apr 1855	11m17d		DET
Glidden, female	01	Jun	1858	26 May 1858	45y4m4d	nee Young	PSOT
Glidden, Jefferson W.	14	Mar	1863	13 Mar 1863			PTIMES
Glidden, Joseph	13	May	1865	07 May 1865	56y11m6d		PTIMES
Glidden, Mary Alice	15	Apr	1859	02 Apr 1859	2y5m1d		DET
Glidden, Mary Alice	20	Apr	1859	02 Apr 1859	2y5m1d		WPT
Glidden, Mary Ellen	18	Mar	1857	15 Mar 1857			WPT
Glidden, Mary Ellen	24	Mar	1857	15 Mar 1857		nee Robinson	PSOT
Glover, Catharina	21	Mar	1856		78		OP
Glover, Catharine	26	Mar	1856	19 Mar 1856	78		WPT
Glover, Elijah	31	Oct	1829	23 Oct 1829	47		WT
Glover, Hester Ann Roe	07	Sep	1820	06 Aug 1820			STEL
Glover, Samuel G.	09	Jul	1853	8 Jul 1853	36		DET
Glover, Samuel G.	11	Jul	1853	08 Jul 1853			PDD
Glover, Samuel G.	13	Jul	1853	08 Jul 1853	36		PT&C
Gness, J.A.	09	Apr	1851	18 Mar 1851			PT&C
Godrey, male	30	Aug	1854	27 Aug 1854			DET
Goff, Christopher	28	Dec	1858	07 Dec 1858	25		PTIMES
Going, Jonathan (Rev.)	21	Nov	1844	09 Nov 1844			TRIB
Golden, Effie Luella	10	Mar	1857	01 Mar 1857	6m		PSOT
Golden, male	06	Jul	1860	04 Jul 1860			DET
Golding, Mary	09	Jul	1851		48		PT&C
Goldsmith, Lewis	03	Mar	1854	28 Feb 1854			PDD
Goldsmith, Sampson	11	May	1853				PDD
Goodman, Emilia	26	Aug	1865	22 Aug 1865	14y8m26d		PTIMES
Goodman, Hermon	07	Aug	1855	07 Aug 1855	9m11d		DET
Goodwin, P. (Dr.)	29	Oct	1859				PTIMES
Goor, Frederick	21	Aug	1854				DET
Gordon, Margaret	28	Sep	1853	19 Sep 1853	48		PDD (S)
Gorsuch, Thomas	18	Oct	1859				DET
Goss, Ellen	11	May	1853				PDD
Gould, female	02	Aug	1854	30 Jul 1854			DET
Gould, Helen M.	27	Jun	1850	12 Jun 1850	2y		PT&C
Gould, John	20	Feb	1864		75		PTIMES
Gould, John F.	16, 20	Oct	1860	04 Oct 1860	44		DET
Gould, Samuel	20	Feb	1864	11 Feb 1864	81		PTIMES
Gouldin, Samuel	22	Mar	1855				DET
Gouldy, male	02	Nov	1858	27 Oct 1858	9		PTIMES
Gouldy, male	02	Nov	1858	27 Oct 1858	12		PTIMES
Gouldy, male	02	Nov	1858	27 Oct 1858	19		PTIMES
Gracie, Wm.	05	Jan	1853	30 Dec 1852	30		PT&C
Graham, Harriet N.	15	Jul	1850	July 1850		nee Scott	PI

Deaths

Name	Notice Date			Death Date	Age	Comment	Paper
Graham, male	01	Dec	1852				PT&C
Graham, male	20	Aug	1851	13 Aug 1851			PT&C
Graham, William	10	Aug	1855				DET
Graham, William Young	16	Feb	1844	09 Feb 1844		alias Clark	TRIB
Gramm, Hellen C.	20	Aug	1856	16 Aug 1856	31		WPT
Gramm, Moses	06	Oct	1855	05 Oct 1855			DET
Grant, Geo.	30	Jul	1851	Jul 1851			PT&C
	06	Aug	1851				
Grant, Jeremiah	06	Aug	1851				PT&C
Grant, Sophia	06	Aug	1851				PT&C
Grant, unknown	28	Jun	1862	21 Jun 1862			PTIMES
Graper, Michael	13	Apr	1855				DET
Graves, Merritt	28	Jul	1852	18 Jul 1852	21		PT&C
Gray, F. C.	01	Aug	1853				DET
Gray, J.S.	10	May	1853	06 May 1853			PDD
Gray, J.W.	31	May	1862	26 May 1862	48		PTIMES
Greathouse, Alexander	03	May	1844	26 Apr 1844			TRIB
Greeden, Betsy	08	Jan	1856	26 Dec 1855	80		DET
Greely, female	04	Aug	1855	27 Jul 1855			DET
Greely, Philip (Hon.)	01	Apr	1854	15 Mar 1854			PDD
Green, A.M. (Esq.)	26	Sep	1844				TRIB
Green, Albert Edward	04, 06	Nov	1854	03 Nov 1854	2y9m		DET
Green, female	19	Jan	1844	04 Jan 1844			TRIB
Green, female	20	Aug	1851	14 Aug 1851			PT&C
Green, female	27	Sep	1854				PDD
Green, Henry Forest (Rev.)	11	Jun	1855	06 May 1855	26		DET
Green, Jas.	27	Apr	1853	15 Apr 1853		Negro	PT&C
Green, John L.	10	May	1855				DET
Green, male	08	Jun	1853				PT&C
Green, Samuel (Col.)	20	Sep	1859	06 Sep 1859	92		PTIMES
Green, Shields	17, 24	Dec	1859	16 Dec 1859			PTIMES
Green, unknown	19	Jan	1844	04 Jan 1844	child		TRIB
Green, unknown	19	Jan	1844	04 Jan 1844	child		TRIB
Green, unknown	19	Jan	1844	04 Jan 1844	child		TRIB
Green, unknown	20	Aug	1851	14 Aug 1851	child		PT&C
Green, unknown	20	Aug	1851	14 Aug 1851	child		PT&C
Green, unknown	20	Aug	1851	14 Aug 1851	child		PT&C
Green, unknown	20	Aug	1851	14 Aug 1851	child		PT&C
Greene, Elizabeth A.	14	Nov	1860		2y9m		WPT
Greene, female	11	Nov	1865	09 Nov 1865			PTIMES
Greene, Frances Ellen	13	Sep	1862	09 Sep 1862	26		PTIMES
Greene, Thomas D.	28	Jan	1865	22 Jan 1865	40		PTIMES
Greenleaf, Mary	09	Jun	1860	Jun 1860			PTIMES
Greenlee, David	09	Feb	1853	23 Jan 1853	45		PT&C

Name	Notice Date			Death Date	Age	Comment	Paper
Greenseig, Otto	03	Mar	1852	27 Feb 1852			PT&C
Gregg, unknown (Major)	29	Mar	1859				PTIMES
Gregory, Mary	22	Apr	1837	19 Apr 1837		nee Tilton	STRIB
Gregory, Phebe Jane	02	May	1850	17 Apr 1850	5		PT&C
Gregory, Phebe Jane	06	May	1850	17 Apr 1850	5		PI
Gregory, Susannah Elizabeth	13	Jun	1829		13m		WT
Gregory, Thomas Tilton	29	Dec	1843	16 Dec 1843	3y3m		TRIB
Gregory, Wm. B.	19	May	1858				WPT
Grey, male	11	May	1853				PT&C
Grier, Rhoda	20	May	1850	19 May 1850	22		PI
Grier, Rhoda	23	May	1850	19 May 1850	22		PT&C
Griesser, George	20	Jul	1858	17 Jul 1858	1y6m9d		PSOT
Grieve, Hanna	14	Nov	1850		17	nee Banks	PT&C
	26	Feb	1851				
Grieve, John	23	Jul	1851				PT&C
Grieve, John	14	Nov	1850				PT&C
	26	Feb	1851				
Griffin, Michael	30	Jul	1851				PT&C
Griffith, female	10	Jan	1854				DET
Griffith, James	12	May	1860	11 May 1860	18y11m		DET
Griffith, James	16	May	1860	11 May 1860	18y11m		WPT
Grimes, Hester	24	Jun	1865	16 Jun 1865	infant		PTIMES
Grimes, Hester A.	24	Jun	1865	12 Jun 1865	20		PTIMES
Grimes, male	17	Oct	1850	12 Oct 1850			PT&C
Griswold, Alexander Viets (Rt.Rev.)	03	Mar	1843	16 Feb 1843	77		TRIB
Griswold, Edwin Churchill	17	Nov	1857	16 Nov 1857	2y11m		DET
Griswold, Edwin Churchill	18	Nov	1857	16 Nov 1857	2y11m		WPT
Griswold, Edwin H. (Dr.)	19	Jun	1860	16 Jun 1860	38		DET
Griswold, Edwin H. (Dr.)	20	Jun	1860	16 Jun 1860	38		WPT
Groff, John R.	07	May	1856	May 1856			WPT
Groniger, Susanna	20	May	1854	18 May 1854	42		DET
Groves, James Madison	31	Mar	1854	25 Mar 1854	5		DET
Groves, Spencer	09	Aug	1854	07 Aug 1854	63		DET
Guild, male	20	Mar	1854				PDD
Guilford, Nathan	21	Dec	1854				DET
Gullen, John	02	Jul	1851				PT&C
Gun, Margaret	27	Jun	1854	23 Jun 1854	21		PDD (S)
Gunn, Clarissa	03	Nov	1852	23 Oct 1852	50		PT&C
Gunn, female	07	Jun	1859				DET
Gunn, Joanna	16	May	1850	14 May 1850	7		PT&C
Gunn, Joanna	20	May	1850	14 May 1850	7		PI
Gunn, Joanna	26	Oct	1858	21 Oct 1858	96		PSOT
Gunn, Joanna	26	Oct	1858	21 Oct 1858	95		DET
Gunn, Joanna	26	Oct	1858	21 Oct 1858	96		PTIMES

Deaths

Name	Notice Date			Death Date	Age	Comment	Paper
Gunn, Samuel W.	10	Aug	1854	10 Aug 1854	2m		DET
Gunnison (or Jennison), J.W. (Capt.)	03, 06	Dec	1853				PDD
Gunnison, J.W. (Capt.)	02, 05	Dec	1853				DET
Guthrie, Aaron	13	May	1825				PG&LA
Guthrie, Alfred C.	07	Mar	1856	01 Mar 1856	33		OP
Guthrie, James	12	Mar	1855		78		DET
Guyotte, Louisa	03	Sep	1851		8		PT&C
Gwinn, Isabel G.	24	Jul	1838	16 Jul 1838			STRIB
Habersham, Francis B.	19	Sep	1854	10 Sep 1854			PDD
Haddleson, unknown	13	Oct	1854	05 Oct 1854	2		PDD (S)
Hagey, Catharine	23	Feb	1861	13 Feb 1861	106		PTIMES
Haggerty, Patrick	08	Jun	1855	05 Jun 1855			DET
Hale, Foster	18	Jan	1859	26 Dec 1858			PTIMES
Haley, female	15	Mar	1854				DET
Hall, Albert McFarland	19	Sep	1863	17 Sep 1863	2y9m19d		PTIMES
Hall, Cornelia	10	Mar	1843	06 Mar 1843	infant		TRIB
Hall, Edwin	23	Jul	1856	Jul 1856			WPT
Hall, Faneuil	03	Aug	1853	28 Jul 1853	3y1m21d		PT&C
Hall, Faneuil	30	Jul	1853	28 Jul 1853	3y1m21d		DET
Hall, Faneul	02	Aug	1853	28 Jul 1853	3y1m21d		PDD
Hall, J.A.	23	Jun	1852	14 Jun 1852			PT&C
Hall, James	25	Nov	1854	22 Nov 1854			DET
Hall, Joshua	30	Aug	1854	10 Aug 1854	12		DET
Hall, male	02	Feb	1859		18		WPT
Hall, male	28	May	1851	24 May 1851			PT&C
Hall, male	28	Jul	1854	26 Jul 1854			DET
Hall, Margaret Kinney	01	Oct	1864	28 Sep 1864	57y7m3d		PTIMES
Hall, Nancy Dickson	22	Sep	1857	10 Sep 1857	71y9m9d		PSOT
Hall, O.V.	10	Feb	1851	6 Feb 1851			PI
Hall, unknown	16	Dec	1853		child		DET
Hall, unknown	16	Dec	1853		child		DET
Hall, unknown	16	Dec	1853		child		DET
Hall, Vilena	21	Nov	1850	09 Nov 1850	28y9m21d		PT&C
Hall, Wm.	18	May	1854	17 May 1854			PDD
Haller, Elizabeth	12	Mar	1855	12 Mar 1855	5		DET
Halley, Henry	16	Mar	1853	08 Mar 1853	35		PT&C
Halsey, Fanny Dean	14	Jun	1859	Jun 1859			PTIMES
Halsey, S.W.	27	Aug	1852	24 Aug 1852			PI
Halterman, John	19	Jul	1859	Jul 1859	20		PTIMES
Halterman, John	27, 28	Jun	1859	26 Jun 1859			DET
Halton, A.B.	14	Mar	1855				DET
Ham, male	28	Jun	1853				PDD
Ham, male	29	Jun	1853				PT&C
Hamblin, Isaac	27	Sep	1859				PTIMES

Name	Notice Date			Death Date	Age	Comment	Paper
Hamblin, Isaac, Sr.	30	Jul	1864				PTIMES
Hamer, Thomas M.	20	Aug	1851				PT&C
Hamilton, Genevieve	05	Nov	1859	04 Nov 1859	6	or Davis	DET
Hamilton, Genevieve	05	Nov	1859	04 Nov 1859	6		PTIMES
Hamilton, Genevieve	09	Nov	1859	04 Nov 1859	6		WPT
Hamilton, J.K.	03	Oct	1860	24 Sep 1860			WPT
Hamilton, unknown	06	Dec	1853		11d		DET
Hamilton, Wm.	19	Mar	1851	07 Jan 1851			PT&C
Hamlin, James G. (M.D.)	13	Aug	1824	04 Aug 1824	28		PG&LA
Hammer, Hiram	30	Dec	1853	22 Dec 1853			PDD
Hammit, S.	14	Nov	1850				PT&C
Hampson, Jno.	17	Sep	1864				PTIMES
Hancok, Denis	01	Jul	1850	30 Jun 1850			PI
Handley, female	28	Jul	1853	11 Jul 1853	17		PDD
Handy, B.S.	05	Jan	1854	19 Dec 1853			PDD
Hanel, Casper	22	Sep	1854	19 Sep 1854			PDD
Haney, male	20	Jan	1855	19 Jan 1855	50		DET
Hanna, Charles Edward	09	Jul	1851	06 Jul 1851	14m22d		PT&C
Hanna, female	11	May	1853				PDD
Hanna, Harriet Maria	04	May	1858	24 Apr 1858	1		PSOT
Hanna, Samuel	12	Dec	1860	06 Dec 1860	28		WPT
Hannah, Shadrach	13	Feb	1856	02 Feb 1856	94		DET
Hannahs, Susannah	19	May	1843	15 May 1843	49		TRIB
Hans, male	28	Jul	1852	26 Jul 1852			PT&C
Haraden, John	18	May	1853	23 Apr 1853			PT&C
Harbor, J.	21	Feb	1863	26 Jan 1863	76		PTIMES
Harcum, male	04	Jul	1850	30 Jun 1850			PT&C
Hardwick, male	06	Aug	1856				WPT
Harge, George	30	Jun	1860				DET
Harley, female	12	May	1853				PDD
Harley, unknown	12	May	1853		6m		PDD
Harman, Henry	22	Apr	1865				PTIMES
Harmon, John	01	Feb	1862	07 Jan 1862			PTIMES
Harover, Milburn	02	Jan	1856				WPT
Harper, Robert Goodloe (Gen.)	04	Feb	1825	11 Jan 1825	60		PG&LA
Harr, Thomas	10	Oct	1863				PTIMES
Harrington, female	18	Jun	1851				PT&C
Harrington, Jonathan	04	Apr	1854		96		DET
Harrington, Jonathan	07	Apr	1854	26 Mar 1854	96		PDD
Harrington, Solon	19	May	1855	17 May 1855			DET
Harris, Elijah L.	22	Mar	1854	18 Mar 1854			PDD
Harris, Elisha W.	07	May	1851	11 Apr 1851			PT&C
Harris, F.F. (Dr.)	13	Mar	1854	30 Feb 1854			PDD
Harris, female	05	Jan	1854	01 Jan 1854			PDD

Name	Notice Date			Death Date	Age	Comment	Paper
Harris, female	17	Mar	1860			Morgan, Mrs.	PTIMES
Harris, Prentice	05	Jan	1854	01 Jan 1854	30		PDD
Harrison, Henry	23	Jul	1856	Jul 1856			WPT
Harsh, Jonathan	06	Aug	1851				PT&C
Harsham (or Clark), Louisa	30	Nov	1853	26 Nov 1853	18		PDD
Hart, Adella	23	Apr	1852	12 Apr 1852	37		PI
Hart, Andrew	15	Jun	1855	30 May 1855	30		DET
Hart, Anna	05	May	1852	26 Apr 1852	11		PT&C
Hart, Joab	01	Dec	1853	25 Nov 1853			PDD
Hart, Joab	30	Nov	1853				DET
	05	Dec	1853				
Hartman, Cutlip	22	Jan	1855				DET
Hartman, unknown	23	May	1863	18 May 1863	child		PTIMES
Hartman, unknown	23	May	1863	18 May 1863	child		PTIMES
Hartman, unknown	23	May	1863	18 May 1863	child		PTIMES
Hartnett, Michael	02	Feb	1853				PT&C
Hartup, male	09	Sep	1865	06 Sep 1865			PTIMES
Harvey, James	15	Jul	1853				PDD
Harvey, male	15	Mar	1860	25 Feb 1860	15		DET
Haskell, Wm. T. (General)	29	Mar	1859	Mar 1859			PTIMES
Haskin, male	08	Jul	1854				PDD
Haskins, female	15	Mar	1854				DET
Haskins, unknown	15	Mar	1854		children		DET
Hassenkauff, unknown	31	Mar	1859				DET
Hatch, Bartlett	09	Nov	1858				PTIMES
Hatch, Willard	16	Aug	1859				DET
Hatcher, unknown (Dr.)	29	Apr	1850				PI
Hatfield, female	26	Mar	1851	Mar 1851			PT&C
Hatfield, female	26	Mar	1851	Mar 1851			PT&C
Hatfield, male	26	Mar	1851	Mar 1851			PT&C
Hatfield, Marion M.	05	Apr	1859	01 Apr 1859			PTIMES
Hathaway, Benjamin	20	Aug	1851	18 Aug 1851			PT&C
Hatings, John	29	Dec	1854				DET
Hatten, John	10	Aug	1853	10 Aug 1853			PT&C
Hatter, A.	13	Oct	1854	11 Oct 1854	29		PDD (S)
Hatton, female	04	Aug	1853	03 Aug 1853			PDD
Hatton, John	03, 08	Aug	1853	03 Aug 1853			DET
Hatton, male	04	Aug	1853	03 Aug 1853			PDD
Have, unknown (Capt.)	26	Oct	1854				DET
Have, unknown (Capt.)	27	Oct	1854				PDD
Haveling, Frederick	29	Jul	1850	25 Jul 1850			PI
Hawes, Griswold	02	Aug	1853				PDD
Hawes, Griswold	03	Aug	1853				PT&C

Name	Notice Date			Death Date	Age	Comment	Paper
Hawk, Malinda	16, 27	Jul	1856	04 Jul 1856	34		WPT
Hawkins, Joseph S. (Esq.)	18	Aug	1852	11 Aug 1852			PT&C
Hawthorne, Nathaniel	28	May	1864	19 May 1864			PTIMES
	04	Jun	1864				
Hayman, S.B.	31	Aug	1855	26 Aug 1855			DET
Haynes, David	14	Nov	1850	02 Nov 1850			PT&C
Hays, John (Lord)	21	May	1855				DET
Hays, Thomas (Capt.)	19	Dec	1863				PTIMES
Hayward, Lafayette	02	Sep	1853	01 Sep 1853			DET
Hazard, Horace H.	12	Apr	1855	06 Apr 1855			DET
Hazlett, Robert (Capt.)	13	Jun	1860		63		DET
Headly, female	30	Aug	1854	27 Aug 1854	11		DET
Heath, Uriah	05	Apr	1862	28 Mar 1862			PTIMES
Heberton, Mahlon Hutchinson	24	Feb	1843				TRIB
Hechinger, Anna Marie	21	Jul	1851	15 Jul 1851			PI
Heenan, Timothy	26	Jan	1861	24 Jan 1861			PTIMES
Hefferman, Ann	13	Oct	1843	17 Sep 1843	101		TRIB
Hefferman, Patrick	03	Dec	1853				PDD
Hellings, John	17	Aug	1820	02 Aug 1820	34		STEL
Hemerstein, male	13	Jun	1859	13 Jun 1859			DET
Henderson, David	22	Aug	1853				DET
Henderson, James	29	Mar	1859	23 Mar 1859			PTIMES
Henderson, James (Esq.)	29	Mar	1844	19 Mar 1844			TRIB
Henderson, male	23	Jul	1856	17 Jul 1856			WPT
Henderson, Robert	05	Apr	1855	16 Mar 1855	70		DET
Hendrixson, Robert	10	Nov	1853	06 Nov 1853			DET
Hennes, Benjamin	23	Dec	1865	16 Dec 1865			PTIMES
Henning, Thomas	08	Jun	1853		25		PDD
Henning, Thomas	15	Jun	1853	03 Jun 1853			PT&C
Henry, female	19	Apr	1860	10 Apr 1860			DET
Henry, James W.	10	Sep	1864				PTIMES
Henry, John	13, 20	Aug	1851	Aug 1851			PT&C
Henry, male	13	Apr	1854	12 Apr 1854	12		DET
Henry, male	19	Apr	1860	10 Apr 1860			DET
Henry, male	22	Jun	1854				DET
Henry, Robert	03	Jun	1854	31 May 1854			DET
Henry, unknown	19	Apr	1860	10 Apr 1860	child		DET
Henry, unknown	19	Apr	1860	10 Apr 1860	child		DET
Henry, unknown	19	Apr	1860	10 Apr 1860	child		DET
Henry, unknown	19	Apr	1860	10 Apr 1860	child		DET
Henshaw, Wm. F. (Col.)	31	Dec	1853	13 Nov 1853	53		DET
Hepburn, Burton (Col.)	27	Jan	1843	05 Jan 1843			TRIB
Hepler, Singleton C.	26	May	1857	05 May 1857	7y9d		PSOT

Deaths

Name	Notice Date			Death Date	Age	Comment	Paper
Hepp, Marcus	18	Oct	1862				PTIMES
Herder, Jacob	21	Dec	1861	14 Dec 1861			PTIMES
Herpst, Joseph	12	Apr	1860	11 Apr 1860			DET
Herriera, unknown	08	Mar	1854	12 Feb 1854		ex-Pres. Mexico	PDD
Herrington, Patrick	15	Apr	1854	13 Apr 1854			PDD
Hershey, Abraham	31	Jan	1863				PTIMES
Hess, Leo	05	Aug	1865	04 Aug 1865	20		PTIMES
Hester, unknown (Dr.)	03	Dec	1853	01 Dec 1853			DET
Hester, unknown (Dr.)	05	Dec	1853	01 Dec 1853			PDD
Hevill, Alex.	21	Jun	1854	17 Jun 1854			PDD
Hews, Daniel	24	Jan	1854	17 Jan 1854			PDD
Hibbard, Martha	02	Jul	1851		20		PT&C
Hibbard, unknown	27	Jul	1853	19 Jul 1853	4		PDD
Hibbs, Jacob	21	Jul	1852	12 Jul 1852	59		PT&C
Hibler, Casper	01	Jul	1857	16 Jun 1857			WPT
Hickee, Elias	09	Jul	1864				PTIMES
Hickey, James	23	Jul	1856	Jul 1856			WPT
Hickle, Elias	23	Jul	1864	29 Jun 1864			PTIMES
Hickman, Christopher	28	May	1851	21 May 1851	17		PT&C
Hicks, Elizabeth	10	May	1853		21		PDD (S)
Hicks, female	14	Nov	1853	11 Nov 1853	3		DET
Hicks, female	14	Nov	1853	11 Nov 1853	13m		DET
Hicks, male	22	Jan	1851				PT&C
Hicks, Simon	23	Feb	1855	24 Jan 1855	99		DET
Higby, E.G. (Lieut.)	20	May	1865	14 May 1865?			PTIMES
Higby, E.J. (Lieut.)	28	May	1864	May 1864			PTIMES
Higgins, Charles W.	01	Oct	1864	29 Sep 1864	48y3m		PTIMES
Higgins, John, Sr.	16	Jun	1857	09 Jun 1857	75		PSOT
Higgins, R.B.	29	Aug	1863	28 Aug 1863	10m		PTIMES
Higgins, Susan Frances	22	Oct	1864	21 Oct 1864	14y11m12d		PTIMES
Hill, Alfred	11	Jun	1851		19		PT&C
Hill, C.G.	11	Feb	1865	04 Feb 1865			PTIMES
Hill, George G.	20	Sep	1854	18 Sep 1854	50		DET
Hill, Jas.	04	Feb	1854				PDD
Hill, Margaret	02	May	1854	24 Apr 1854	64		PDD (S)
Hill, Susannah	11	Feb	1865	04 Feb 1865			PTIMES
Hill, Wm.	16	Feb	1854				PDD
Hindman, R.T. (Dr.)	03	Mar	1860	12 Feb 1860			PTIMES
Hine, male	04	Feb	1852				PT&C
Hinshaw, male	15	Mar	1854				DET
Hinton, R.C.	19	Jun	1860	16 Jun 1860			DET
Hirsh, Nathan	09	May	1857	06 May 1857			DET
Hirsh, Nathan	13	May	1857	06 May 1857			WPT
Hitchcock, Peter (Hon.)	09	Mar	1853	05 Mar 1853			PT&C

Name	Notice Date			Death Date	Age	Comment	Paper
Hite, Jonathan F.	30	Jul	1864	20 Jul 1864			PTIMES
Ho_t, unknown	21	Mar	1854	14 Mar 1854	3		PDD (S)
Hobbie, unknown (Major)	27	Mar	1854	23 Mar 1854			PDD
Hobbs, Charles Webster	12	May	1858	12 May 1858	1y8m8d		DET
Hochbliss, William C.	01	Feb	1862	21 Nov 1861			PTIMES
Hodge, Samuel	27	Apr	1853	07 Apr 1853			PT&C
Hodges, Irvine	31	Jul	1845				TRIB
Hodges, J.J.	02	Mar	1859	27 Feb 1859			DET
Hodgkins, Rachel A.	30	Jul	1856	29 Jul 1856	10m10d		WPT
Hoffman, J.	06	Jun	1863	16 May 1863			PTIMES
Hoffman, Pleasant M.	21	Nov	1853	02 Nov 1853			DET
Hoffman, William O.	20	Apr	1854				DET
Hoffman, William O.	21	Apr	1854	13 Apr 1854			PDD
Hoke, Michael (Esq.) (Col.)	26	Sep	1844				TRIB
Holbeck, C. (Corp.)	06	Jun	1863	16 May 1863			PTIMES
Holbert, George	11	Feb	1852	28 Jan 1852	19		PT&C
Holbert, George	30	Jan	1852	28 Jan 1852	19		PI
Holcomb, Abigal	31	Dec	1853	18 Dec 1853	14		DET
Holland, Stewart	16	Nov	1854				DET
Holliday, Amos	11	May	1853	09 May 1853	106y3m15d		PT&C
Hollingsworth, Sarah	13	Aug	1864		110		PTIMES
Hollinsworth, Thomas	20	Jun	1853	15 Jun 1853			DET
Hollis, Ebenezer	22	Mar	1859	17 Mar 1859			PTIMES
Holly, female	03	Dec	1859			nee Hamilton	PTIMES
Holly, John	21	May	1858	15 May 1858	36		DET
Holly, John	25	May	1858	15 May 1858	36		PSOT
Holly, John	26	May	1858	15 May 1858	36		WPT
Holmes, Enos A. (Lieut)	01	Feb	1862	24 Dec 1861			PTIMES
Holmes, John (Hon.)	28	Jul	1843				TRIB
Holmes, Mary Jane	09	May	1855	18 Apr 1855	2		DET (S)
Holmes, Mary Jane	17	Apr	1855	17 Apr 1855	2y7m		DET
Holmes, W.R.	03	Apr	1858	02 Apr 1858	70		DET
Holt, James	14	Oct	1865	08 Oct 1865	40		PTIMES
Hood, Charles Francis	10	May	1862	02 May 1862	1y1m18d		PTIMES
Hooft, A.	09	Jun	1860	Jun 1860			PTIMES
Hooper, Thomas W.	29	Mar	1855	27 Mar 1855			DET
Hoover, Garrett	04	Nov	1857	22 Oct 1857			WPT
Hopkins, George	21	Jun	1862	03 Jun 1862			PTIMES
Hopkins, J.W.	15	Jul	1850	13 Jul 1850			PI
Hopkins, S.H.	14	Nov	1853	23 Oct 1853			DET
Horton, female	15	Mar	1854				DET
Horton, John	15	Mar	1854				DET
Horton, unknown	15	Mar	1854			child	DET

Deaths

Name	Notice Date			Death Date	Age	Comment	Paper
Horton, unknown	15	Mar	1854		child		DET
House, female	19	Jul	1854				DET
Housman, female	12	Jan	1844	Dec 1843	27	nee Van Pelt	TRIB
Housman, unknown	12	Jan	1844	Dec 1843	18m		TRIB
Houtchins, Christopher	21	Jun	1862				PTIMES
Hover, unknown	19	May	1858		child		WPT
Hovey, Alfred	04	Apr	1854	31 Mar 1854	76		PDD
Howard, Clarence S.	27	Jul	1860	24 Jul 1860	13		DET
Howard, H.B.	11	Jun	1851				PT&C
Howard, Henry	04	Oct	1862	14 Sep 1862			PTIMES
Howard, Tilghman A. (Hon.)	26	Sep	1844	16 Sep 1844			TRIB
Howard, unknown (Col.)	23	Jun	1852	02 Jun 1852			PT&C
Howe, Abel	31	Mar	1854	25 Mar 1854			PDD
Howe, Joseph	22	Mar	1855				DET
Howe, Pulaski	22	Nov	1862				PTIMES
Howell, A.	19	Jan	1844	04 Jan 1844			TRIB
Howell, Hester	17	Sep	1841	11 Sep 1841	50		TRIB
Howells, Seth (Rev.)	03	Mar	1858				WPT
Howland, Sylvia Ann	22	Jul	1865	16 Jul 1865	59		PTIMES
Howland, Wm.	08	Aug	1854				PDD
Hoy, C.W.	08	Jul	1857				WPT
Hoylan, Robert	13	Aug	1864	22 Jul 1864			PTIMES
Hoyt, A.B.	09	Dec	1854	07 Dec 1854			DET
Hubbard, C.D.	06	Jun	1863	16 May 1863			PTIMES
Hudson, Mary Emma	08	Aug	1863	30 Jul 1863	18m		PTIMES
Huffman, Joseph	11	Jul	1855	06 Jul 1855			DET
Hughes, Amanda Pursell	12	Mar	1864	08 Mar 1864	5y1m22d		PTIMES
Hughes, Hannah	03	Dec	1853		16		PDD
Hughes, Hannah	12	Dec	1853		16		DET
Hughes, Hannah	14	Dec	1853		16		WPT
Hughes, Joseph	31	Mar	1843	17 Mar 1843			TRIB
Hughes, male	31	Oct	1844	Oct 1844			TRIB
Hughes, Thomas	22	Mar	1854	10 Mar 1854			PDD
Hughes, Tom (Col.)	08	Sep	1853	28 Aug 1853			DET
Hull, Isaac (Commodore)	24	Feb	1843		68		TRIB
Humphreys, George Ella	21	Jul	1851	15 Jul 1851			PI
Huntemuler, H.F.D.	11	Jun	1855	09 Jun 1855	22		DET
Hunter, Charles	21	Nov	1854	24 Oct 1854	30		DET
Hunter, John	04	Apr	1863		92		PTIMES
Hunter, John	20	Sep	1858	20 Sep 1858	53		DET
Hunter, John	22	Sep	1858	20 Sep 1858	53		WPT
Huntington, Elijah (Esq.)	03	Aug	1854				DET
Hurd, John R.	12	May	1852	12 May 1852	1y2m3d		PT&C

Name	Notice Date			Death Date	Age	Comment	Paper
Hurd, Mary	24	Sep	1852	19 Sep 1852	62		PI
Hurley, John	28	May	1864	May 1864			PTIMES
Huston, Andrew	20	Mar	1854				DET
Huston, Benj. Franklin	22	Sep	1843	15 Sep 1843	2		TRIB
Huston, Giles	10	Mar	1843	07 Mar 1843	infant		TRIB
Huston, James L.O.	22	Apr	1865	20 Apr 1865	20y5m2d		PTIMES
	27	May	1865				
Hutchins, unknown	18	Jun	1851		24		PT&C
Hutchinson, Jesse	25	May	1853	22 May 1853			PT&C
Hutchison, T.M.	11	May	1853				PDD
Hutton, Milton	10	May	1862	03 May 1862	24		PTIMES
Hyatt, Elvin	22	Apr	1865	15 Apr 1865	68y7m12d		PTIMES
Hyatt, male	20	Apr	1853				PT&C
Hyatt, unknown	13	Mar	1855	28 Jan 1855	2		DET (S)
Hyer, Tom	09	Jul	1864	26 Jun 1864			PTIMES
Hysell, Heywood	06	Feb	1854	06 Feb 1854			PDD
Idler, Samuel	28	Jun	1855	25 Jun 1855			DET
Iliffe, Alice	29	Oct	1859	22 Oct 1859	22y6m23d	nee Smith	PTIMES
Iliffe, Alice G.	27	Oct	1859	26 Oct 1859	22y6m23d	nee Smith	DET
Ingalls, male	20	Mar	1854				PDD
Ingalls, William	09	Dec	1850	7 Dec 1850			PI
Ingersoll, Charles Jared	24	May	1862	14 May 1862	18		PTIMES
Ingles, Harriet	09	May	1855	19 Apr 1855			DET (S)
Innis, Anna	18	Jun	1851	12 May 1851			PT&C
Irby, unknown (Dr.)	26	Jan	1854				PDD
Irving, Washington	01	Dec	1859		79		DET
Irving, Washington	10	Dec	1859	05 Dec 1859	76		PTIMES
Irving, William	08	Aug	1854	30 Jul 18554			PDD
Irwin, Demara	17	Sep	1856	08 Sep 1856	6m26d		WPT
Irwin, Julia H.	28	Jul	1854	21 Jul 1854			DET
Irwin, male	28	Jan	1852				PT&C
Irwin, Sarah	06	Jul	1858	22 Jun 1858	33		PSOT
Irwin, Wm.	13	Oct	1852				PT&C
Irwine, G. (Serg't)	06	Jun	1863	16 May 1863			PTIMES
Isaacs, female	06	Apr	1853				PT&C
Isem, Jo	31	Mar	1843	17 Mar 1843			TRIB
Isham, Asa W. (Dr.)	06	Jun	1853		53		PDD
Iverson, Knud	10	Nov	1853	09 Aug 1853			DET
	29	Dec	1853				
Jack, James	23	Sep	1854	16 Sep 1854			DET
Jack, Laura Virginia	01	Aug	1857	31 Jul 1857	3m18d		DET
Jack, Laura Virginia	05	Aug	1857	31 Jul 1857	3m18d		WPT
Jackman, Robert	13	Aug	1851	09 Aug 1851			PT&C
Jackson, Andrew, Jr.	29	Apr	1865		56		PTIMES
Jackson, Cynthia	10	Jun	1852	9 Jun 1852	23		PI

Deaths

Name	Notice Date			Death Date	Age	Comment	Paper
Jackson, James	05	Sep	1855	29 Aug 1855			DET
Jackson, Stonewall	16	May	1863	10 May 1863			PTIMES
Jackson, unk. (Capt.)	25	Mar	1859				DET
Jackson, unk. (Capt.)	30	Mar	1859				WPT
Jackson, Wells A.H.	06	Oct	1860	02 Oct 1860			PTIMES
Jacobs, female	28	May	1851	24 May 1851			PT&C
Jacobs, Hans	27	Aug	1851	23 Aug 1851			PT&C
Jacobs, Mathias	20	Jul	1858	16 Jul 1858			DET
Jacobs, unknown	28	May	1851	24 May 1851	child		PT&C
Jahue, female	02,07, 11	Nov	1854				DET
James, George W.	28	May	1864	May 1864			PTIMES
James, John	28	May	1864	May 1864			PTIMES
Jaynes, Betsy Ann	01	Apr	1854	27 Mar 1854	23	nee Kelley	DET
Jefferson, John Randolph	16	Aug	1862	06 Jul 1862	71		PTIMES
Jefferson, Laura Susan	15	Jul	1850	11 Jul 1850	5		PI
Jefferson, male	02	Dec	1850		11		PI
Jefferson, male	28	Nov	1850	26 Nov 1850			PT&C
Jefferson, Thomas	20	Jul	1826	04 Jul 1826	80	ex-Pres.	WT
Jeffords, Isabella	27	Sep	1828	20 Sep 1828	13		WT
Jenkins, Ebenezer	26	Jan	1854	20 Jan 1854			PDD
Jenkins, female	01	Aug	1850	26 Jul 1850			PT&C
Jenkins, Samuel	11	Aug	1858				WPT
Jenkins, unknown	19	May	1858			Negro	WPT
Jenkison, male	07	Jan	1852				PT&C
Jennet, J. (Rev.)	14	Jan	1852	31 Dec 1851	85		PT&C
Jennings, John	29	Dec	1843				TRIB
Jennings, Simeon	09	Dec	1865				PTIMES
Jennings, unknown	11	Jan	1854	05 Jan 1854			DET
Jennison (or Gunnison), J.W. (Capt.)	03, 06	Dec	1853				PDD
Jewell, David	28	Mar	1854	24 Mar 1854			PDD
Jewitt, Jonathan	22	Mar	1855				DET
Johnson, Benjamin H.	04	Aug	1854				DET
Johnson, Bill	27	Oct	1843				TRIB
Johnson, David	15	Aug	1850	09 Aug 1850	70		PT&C
Johnson, Edward	05	Feb	1851		child		PT&C
Johnson, Elias S.	12	Jan	1854	29 Dec 1853			PDD
Johnson, female	17	May	1859	May 1859	7		PTIMES
Johnson, Frank	03	May	1844				TRIB
Johnson, J.M.	03	Sep	1851				PT&C
Johnson, James	29	Jul	1850	21 Jul 1850	17m		PI
Johnson, James	31	Dec	1851	23 Dec 1851	38		PT&C
Johnson, Joseph	23	Jul	1856	Jul 1856	100	Negro/aka Capt. Bunkry	WPT

Name	Notice Date			Death Date	Age	Comment	Paper
Johnson, Lawrence (Esq.)	09	May	1860	26 Apr 1860			WPT
Johnson, Matthias	06	Apr	1853	28 Mar 1853			PT&C
Johnson, Nancy	02	May	1863	23 Apr 1863	20		PTIMES
Johnson, Peter	25	Aug	1854	22 Aug 1854			DET
Johnson, Priscilla	18	Mar	1820				STEL
Johnson, R.M.	21	Nov	1850				PT&C
Johnson, Robert	18	May	1853	13 May 1853	64		PT&C
Johnson, Robert (Rev.)	25	Jan	1862				PTIMES
Johnson, Thomas A. (Act'g Adj't)	01	Feb	1862	11 Jan 1862			PTIMES
Johnson, unknown	17	Aug	1854	04 Aug 1854	2		DET (S)
Johnson, Wm.	20	Apr	1854		45		PDD
Johnson, Wm.	20	Jun	1860	15 Jun 1860	65		WPT
Johnson, Wm.	23	Jun	1860	15 Jun 1860	65		PTIMES
Johnston, Benj. (Judge)	11	Jul	1863	04 Jul 1863	61		PTIMES
Johnston, Ddelia	06	May	1854	01 May 1854	17		PDD
Johnston, Jacob H.	20	Jul	1854	08 Jul 1854	40		DET
Johnston, John (Major)	14	Dec	1826	21 Nov 1826	80		WT
Joice, James T.	05	Feb	1851		child		PT&C
Jones, Alpheus	06	Jul	1853				PT&C
Jones, Elizabeth H.	20	Aug	1851	05 Aug 1851	37y8d		PT&C
Jones, Francis M.	16	Mar	1853				PT&C
Jones, Francis M.	18	Mar	1853		25		PI
Jones, Gideon	30	Dec	1858	29 Dec 1858	19		DET
Jones, J.G. (Dr.)	18	Mar	1857	14 Mar 1857			WPT
Jones, Jacob	08	Sep	1851	3 Sep 1851			PI
Jones, Jacob	10	Sep	1851	03 Sep 1851	42		PT&C
Jones, Jane	14	Jul	1855	13 Jul 1855			DET
Jones, Joel	29	Dec	1854	22 Dec 1854	40		DET
Jones, M.	22	Aug	1850				PT&C
Jones, male	11	Jun	1855		14		DET
Jones, male	22	Apr	1865		2		PTIMES
Jones, Sarah Ann	20	Feb	1852	12 Feb 1852		nee Warner	PI
Jones, Thomas Walter	22	Aug	1853				DET
Jones, Thomas Walter	24	Aug	1853				PT&C
Jones, unknown	05	Apr	1859		2		DET
Jones, Vennette Stevens	26	May	1860	21 May 1860	5		PTIMES
Jones, Walter R.	12	Apr	1855				DET
Jones, William	11	Mar	1859	04 Mar 1859	84		DET
Jones, Wm.	08	Mar	1859	04 Mar 1859	84		PTIMES
Jones, Wm.	16	Mar	1859	04 Mar 1859	84		WPT
Jones, Wm.	29	Jun	1853		13		PDD
Jones, Yennette Stevens	22	May	1860	21 May 1860	5		DET
Jordan, Jerman	18	Feb	1865		75		PTIMES

Name	Notice Date			Death Date	Age	Comment	Paper
Jordan, Mary Emma	19	Nov	1864	15 Nov 1864	10m17d		PTIMES
Jordon, Berthia	02	Jan	1855	29 Dec 1854	62		DET
Jordon, male	08	Feb	1854	23 Dec 1853			PDD
Joyce, Isabelle	01	Jul	1865				PTIMES
Joyce, male	01	Jul	1865				PTIMES
Joyce, Michael	07	Mar	1860	04 Mar 1860			DET
Judevine, Alfred	05	Aug	1865	29 Jul 1865			PTIMES
Kamehameha III	06	Feb	1855	15 Dec 1854	41y9m	King	DET
Kane, female	29	Nov	1854	26 Nov 1854			DET
Kane, Francis	02	Oct	1860	28 Sep 1860			DET
Kane, John	13	Mar	1855	10 Mar 1855			DET
Kane, Patrick	29	Nov	1854	26 Nov 1854			DET
Kane, William	11	May	1853				PT&C
Kapps, Casper	17	Dec	1857	16 Dec 1857	60		DET
Kaskingo (Kaw or Kansas Chief)	11	Feb	1857	17 Jan 1857		Indian	WPT
Kauffman, David S. (Hon.)	12	Feb	1851	07 Feb 1851			PT&C
Kavanah, male	11	Jun	1855	07 Jun 1855			DET
Kean, Tho.	26	Jun	1854	18 Jun 1854			DET
Kearney, Jas. (Col.)	18	Jan	1862				PTIMES
Kearney, Wylie	05	Nov	1853				DET
Keating, male	16	Sep	1865				PTIMES
Keefe, male	20	Jul	1854	18 Jul 1854			DET
Keese, John	02	Jun	1854	31 May 1854			PDD
Kehoe, Annie Carey	15	Jun	1859	07 Jun 1859	3		WPT
Kehoe, Caroline	13	Oct	1854	08 Oct 1854	16		PDD (S)
Kehoe, Caroline C.	10	Oct	1854	07 Oct 1854	18y5m		DET
Kehoe, female	19	Aug	1850	15 Aug 1850	infant		PI
Kehoe, M.E.	17	Aug	1854	12 Aug 1854	14		DET (S)
Kehrer, Caroline Sophia	08	Oct	1851	06 Oct 1851	11m		PT&C
Kehrer, Caroline Sophia	10	Oct	1851	6 Oct 1851	11m		PI
Keiningham, unknown	16	May	1855	11 May 1855			DET
Keller, Thomas	15	Nov	1853	11 Nov 1853	26		PDD (S)
Kelley, female	07	Jan	1852				PT&C
Kelley, G.W.	17	Oct	1860	31 Sep 1860	48	aka "Wash"	WPT
Kelley, G.W.	05	Oct	1860	31 Sep 1860	48	aka "Wash"	DET
Kelley, George T.	14	Feb	1854	3 Feb 1854	25		DET
Kelley, Harriet	02	May	1860	20 Apr 1860	18		WPT
Kelley, James	23	Aug	1853	18 Aug 1853	13		PDD
Kelley, John	11	Apr	1859	30 Mar 1859	78		DET
Kelley, Michael	10	May	1853	08 May 1853	24		PDD
Kelley, Michael	11	May	1853	08 May 1853	24		PT&C
Kelley, unknown	03	Mar	1843	Feb 1843			TRIB
Kelley, William S.	06	Aug	1856				WPT

Name	Notice Date			Death Date	Age	Comment	Paper
Kellogg, William W.	20	Jun	1844	16 Jun 1844			TRIB
Kelly, Alfred	10	Dec	1859	08 Dec 1859	70		PTIMES
Kelly, J.F.	24	Jul	1854				PDD
Kelly, John	06	Jul	1853	11 Jun 1853	93		PT&C
Kelly, John (Rev.)	19	Apr	1859	30 Mar 1859	79		PTIMES
Kelly, Mary J.	10	Nov	1860	06 Nov 1860	13		PTIMES
Kelly, Patrick	11	Aug	1860	05 Aug 1860	25		PTIMES
Kelly, Whitfeld	20	Jan	1860	17 Jan 1860	52		DET
Kelly, Whitfeld	25	Jan	1860	20 Jan 1860	52		WPT
Kendall, Ida E.	23	Aug	1860	23 Aug 1860	10m9d		DET
Kendall, Ida E.	29	Aug	1860	23 Aug 1860	10m9d		WPT
Kendall, Milton	25	Jun	1851	21 Jun 1851	16m		PT&C
Kennedy, Charles	06	Apr	1853	02 Apr 1853			PT&C
Kennedy, female	13	Aug	1855		5		DET
Kennedy, Jane	04	Jan	1854	27 Nov 1853	14		DET
Kennedy, male	13	Aug	1855		8		DET
Kennedy, male	13	Aug	1855		20m		DET
Kennedy, Nancy	04	Jan	1854	27 Nov 1853	11		DET
Kennedy, Samuel	17	Nov	1859	14 Nov 1859			DET
Kennedy, Thomas Henry	04	Jan	1854	20 Nov 1853	9		DET
Kennon, unk. (Commodore)	08	Mar	1844	28 Feb 1844			TRIB
Keogh, James	17, 18, 23	May	1860	17 May 1860	10		DET
Kephart, Charles Fenelon	11	Nov	1857	03 Nov 1857	27		DET
Kepler, Mitchel	19	Feb	1851	13 Feb 1851			PT&C
Kerley, Sidney	04	Oct	1853	03 Oct 1853			DET
Kerne, R.H.	03, 06	Dec	1853				PDD
Kerne, R.H. (Capt.)	02, 05	Dec	1853				DET
Kerr, female	03	Jun	1850	29 May 1850			PI
Kerr, female	06	Jun	1850	29 May 1850			PT&C
Kerr, Franklin C.	30	May	1863	20 May 1863	23		PTIMES
Kerr, Mary	15	Aug	1850	14 Aug 1850	66		PT&C
Kerr, Mary	19	Aug	1850	14 Aug 1850	66		PI
Kerr, William R., Jr.	16	Dec	1850	5 Dec 1850	16		PI
Ketcham, John	12	Dec	1850	09 Dec 1850	61		PT&C
Key, male	09	Mar	1859				WPT
Key, Philip Barton	01, 08	Mar	1859	27 Feb 1859			PTIMES
Key, Philip Barton	02, 03, 18, 19, 21	Mar	1859				DET
Keyes, Catharine	08	Jun	1858	07 Jun 1858	50		DET
Keyes, Catharine	09	Jun	1858	07 Jun 1858	50		WPT
Keys, John	03	Jun	1854	31 May 1854			DET
Keys, John	29	Sep	1852	28 Sep 1852		Negro	PT&C
Keys, male	19	Dec	1853		child		PDD

Deaths

Name	Notice Date			Death Date	Age	Comment	Paper
Kidd, Margaret J.	10, 12	Nov	1853	22 Oct 1853	22	nee Ross	DET
Kiel, female	20	Aug	1851	29 Jul 1851		nee Mason	PT&C
Kierman, John	05	Dec	1853	Oct 1853			DET
Killen, Robert L.	26	Jul	1855	26 Jul 1855	2		DET
Kilpatrick, Hugh	11	Mar	1865				PTIMES
Kimball, female	16	Mar	1860				DET
Kimberly, Wollaston	31	Aug	1853	29 Aug 1853			DET
	03	Sep	1853				
King, male	27	Apr	1853	Apr 1853			PT&C
King, male	29	Jul	1853				DET
King, male	29	Jul	1853				DET
King, Nathaniel, Jr.	11	May	1853				PDD
King, Preston (Hon.)	18	Nov	1865				PTIMES
King, William R.	26	Apr	1853	18 Apr 1853		V.P. of U.S.	PDD
	01	Jun	1853			under Pierce	
Kingsbury, Cornelia	13	May	1858	03 May 1858	29	nee Brown	DET
Kingsbury, Cornelia	26	May	1858	03 May 1858	29	nee Brown	WPT
Kingsbury, Francis	19	May	1852	11 May 1852	6		PT&C
Kingsbury, Lewis B.	03	Apr	1854				PDD
Kinney, male	14	Apr	1857		83		PSOT
Kinney, Mary	03	Jul	1854		4		DET
Kirby, James (Col.)	03	Jul	1854	28 Jun 1854	69		DET
Kirby, Moses	31	Oct	1844	Oct 1844			TRIB
Kirker, Thomas	11	Mar	1837	19 Feb 1837	77		STRIB
Kirker, William	17	Feb	1857	10 Feb 1857	66y16d		PSOT
Kirkpatrick, Clarinda	24	Oct	1829		20		WT
Kissel, male	31	Aug	1853				DET
Klaus, Valentine	06	May	1854	23 Apr 1854			PDD
Kleine, Morris	13	Jul	1853				DET
Kleine, Morris	20	Jul	1853	14 Jul 1853			PT&C
Knight, unknown (Gov.)	25	Apr	1854				PDD
Koehler, Fred (Corp.)	23	May	1863				PTIMES
Kopf, John	06	Aug	1851				PT&C
Kossuth, female	05	Jul	1854				DET
Kossuth, female	14	Jan	1852	12 Dec 1851			PT&C
Kouns, George W.	12	Dec	1860	25 Nov 1860			WPT
Kouns, S.E. (Mrs.)	26	Mar	1856	09 Mar 1856	28		WPT
Kountz, unknown (Capt.)	26	Jun	1854	23 Jun 1854			DET
Kountz, unknown (Capt.)	26	Jun	1854	23 Jun 1854			PDD
Kraiser, Margaret	06	May	1854	23 Apr 1854	21		PDD
Kramer, John	19	Aug	1857	17 Aug 1857			WPT
Kramer, Louis	21	Jan	1865				PTIMES
Kramer, unknown (Corp.)	24	Aug	1853				PT&C
Kramer, unknown (Corp.)	19	Aug	1853	15 Aug 1853			DET

Name	Notice Date			Death Date	Age	Comment	Paper
Krat, Amos	03	Mar	1858				WPT
Kraylor, female	23	Mar	1853				PT&C
Kraylor, unknown	23	Mar	1853		infant		PT&C
Kreider, M.Z. (Dr.)	23	Jul	1855				DET
Kreninger, John	25	May	1853	22 May 1853			PT&C
Kroger, male	11	May	1854				PDD
Krous, male	31	May	1854	28 May 1854	1y8m		PDD
Kyler, John	21	Sep	1854	18 Sep 1854			DET
Lacey, W.P.	29	Aug	1853	20 Aug 1853	34		PDD
Lackey, James	31	Dec	1853	8 Dec 1853	84		DET
Ladue, Emeline	17	Mar	1852				PT&C
Lafferty, Caroline	30	Jul	1851	Jul 1851			PT&C
	06	Aug	1851				
Lafferty, James	03	Oct	1860	24 Sep 1860			WPT
Lafferty, Mary	23	Jul	1851	11 Jul 1851	78		PT&C
Laforge, Matilda	22	Nov	1853	13 Nov 1853	26		PDD (S)
Laguiref, J. Davidson	08	Aug	1853				PDD
Laidlow, James W.	12	May	1854				DET
Lally, Thos.	03	Jun	1854	31 May 1854			DET
Lamar, female	10	Aug	1854				PDD
Lamb, Reuben	14	Feb	1854	19 Jan 1854	37		DET
Lamb. Persis	14	Feb	1854	17 Jan 1854	86		DET
Lamme, Peter	13	Jun	1854	08 Jun 1854	32		PDD (S)
Lampton, Anna Barr	21	Jan	1857	06 Dec 1856	5y7m11d		WPT
Lampton, Isaac Newton	14	Jan	1854	8 Jan 1854	8		DET
Lampton, Susan	31	Aug	1859	22 Aug 1859	68		DET
Landress, female	11	May	1853				PDD
Lane, male	14	Jul	1852	25 Jun 1852			PT&C
Lanegan, Edward	20	Jun	1853	13 Jun 1853			PDD
Lang, Ann	12	May	1853				PDD
Lang, Anna B.	11	May	1853				PDD
Lang, female	12	May	1853				PDD
Lang, Francis	27	Aug	1856	19 Aug 1856			WPT
Lang, Henry	12	Jan	1853	07 Jan 1853	30		PT&C
Lang, Martin	12	May	1853				PDD
Lants, Christian	31	Jan	1854	16 Jan 1854	73		DET
Lapham, D. (Esq.)	25	Jul	1850	20 Jul 1850			PT&C
Lardner, unknown (Dr.)	31	May	1859		59		PTIMES
Larier, B.F.	12	May	1853				PDD
Larimer, Mary	20	May	1854	19 May 1854			DET
Lasalle, unknown (Gen.)	24	Feb	1843	23 Jan 1843	66		TRIB
Lassiter, male	12	Jan	1853				PT&C
Latham, W.A. (Col.)	12	Jul	1859	13 Jun 1859			DET
Latham, W.A. (Col.)	13	Jul	1859	13 Jun 1859			WPT
Lathom, Patrick	27	Jun	1854	17 Jun 1854	3		PDD (S)

Name	Notice Date			Death Date	Age	Comment	Paper
Lathrop, J.T.K.	26	Sep	1844	14 Aug 1844			TRIB
Latimer, male	13	Dec	1853		70		PDD
Lattimore, John	29	Oct	1859	Oct 1859	83		PTIMES
Laughlin, Catharine	25	Nov	1854				DET
Laughlin, female	09	Nov	1854				PDD
Laughlin, female	25	Nov	1854				DET
Laughlin, Robert	04	Aug	1855	04 Aug 1855	50		DET
Laughlin, unknown	25	Nov	1854		child		DET
Laughlin, unknown	25	Nov	1854		child		DET
Laughlin, William	15	Oct	1851				PT&C
Laughlin, Wm. C.	25	Nov	1854				DET
Laur, George	02	May	1855		18		DET
Lavering, John	04	Mar	1859	19 Feb 1859	9		DET
Lawson, A.W.	27	Apr	1853	06 Apr 1853			PT&C
Lawson, Franklin	22	Jul	1825	17 Jul 1825	1y9m		PG&LA
Lawson, John	05	Oct	1859	15 Sep 1859	69		DET
Lawson, Thomas E.	09	Apr	1860	09 Apr 1860	23		DET
Lawson, William	21	Mar	1832	18 Mar 1832	72		PC
Lazell, female	16	Dec	1859				DET
Leak, Cordelia M.	28	Jul	1858	22 Jul 1858		nee Scott	WPT
Leary, Dennis	13	Feb	1860	04 Feb 1860			DET
Lebaum, female	09	May	1854	16 Apr 1854		nee Thomas	PDD
Ledbetter, Georgiana	12	Aug	1854	11 Aug 1854			DET
Leddy, female	27	Apr	1853	23 Apr 1853			PT&C
Lee, Ann	16	Jul	1852	11 Jul 1852			PI
Lee, Eleanor	27	Dec	1853	18 Dec 1853			DET
Lee, male	26	Jul	1853				PDD
Lee, male	28	Jul	1860				PTIMES
Lee, Thomas	19	Nov	1864				PTIMES
Leet, female	22	Dec	1854				DET
Leet, Frank Herndon	22	Feb	1859	21 Feb 1859	7m2d		PTIMES
Leet, M. Frank	21	Feb	1859	21 Feb 1859	7m		DET
Leete, Uriah	30	May	1863	15 May 1863	73		PTIMES
Legare, Davidson	13	Aug	1853				DET
Legare, Davidson	17	Aug	1853				PT&C
Lehmann, Caroline	22	Mar	1854		55		SVREP
Leichner, Conrad	11	Jan	1862	08 Jan 1862			PTIMES
Leister, Peter	10	Jun	1854	03 Jun 1854			DET
Lene, male	06	Aug	1853				PDD
Lenox, Lawrence	11	Feb	1865	04 Feb 1865			PTIMES
Leonard, Elizabeth	06	Nov	1838	11 Oct 1838	65		STRIB
Lester, J.J.	22	Mar	1855				DET
Letcher, Robert P.	02	Feb	1861	31 Jan 1861			PTIMES
Letz, Frederick	07	Feb	1863	23 Jan 1863			PTIMES

Name	Notice Date			Death Date	Age	Comment	Paper
Levi, Joseph	10	Nov	1860				DET
Lewellyn, male	28	Jun	1855	22 Jun 1855			DET
Lewis, Charles	24	Jan	1854				DET
Lewis, Francis Cotton	11	Jul	1857	11 Jul 1857	6m16d		DET
Lewis, James	25	May	1854	23 May 1854			DET
Lewis, John	04	Feb	1854	16 Jan 1854			DET
Lewis, John	16	Aug	1859				PTIMES
Lewis, John	29	Dec	1843				TRIB
Lewis, male	11	May	1855	06 May 1855			DET
Lewis, Maria	01	Sep	1852				PT&C
Lewis, Rachel	15	Jan	1831	09 Jan 1831	37		PC
Lewis, Robert	25	Sep	1855				DET
Lewis, Samuel (Hon.)	03	Aug	1854				DET
Lewis, Sherrod	29	Mar	1859	Mar 1859			PTIMES
Lewis, William	12	Nov	1853	2 Nov 1853	91		DET
Liggett, John	03	Oct	1853				DET
Lilly, Mary	23	Jul	1856	Jul 1856			WPT
Lincoln, Abraham (President)	22	Apr	1865	15 Apr 1865	56		PTIMES
Lindermood, George	21	Feb	1863	14 Feb 1863			PTIMES
Lindley, Angeline	25	Nov	1850	16 Nov 1850			PI
Lindley, Angeline	28	Nov	1850	16 Nov 1850			PT&C
Lindley, unknown	12	Feb	1851		5		PT&C
Lindsey, Abagail	18	Nov	1853		53		DET
Linn, Ann Elizabeth	03	Sep	1852	Sep 1852	1m25d		PI
Linn, Ann Elizabeth	13	Aug	1852	Aug 1852	26		PI
Linn, Lewis F. (Hon.)	20	Oct	1843	03 Oct 1843			TRIB
Linn, Sarah Jane	04	Aug	1851	2 Aug 1851			PI
Linn, Sarah Jane	06	Aug	1851	02 Aug 1851	infant		PT&C
Liplarett, unknown	05	Dec	1853				DET
Liplarett, unknown	03, 06	Dec	1853				PDD
List, Conrad	06	Jul	1853	05 Jul 1853			PDD
Little, David	04	Jun	1864				PTIMES
Little, Mary Jane	20	Oct	1855	20 Oct 1855			DET
Littlejohn, Typhosa	23	Jul	1851	14 Jul 1851	18		PT&C
Littlejohn, Typhosa	28	Jul	1851	14 Jul 1851	18		PI
Livingston, Barker	15	Jul	1850	13 Jul 1850	2		PI
Livingston, Simon	08	Jul	1857	03 Jul 1857			WPT
Lloyd, Ann Adele	01	Jul	1850	26 Jun 1850	11m		PI
Lloyd, Ann Adele	27	Jun	1850	26 Jun 1850	11m		PT&C
Lock, Mary Boynton	05	Aug	1825		14m		PG&LA
Lockard, Geo.	21	Apr	1852				PT&C
Locke, Benjamin	13	Feb	1864	07 Feb 1864	73y2m12d		PTIMES
Lockhead, James	11	Feb	1865				PTIMES
Locquet, male	26	Mar	1859	11 Mar 1859			DET

Name	Notice Date			Death Date	Age	Comment	Paper
Locquet, male	30	Mar	1859	11 Mar 1859			WPT
Locy, Nanch	09	May	1855	20 Apr 1855	9		DET (S)
Lodwick, Eggleston	23	Feb	1861	21 Feb 1861	6y6m		PTIMES
Lodwick, Erastus Burr	09	Apr	1864	03 Apr 1864	2y2m		PTIMES
Lodwick, Fannie	15	Jul	1865	07 Jul 1865	30		PTIMES
Lodwick, Henry C.	29	Dec	1860	11 Dec 1860			PTIMES
Lodwick, James	05	Mar	1851	03 Mar 1851	3y3m10d		PT&C
Lodwick, James	10	Mar	1851	Mar 1851	3y3m10d		PI
Lodwick, Jane	11	Mar	1865	08 Mar 1865	64		PTIMES
Lodwick, Maggie	28	Nov	1863	27 Nov 1863	3y7m19d		PTIMES
Long, Abner	22	Dec	1852	14 Dec 1852			PT&C
Long, Janetta M.	04	Feb	1854	1 Feb 1854	21y11m	nee Ray	DET
Long, John	25	Aug	1851	22 Aug 1851			PI
Long, John	27	Aug	1851	22 Aug 1851			PT&C
Long, Richard (Sen.)	10	Dec	1856				WPT
Long, William	19	Nov	1864				PTIMES
Longworth, Nicholas	21	Feb	1863	17 Feb 1863	81		PTIMES
Looker, James H.	20	Oct	1843	05 Oct 1843	63		TRIB
Loomis, female	03	Jan	1854				DET
Loring, male (Col.)	04	Aug	1854	01 Aug 1854			DET
Loring, unknown (Col.)	05	Aug	1854	01 Aug 1854			PDD
Loucks Jon	22	Jan	1855	15 Jan 1855			DET
Louden, female	11	Feb	1865	04 Feb 1865			PTIMES
Louderbach, male	16	Mar	1855				DET
Louderbaugh, female	11	Apr	1863	06 Apr 1863			PTIMES
Louis, Franky	04	Nov	1865	02 Nov 1865	6y11m2d		PTIMES
Love, Eliza	02	Aug	1853				PDD
Love, Robert	13	Feb	1854	11 Feb 1854			PDD
Lovejoy, Owen	02, 09	Apr	1864	25 Mar 1864			PTIMES
Lovett, F.W. (Capt.)	23	Aug	1854				PDD
Low, Emory	28	Jul	1852	22 Jul 1852			PT&C
Low, male	09	Jan	1851				PT&C
Lucas, John	30	Jul	1864	20 Jul 1864			PTIMES
Lucas, John (Lt.Col.)	05	Aug	1825	30 Jul 1825			PG&LA
Lucas, William	22	Mar	1854		60		SVREP
Luce, unknown (Capt.)	21	May	1855				DET
Luckett, Otho H.W. (Col.)	12	Jul	1854	05 Jul 1854	72		DET
Ludwig, Fredrick	28	Aug	1854	18 Aug 1854			DET
Lukens, Samuel S.	12	Mar	1851	Feb 1851			PT&C
Lundy, Sampson	01	Feb	1862	13 Dec 1861			PTIMES
Lusk, Charles W.	23	Jan	1855	23 Jan 1855	3m		DET
Lusk, Elizabeth	21	Sep	1853	17 Sep 1853	68		PDD (S)
Lusk, male	03	Sep	1851				PT&C
Lusk, unknown	13	Mar	1855	24 Jan 1855	infant		DET (S)
Lusk, William McDowell	29	Jun	1853	21 Jun 1853	9m		PT&C

Name	Notice Date			Death Date	Age	Comment	Paper
Lusk, William Mead	27	Aug	1851	21 Aug 1851	14		PT&C
Luster, male	10	Sep	1851				PT&C
Luther, unknown	13	Mar	1855	06 Mar 1855	7m		DET (S)
Lutz, Marcus	26	Jul	1859		13		DET
Lyle, William	02	Jun	1854		77		PDD
Lynch, Ellen	16	Mar	1853				PT&C
Lynch, female	23	Apr	1851				PT&C
Lynch, James	02	Aug	1854	30 Jul 1854			DET
Lynch, James	03	Aug	1854	30 Jul 1854			PDD
Lynch, John	04	Jun	1851	02 Jun 1851			PT&C
Lynn, Anna Neill	13	Feb	1864	10 Feb 1864	4m28d		PTIMES
Lyons, James	20	Sep	1855	20 Sep 1855	20		DET
Lyons, Joseph	10	Nov	1853	06 Nov 1853			DET
Lytle, Andrew, Jr.	15	Jun	1855				DET
Lytle, Elizabeth	16	Jul	1851				PT&C
	06	Aug	1851				
Mabee, Edmun(t)d (Rev.)	25, 27, 29	Jun	1855	24 Jun 1855			DET
Macdonald, William	23	Oct	1854	13 Oct 1854			PDD
Mace, John (Col.)	07	Oct	1857				DET
Mack, Thomas B.	29	Oct	1851	13 Oct 1851			PT&C
Mack, unknown	19	May	1858		child		WPT
Mack, unknown	19	May	1858		child		WPT
Mackay, male	07	Nov	1844				TRIB
Mackoy, Harriet Levernia	20	Aug	1855	20 Aug 1855	10m15d		DET
Macracon, John	21	Aug	1854				DET
Macy, Virgil (Hon.)	08	Mar	1844	28 Feb 1844			TRIB
Maddock, Ella H.	19	Mar	1864	12 Mar 1864	25y9m		PTIMES
Maddox, William	13	May	1865				PTIMES
Maffit, John Newland (Rev.)	13	Jun	1850	25 May 1850			PT&C
Magee, female	22	Sep	1854				DET
Maguire, Thomas	15	Jun	1854	13 Jun 1854			DET
Mahon, William	07	Jul	1853				DET
Mahon, Wm.	13, 20	Jul	1853				PT&C
Mahoney, Honora	03	Sep	1851	29 Aug 1851			PT&C
Mallen, Mary Ann	16	Aug	1855	16 Aug 1855	33		DET
Mallin, Isabella	19	Sep	1854	18 Sep 1854	8m3d		DET
Mallin, Joseph D.	25	Jun	1864	24 Jun 1864	43		PTIMES
Mallin, Rosa	05	Sep	1855	05 Sep 1855	6y10d		DET
Mallory, William	08	Aug	1860		80		DET
Mallory, Wm.	15	Aug	1860		80		WPT
Manley, Geo. W.	01	Aug	1855	16 Jul 1855			DET
Mann, Alvah (Col.)	12	Jul	1855	09 Jul 1855			DET
Manring, G.W.	06	Jun	1863	16 May 1863			PTIMES

Name	Notice Date			Death Date	Age	Comment	Paper
Mansfield, male	19	Aug	1854	Aug 1854	4		DET
Mantle, John	25	Aug	1852	21 Aug 1852			PT&C
Manypenny, Robert L.	19	Jul	1853	23 Jul 1853	18		PDD
Maratta, Robert Franklin	11	Dec	1855	11 Dec 1855	16m		DET
Maratta, Robert Franklin	12	Dec	1855	11 Dec 1855	16m		WPT
Marcy, unknown (Capt.)	25	Aug	1852				PT&C
Mardlow, unk. (Lieut.)	26	Oct	1854				DET
Mardlow, unk (Lieut.)	27	Oct	1854				PDD
Marion, Elizabeth	13	Jun	1854	10 Jun 1854	22		PDD (S)
Marker, female	21	Jun	1862	19 Jun 1862			PTIMES
Markham, male	09	Feb	1855				DET
Markin, Samuel	06	Jul	1858	14 Jun 1858	23		PSOT
Marklin, unknown	19	Oct	1853	11 Oct 1853	9m		PDD (S)
Marsell, female	31	Aug	1854				DET
Marsh, David	24	Nov	1852	03 Nov 1852			PT&C
Marsh, Rhoda Francis	11	Mar	1858	08 Mar 1858	3		DET
Marsh, Rhoda Francis	16	Mar	1858	08 Mar 1858	3		PSOT
Marsh, Rhoda Francis	17	Mar	1858	08 Mar 1858	3		WPT
Marshall, female	21	Jan	1852	Dec 1851	6		PT&C
Marshall, Joseph G. (Hon.)	12	Apr	1855	06 Apr 1855			DET
Marshall, Thomas (Gen.)	06	Apr	1853				PT&C
Marshall, W.C.	28	Apr	1852	14 Apr 1852			PT&C
Marshall, W.G.	06	Jun	1863	16 May 1863			PTIMES
Martin, female	30	Aug	1854	27 Aug 1854			DET
Martin, Frank	15	Aug	1853	14 Aug 1853	36		DET
Martin, Frank	16	Aug	1853	15 Aug 1853	36		PDD
Martin, Frank	17	Aug	1853		36		PT&C
Martin, Frank	23	Aug	1853	16 Aug 1853	35		PDD
Martin, Lucy Lorette	28	Nov	1853	19 Nov 1853	14d		DET
Martin, Luther (Hon.)	03	Aug	1826	08 Jul 1826	82		WT
Martin, M.	15	Mar	1854				DET
Martin, Sarah	11	Feb	1852	05 Feb 1852	19	nee Barnes	PT&C
Martin, unknown	25	Jun	1851	03 Jun 1851	child		PT&C
Martz, male	02	May	1860				WPT
Mason, female	20	Aug	1851	29 Jul 1851			PT&C
Mason, J. M.	26	Jan	1853	23 Jan 1853	38		PT&C
Mason, John Y.	22	Oct	1859	03 Oct 1859			PTIMES
Mason, Stevens Thompsen	27	Jan	1843	04 Jan 1843	31		TRIB
Massie, female	12	Aug	1854				DET
Massie, Henry	29	Mar	1862	10 Mar 1862			PTIMES
Mather, George	07	Jan	1852				PT&C
Mather, Wm. W. (Prof.)	01	Mar	1859	25 Feb 1859	60		DET
Mathews, Hugh H.	12	May	1855	03 May 1855			DET

Name	Notice Date			Death Date	Age	Comment	Paper
Mathias, Benjamin	18	Aug	1852	14 Aug 1852			PT&C
Matlock, male	31	Oct	1844	Oct 1844			TRIB
Matney, Thomas	27	Feb	1864				PTIMES
Matson, Wm.	30	May	1850	May 1850			PT&C
Matthews, male	16	Nov	1859				DET
Matthews, Phineas	18	May	1854		85		DET
Matthews, unknown	21	Feb	1859		child		DET
Matthews, unknown	21	Feb	1859		child		DET
Mauk, John	22	Jun	1860				DET
Maule, Magdalene Stemshorn	31	May	1853	27 May 1853	7		PDD
Maule, Margaret	30	Jul	1855	29 Jul 1855	61		DET
Maupin, Mary Eugenia	17	Dec	1853	9 Dec 1853	4y14d		DET
Maury, unknown	05	Feb	1855	02 Feb 1855		ex-Mayor	DET
May, male	13	Aug	1864	06 Aug 1864	7		PTIMES
Mayberry, male	20	Jul	1855				DET
Mayer, Judge	14	Jun	1855		20	slave	DET
Mayo, Edward C.	23	Jun	1852	05 Jun 1852			PT&C
McAdams, Robert	09	Jun	1858				WPT
McAndrew, Thomas	10	Feb	1854	04 Feb 1854			PDD
McArthur, Allen C.	04	May	1858	21 Apr 1858	50		PSOT
McAuley, William	18	Aug	1858				WPT
McBeth, female	15	Feb	1859				PTIMES
McBrayer, female	27	May	1854			nee Bond	PDD
McBride, Edward	21	Apr	1855				DET
McBride, male	24	May	1854				PDD
McBride, male	30	Aug	1854	27 Aug 1854			DET
McBride, unknown	30	Aug	1854	27 Aug 1854	child		DET
McCann, Mike	30	Dec	1859				DET
McCarrell, James Wallace	14	Apr	1851	12 Feb 1851	10m5d		PI
McCarrell, Mary Isabelle	14	Apr	1851	6 Apr 1851	1		PI
McCarthy, Peter	02	Oct	1860	28 Sep 1860			DET
McCarthy, Thomas	15	Sep	1854	Sep 1854			PDD
McCarty, Richard	06	Jun	1863	01 May 1863			PTIMES
McCaulsen, A. Wray	26	Sep	1863	20 Sep 1863			PTIMES
McCauly, Catharine	30	Jul	1851	Jul 1851			PT&C
	06	Aug	1851				
McCauly, Margaret	30	Jul	1851	Jul 1851			PT&C
	06	Aug	1851				
McCerren, Robt. (Capt.)	01	Dec	1854	28 Nov 1854			DET
McChesney, Richard J.	18	Oct	1862				PTIMES
McClain, James (Esq.)	30	Jun	1852				PT&C
McClellen, unk. (Capt.)	25	Aug	1852				PT&C
McClinteck, Jacob	19	Jan	1859	01 Jan 1859	31		WPT

Name	Notice Date			Death Date	Age	Comment	Paper
McClintick, James (Sheriff)	04	May	1858		61		PSOT
McClosky, male	30	Jun	1853				PDD
McCloud, Marie Lutisia	20	Aug	1851	16 Aug 1851			PT&C
McCloud, Samuel J.	11	Nov	1850	9 Nov 1850	63		PI
McCloud, Vianna	23	Jan	1854	20 Jan 1854	60		PDD
McClurg, James	23, 24	Jul	1855	18 Jul 1855	55		DET
McClusky, Patrick	12	Nov	1851	30 Oct 1851			PT&C
McCollister, Dorinda	28, 30	Jan	1854	25 Jan 1854	36		DET
McCollister, Henry	02	Jun	1860	26 May 1860			PTIMES
McCollister, Henry	28	May	1860	26 May 1860			DET
McCollister, Henry	30	May	1860	26 May 1860			WPT
McCollister, John Milton	04	Feb	1860	30 Jan 1860	24y1m14d		PTIMES
McCollister, John Milton	31	Jan	1860	30 Jan 1860	24y1m14d		DET
	08	Feb	1860				
McCollister, Maggie	06	Dec	1862	03 Dec 1862	23y9m8d	nee Shellieg	PTIMES
McColm, James A.	22	Oct	1855	08 Oct 1855			DET
McColm, William	12	Sep	1850	07 Sep 1850	53		PT&C
McColm, William	09, 23	Sep	1850	7 Sep 1850	53		PI
McComas, J. Parker	20	Aug	1853		17		DET
McComas, Parker	24	Aug	1853				PT&C
McComb, Julia Ann	16	Jan	1864	23 Dec 1863	61		PTIMES
McComb, William	09	Jul	1864	30 Jun 1864	32		PTIMES
McConnell, Thomas (Hon.)	02	Feb	1844	13 Nov 1844			TRIB
McCook, Dan (Col.)	23	Jul	1864	17 Jul 1864			PTIMES
McCook, Daniel (Maj.)	25	Jul	1863				PTIMES
McCormick, John	03	Feb	1860	23 Jan 1860	103y6m14d		DET
McCormick, John	08	Feb	1860	23 Jan 1860	103y6m14d		WPT
McCowan, H.H.	06	Jun	1863	16 May 1863			PTIMES
McCoy, William	19	Feb	1856	04 Feb 1856			DET
McCoy, Wm.	20	Feb	1856				WPT
McCreary, James (Rev.)	07	Nov	1844	Oct 1844			TRIB
McCullough, unknown	16	May	1863				PTIMES
McCullum, male	05	Sep	1850	31 Aug 1850			PT&C
McCutcheon, John	03	Oct	1860	24 Sep 1860			WPT
McDermott, Thos.	03	Oct	1860	24 Sep 1860			WPT
McDonal, James	17	Mar	1851	27 Feb 1851	74		PI
McDonald, female	23	Jun	1855	19 Jun 1855			DET
McDonald, Wm.	20	Oct	1854	13 Oct 1854			DET
McDonnold, Solomon	06	Apr	1848				DENQ
McDonough, John	21	Nov	1850				PT&C
McDougal, male	25	Jul	1863				PTIMES
McDowell, Eliza	14	Jan	1852	12 Jan 1852	infant		PT&C
McDowell, Wm.	22	Jun	1853	21Jun 1853	9m	son of Lusk	DET

Name	Notice Date			Death Date	Age	Comment	Paper
McDuffie, George (Gen.)	26	Mar	1851				PT&C
McElroy, Mary Ann	20	Jun	1853				PDD
McElroy, R.A.	22	Dec	1855	15 Dec 1855	40		DET
McElroy, R.A.	26	Dec	1855	15 Dec 1855	40		WPT
McElroy, Thomas	11	Feb	1865	04 Feb 1865			PTIMES
McElvaine, Joseph	10	Feb	1858	06 Feb 1858	65		DET
McFann, Andrew J., Jr.	16	Jul	1864				PTIMES
McFarland, A.B.	25	Aug	1854	18 Aug 1854			PDD
McFarland, Rachel	28	Oct	1865	21 Oct 1865	65		PTIMES
McFarlin, James S.	29	Mar	1862	25 Mar 1862	5m		PTIMES
McGilligan, Hannah	22	Dec	1853	22 Dec 1853	33		DET
McGinnis, John	22	Sep	1858				WPT
McGintey, Martin	26	Nov	1859	20 Nov 1859			PTIMES
McGinty, Martin	26	Nov	1859	20 Nov 1859			DET
McGowan, Jno.	30	Aug	1854	27 Aug 1854			DET
McGrady, I.V.	20	Mar	1854				PDD
McGraw, Archibald	16	Aug	1855				DET
McHale, female	22	Oct	1859		child		PTIMES
McIntire, Davis	24	Sep	1851				PT&C
McIntire, James	09	Apr	1859	16 Mar 1859			DET
McIntire, Samuel	01	Sep	1853				DET
McIntosh, male	11	Nov	1859		10		DET
McIntyre, Henry (Lieut.)	23	Jul	1864	01 Jul 1864	23		PTIMES
McKay, Alexander	05	May	1854				PDD
McKay, Daniel	05	May	1854				PDD
McKay, James J.	22	Sep	1853	15 Sep 1853			DET
McKean, Andrew	29	Sep	1843	27 Sep 1843			TRIB
McKean, Wm. (Capt.)	28	May	1864	May 1864			PTIMES
McKee, Amos	18	Jan	1862				PTIMES
McKee, Arthur	02	Jul	1864	27 Jun 1864	70		PTIMES
McKee, David	03	Jun	1854		43		DET
McKenzie, male	15	Oct	1851				PT&C
McKinney, L. B.	12	Nov	1853	02 Oct 1853	28		DET
McKinney, male	03	Mar	1843				TRIB
McKinney, William	22	May	1860	21 May 1860	40		DET
McKinney, William	23	May	1860	21 May 1860	40		WPT
McKinney, William J.	01	Apr	1854	25 Mar 1854			PDD
McLaughlin, John	19	Aug	1854	12 Aug 1854	69		DET
McLaughlin, Levi	13	Jun	1854	Oct 1853			DET
McLean, male	10	Mar	1852	27 Feb 1852	7		PT&C
McLeland, male	30	Aug	1854	27 Aug 1854			DET
McLellan, Andrew	31	Mar	1843	17 Mar 1843			TRIB
McLellan, Moses (Capt.)	07	Jun	1855	02 Jun 1855			DET
McLure, D.A.	25	Apr	1863		2y4m		PTIMES
McMahon, James	02	Oct	1860	28 Sep 1860			DET

Name	Notice Date			Death Date	Age	Comment	Paper
McManus, Edward	23	Aug	1854				DET
McManus, Edward	24	Aug	1854	20 Aug 1854			PDD
McMelan, Wm.	03	Oct	1860	24 Sep 1860			WPT
McMicken, unk. (Col.)	28	May	1860				DET
McMullen, Jane	20	Jan	1855	17 Jan 1855			DET
McMullen, male	09	Dec	1853	04 Dec 1853			PDD
McMullen, unknown	15	Mar	1854		child		DET
McMullen, unknown	15	Mar	1854		child		DET
McMullen, unknown	15	Mar	1854		child		DET
McMullen, unknown	15	Mar	1854		child		DET
McNabb, Robt. (Rev.)	05	Nov	1851	17 Oct 1851			PT&C
McNairin, Joseph	17	Dec	1855	16 Dec 1855	72		DET
McNairin, Joseph	19	Dec	1855	16 Dec 1855	72		WPT
McNairn, Eliza R.	03	Mar	1843	28 Feb 1843			TRIB
McNally, Thomas (Dr.)	25	Jun	1864				PTIMES
McNeal, A., Jr.	23	Aug	1862	08 Aug 1862			PTIMES
McNeal, Washington	21	Aug	1854				DET
McNeil, Elizabeth	05	Apr	1855		68		DET
McNulty, female	19	Jan	1854	16 Jan 1854			PDD
McNulty, female	23	Jan	1854	16 Jan 1854		nee Arnold	DET
McNulty, John	12	May	1854	28 Apr 1854			PDD
McRoberts, Samuel (Hon.)	14	Apr	1843	27 Mar 1843			TRIB
McVey, Jane Andrews	16	Feb	1844	11 Feb 1844	infant		TRIB
McVey, Nathaniel W.	04	Jun	1858	04 Jun 1858	20		DET
McVey, Nathaniel W.	09	Jun	1858	04 Jun 1858	20		WPT
McVey, William (Col.)	03	Feb	1857	22 Jan 1857	80		PSOT
McWhirt, George	20	Feb	1864	05 Feb 1864			PTIMES
Meach, Robert	19	Feb	1851				PT&C
Meacham, Eliza	01	Sep	1855	26 Aug 1855	9m7d		DET
Meaney, Margaret	23	Jul	1856	Jul 1856			WPT
Means, Esther E.	29	Aug	1860	19 Aug 1860	20		DET
Means, female	30	Jul	1851				PT&C
Means, James W.	27	May	1854				DET
Medary, Samuel	12	Nov	1864			ex-Gov.	PTIMES
Medill, William	09	Sep	1865	02 Sep 1865		ex-Gov.	PTIMES
Meeker, Jacob	07	Nov	1844	Oct 1844			TRIB
Meeker, male	01	Aug	1850	10 Jul 1850			PT&C
Meeker, male	01	Aug	1850	10 Jul 1850			PT&C
Meigs, Jno. R. (Lieut.)	15	Oct	1864				PTIMES
Melcher, George Henry	08	Mar	1844	03 Mar 1844	9y11m		TRIB
Melcher, James Johnson	25	Jul	1850	21 Jul 1850	17m		PT&C
Melcher, Joseph C.	01	Sep	1843	29 Aug 1843	25		TRIB
Menager, Mary	18	Dec	1854	17 Dec 1854			DET
Mercer, Henry	28	May	1864	May 1864			PTIMES

Name	Notice Date			Death Date	Age	Comment	Paper
Merrill, Addison	18	May	1859	05 May 1859	25		DET
Merrill, Addison	24	May	1859	05 May 1859	25		PTIMES
Merrill, Adison	25	May	1859	05 May 1859	25		WPT
Merrill, John	27	Mar	1854	24 Mar 1854			DET
Merrill, John B.	08	Feb	1859	03 Feb 1859	51		PTIMES
Merrill, John B.	09	Feb	1859	03 Feb 1859	51		WPT
Merriman, Henry	03	Jul	1854		13		DET
Merrit, F.	27	Sep	1854	24 Sep 1854	30		DET (S)
Merrit, F.	27	Sep	1854	24 Sep 1854	30		PDD (S)
Merritt, Elizabeth	11	Feb	1865	04 Feb 1865			PTIMES
Merritt, Enos	29	Mar	1859	Mar 1859			PTIMES
Merritt, Tom	10	Feb	1843				TRIB
Mershon, Henry Sr.	26	Dec	1860	18 Dec 1860	74		WPT
Mershon, Henry, Sr.	29	Dec	1860	18 Dec 1860	74		PTIMES
Messenger, Henry C. (Capt.)	23	May	1863	20 Apr 1863			PTIMES
Messenger, W.	13	Mar	1855	02 Feb 1855	69		DET (S)
Metcalf, Benjamin (Hon.)	18	Mar	1865	27 Feb 1865			PTIMES
Metcalf, Frances Adelia	07	Apr	1852	01 Apr 1852	4		PT&C
Metcalf, J.F.	12	Mar	1852	8 Mar 1852	30		PI
Metcalf, male	06	Aug	1856				WPT
Metcalf, unknown	22	Aug	1855	18 Aug 1855		ex-Gov.	DET
Meyer, Rosa	27	Jul	1856	20 Jul 1856	18		WPT
Meyle, Augustus	09	Jun	1860	Jun 1860			PTIMES
Meyle, unknown	09	Jun	1860	Jun 1860	child		PTIMES
Meynter, male	07	Feb	1854	20 Jan 1854			PDD
Michaels, female	24	Dec	1853				PDD
Middleton, male	25	Apr	1855				DET
Milam, unknown (Col.)	03	Mar	1843				TRIB
Miles, John	06	Nov	1838	31 Aug 1838			STRIB
Miles, Sally	04	Nov	1865	30 Oct 1865	67		PTIMES
Milford, William	20	Nov	1854	17 Nov 1854			DET
Miller, Abraham	22	Dec	1852	14 Dec 1852	18		PT&C
Miller, Abraham M.	17	Dec	1852	11 Dec 1852	21		PI
Miller, Carlton	10	Jan	1829	13 Dec 1828	25		WT
Miller, Charles S.	23	Jun	1859	23 Jun 1859	3y2m		DET
Miller, child	17	Dec	1851				PT&C
Miller, female	04	Aug	1853				DET
Miller, female	04	Aug	1853				DET
Miller, female	10	Aug	1853				PT&C
Miller, female	10	Aug	1853				PT&C
Miller, Francis	03	Oct	1851	30 Sep 1851			PI
Miller, George W.	05	Nov	1864	04 Nov 1864	19y3m8d		PTIMES
Miller, Harvey	06	Aug	1864	03 Aug 1864	5		PTIMES
Miller, Horace	12	Aug	1853	10 Aug 1853			DET

Deaths

Name	Notice Date			Death Date	Age	Comment	Paper
Miller, Horace (Capt.)	15	Aug	1853				PDD
Miller, Horace (Capt.)	17	Aug	1853	10 Aug 1853			PT&C
Miller, Jesse	21	Jan	1852				PT&C
Miller, John	09	Sep	1854	05 Sep 1854			PDD
Miller, John	13	Jan	1857	12 Jan 1857	76		PSOT
Miller, John G.	24	Sep	1852	Sep 1852			PI
Miller, John W.	21	Jan	1857	12 Jan 1857	75		WPT
Miller, Lydia	14	Jan	1852	01 Jan 1852			PT&C
Miller, Michael	01	Aug	1853	26 Jul 1853			PDD
Miller, Parmelia Ann	18	Apr	1859	17 Apr 1859	34		DET
Miller, Parmelia Ann	20	Apr	1859	17 Apr 1859	34		WPT
Miller, Peter	11	Aug	1853				DET
Miller, Peter	18	Aug	1853	15 Aug 1853			PDD
Miller, William A.	11	Jul	1863	03 Jul 1863			PTIMES
Miller, Wm.	05	Sep	1863	30 Aug 1863			PTIMES
Millham, John S.	18	Mar	1854				PDD
Mills, Edward H.	22	Sep	1855	04 Sep 1855	23		DET
Mills, male	02	Aug	1853				PDD
Mills, male	03	Aug	1853		40		PT&C
Millson, Eli	09	Jun	1860	Jun 1860			PTIMES
Milton, unknown	05	Dec	1853				DET
Milton, unknown	03, 06	Dec	1853				PDD
Minford, Mary	18	Aug	1851	10 Aug 1851	61		PI
Mink, John	02	Jun	1852	28 May 1852			PT&C
Misner, Eliza Jane	12	Nov	1855	29 Oct 1855	23y2m10d		DET
Misner, Eliza Jane	14	Nov	1855	29 Oct 1855	23y2m10d		WPT
Mitchel, John	19	Aug	1850				PI
Mitchell, Amasia	19	Mar	1851	12 Feb 1851	90		PT&C
Mitchell, Desire	26	Mar	1851	04 Feb 1851	87		PT&C
Mitchell, Edmund	17	Oct	1850				PT&C
Mitchell, Henry	13	Sep	1859				DET
Mitchell, John	15	Aug	1850	12 Aug 1850			PT&C
Mitchell, John W.	28	May	1864	May 1864			PTIMES
Mitchell, Misa	11	May	1853				PDD
Mitchell, Susan	26	Mar	1851	02 Feb 1851	82		PT&C
Mitchell, unknown	07	Jul	1854		17		PDD
Mitchell, unknown (Gen.)	08	Nov	1862	30 Oct 1862			PTIMES
Molen, unknown (Capt.)	04	Apr	1860	30 Mar 1860	58		WPT
Mollier, female	21	Jun	1855	18 Jun 1855			DET
Molma, Don Felipe	03	Feb	1855	01 Feb 1855			DET
Monahan, William	17	Apr	1860	11 Apr 1860			DET
Monck, unknown (Capt.	26	Oct	1854				DET
Monck, unknown (Capt.	27	Oct	1854				PDD
Monk, male	15	Apr	1865	12 Apr 1865	12		PTIMES
Monroe, Daniel B.	26	Mar	1864	16 Mar 1864			PTIMES

Name	Notice Date			Death Date	Age	Comment	Paper
Monroe, G.B.	06	Apr	1855	05 Apr 1855			DET
Montague, unk. (Lieut.)	26	Oct	1854				DET
Montague, unk. (Lieut.)	27	Oct	1854				PDD
Montgomery, C.P. (Cath. Priest)	18	Apr	1860	16 Apr 1860			WPT
Montgomery, C.P. (Cath. Priest)	19	Apr	1860	16 Apr 1860			DET
Montgomery, Joseph S.	12	Aug	1865	08 Aug 1865	30y5m		PTIMES
Montgomery, male	09	Jun	1852				PT&C
Montgomery, Rebecca	08	Apr	1857	31 Mar 1857	81		WPT
Moodie, Jackson	02	Nov	1860	02 Nov 1860	19		DET
Moodie, Nicholas	02	Nov	1860	02 Nov 1860	35		DET
Moodie, Nicholas	12	Dec	1860	02 Nov 1860			WPT
Moody, Nancy	25	Aug	1852	08 Jul 1852	30		PT&C
Moor, David	18	Dec	1854		80		DET
Moore, Anna Laura	18	Mar	1865	12 Mar 1865	2		PTIMES
Moore, Emma	21	Mar	1855				DET
Moore, H.	19	May	1858				WPT
Moore, H.A.	26	Apr	1844	03 Apr 1844			TRIB
Moore, Hannah	28	Nov	1851	21 Nov 1851	26		PI
Moore, James H. (Dr.)	03	Mar	1858	26 Feb 1858			WPT
Moore, John	18	Jun	1853	14 Jun 1853			PDD
Moore, Joseph W.	07	Apr	1854	30 Mar 1854			PDD
Moore, Levi	06	May	1865	27 Apr 1865	72		PTIMES
Moore, Levina	23	Sep	1831	25 Aug 1831			PC&WT
Moore, Milton	20	Oct	1855	30 Sep 1855	37		DET
Moore, Samuel	03	May	1854		50		PDD
Moore, Thomas	17	Mar	1852	26 Feb 1852	72		PT&C
Moore, William	19	Dec	1854		70		DET
Moran, J.	17	Aug	1854	03 Aug 1854	62		DET (S)
Moran, James	07	Aug	1854	02 Aug 1854	63		DET
Moran, Jas.	04	Aug	1854	02 Aug 1854	63		PDD
Morehead, Charles D.	03	Oct	1853	22 Aug 1853			DET
Morehead, Charles Edwin	03	Oct	1853	19 Aug 1853			DET
Morehead, Eliza	03	Oct	1853	26 Aug 1853			DET
Morehead, Emma A.	03	Oct	1853	22 Aug 1853			DET
Morehead, John H.	22	Jun	1854				PDD
Morehead, unknown	16	Jun	1855			Ex-Gov.	DET
Moreland, David	20	Jul	1854				PDD
Morford, Kennard	12	Aug	1857	07 Aug 1857	57		WPT
Morford, Thomas J.	07	Nov	1857	20 Oct 1857	22m9d		DET
Morgan, female	26	Mar	1851				PT&C
Morgan, John	10	Sep	1864				PTIMES
Morgan, Mahale	06	Aug	1824	02 Aug 1824	12		PG&LA
Morgan, male	06	Aug	1856	02 Aug 1856			WPT

Deaths

Name	Notice Date			Death Date	Age	Comment	Paper
Morgan, male	19	Feb	1851	17 Feb 1851			PT&C
Morris, David	16	Apr	1851		18		PT&C
Morris, Enoch	21	May	1864	17 May 1864	30		PTIMES
Morris, female	09	Jun	1860	Jun 1860			PTIMES
Morris, George P.	09	Jul	1864		64		PTIMES
Morris, Isaac	19	Feb	1855				DET
Morris, John	27	Mar	1854	24 Mar 1854			DET
Morris, male	09	May	1850	14 Apr 1850			PT&C
Morris, Thomas	28	May	1864	04 May 1864			PTIMES
Morris, Thomas (Hon.)	26	Dec	1844	07 Dec 1844			TRIB
Morrisey, unknown	17	Oct	1853				DET
Morrison, male	23	Apr	1851	17 Apr 1851	child		PT&C
Morrison, Wm. P.	17	Mar	1854	06 Mar 1854			DET
Morrow, Mary	05	Dec	1853	14 Nov 1853	16		DET
Morrow, Mary	06	Dec	1853	04 Dec 1853	16		PDD
Morrow, Nancy	20	May	1850	11 May 1850			PI
Morton, Daniel O.	09	Dec	1859	05 Dec 1859			DET
Morton, Daniel O.	10	Dec	1859	05 Dec 1859			PTIMES
Morton, Ellennora	12	Dec	1863	01 Nov 1863	4y6m10d		PTIMES
Morton, female	25	Jun	1851	25 Jun 1851	12		PT&C
Morton, Josiah	27	Feb	1838	25 Feb 1838			STRIB
Morton, Lettie	09	Jul	1864	30 Jun 1864	19		PTIMES
Moss, female	26	Feb	1851	22 Feb 1851			PT&C
Moss, J.	25	Aug	1854				PDD
Moss, John	10	May	1853	06 May 1853			PDD
Moss, John	22	Oct	1857	13 Sep 1857	34		DET
Moss, Lemuel	06	Apr	1853	01 Apr 1853			PT&C
Moss, Martha	03	Mar	1851	22 Feb 1851			PI
Moss, unknown	14	Oct	1853	Aug 1853			DET
Mouhat, Isaac	15	Nov	1853	06 Nov 1853	21		PDD (S)
Mountjoy, female	14	Dec	1861				PTIMES
Mower, Columbus	17	Dec	1851	10 Dec 1851			PT&C
Moxie, Sophia A.	12	Feb	1858	09 Feb 1858	11d		DET
Moxley, Sophia A.	16	Feb	1858	09 Feb 1858	11d		PSOT
Moyer, Peter	08	Jun	1853	29 May 1853			PT&C
Muhlenberg, Henry A.	22	Aug	1844	18 Aug 1844			TRIB
Muhlenburg, Henry (Hon.)	11	Jan	1854	09 Jan 1854			DET
Muhlheisser, Barbara	15	Aug	1850	14 Aug 1850	2		PT&C
Muhlheisser, Barbara	19	Aug	1850	14 Aug 1850	2		PI
Mulky, Nancy	31	Dec	1851	25 Nov 1851			PT&C
Mullagan, Samuel	30	Oct	1854				DET
Mullen, male	03	Dec	1851				PT&C
Mulligan, Edward	05	Mar	1864	04 Mar 1864	66		PTIMES
Mulliken, Nathan	19	Nov	1851	01 Nov 1851			PT&C

Name	Notice Date			Death Date	Age	Comment	Paper
Mullin, Emma B.	19	Sep	1863		14		PTIMES
Mundell, female	06	Aug	1855				DET
Munn, D.C. (Dr.)	04	Mar	1865	27 Feb 1865	47		PTIMES
Munn, Wesley	16	May	1854	15 May 1854			DET
Munn, Wesley	17	May	1854	15 May 1854			PDD
Munroe, female	01	Jun	1853				PT&C
Munroe, James	01	Jun	1853				PT&C
Munroe, unknown	01	Jun	1853		child		PT&C
Munroe, unknown	01	Jun	1853		child		PT&C
Murfin, Helen Ruby	08	Jul	1857	29 Jun 1857	2y7m		DET
Murfin, Jacob F.	01	Feb	1862	29 Nov 1861			PTIMES
Murphey, male	28	Apr	1854	Apr 1854			PDD
Murphy, A.B.	02	Mar	1859	27 Feb 1859			DET
Murphy, Andrew	06	Apr	1853	01 Apr 1853			PT&C
Murphy, Jeremiah	21	Jan	1852	Jan 1852			PT&C
Murphy, male	19	Jul	1827	12 Jul 1827	2		WT
Murphy, male	19	Jul	1827	12 Jul 1827	1		WT
Murphy, Michael	23	Mar	1855	17 Mar 1855			DET
Murphy, Nellie	27	Apr	1853				PT&C
	04	May	1853				
Murphy, Nelly	28	Apr	1853	24 Apr 1853			PDD
Murphy, Patrick	10	Aug	1855				DET
Murphy, unknown (Gen.)	26	Sep	1844				TRIB
Murray, female	10	Oct	1844	23 Sep 1844			TRIB
Murray, Harriett Ardelia	20	Jul	1853	12 Jul 1853	8m		PT&C
Murray, Harriett Ardella	13	Jul	1853	12 Jul 1853	8m		DET
Murray, John	13	Feb	1856	09 Feb 1856			WPT
Murray, John E.	15	Dec	1853				DET
Murrell, John A.	09	Jan	1845	01 Dec 1844			TRIB
Murrey, (slave of, Tom)	11	May	1853	07 May 1853		Slave	PT&C
Musser, Patience	20	Jun	1850	Jun 1850	7		PT&C
Mussey, Frank	18	Aug	1854	16 Aug 1854	7y10d		DET
Mussey, Mary Lucretia	22	Apr	1857	17 Apr 1857	2y6m		WPT
Myers, Bartley J.	08	Mar	1854	06 Mar 1854	35		PDD
Myers, Bartley J.	21	Mar	1854	08 Mar 1854	33		PDD (S)
Myers, Bartly J.	08	Mar	1854	06 Mar 1854	35		SVREP
Myers, John	02	Mar	1861	07 Jan 1861	38y6m		PTIMES
Myers, male	26	May	1860	21 May 1860			PTIMES
Myers, Sarah E.	26	Nov	1864	24 Nov 1864	32y8m26d	nee Montgomery	PTIMES
Myers, unknown	30	Jul	1851	Jul 1851	child		PT&C
Myres, female	16	Nov	1854	22 Feb 1852	infant		DET
M'Cartney, female	29	Aug	1863		47		PTIMES
M'Collister, Martha	30	Aug	1853	26 Aug 1853	28		PDD
M'Cormick, Ellis C.	11	May	1853				PT&C

Deaths

Name	Notice Date			Death Date	Age	Comment	Paper
M'Coy, B.F. (Dr.)	20	Oct	1852	09 Jul 1852			PT&C
M'Donald, Nathaniel W.	08	Sep	1853	5 Sep 1853	25		DET
M'Donnel, Patrick	09	May	1855	23 Apr 1855			DET (S)
M'Dugal, Nancy	23	Sep	1818	31 Aug 1818	65		PGAZ
M'Erlain, Mary	23	Jul	1856	Jul 1856			WPT
M'Farland, A.B.	24	Aug	1854				DET
M'Farlin, unknown	06	Sep	1853	30 Aug 1853	13m		PDD (S)
M'Farlin, unknown	14	Sep	1853	06 Sep 1853	13m		PDD (S)
M'Farlin, unknown	19	Oct	1853	09 Oct 1853	5		PDD (S)
M'Farlin, unknown	19	Oct	1853	10 Oct 1853	5		PDD (S)
M'Farlin, unknown	30	Aug	1853	24 Aug 1853	2y6m		PDD (S)
M'Gire, Kate	23	Jul	1856	Jul 1856			WPT
M'Guigan, Sarah	23	Jul	1856	Jul 1856			WPT
M'Guire, Jno.	23	Jul	1856	Jul 1856			WPT
M'Inteer, Elizah	23	Aug	1827		38		WT
M'Intyre, Jas.	23	Jul	1856	Jul 1856			WPT
M'Lewis, Jacob	19	Jun	1838	14 Jun 1838	50		STRIB
M'Querk, Catherine	23	Jul	1856	Jul 1856			WPT
M'Vean, Chas.	19	Mar	1851	12 Mar 1851			PT&C
Nagler, Leonard	04	Oct	1862	14 Sep 1862			PTIMES
Nail, H.	06	Jun	1863	16 May 1863			PTIMES
Nathaway, unknown	30	Jan	1854	24 Dec 1853	child		DET
Nathaway, unknown	30	Jan	1854	24 Dec 1853	child		DET
Nathaway, unknown	30	Jan	1854	24 Dec 1853	child		DET
Nathaway, unknown	30	Jan	1854	24 Dec 1853	child		DET
Natthews, unknown	21	Feb	1859		child		DET
Neill, William	28	Nov	1857	28 Nov 1857	infant		DET
Nelson, Emily	31	Mar	1854	26 Mar 1854	17		PDD
Nelson, John	28	Sep	1855	22 Sep 1855	24		OP
Nelson, Joseph Washington	07	Jan	1859	22 Dec 1858	35		DET
Nelson, Raleigh	12	Sep	1853				DET
Nelson, Simon	15	Apr	1865	07 Apr 1865			PTIMES
Nesbit, male	09	Apr	1851				PT&C
Nesbit, male	09	Apr	1851				PT&C
Neuanburger, Mary	09	May	1855		2		DET (S)
Neudoerfer, Margaret	23	Jul	1851	23 Jul 1851	24		PT&C
Newland, (Rev.)	14	Jan	1852		50		PT&C
Newman, Catherine	27	Jul	1856	08 Jul 1856	47		WPT
Newman, Henry Carpenter	23	Jul	1852	17 Jul 1852	10m3d		PI
Newman, male	17	Mar	1843				TRIB
Newson, Robert	09	Jul	1855				DET
Newton, Cynthia	22	Sep	1857	02 Sep 1857	32		PSOT
Newton, Isaac	29	Jul	1850	24 Jul 1850	15m		PI

Name	Notice Date			Death Date	Age	Comment	Paper
Newton, Nancy G.	09	Apr	1856	29 Mar 1856	34	nee Bell	WPT
Nibit, Soloman	28	Sep	1820		143(?)		STEL
Nicholr, Samuel	22	Sep	1854	18 Sep 1854			PDD
Nichols, female	12	Jul	1860	05 Jul 1860			DET
Nichols, H.M.	12	Jul	1860	05 Jul 1860			DET
Nichols, Thomas	15	Mar	1862	11 Mar 1862	71		PTIMES
Nichols, unknown	12	Jul	1860	05 Jul 1860	child		DET
Nickells, Clara	03	Mar	1860	24 Feb 1860	3y8m		PTIMES
Nickells, Clara	28	Feb	1860	24 Feb 1860	3y8m		DET
Nickells, Clara	29	Feb	1860	24 Feb 1860	3y8m		WPT
Nickols, Clarence Ivey	03	Mar	1860	02 Mar 1860	4y2m23d		DET
Nickols, Clarence Ivey	07	Mar	1860	02 Mar 1860	4y2m23d		WPT
Nigh, Michael	06	Aug	1855	26 Jul 1855	70		DET
Nigh, Reese	19	Sep	1850	08 Sep 1850	1y9m		PT&C
Noble, unknown	23	Feb	1844	08 Feb 1844		ex-Gov.	TRIB
Noel, Catherine Ann	05	Mar	1864	25 Feb 1864	49		PTIMES
Noel, Harriet	19	Feb	1851	13 Feb 1851		nee Oldfield	PT&C
Noel, Jacob	14	Jun	1828	07 Jun 1828	50		WT
Noel, John	01	Apr	1837		49		STRIB
Noel, John	15	Apr	1854	15 Apr 1854	8		DET
Noel, John W. (Hon.)	21	Mar	1863	14 Mar 1863			PTIMES
Noel, male	17	Apr	1854	15 Apr 1854	8		PDD
Noel, Mary M.	30	Jul	1858	30 Jul 1858			DET
Noel, Milton	14	Nov	1855	14 Nov 1855			WPT
Noel, Robert	17	Aug	1826		9		WT
Noland, female	16	Dec	1854	11 Dec 1854			DET
Nolin, John	22	Jul	1854	17 Jul 1854			PDD
Nolner, Jacob	07	Nov	1844	Oct 1844			TRIB
Norris, Clarissa Ann	21	Nov	1844	16 Nov 1844	19		TRIB
Norris, male	07	Nov	1844	Oct 1844			TRIB
Norris, Thomas	11	Mar	1854				PDD
Norris, Thomas	27	Feb	1854		31		DET
Norris, Thomas F.	31	Dec	1853				PDD
North, male	25	Jun	1855				DET
Norton, Daniel S.	12	Nov	1859		72		PTIMES
Norton, Ellen	30	Sep	1854				DET
Norton, male	01	Jan	1853		child		PDD
Nuedoerfer, Margaret	21	Jul	1851	17 Jul 1851			PI
Nurse, Isaiah	13	Apr	1854	07 Apr 1854	60		PDD
Nurse, Joshua	13	Jul	1853	11 Jul 1853	53		DET
Nurse, Joshua	20	Jul	1853	11 Jul 1853	53		PT&C
Nurse, Morrison	31	May	1854	27 May 1854	30		PDD
Nye, Daniel (Pvt.)	30	Jul	1864	04 Jul 1864			PTIMES
Nye, Horace	15	Mar	1859	Mar 1859			PTIMES
Nye, J.A.	21	Jan	1857	09 Jan 1857	67		WPT

Name	Notice Date			Death Date	Age	Comment	Paper
Nye, James C.	04	Jun	1864				PTIMES
Nye, Theodore	17	Mar	1852	25 Feb 1852			PT&C
Nye, unknown (Judge)	05	Aug	1865				PTIMES
Odbert, James	28	Feb	1850				PT&C
Odell, Noah	27	Sep	1853	25 Sep 1853	60		DET
Offnere, J. (Dr.)	13	Dec	1859	12 Dec 1859	85		DET
Offnere, J. (Dr.)	14	Dec	1859	12 Dec 1859	85		WPT
Offnere, J. (Dr.)	17	Dec	1859	12 Dec 1859	85		PTIMES
Offnere, Jacob (Dr.)	14	Apr	1843	09 Apr 1843	65		TRIB
Ogden, Samuel G.	21	Apr	1860	Apr 1860	81		PTIMES
Ogden, unknown (Capt.)	13	Aug	1855				DET
Ohe, John	03	Mar	1843	25 Feb 1843			TRIB
Old Milly	20	Jan	1854	16 Jan 1854	114		DET
Olds, Catharine	03	Aug	1853	05 Jul 1853			PT&C
Olds, Eliza	03	Aug	1859	27 Jul 1859			WPT
Olds, Eliza	28	Jul	1859	27 Jul 1859		nee Crichton	DET
Olds, Mary	26	Dec	1859	22 Dec 1859			DET
Olds, unknown	03	Aug	1853	05 Jul 1853	3m		PT&C
Oliver, male	09	Sep	1865	06 Sep 1865			PTIMES
Oman, Jacob S.	09	May	1855	01 May 1855	23m		DET (S)
Onacker, male	27	Aug	1851	19 Aug 1851	16		PT&C
Onacker, male	27	Aug	1851	19 Aug 1851	14		PT&C
Onacker, male	27	Aug	1851	19 Aug 1851	12		PT&C
Onacker, male	27	Aug	1851	19 Aug 1851	11		PT&C
Onacker, male	27	Aug	1851	19 Aug 1851	2		PT&C
Onkst, Joseph	31	Jan	1863	30 Jan 1863	18		PTIMES
Opdyke, William	09	Jul	1851	01 Jul 1851	38		PT&C
Oppy, Christopher	22	Oct	1864	Sep 1864			PTIMES
Orm, John	04	Aug	1851				PI
Orm, John	30	Jul	1851	28 Jul 1851			PT&C
Ormsby, Kaye Birdee	04	Nov	1859	28 Oct 1859			DET
Orr, Presly	15	Jun	1854				PDD
Osborn, Ebenezer Francis	23	May	1857				DET
Osborn, Low	14	Aug	1858	11 Aug 1858	25		DET
Osborn, Low	18	Aug	1858	11 Aug 1858	25		WPT
Osbourn, William C.	01	Feb	1862	15 Nov 1861			PTIMES
Ovaton, male	03	Aug	1854				DET
Ovaton, male	03	Aug	1854				DET
Overturf, Rhoda	22	Apr	1837	19 Apr 1837		nee Kendall	STRIB
Owen, Eliziannah	06	Aug	1851				PT&C
Owen, Mary	06	Aug	1851				PT&C
Owen, Samuel	07	Oct	1865				PTIMES
Owen, Samuel	11	Apr	1854		80		PDD

Name	Notice Date			Death Date	Age	Comment	Paper
Owens, John	11	Feb	1860				PTIMES
Owens, Richard	21	Dec	1858	17 Dec 1858			PTIMES
Owster, James	09	Jul	1860	07 Jul 1860			DET
O'Conner, George	28	May	1864	May 1864			PTIMES
O'Conner, Michael	15	Jun	1855	10 Jun 1855			DET
O'Donnell, John B.	05	May	1854	03 May 1854			PDD
O'Donohoe, Patrick	03	Feb	1854	29 Jan 1854			PDD
O'Keef, male	24	Feb	1854				PDD
O'Neal, Nancy	19	Oct	1853	07 Oct 1853	50		PDD (S)
O'Neil, Patrick	22	Mar	1854	17 Mar 1854			PDD
O'Neil, Samuel	10	Jul	1860				DET
Paden, Angeline C.	26	Nov	1859	25 Nov 1859	6y5m25d		DET
Page, T.N. (Major)	07	Apr	1860	25 Mar 1860			DET
Paige, Barney R.	24	Jun	1853	17 Jun 1853			PDD
Paine, unknown	03	Aug	1853	06 Jul 1853			DET
Paine, unknown	10	Aug	1853	06 Jul 1853		Ex-Gov./VT	PT&C
Paine, Wm. V. (Dr.)	16	Aug	1855				DET
Palmer, male	03	Apr	1855				DET
Palmer, male	29	Dec	1853				DET
Parish, female	13	Aug	1864		child		PTIMES
Parish, Orris	22	Apr	1837	17 Apr 1837	45		STRIB
Parke, John B.	12	May	1843				TRIB
Parker, Elizabeth D.	04	Aug	1851	28 Jul 1851	28		PI
Parker, Elizabeth D.	30	Jul	1851	28 Jul 1851	28	nee Bockwalter	PT&C
Parker, male	06	Feb	1854				PDD
Parker, Richard	20	Sep	1854				DET
Parker, Samuel C. (Rev.)	27	Oct	1858	10 Oct 1858			WPT
Parker, Tamar	04	May	1858	10 Apr 1858	68		PSOT
Parker, Theodore (Rev.)	06	Jun	1860	10 May 1860			WPT
Parker, unknown	06	Feb	1854		child		DET
Parker, unknown	06	Feb	1854		child		DET
Parker, unknown	06	Feb	1854		child		DET
Parker, unknown	06	Feb	1854		child		DET
Parker, unknown	20	Feb	1854		child		PDD
Parker, unknown	20	Feb	1854		child		PDD
Parker, unknown	20	Feb	1854		child		PDD
Parker, Walker	10	May	1853	06 May 1853			PDD
Parker, Willie	18	Aug	1851	13 Aug 1851			PI
Parks, Beverly	11	May	1853				PDD
Parnell, John W.	21	Jun	1855	19 Jun 1855	8m		DET
Parratt, Alfred A.	25	Jan	1854	17 Jan 1854	23		DET
Parsons, male	03	Feb	1860	22 Jan 1860			DET
Parsons, unknown (Dr.)	30	Mar	1855				DET
Partloe, George	13	Apr	1858	01 Apr 1858	86y21d		PSOT

Deaths

Name	Notice Date			Death Date	Age	Comment	Paper
Partridge, Alden (Capt.)	23	Jan	1854	19 Jan 1854			PDD
Patch, female	30	Aug	1854		80		DET
Patch, female	31	Aug	1854		80		PDD
Paterson, female	25	Jun	1851	03 Jun 1851			PT&C
Paterson, unknown	25	Jun	1851	03 Jun 1851	child		PT&C
Paton, James Downey	18	Aug	1851	16 Aug 1851	2y6m		PI
Patten, female	12	May	1860		5		PTIMES
Patterson, Augusta	05	Jun	1854	26 May 1854			DET
Patterson, Caroline	14	Oct	1865	11 Oct 1865	30y3m6d		PTIMES
Patterson, Horace	24	Apr	1854		21		DET
Patterson, Linton A.	10	Feb	1858	06 Feb 1858	9		WPt
Patterson, R. (Col.)	17	Nov	1852	02 Nov 1852			PT&C
Patton, Catharine	01	Jun	1820	16 May 1820	54		STEL
Patton, John	27	Jul	1853	24 Jul 1853			PT&C
Paxton, Michael	07	Jun	1859	26 May 1859	65		PTIMES
Payne, John (Gen.)	28	Jan	1854				PDD
Payne, Joshua (Rev.)	23	Sep	1854				PDD
Payne, male (ex-Gov.)	04	Aug	1853				PDD
Payne, Woodford	11	Feb	1852				PT&C
Peabody, Charles H.	14	Aug	1854	Jul 1854			PDD
Pearce, Elgar B.	25	Jun	1864	08 Jun 1864	32		PTIMES
Pearce, unknown	12	Dec	1850	07 Dec 1850	7w		PT&C
Pearson, male	28	May	1851	12 May 1851	5		PT&C
Peatling, Edward C.	18	Oct	1862				PTIMES
Peck, George	15	Jul	1850	13 Jul 1850			PI
Peck, Margaret	24	Feb	1851	17 Feb 1851			PI
Peck, Mary Cotlin	04	Nov	1831	02 Nov 1831	infant		PC&WT
Peck, Mary Emma	16	Feb	1847		14m4d		CLIPPER
Peck, Myron H.	06	May	1858	30 Apr 1858	40		DET
Pegram, J.W. (Gen.)	31	Oct	1844	Oct 1844			TRIB
Pelhank, Frederick	27	May	1865	22 May 1865	64y9m5d		PTIMES
Penisten, Isaac	05	Nov	1858	18 Oct 1858	59		SVREP
Pepper, Phillip	09	Jun	1860	Jun 1860			PTIMES
Perkins, Angelique	02	Feb	1853				PT&C
Perkins, Apollis	21	Nov	1850				PT&C
Perkins, unknown	24	Dec	1853	23 Dec 1853	child		DET
Perry, Caleb (Capt.)	10	Feb	1855				DET
Perry, male	26	Dec	1850	14 Dec 1850			PT&C
Peters, Clinton J.	28	May	1864	May 1864			PTIMES
Petit, male	22	Aug	1829	14 Aug 1829			WT
Pettit, Thos. McKean	04	Jun	1853	31 May 1853			PDD
Phelps, Anson G.	03	Dec	1853	30 Nov 1853	74		PDD
Phelps, female	17	Apr	1854				DET
Philips, Eliza	28	May	1851	08 May 1851			PT&C
Philips, James	02	Feb	1853				PT&C

Name	Notice Date			Death Date	Age	Comment	Paper
Phillippi, Catharine	13	Jun	1854	04 Jun 1854	47		PDD (S)
Phillips, James	27	Jan	1854	24 Jan 1854			PDD
Phillips, Jonathan (Maj.)	26	Jul	1854	23 Jul 1854			DET
Phillips, William	05	Jan	1860				DET
Phister, female	08	Jul	1857	07 Jul 1857	9		WPT
Pickerill, Samuel	06	Jun	1850	May 1850	100		PT&C
Pickering, Timothy	21	Feb	1829	29 Jan 1829	84		WT
Pierce, James	08	Jun	1855	05 Jun 1855			DET
Pierce, male	19	Jan	1853	06 Jan 1853			PT&C
Pierpoint, A.G. (Dr.	11	May	1853				PDD
Pierson, Able L.	11	May	1853				PDD
Pierson, male	17	Aug	1853				DET
Pifer, unknown	31	Mar	1852		11		PT&C
Pilchard, female	02	Jul	1855		18		DET
Pilchard, male	02	Jul	1855		25		DET
Pilchard, male	02	Jul	1855		13		DET
Pinkerton, William	01	Feb	1862	27 Dec 1861			PTIMES
Pinkman, Patrick	23	Aug	1854				DET
Pinkman, Patrick	24	Aug	1854	20 Aug 1854			PDD
Pitts, Joseph	08	Oct	1853	06 Oct 1853			DET
Pixley, Seymour	07	Nov	1860	Oct 1860			WPT
Pixley, Seymour	09	Nov	1860				DET
Plaukhaup, Peter	15	Nov	1853		63		DET
Plaukhaup, Peter	17	Nov	1853	09 Nov 1853	63		PDD
Poe, Adam (Deacon)	19	Jan	1859	12 Jan 1859			WPT
Poe, Archibald Alexander	03	Oct	1857	01 Oct 1857	6y5m		DET
Poe, Lucy Alice Anna	16	Aug	1860	16 Aug 1860	22m9d		DET
Poe, Lucy Alice Anna	22	Aug	1860	16 Aug 1860	22m9d		WPT
Poken, male	20	Aug	1855	08 Aug 1855			DET
Pollard, James	08	Jan	1846				TRIB
Pollock, F.A.	06	Aug	1851	17 Jul 1851			PT&C
Polluck, Lewis	15	Mar	1854				DET
Pomeroy, unk. (Lieut.)	10	Sep	1864				PTIMES
Pool, Sarah	11	Mar	1857	01 Mar 1857	67		WPT
Pool, Susannah E.	15	Mar	1854				DET
Pool, Timothy	29	Aug	1853	24 Aug 1853			PDD
Poorman, Lydia C.	04	Feb	1860	23 Jan 1860	18		PTIMES
Porter, Alex.	09	Feb	1844	12 Jan 1844			TRIB
Porter, John	10	Oct	1863				PTIMES
Porter, Peter B. (Gen.)	05	Apr	1844	20 Mar 1844	71		TRIB
Porter, W.G.	06	Jun	1863	16 May 1863			PTIMES
Porter, William	02	Dec	1853				DET
Porter, Wm.	03	Dec	1853				PDD
Postlethwaite, unknown	01	Jun	1853	29 May 1853	23y3m7d		PT&C
Postlethwaite, unknown	08	Jun	1853	29 May 1853	23y3m7d		PT&C (S)

Name	Notice Date			Death Date	Age	Comment	Paper
Postlethwaite, William	31	May	1853	29 May 1853	23y3m7d		PDD
Postlethwaite, Wm.	07	Jun	1853	30 May 1853	23		DET
Pottenger, Mary	07	Apr	1854	27 Mar 1854	88	nee Buchanan	PDD
Potterfield, Rob't. (Gen.)	31	Mar	1843	13 Feb 1843	91		TRIB
Powell, Elizabeth Ann	24	Nov	1852	18 Nov 1852	25		PT&C
Powell, Elizabeth Ann	26	Nov	1852	18 Nov 1852	25		PI
Powell, Lucy	31	Jan	1854	4 Jan 1854	23		DET
Powell, Matilda	17	Aug	1826	29 Jul 1826	25		WT
Powell, Michael	13	May	1865				PTIMES
Powers, L.G.	28	Jan	1860	23 Jan 1860	51		PTIMES
Powlhill, unknown (Lieut.)	26	Oct	1854				DET
Powlhill, unknown (Lieut.)	27	Oct	1854				PDD
Poynter, James Lucien	14	Jan	1852	02 Jan 1852	18m		PT&C
Pratent, Adaline	27	Jun	1854	24 Jun 1854	14		PDD (S)
Prather, Alice	06	Aug	1851				PT&C
Prather, Ann Oleivia	23	Jul	1851	14 Jul 1851	14		PT&C
	06	Aug	1851				
Prather, female	30	Dec	1857				WPT
Prather, Mary O.	06	Aug	1851				PT&C
Prather, Silas D. (Corp.)	12	Dec	1863	Nov 1863			PTIMES
Prather, Thomas	23	Jul	1851	14 Jul 1851	4		PT&C
	06	Aug	1851				
Prather, unknown	30	Jul	1851	Jul 11851	child		PT&C
Prather, Wilson	23	Jul	1851	14 Jul 1851			PT&C
	06	Aug	1851				
Prentice, unknown	24	Mar	1859		child		DET
Prentice, unknown	24	Mar	1859		child		DET
Prentice, unknown	24	Mar	1859		child		DET
Prentice, unknown	30	Mar	1859	Mar 1859	child		WPT
Prentice, unknown	30	Mar	1859	Mar 1859	child		WPT
Prentice, unknown	30	Mar	1859	Mar 1859	child		WPT
Prescott, female	13	Aug	1852	9 Aug 1852			PI
Prescott, O.G. (Dr.)	16	Dec	1857	14 Dec 1857			WPT
Prescott, Wm. H.	02	Feb	1859	29 Jan 1859			WPT
Pretchard, unknown	06	Jun	1853		2		PDD
Prettyman, William Jameson	24	Mar	1857	18 Mar 1857	9m		PSOT
Price, David	22	May	1860	21 May 1860	35		DET
Price, David	26	May	1860	21 May 1860	35		PTIMES
Price, Elizabeth	22	May	1858	22 May 1858	72		DET
Price, Elizabeth	26	May	1858	22 May 1858	72		WPT
Price, John (Judge)	18	Mar	1865				PTIMES
Price, Sam'l	27	May	1854				DET
Price, unknown (Col.)	30	Apr	1864				PTIMES
Price, Willie	28	Dec	1859	26 Dec 1859	3y9m20d		DET

Name	Notice Date			Death Date	Age	Comment	Paper
Pritchard, male	08	Jun	1853	03 Jun 1853	3 or 4		PT&C
Pry, Daniel (Priv.)	12	Dec	1863	Nov 1863			PTIMES
Pry, Henry	10	Oct	1863				PTIMES
Puffet, William	11	Mar	1854		70		PDD
Pugh, male	13	Aug	1851		4		PT&C
Purdam, E.	28	Mar	1854	21 Mar 1854	36		PDD
Purdom, Eliza	22	Mar	1854	20 Mar 1854	35	nee Radcliff	SVREP
Purdum, Eliza	20	Mar	1854	20 Mar 1854		nee Ratliffe	DET
Pursell, Emma Loretta	05	Mar	1851	03 Mar 1851	2		PT&C
Pursell, Emma Loretta	10	Mar	1851	3 Mar 1851	2		PI
Pursell, James	26	Mar	1856	22 Mar 1856	39		WPT
Pye, female	23	Jul	1851				PT&C
Pyles, Peter	30	Jul	1864	20 Jul 1864			PTIMES
Quartz, S.B.	06	Jun	1863	16 May 1863			PTIMES
Querry, female	20	Mar	1854	17 Feb 1854			PDD
Quick, Jacob	06	Oct	1852		23		PT&C
Quick, Jacob	29	Sep	1852		23		PT&C
Quigley, Ann Eliza	13	Feb	1838	Feb 1838	4		STRIB
Quigley, Catherine	21	Oct	1853	09 Oct 1853	13		DET
Quinn, Francis	10	Aug	1855				DET
Quirk, James	16	Aug	1855		10		DET
Rabbe, John Augustus	21	Mar	1854	07 Mar 1854			PDD
Rachel, female	23	Feb	1853				PT&C
Rachel, male	23	Feb	1853				PT&C
Rachel, unknown	23	Feb	1853		child		PT&C
Radcliff, Isham Perry	24	Sep	1855		10y		DET
Radcliff, Thomas Jefferson	24	Sep	1855		13y7m20d		DET
Radcliff, unknown (Lieut.)	26	Oct	1854				DET
Radcliff, unknown (Lieut.)	27	Oct	1854				PDD
Radcliffe, Wm.	06	Jun	1863	16 May 1863			PTIMES
Rader, Wm.	02	Jan	1854	31 Dec 1853			PDD
Rader, Wm. S.	31	Dec	1853	24 Dec 1853	16		DET
Radford, Isaac	13	Aug	1864	25 Jul 1864			PTIMES
Ragin, J.M.	18	Nov	1853	16 Nov 1853			DET
Raglan, (Field Marshal) (Lord)	18, 20	Jul	1855		67		DET
Railman, Elizabeth	27	Sep	1854	17 Sep 1854	28		DET (S)
Railman, Elizabeth	27	Sep	1854	17 Sep 1854	28		PDD (S)
Rainey, George T.	07	Jan	1854	03 Jan 1854	20		PDD
Rainey, John C.	22	Apr	1865	30 Mar 1865	57		PTIMES
Rains, female	06	Aug	1853				DET
Rains, female	28	Apr	1852				PT&C
Ralston, male	31	Dec	1851		6		PT&C
Ralston, unknown	31	Dec	1851		child		PT&C

Deaths

Name	Notice Date			Death Date	Age	Comment	Paper
Ramsey, unknown	30	Aug	1854	14 Aug 1854	13m		DET
Ramsey, Wm.	06	Aug	1851	20 Jul 1851			PT&C
Randolph, Richard	15	Mar	1859	31 Jan 1859			PTIMES
Rankin, Calla M.	19	Dec	1854	18 Dec 1854	2y10m4d		DET
Rankin, male	13	Mar	1855	07 Mar 1855	5		DET (S)
Rankin, Mary	20	Apr	1858	14 Apr 1858	29y3m24d		DET
Ransom, Mary	13	Aug	1824				PG&LA
Ratcliff, Harriet A.	30	Jun	1843	26 Jun 1843	22		TRIB
Ratcliff, John	19	Mar	1864	12 Mar 1864	74		PTIMES
Ratcliffe, John	01	Sep	1843	31 Aug 1843	19		TRIB
Ratcliffe, Thomas	27	Mar	1854	24 Mar 1854			DET
Rathbone, Elizabeth	09	Jun	1860	Jun 1860			PTIMES
Raton, unknown	03, 06	Dec	1853				PDD
Rauch, Peter	23	Dec	1865	12 Dec 1865			PTIMES
Rav, George	13	Oct	1854	09 Oct 1854	55		PDD (S)
Ray, Catharine	02	Jul	1855	29 Jun 1855			DET
Ray, male	09	Oct	1854				DET
Raymond, Jane	20	Feb	1854	16 Feb 1854	65		DET
Raynor, female	20	Aug	1864	18 Aug 1864			PTIMES
Read, T.B.	26	Jul	1855				DET
Read, unknown (Judge)	31	Jan	1854	27 Dec 1853			PDD
Ream, Jonathan	26	Sep	1854	22 Sep 1854			DET
Redd, Travis	26	Jul	1827	Jul 1827			WT
Redkey, Basil	17	May	1859	May 1859			PTIMES
Redmon, female	17	Jun	1854				PDD
Redmond, John	12	Apr	1859	Apr 1859			PTIMES
Redmond, John	01, 04	Apr	1859	29 Mar 1859			DET
Reed, A.B.	04	May	1853	21 Apr 1853			PT&C
Reed, Adeline	24	Mar	1858	24 Mar 1858	25		DET
Reed, Adeline	31	Mar	1858	24 Mar 1858	25		WPT
Reed, Amos	11	Oct	1862	07 Oct 1862			PTIMES
Reed, Geo. W.	21	Feb	1855	18 Feb 1855			DET
Reed, George	05	Mar	1859	25 Feb 1859	45		DET
Reed, George	08	Mar	1859	25 Feb 1859	45		PTIMES
Reed, George	09	Mar	1859	25 Feb 1859	45		WPT
Reed, Henry (Prof.)	16	Oct	1854				DET
Reed, John C.	14	Dec	1857	12 Dec 1857	37		DET
Reed, John C.	16	Dec	1857	12 Dec 1857	37		WPT
Reed, Madison	12, 19	Mar	1851	03 Mar 1851	40		PT&C
Reed, male	27	Jul	1854	26 Jul 1854			DET
Reed, Myron	29	Mar	1859	12 Mar 1859			PTIMES
Reed, William	01	Sep	1855	27 Aug 1855	26		DET
Reed, Wm.	21	Apr	1855				DET
Reedch, Wm. F.	09	May	1855	15 Apr 1855	53		DET (S)
Reeder, John M.	01	Feb	1862	06 Dec 1861			PTIMES

Name	Notice Date			Death Date	Age	Comment	Paper
Reese, Jacob	19	Sep	1854				PDD
Reese, James	08	Jun	1853				PT&C
Reese, Julin	02	Jun	1854	31 May 1854			DET
Reeside, Gillen	17	Mar	1852	11 Mar 1852	infant		PT&C
Reeves, female	18	Mar	1857				WPT
Reid, female	28	Aug	1855	19 Aug 1855		nee Jennings	DET
Reid, Samuel	10	Sep	1851				PT&C
Reieh, female	22	Feb	1860		2		DET
Reilly, Thomas Devin	18	Mar	1854				PDD
Reiner, Geo.	15	Aug	1850	12 Aug 1850			PT&C
Reiniger, unknown	02	Sep	1845	30 Aug 1845	3y11m10d		CLIPPER
Renick, Mortimer	24	Feb	1855	17 Feb 1855	27		DET
Reniger, unknown	23	Aug	1853	14 Aug 1853	4		PDD
Renner, Jacob	04	Aug	1852				PT&C
Renshaw, female	06	Aug	1856				WPT
Resler, unknown	21	Mar	1854	18 Mar 1854	2		PDD (S)
Rey, male	01	Dec	1852		child		PT&C
Reynolds, Chancy H.	10	Mar	1854	27 Feb 1854			PDD
Rhodes, Alvin	03	Oct	1850	30 Sep 1850			PT&C
Rhodes, C.	31	Mar	1843				TRIB
Rhodes, Francis M.	28	May	1864	May 1864			PTIMES
Rhodes, George L.	20	Oct	1852	10 Oct 1852	3y6m		PT&C
Rhodes, James S.	20	Oct	1852	14 Oct 1852	1y2m		PT&C
Rhodes, Theodore	10	Aug	1855		30		DET
Rice, Israel C. (Esq.)	14	Dec	1853				PDD
Rice, N. (Sergeant)	19	Mar	1864	07 Mar 1864	25		PTIMES
Richards, H.	06	Jun	1863	16 May 1863			PTIMES
Richards, Margaline	21	Sep	1853	12 Sep 1853	56		PDD (S)
Richards, unk. (Capt.)	31	Aug	1855	26 Aug 1855			DET
Richardson, Cornelia H.	30	Apr	1864	22 Apr 1864			PTIMES
Richardson, George Francis	02	Aug	1854	02 Aug 1854	1y4m		DET
Richardson, Isabella Jane	09	May	1863	30 Apr 1863	7y10m12d		PTIMES
Richardson, J.B. (Maj.Gen.)	15	Nov	1862	03 Nov 1862			PTIMES
Richardson, Robert	16	Nov	1859	15 Nov 1859	9y10m23d		DET
Richardson, unknown	16	May	1863				PTIMES
Richardson, Walter	19	May	1852	14 May 1852	15		PT&C
Richardson, Winthrop (Capt.)	30	Jun	1853	25 Jun 1853			DET
Richardson, Wm.G.	08	Jul	1857				WPT
Richerson, unknown	17	Aug	1854	03 Aug 1854	4		DET (S)
Richey, Rebecca	19	Nov	1853	14 Nov 1853	23		DET
Richie, Thomas (Gen.)	21	Mar	1863				PTIMES

Name	Notice Date			Death Date	Age	Comment	Paper
Richmond, female	09	Jun	1860	03 Jun 1860			PTIMES
Richter, Cornelius	09	Feb	1853	05 Feb 1853			PT&C
Ricketts, Girard (Dr.)	14	Mar	1859	06 Mar 1859	40		DET
Ricketts, Girard C. (Dr.)	16	Mar	1859	06 Mar 1859	40		WPT
Rickoff, Elizabeth B.	24	Sep	1852	3 Sep 1852	26		PI
Rickoff, Elizabeth B.	29	Sep	1852	03 Sep 1852			PT&C
Ridgely, Harry	23	Apr	1855				DET
Ridgway, David	09	May	1853	28 Apr 1853	21		PDD
Ridgway, Jacob	19	May	1843	30 Apr 1843			TRIB
Ridgway, Jos. Jr.	29	Aug	1850				PT&C
Riely, Ann	09	Jul	1851		20	nee Golding	PT&C
Rife, G. (Serg't)	06	Jun	1863	16 May 1863			PTIMES
Rigden, George H.	02	Dec	1854	30 Oct 1854	18		DET
Riggs, Charles	09	Sep	1857	24 Aug 1857			WPT
Riggs, Rebecca G.	05	Apr	1862	02 Apr 1862	61y1m15d		PTIMES
Riley, Charles	19	Jan	1853	06 Jan 1853			PT&C
Riley, David	25	Aug	1854	22 Aug 1854	8		DET
Riley, James	19	Nov	1851				PT&C
Riley, male	29	Mar	1855	17 Mar 1855			DET
Riley, Margaret	25	Aug	1854	22 Aug 1854	10		DET
Riley, unknown	09	Jun	1860	Jun 1860	child		PTIMES
Riley, unknown	09	Jun	1860	Jun 1860	child		PTIMES
Rily, David	26	Aug	1854	22 Aug 1854	8		PDD
Rily, Margaret	26	Aug	1854	22 Aug 1854	10		PDD
Riners, Jno.	23	Jul	1856	Jul 1856			WPT
Ring, N., Jr.	01	Jun	1853				PT&C
Ringgold, Thomas L. (Capt.)	26	May	1854	11 May 1854			PDD
Ringley, unknown (Lieut.)	26	Oct	1854				DET
Ringley, unknown (Lieut.)	27	Oct	1854				PDD
Ringo, female	17	Oct	1850	Oct 1850			PT&C
Ringo, William	17	Oct	1850	Oct 1850			PT&C
Rings, Martha	21	Jul	1854	18 Jul 1854	18		DET
Ripley, William P.	25	Dec	1845	18 Dec 845	60		TRIB
Ritcherson, Johnathan	06	Jul	1854	01 Jul 1854			PDD
Ritchie, Matthew	10	May	1827	08 May 1827	23		WT
Ritchie, Thomas	05	Jul	1854	03 Jul 1854			DET
Ritchie, Thomas	06	Jul	1854	03 Jul 1854			PDD
Ritchie, Thomas (Father)	08	Jul	1854	03 Jul 1854			PDD
Robb (?), A.C.	22	Nov	1858		27		DET
Robbins, female	11	May	1853				PDD
Robbins, Mary H.	11	May	1853				PDD
Robe, A.C.	24	Nov	1858	Nov 1858	27		WPT
Robert, Cordelia Eliza	23	Jun	1854		12y9m		DET

Name	Notice Date			Death Date	Age	Comment	Paper
Robert, Cordella Eliza	23	Jun	1854	22 Jun 1854	12y9m		PDD
Roberts, D.	01	Dec	1853	22 Nov 1853			DET
Roberts, D.	01	Dec	1853				PDD
Roberts, female	05	Sep	1859	01 Sep 1859			DET
Roberts, female	07	Sep	1859	01 Sep 1859			WPT
Roberts, female	13	Sep	1859	08 Sep 1859			PTIMES
Roberts, J.H. (Capt.)	15	Sep	1859	08 Sep 1859			DET
Roberts, Jas. H. (Capt.)	20, 27	Sep	1859	08 Sep 1859			PTIMES
Roberts, Julius W.	30	Apr	1851	19 Apr 1851	23		PT&C
Roberts, unk. (Bishop)	21	Apr	1843				TRIB
Robertson, George W.	02	Aug	1854	30 Jul 1854	37		DET
Robertson, James (Dr.)	03	Aug	1854				DET
Robins, female	19	Jun	1854				DET
Robins, male	12	Jul	1855				DET
Robins, Terence	29	Sep	1843				TRIB
Robinson, Hannah	23	Apr	1864	18 Apr 1864			PTIMES
Robinson, J.V.	14	Jan	1865	08 Jan 1865	74y2m20d		PTIMES
Robinson, J.V., Jr. (Major)	29	Mar	1862	23 Mar 1862	42		PTIMES
Robinson, John	07	Jul	1852				PT&C
Robinson, male	07	Jul	1852		3		PT&C
Robinson, male	29	Oct	1851		25		PT&C
Robinson, unk. (Judge)	26	May	1843	26 Apr 1843			TRIB
Robson, John	03	Feb	1855				DET
Robson, Mary	15	Nov	1853	14 Nov 1853	8		DET
Rodgers, A.	30	Mar	1855				DET
Rodgers, Margaret Anna	22	Sep	1857	08 Sep 1857	3y3m		PSOT
Rodgers, Milton	11	Apr	1855	06 Apr 1855	child		DET
Rodgers, unknown	27	Sep	1854	18 Sep 1854	1		PDD (S)
Rodney, Wm.	22	Oct	1851	10 Oct 1851			PT&C
Rogers, Ada Ann	20	Jan	1854	13 Jan 1854	1		DET
Rogers, Anna	25	Jan	1826		78		WT
Rogers, male	01	Jun	1853				PT&C
Rogers, male	17	Oct	1850	13 Oct 1850			PT&C
Rogers, unknown	27	Sep	1854	18 Sep 1854	1		DET (S)
Rohan, Peter	31	Dec	1859	29 Dec 1859			PTIMES
Rohn, Peter	30	Dec	1859				DET
Roosa, female	07	Jan	1865	02 Jan 1865			PTIMES
Roosa, unknown	07	Jan	1865	02 Jan 1865	child		PTIMES
Roosa, unknown	07	Jan	1865	02 Jan 1865	child		PTIMES
Rordan, Thomas	14	May	1855	07 May 1855			DET
Rose, E.M.P.	14	Jan	1860	13 Dec 1859	40		PTIMES
Rose, John	11	May	1855				DET
Rose, John	15	Jan	1855	09 Jan 1855			DET
Rose, John	26	Jun	1855				DET

Name	Notice Date			Death Date	Age	Comment	Paper
Rose, male	02	Dec	1859	25 Nov 1859	16		DET
Rose, Nancy	17	Aug	1854	06 Aug 1854	82		DET (S)
Rose, unknown (Major)	26	Oct	1854				DET
Rose, unknown (Major)	27	Oct	1854				PDD
Rosenthal, Bartta	17	Nov	1855	16 Nov 1855	18		DET
Ross, E.S.	02	May	1850	28 Apr 1850			PT&C
Ross, E.S.	29	Apr	1850	28 Apr 1850			PI
Ross, Jacob (Corp.)	04	Jun	1864				PTIMES
Ross, Jesse Latimer	05	Jul	1859	03 Jul 1859			DET
Ross, Jesse Latimer	06	Jul	1859	03 Jul 1859			WPT
Ross, male	09	Sep	1857	24 Aug 1857			WPT
Ross, male	09	Sep	1857	24 Aug 1857			WPT
Ross, Martha D.	02	Jul	1852	27 Jun 1852			PI
Ross, Martha D.	30	Jun	1852	27 Jun 1852			PT&C
Ross, Mary K.	24	Nov	1852	22 Nov 1852	3y2m		PT&C
Ross, Mary R.	26	Nov	1852	Nov 1852	3		PI
Ross, S.M. Tracy	23	May	1848	18 May 1848	2y10m27d		DENQ
Ross, William J.	09	Jun	1859	09 Jun 1859	9		DET
Ross, William J.	15	Jun	1859	09 Jun 1859	9		WPT
Roster, male	29	Dec	1854		6		DET
Rosy, G.W.	03	Feb	1843				TRIB
Rothaupt, Powell	10	Aug	1855				DET
Rothschild, Solomon (Baron)	23	Aug	1855		82		DET
Roughton, Harriet	31	Mar	1854	25 Mar 1854	19		DET
Rouse, Catharine	14	Sep	1853	04 Sep 1853	40		PDD (S)
Roush, John	03	Sep	1856				WPT
Roussel, Charles	16	Apr	1851				PT&C
Row, Charles	12	Aug	1854	12 Aug 1854			DET
Row, Lucina	09	Jul	1851	06 Jul 1851	13m6d		PT&C
Row, unknown	17	Aug	1854	11 Aug 1854	14m		DET (S)
Rowan, John (Hon.)	28	Jul	1843				TRIB
Roworth, Geo.	09	Jun	1860	03 Jun 1860			PTIMES
Roy, Jas.	23	Jul	1856	Jul 1856			WPT
Royal, Ann	10	Oct	1854	08 Oct 1854			DET
Royce, male	23	Jul	1856	Jul 1856			WPT
Royce, male	23	Jul	1856	Jul 1856			WPT
Rubel, Martin	26	Jan	1861	19 Jan 1861			PTIMES
Ruckman, Lovina	11	Nov	1853	5 Nov 1853	8m		DET
Ruffin, Edward	01	Jul	1865	Jun 1865			PTIMES
Ruffner, M.	23	Apr	1856	18 Apr 1856			WPT
Ruggles, Titus	16	Jul	1851				PT&C
Rumsey, Harriet	07	Oct	1865	06 Oct 1865	10m21d		PTIMES
Runyan, John	09, 15	Jul	1853	02 Jul 1853			PDD
Runyon, John	08	Jul	1853	02 Jul 1853			DET

Name	Notice Date			Death Date	Age	Comment	Paper
Runyon, John	13	Jul	1853				PT&C
Ruprecht, Paulus	05	Apr	1859	31 Mar 1859			PTIMES
Rush, William L.	22	Mar	1854	12 Mar 1854	29y11m5d		DET
Russell, Eliza	06, 08	Feb	1855	03 Feb 1855			DET
Russell, James	03	Nov	1843	17 Oct 1843			TRIB
Russell, Nancy	03	Mar	1857	22 Feb 1857	66		PSOT
Russell, Nancy	04	Mar	1857	22 Feb 1857	66		WPT
Russell, unknown	01	Aug	1855	25 Jul 1855	3		DET
Russell, unknown	07	Jan	1854	28 Dec 1853	5w		PDD
Russell, William	31	May	1828		57		WT
Rust, Henry M.	07	Dec	1861				PTIMES
Ryan, female	13	Jul	1853	12 Jul 1853			PDD
Ryan, Jeremiah	26	Nov	1851				PT&C
Ryan, male	15	Mar	1844	29 Feb 1844			TRIB
Ryan, Mary	29	Dec	1853	16 Dec 1853			PDD
Ryder, female	09	Jun	1860	Jun 1860			PTIMES
Ryder, James	20	Aug	1851	16 Aug 1851			PT&C
Sacket, Susannah	16	Apr	1856	08 Apr 1856		nee Hoge	WPT
Salisbury, Wesley	18	Mar	1865		60		PTIMES
Salsburry, William	07	Aug	1854	06 Aug 1854			PDD
Salsbury, female	30	Aug	1854	27 Aug 1854			DET
Salsbury, Julia	27	Aug	1859	27 Aug 1859	9		DET
Salsbury, Julia	31	Aug	1859	27 Aug 1859	9		WPT
Salsbury, W.	17	Aug	1854	07 Aug 1854	32		DET (S)
Salsbury, William	07	Aug	1854	06 Aug 1854	32		DET
Salter, Fannie	31	Jul	1854	30 Jul 1854	infant		DET
Samuel Pickerill	03	Jun	1850	May 1850	100		PI
Sanders, Edward	01	Feb	1862	09 Nov 1861			PTIMES
Sanders, Lewis	06	Aug	1851				PT&C
Sanford, Julia	29	Jul	1854	26 Jul 1854	33		DET
Sanford, male	17	Mar	1843				TRIB
Sanor, Benjamin F.	18	Feb	1860				PTIMES
Sansom, female	23	Jan	1864		child		PTIMES
Santer, Wm.	30	Jul	1851	Jul 1851			PT&C
	06	Aug	1851				
Sargeant, James	30	Aug	1854	24 Aug 1854	76		DET
Sattenbury, D.	09	Jun	1860	Jun 1860			PTIMES
Saunders, Cora Alice	18	Jul	1859	17 Jul 1859	5y1m17d		DET
Saunders, Cora Alice	20	Jul	1859	17 Jul 1859	5y1m17d		WPT
Saunders, John E.	22	Jan	1851				PT&C
Saunders, Louis	30	Jul	1851	Jul 1851			PT&C
Savage, Josiah Merrill	06	Nov	1858	02 Nov 1858	23		DET
Savage, Josiah Merrill	09	Nov	1858	02 Nov 1858	23		PSOT
Savage, Josiah Merrill	09	Nov	1858	02 Nov 1858	23		PTIMES
Savage, Sarah H.	21	Jun	1855	16 Jun 1855	18		DET

Name	Notice Date			Death Date	Age	Comment	Paper
Sawyer, female	02	Jun	1852	24 May 1852			PT&C
Sawyer, male	02	Jun	1852	24 May 1852			PT&C
Sayley, Francis W.	11	May	1853				PDD
Scanlin, female	22	Apr	1865				PTIMES
Scarborough, Mary	16	Feb	1853	11 Feb 1853			PT&C
Scavits, Francis	18	Feb	1852	11 Feb 1852			PT&C
Schaffer, Charles F.	28	May	1864	May 1864			PTIMES
Schamyl, unknown	13	Aug	1855				DET
Schaw, unknown (Capt.)	26	Oct	1854				DET
Schaw, unknown (Capt.)	27	Oct	1854				PDD
Schell, Augustus	15	Dec	1852				PT&C
Schlessinger, unknown	20	Jun	1854				DET
Schlessinger, unknown	20	Jun	1854				PDD
Schoch, Benjamin	09	Jun	1858	01 Jun 1858	60		WPT
Scholton, female	06	Aug	1851				PT&C
Schoolcraft, Henry	14	Oct	1854				PDD
Schooley, Catharine	14	Jul	1855	05 Jul 1855	39		DET
Schoonover, male	02	May	1854	01 May 1854			DET
Schoonover, male	02	May	1854	01 May 1854			PDD
Schoppe, male	03	Dec	1851				PT&C
Schwartz, John (Hon.)	27	Jun	1860	20 Jun 1860	65		WPT
Scotch, Giant	04	Aug	1854				DET
Scott, Andrew	24	Mar	1852	20 Mar 1852		Negro	PT&C
Scott, Benjamin	12	Nov	1856				WPT
Scott, Benjamin F.	26	Aug	1859	16 Aug 1859	14m7d		DET
Scott, Benjamin F.	31	Aug	1859	16 Aug 1859	14m7d		WPT
Scott, Catharine	16	Jul	1858	04 Jul 1858	80		DET
Scott, Elizabeth	08	Oct	1864	05 Oct 1864	57	nee Kerr	PTIMES
Scott, Jane	31	May	1828	22 Mar 1828			WT
Scott, Jennie	21	Jun	1862	17 Jun 1862			PTIMES
Scott, male	22	Dec	1853	16 Dec 1853			PDD
Scott, Nancy	04	May	1858	24 Apr 1858		nee Hammond	PSOT
Scott, Samuel (Col.)	03	Mar	1855				DET
Scott, Thomas Winter	18	Mar	1865	13 Mar 1865	16m		PTIMES
Scott, unknown	12	Mar	1855				DET
Scott, William C. (Judge)	31	May	1862	17 May 1862	79		PTIMES
Scott, Winfield	09	Apr	1855	07 Apr 1855	9m2w		DET
Seal, George	21	May	1864		40		PTIMES
Seal, unknown	27	Sep	1854	01 Sep 1854	2		DET (S)
Seal, unknown	27	Sep	1854	01 Sep 1854	2		PDD (S)
Seaman, Margaret	19	Sep	1860	14 Sep 1860			WPT
Sears, male	13	Mar	1855	08 Feb 1855	18m		DET (S)
Seavens, Joel	04	May	1853				PT&C
Seaver, male	15	Dec	1852				PT&C

Name	Notice Date			Death Date	Age	Comment	Paper
Secoy, unknown	16	Aug	1859				DET
Secrist, female	23	Sep	1853				DET
Sedgwick, unknown (Maj.Gen.)	14	May	1864	10 May 1864			PTIMES
Seele, male	10	Dec	1851	26 Nov 1851			PT&C
Seidenbach, L.	17	Jan	1863				PTIMES
Seifurt, Adam	29	Jul	1850	26 Jul 1850			PI
Selfridge, E.C.	18	Feb	1852	15 Feb 1852	24		PT&C
Sellers, George	12	Jul	1853	21 Jun 1853	17 or 18		DET
Sellers, George	13	Jul	1853	21 Jun 1853	17 or 18		PT&C
Sellers, George	13	Jul	1853	21 Jun 1853	17 or 18		PDD
Senate, male	20	Mar	1854				PDD
Sergeant, John (Hon.)	01	Dec	1852	23 Nov 1852	73		PT&C
Seward, female	24	Jun	1865	21 Jun 1865			PTIMES
Seymour, J.W.	02	Mar	1859	27 Feb 1859			DET
Shackleford, Daniel	22	Oct	1851	20 Oct 1851	3y11m12d		PT&C
Shackleford, Hattie	14	Oct	1865	10 Oct 1865	child		PTIMES
Shackleford, John	18	Aug	1854				PDD
Shackleford, male	08	Dec	1854				DET
Shackleford, Sam.	21	Aug	1854				DET
Shackleford, Wm.	18	Aug	1854				PDD
Shackleford, Wm.	21	Aug	1854				DET
Shaffels, Jas.	13	Oct	1854	29 Sep 1854	17		PDD (S)
Shaffer, Joseph	21	Nov	1855				DET
Shaffer, unknown	14	Sep	1853	06 Sep 1853	13m		PDD (S)
Shakes, John	27	Oct	1860	20 Oct 1860	87		PTIMES
Shambert, I.	09	May	1855	24 Apr 1855	6m		DET (S)
Shane, George	07	Apr	1852	01 Apr 1852	55		PT&C
Shannon, Hugh	14	Apr	1858	Apr 1858			WPT
Shannon, Patrick	03	Nov	1852	30 Oct 1852			PT&C
Shannon, Thomas (Hon.)	14	Apr	1843	16 Apr 1843			TRIB
Shape, John	03	Dec	1851	25 Nov 1851			PT&C
Sharp, female	27	Jul	1860	22 Jul 1860	16		DET
Sharp, G.	16	Sep	1854	02 Sep 1854	30		DET
Sharp, George W.	21	Sep	1854	19 Sep 1854			DET
Shaw, Emily	06	Sep	1828	03 Sep 1828	18		WT
Shaw, George W. (Capt.)	19	Sep	1854				DET
Shaw, Hannah	16	Mar	1853				PT&C
Shaw, Tristam	31	Mar	1843	14 Feb 1843			TRIB
Shawley, William	14	Nov	1859	14 Nov 1859			DET
	18	Feb	1860				
Shawney, male	01	Aug	1853	22 Jul 1853			DET
Shea, Patrick	02	Aug	1854				DET
Shea, Patrick	03	Aug	1854	29 Jul 1854			PDD
Shearer, P.S.	23	Sep	1857		43		WPT

Deaths

Name	Notice Date			Death Date	Age	Comment	Paper
Sheckler, male	17	Mar	1852		3y6m		PT&C
Shed, John	31	Mar	1860	02 Mar 1860	102		PTIMES
Sheeley, Jacob	24	Jun	1854	17 Jun 1854			DET
Sheely, Elizabeth	12	Aug	1818		37		PGAZ
Shelby, Isaac (Hon.)	03	Aug	1826	18 Jul 1826	76		WT
Sheldon, Thomas C.	21	Jun	1854	13 Jun 1854	60		PDD
Sheldon, unknown	03	Sep	1851				PT&C
Shellieg, Mary Jane	28	Apr	1857	19 Apr 1857	26		PSOT
Shellige, Mary	03	Apr	1855	02 Apr 1855	34		DET
Shelly, Isaac	03	Aug	1826	18 Jul 1826	76		WT
Shenk, Andrew J.	05	May	1854				PDD
Shepard, Charles C.	03	Mar	1855	22 Feb 1855			DET
Shepard, Hezekiah	02	Dec	1865	Nov 1865			PTIMES
Shepherd, female	01	Aug	1853	25 Jul 1853	10		DET
Shepherd, female	03	Aug	1853	25 Jul 1853	10		PT&C
Shepherd, William	30	Nov	1859				WPT
Sheppard, unknown	24	Sep	1851		child		PT&C
Sheppard, Wm. B.	24	Aug	1854				DET
Sherer, Joseph	07	Jun	1853	31 May 1853			DET
Sherer, Joseph	08	Jun	1853	04 Jun 1853			PT&C
Sheridan, David (Rev.)	23	Jul	1856	Jul 1856			WPT
Sheridan, John	17	Mar	1854				PDD
Sherman, unknown	28	Jan	1860				PTIMES
Sherman, unk. (Capt.)	23	Jan	1860				DET
Sherman, unknown (Col.)	24	Jul	1855				DET
Sherrard, James	07	May	1851	16 Apr 1851			PT&C
Shewell, Edward	31	Oct	1854	30 Oct 1854	47		PDD
Shiddell, male	25	Feb	1852	19 Feb 1852			PT&C
Shields, Jno.	09	Aug	1854				PDD
Shields, Laura	27	Jul	1853	04 Jul 1853			PT&C
Shields, Michael	28	May	1864	May 1864			PTIMES
Shields, Theodore F.	10	Jan	1855		45		DET
Shinn, Charles Samuel	06, 08	Feb	1855	03 Feb 1855			DET
Shinn, F.	16	Jul	1851				PT&C
Shinn, Francis	06	Aug	1851				PT&C
Shinn, Francis A.G.	06	Aug	1851				PT&C
Shinn, George	06	Aug	1851				PT&C
Shipman, Hannah	16	Mar	1860	28 Feb 1860		nee Cotton	DET
Shipman, Hannah	21	Mar	1860	28 Feb 1860		nee Cotton	WPT
Shipp, female	28	Jul	1854		10		DET
Shirley, unknown	08	Jun	1860		18		DET
Shoenberger, Peter (Dr.)	06	Jul	1854	18 Jun 1854	72		PDD
Short, Daniel	30	Jul	1864	20 Jul 1864			PTIMES
Short, Josiah M.	24	Oct	1850	05 Oct 1850			PT&C
Short, male	16	Sep	1854				DET

Name	Notice Date			Death Date	Age	Comment	Paper
Short, male	20	Jan	1855	19 Jan 1855	42		DET
Short, male	23	Sep	1854				PDD˙
Shoubertz, Peter	04	Oct	1862				PTIMES
Shoup, female	17	Jul	1860				DET
Shrivel, unknown	02	May	1854	29 Apr 1854			PDD (S)
Shrum, Samuel	15	Sep	1859	09 Sep 1859			DET
Shultz, John	11	Jul	1848	05 Jul 1848			DENQ
Shy, Albrin Brisco	24	Dec	1853	20 Dec 1853			DET
Sidner, Samel	07	Mar	1854	04 Mar 1854	23		PDD (S)
Sigourney, Lydia H.	17	Jun	1865	10 Jun 1865	76		PTIMES
Sigsby, Christian	02	May	1853				PDD
Sigsby, Christiana	04	May	1853	Apr 1853			PT&C
Sikes, unknown	14	Sep	1853	06 Sep 1853	7m		PDD (S)
Sill, Eytge	05	May	1843	28 Apr 1843	78		TRIB
Sill, Joshua W. (Gen.)	10	Jan	1863	03 Jan 1863	31		PTIMES
	07	Feb	1863				
Sill, Richard (Esq.)	05	Sep	1844	04 Sep 1844			TRIB
Silliman, Benjamin, Sr. (Prof.)	03	Dec	1864	24 Nov 1864	84		PTIMES
Silver, Stephen W.	25	Aug	1852	21 Jun 1852	29		PT&C
Simon, unknown (Capt.)	23	Jan	1864				PTIMES
Simonton, unknown	18	Aug	1852		child		PT&C
Simpson, Mary	07	Aug	1854	30 Jul 1854	49		DET
Simpson, Mary	16	Sep	1865	29 Aug 1865	88		PTIMES
Simpson, Willie	09	Apr	1864	07 Apr 1864	8		PTIMES
Sims, Mary Jane	20	Apr	1858	15 Apr 1858	35		DET
Sims, Mary Jane	20	Apr	1858	15 Apr 1858	35		PSOT
Skeen, Josiah K.	16	Jul	1851				PT&C
Slagle, David W.	30	Jul	1864	20 Jul 1864			PTIMES
Slavens, Wm.	22	Aug	1850	20 Aug 1850			PT&C
Sleigh, male	08	Sep	1843	19 Aug 1843			TRIB
Sloan, Jonathan (Hon.)	09	May	1854				PDD
Sloane, Jas.	22	Oct	1851	27 Sep 1851			PT&C
Slocomb, George L.	27	Apr	1860				DET
Slocum, Cyrus	23	Jul	1851	22 Jul 1851			PT&C
Slocum, Sarah Ann	21	May	1851	16 May 1851			PT&C
Slusser, J.A	25	Apr	1860				WPT
Sly, unknown	13	Mar	1855	31 Jan 1855			DET (S)
Smart, William	24	Apr	1860	19 Apr 1860			DET
Smiley, Polly	21	Jan	1857	05 Dec 1856	95		WPT
Smiley, Walter	24	Sep	1852	19 Sep 1852	45		PI
Smith, A.L. (Judge)	10	Jun	1865				PTIMES
Smith, Allen	31	Mar	1852				PT&C
Smith, Andrew	22	Feb	1854				PDD
Smith, Anthony	22	Dec	1852	02 Dec 1852	57		PT&C

Name	Notice Date			Death Date	Age	Comment	Paper
Smith, Caleb B. (Hon.)	16	Jan	1864	14 Jan 1864	56		PTIMES
Smith, Charles	17	Feb	1854				PDD
Smith, D.E.	05	Apr	1854	31 Mar 1854			DET
Smith, Daniel B.	03	Jan	1855	24 Dec 1854	27		DET
Smith, E.W.	08	Jul	1857	25 Jun 1857	54		WPT
Smith, E.W.	26	Jun	1857	25 Jun 1857	54		DET
Smith, Elizabeth	12	Aug	1825	10 Aug 1825			PG&LA
Smith, Elizabeth	13	Jun	1829		25		WT
Smith, Elizabeth	18	May	1855		42		DET
Smith, female	01	Nov	1854				PDD
Smith, female	03	Sep	1855				DET
Smith, female	15	Mar	1854				DET
Smith, female	24	Jan	1854				PDD
Smith, Frank	14	Jul	1855	13 Jun 1855	10		DET
Smith, Gideon B.	11	Feb	1852	28 Jan 1852	33		PT&C
Smith, Gideon B.	13	Feb	1852	28 Jan 1852	33		PI
Smith, Hiram B.	15	Dec	1854	15 Dec 1854	21		DET
Smith, Horace	01	Aug	1853	26 Jul 1853			DET
Smith, Horace	03	Aug	1853				PT&C
Smith, J.	26	Jan	1855	08 Jan 1855			DET
Smith, James	02	Dec	1859	26 Nov 1859			DET
Smith, James	21	Oct	1854				DET
Smith, James Haddock	08	Feb	1862	03 Feb 1862			PTIMES
Smith, James M.	26	Jan	1854				PDD
Smith, Jane	09	Jun	1854		29	nee Slaney	PDD
Smith, Jefferson	09	Dec	1865				PTIMES
Smith, Joe	11	Jun	1844	Jun 1844			TRIB
Smith, John	02	Jan	1845	01 Jan 1845	65		TRIB
Smith, John	07	Sep	1826	04 Sep 1826	35		WT
Smith, John Adam	10	Sep	1856				WPT
Smith, John F.	11	Oct	1859	07 Oct 1859	2y9m27d		PTIMES
Smith, John Speed (Col.)	12	Jun	1854	06 Jun 1854			PDD
Smith, John W.	16	Sep	1865	09 Sep 1865	12		PTIMES
Smith, John Walter	25	Aug	1851	22 Aug 1851			PI
Smith, John Walter	27	Aug	1851	22 Aug 1851			PT&C
Smith, Louisa	07	Jan	1825	28 Dec 1824			PG&LA
Smith, male	01	Nov	1854				PDD
Smith, male	05	Feb	1855	1839			DET
Smith, male	06	Jul	1853	28 Jun 1853			PT&C
Smith, male	11	Jun	1844	Jun 1844			TRIB
Smith, male	14	Oct	1865	30 Aug 1865			PTIMES
Smith, male	15	Mar	1854				DET
Smith, Milton O. (Corp.)	30	Jul	1864	04 Jul 1864			PTIMES
Smith, Polly	20	Jan	1860	Dec 1859	90	nee Bent	DET
Smith, Samuel	09	May	1855	30 Apr 1855			DET (S)

Name	Notice Date			Death Date	Age	Comment	Paper
Smith, Samuel	15	Jul	1850	14 Jul 1850			PI
Smith, Samuel E. (Hon.)	17	Mar	1860	Mar 1860	72		PTIMES
Smith, Stephen	14	Nov	1859	14 Nov 1859			DET
Smith, Thomas	16	Jun	1852				PT&C
Smith, unknown	24	Jan	1854		child		PDD
Smith, unknown	24	Jan	1854		child		PDD
Smith, unknown (Com.)	08	Sep	1855				DET
Smith, unknown (Corp.)	24	Jan	1854				PDD
Smith, unknown (Dr.)	10	May	1853	06 May 1853			PDD
Smith, William	30	Apr	1855	26 Apr 1855			DET
Smith, Wm.	30	Nov	1861				PTIMES
Smith, Wm. R.	01, 02	Mar	1854	25 Feb 1854			PDD
Smyser, Jacob	09	Sep	1854	05 Sep 1854			PDD
Snaget, male	19	Jul	1853				PDD
Snapp, George	28	Feb	1860		95		DET
Sneider, Henry	25	Jun	1853	22 Jun 1853			DET
Sneider, Henry	29	Jun	1853	22 Jun 1853			PT&C
Snell, female	19	Jan	1844	04 Jan 1844			TRIB
Snell, male	19	Jan	1844	04 Jan 1844			TRIB
Snodgrass, male (Rep.)	13	Jun	1854				DET
Snow, male	14	May	1851		18		PT&C
Snyder, Andrew	31	Jul	1854	28 Jul 1854	13		DET
Snyder, unknown	13	Mar	1855	02 Feb 1855	6		DET (S)
Snydey, Arhart	21	Mar	1854	14 Mar 1854	46		PDD (S)
Sohor, unk. (Rev. Mr.)	10	May	1853	06 May 1853			PDD
Somerlott, John	14	Oct	1853	Aug 1853			DET
Sontag, unknown (Madame)	29	Jun	1854	16 Jun 1854			PDD
Soule, Joseph (Dr.)	05	Sep	1853	17 Aug 1853			DET
Sowash, Geo. (Priv.)	12	Dec	1863	Nov 1863			PTIMES
Spahr, Mary Douglas	21	Nov	1855	18 Nov 1855	1y2m29d		WPT
Sparks, male	11	May	1853				PDD
Spencer, Cordelia	21	Oct	1854			nee Leonard	DET
Spencer, Cordelia	23	Oct	1854			nee Leonard	PDD
Spencer, female	10, 11	Nov	1854				DET
Spencer, George	19	Mar	1851	17 Mar 1851			PT&C
Spink, Cyrus	08	Jun	1859				WPT
Sprague, Amasa	12	Jan	1844	31 Dec 1843			TRIB
Spragus, John W. (Col.)	20	May	1865	04 May 1865	60		PTIMES
Sprangler, Isaac (Dr.)	06	Jan	1858	01 Jan 1858	55		WPT
Spring, Wm. O.	25	Feb	1852	11 Feb 1852			PT&C
Sproat, John	22	Aug	1853	21 Aug 1853	12		PDD
Spry, John Henry	21	Jul	1857	11 Jul 1857	4m9d		PSOT
Squires, John	26	Sep	1853	25 Sep 1853	58		DET

Deaths

Name	Notice Date			Death Date	Age	Comment	Paper
Squires, John	27	Sep	1853	24 Sep 1853	30		PDD
St. Arnaud, Marshal	28	Oct	1854				DET
St. Peter, Joseph	18	May	1853	10 May 1853			PT&C
St. Williams, male	02	Dec	1854				DET
Stacey, Byran	18	Apr	1854	Apr 1854			PDD
Stacy, Joseph	09	Jun	1852	02 Jun 1852			PT&C
Stafford, male	23	Jun	1852				PT&C
Stage, Garret	14	Aug	1854		33		PDD
Stall, Agnes	08	Oct	1851	01 Oct 1851	55		PT&C
Stallcup, John	16	Nov	1854	01 Nov 1854			DET
Stamford, George	06	Sep	1853	03 Sep 1853	23		PDD (S)
Stanbury, unknown (Dr.)	31	Jan	1854	20 Jan 1854			PDD
Stapleton, male	21	Aug	1855				DET
Star, E.	18	Mar	1865	06 Mar 1865	50		PTIMES
Starkweather, Ella	05	Aug	1865		17		PTIMES
Starkweather, female	05	Aug	1865		46		PTIMES
Start, William	14	Nov	1844	09 Nov 1844			TRIB
Stedman, Charles J.	30	Sep	1858	22 Sep 1858			DET
Steele, John	04	Nov	1850	25 Oct 1850			PI
Steele, John	30	Jul	1864	20 Jul 1864			PTIMES
Steele, John	31	Oct	1850	25 Oct 1850			PT&C
Stein, male	11	Mar	1865	05 Mar 1865			PTIMES
Stemshorn, Harry	12	Aug	1865	08 Aug 1865	5w3d		PTIMES
Stemshorn, Magdalene	01	Jun	1853	27 May 1853	7		PT&C
Stephens, male	11	Oct	1859				PTIMES
Stephenson, Mary C.	19	Nov	1853	30 Oct 1853	13		DET
Stephenson, Rachel	05	Jan	1853	24 Nov 1852	79		PT&C
Stetson, male	13	Aug	1853				DET
Stevens, Cyrus Martin	02	Jun	1854	31 May 1854	22		DET
Stevens, Harrison	15	Aug	1850	12 Aug 1850			PT&C
Stevens, Harrison	19	Aug	1850				PI
Stevens, Hon. A.	13	Jun	1853	07 Jun 1853			PDD
Stevens, John	27	Aug	1851	14 Aug 1851			PT&C
Stevens, male	20	Feb	1855	14 Feb 1855			DET
Stevenson, Edward O.	19	May	1852	12 May 1852			PT&C
Stevenson, female	06	Apr	1853				PT&C
Stevenson, Richard (Capt.)	20	Jul	1826	16 Jul 1826	59		WT
Stewart, Charles W.	15	Nov	1854	12 Nov 1854			DET
Stewart, female	25	Feb	1860				PTIMES
Stewart, Fletcher	05	Jul	1862				PTIMES
Stewart, J.H.	12	Jan	1854				PDD
Stewart, J.H.	29	Dec	1853				DET
Stewart, Mildred E.	07	Jan	1859	13 Dec 1858	25	nee Dalton	DET
Stewart, Walter P.	15	Jul	1865	09 Jul 1865	20		PTIMES

Name	Notice Date			Death Date	Age	Comment	Paper
Stewart, William	17	Dec	1856				WPT
Stickney, male	01	Jun	1853				PT&C
Stigler, Joseph	30	May	1854				PDD
Stillwell, Wm.	23	Sep	1857	Sep 1857			WPT
Stilwell, Adeline Louisa	06	Aug	1851	04 Aug 1851			PT&C
Stockwell, D.C.	19	Jan	1854				PDD
Stockwell, unk. (Ensign)	26	Oct	1854				DET
Stockwell, unk. (Ensign)	27	Oct	1854				PDD
Stone, A.P. (Hon.)	05	Aug	1865	02 Jul 1865			PTIMES
Stone, Chloeette	22	Dec	1855	19 Dec 1855	22y5m23d		DET
Stone, Chloeette	26	Dec	1855	19 Dec 1855	22y5m23d		WPT
Stone, Ethan	28	Apr	1852	21 Apr 1852	85		PT&C
Stone, John	22	Oct	1864	21 Oct 1864	27		PTIMES
Stone, Oliver B.	18	Mar	1859	13 Mar 1859			DET
Stone, Oliver B.	23	Mar	1859				WPT
Stoopfull, male	19	Sep	1860	14 Sep 1860			WPT
Storms, Jacob	18	Jul	1850	Jul 1850			PT&C
Storms, Thomas	15	Aug	1850	10 Aug 1850			PT&C
Story, Albert J.	23	Dec	1853				PDD
Stotenburg, female	09	Jun	1860	Jun 1860			PTIMES
Stout, James M.	08	Apr	1854	04 Apr 1854			PDD
Stover, John	06	Jul	1820	01 Jul 1820			STEL
Stowell, James Wright	21	Feb	1855	12 Feb 1855	40		DET
Strain, Pat.	09	Aug	1854				PDD
Streen, Patrick	14	Aug	1854		35		PDD
Strible, female	01	Aug	1853				DET
Strible, female	01	Aug	1853	Jun 1853			PDD
Strong, male	09	Apr	1851				PT&C
Strother, Wm.	25	Nov	1857				WPT
Struther, unk. (Lieut.)	26	Oct	1854				DET
Struther, unk. (Lieut.)	27	Oct	1854				PDD
Stuart, J.E.B.	28	May	1864	15 May 1864			PTIMES
Stump, unknown	13	Jun	1854	04 Jun 1854	9m		PDD (S)
Sullivan, Daniel	17	Nov	1852	09 Nov 1852			PT&C
Sullivan, Timothy	11	Apr	1860	08 Apr 1860	26		WPT
Sullivan, Timothy	14	Apr	1860	08 Apr 1860	26		PTIMES
Sullivan, Timothy	09, 25	Apr	1860	08 Apr 1860	26		DET
Sult, Conrad	03	Dec	1851				PT&C
Sulzmann, J. Christian	01	Apr	1865	24 Mar 1865	59y4m7d		PTIMES
Summons, unk. (Capt.)	03	Mar	1858	27 Feb 1858			WPT
Sunderland, K.G.	12	Jun	1855	09 Jun 1855			DET
Sutliff, Lyman	09	Jun	1854				DET
Sutor, male	10	Feb	1854				PDD
Sutphen, male	04	Apr	1854	29 Mar 1854	11		PDD
Sutphen, male	04	Apr	1854	29 Mar 1854	9		PDD

Name	Notice Date			Death Date	Age	Comment	Paper
Sutton, unknown	16	Aug	1853		2y6m		PDD
Swain, Seth	12	May	1852				PT&C
Swartz, William	11	Aug	1853	30 Jul 1853			DET
Swartzwelder, Elizabeth	16	Apr	1856	05 Apr 1856	20m18d		WPT
Sweeney, male	30	Aug	1854	27 Aug 1854			DET
Sweeny, Ellen	17	Jun	1865		18		PTIMES
Symmes, John Cleves	20	Jun	1829				WT
Sypes, Wm.	06	Aug	1851	17 Jul 1851			PT&C
Tacon, female	03	Dec	1853	22 Nov 1853			PDD
Tagart, Samuel	25	Jun	1864	06 Jun 1864	78		PTIMES
Talbott, Catharine	23	Nov	1854	21 Nov 1854	23		DET
Talbott, male	19	Nov	1851				PT&C
Talfourd, Thomas Noon	07	Apr	1854	12 Mar 1854			PDD
Tallman, Nelson	28	Nov	1855	26 Nov 1855			DET
Tanner, Robert Passmore	09	Feb	1853	25 Jan 1853	10		PT&C
Tarver, Levi	21	May	1853				PDD
Tate, James	20	Aug	1852	30 Jul 1852	25		PI
Tatman, William	02	May	1854	30 Apr 1854			PDD
Taylor, Caleb	03	Mar	1843	25 Feb 1843			TRIB
Taylor, Catharine Mariah	24	Sep	1855	13 Sep 1855	11m		DET
Taylor, female	29	Jul	1865	18 Jul 1865		nee Harrison	PTIMES
Taylor, George Washington	11	Aug	1852	03 Aug 1852	child		PT&C
Taylor, Harriet Wilmina	04	Oct	1853		2m9d		PDD
Taylor, Howard T.	03	Sep	1851				PT&C
Taylor, John S., Jr.	09	Feb	1856	06 Feb 1855	32		DET
Taylor, John S., Jr.	13	Feb	1856	06 Feb 1856	32		WPT
Taylor, Mark P.	02	Aug	1853	01 Aug 1853			DET
Taylor, Mark P.	03	Aug	1853				PT&C
Taylor, Mark P.	30	Jul	1853	26 Jul 1853			PDD
Taylor, Oliver C.	23	Apr	1864		28		PTIMES
Taylor, Richard M.	29	Jul	1865	24 Jul 1865			PTIMES
Taylor, unknown (Capt.)	04	Jun	1864	16 May 1864			PTIMES
Taylor, Zachery (Pres.)	22	Jul	1850				PI
Taylor, Zachery (Pres.)	11, 18	Jul	1850	09 Jul 1850			PT&C
Telford, Andrew	19	Jan	1853	Jan 1853			PT&C
Templeton, female	28	Jan	1860				DET
Tenny, male	19	Jan	1854				PDD
Terrell, female	01	Apr	1851				PT&C
Terry, male	02	Jul	1851				PT&C
Terry, Thomas W. (Lieut.)	12	Mar	1864	03 Mar 1864	23		PTIMES
Terry, William W.	02	Mar	1860	13 Feb 1860	30		DET
Terry, William W.	17	Mar	1860	13 Jan 1860	30		PTIMES
Terry, Wm. W.	25	Feb	1860	13 Feb 1860	30		PTIMES

Name	Notice Date			Death Date	Age	Comment	Paper
Tewksbury, Sarah Wells	30	Jul	1851	22 Jun 1851	26	nee Linn	PT&C
Thomas, Charles F. (Capt.)	21	Nov	1855	24 Oct 1855	83		WPT
Thomas, David	29	Jan	1855		60		DET
Thomas, female	20	Feb	1864		101		PTIMES
Thomas, Henry	16	Jul	1853	12 Jul 1853	10		PDD
Thomas, John	06	Jul	1854		54		PDD
Thomas, John	05	Mar	1851	14 Feb 1851		or alias	PT&C
Thomas, Mary	06	Jan	1854	31 Dec 1853	45		PDD (S)
Thomas, N.W.	02	Apr	1864	27 Mar 1864			PTIMES
Thomas, Rebecca	16	Jul	1855	15 Jul 1855			DET
Thomas, Richard	06	Jun	1853				PDD
Thomason, male	15	Mar	1854				DET
Thompson, Andrew	19	Aug	1854	12 Aug 1854	20		DET
Thompson, Ellen	05	Aug	1859	30 Jul 1859	11m11d		DET
Thompson, Ellen	10	Aug	1859	30 Jul 1859	11m11d		WPT
Thompson, female	04	Nov	1857				WPT
Thompson, George	18	Aug	1854				DET
Thompson, J.C. (Prof.)	20	Feb	1856				WPT
Thompson, J.P.	29	Jun	1854	24 Jun 1854	36		PDD
Thompson, James	14	Aug	1854		50		PDD
Thompson, John J.Y.	26	Aug	1865		60y6m11d		PTIMES
Thompson, John N.	08	Nov	1853	18 Oct 1853	28		DET
Thompson, male	06	Jul	1855	04 Jul 1855			DET
Thompson, male	16	Mar	1854				PDD
Thompson, male	18	Jul	1855	14 Jul 1855			DET
Thompson, male	28	Jun	1854				DET
Thompson, Sarah	19	Jun	1854	18 Jun 1854			DET
Thompson, Sarah	27	Jun	1854	21 Jun 1854	68		PDD (S)
Thompson, Smith (Judge)	29	Dec	1843	18 Dec 1843	77		TRIB
Thompson, unknown	18	Nov	1850		30		PI
Thompson, unknown	18	Jul	1855	14 Jul 1855	child		DET
Thompson, unknown	18	Jul	1855	14 Jul 1855	child		DET
Thompson, unknown	18	Jul	1855	14 Jul 1855	child		DET
Thompson, unknown	29	Oct	1859		70	Negro	DET
Thompson, Washington	04	Jul	1863	29 Jun 1863			PTIMES
	08	Aug	1863				
Thompson, Wm. H.	05, 19	Mar	1851	02 Mar 1851		aka One-Eyed Thompson	PT&C
Thomson, female	23	Jan	1864		43	nee Bartley	PTIMES
Thornburg, Solomon	09	Jan	1855	30 Dec 1854	64		DET
Thornley, John	14	Dec	1854				DET
Thornton, Drusilla	17	Aug	1854	11 Aug 1854	8m27d		DET
Thornton, Giles	19	Aug	1857	Jul 1857	29		WPT

Name	Notice Date			Death Date	Age	Comment	Paper
Thornton, Sally	10	Dec	1851	06 Dec 1851			PT&C
Thoroman, Eliza Jane	19	May	1843	15 May 1843	16		TRIB
Thoroman, Oliver C.	30	Sep	1837	28 Sep 1837	40		STRIB
Thoroman, Rebecca	19	May	1843	13 May 1843	39		TRIB
Thoroman, Sophia	05	Mar	1851	01 Mar 1851	30		PT&C
Thrall, Jesse	05	Jan	1844	16 Dec 1843			TRIB
Thrall, Thomas B. (Dr.)	04	Nov	1858	28 Oct 1858	26		DET
Thrall, Thomas B. (Dr.)	10	Nov	1858	28 Oct 1858	26		WPT
Thurman, James T.	10	Sep	1851	07 Sep 1851	31		PT&C
Thurston, Ira J.	11	Mar	1859				DET
Thurston, male	15	Mar	1859	16 Sep 1858			PTIMES
Tidd, unknown	05	Jan	1854				PDD
Tiffin, Edward P. (M.D.)	08	Oct	1853		31		DET
Tiller, female	27	Feb	1854	24 Feb 1854			PDD
Tillow, Clara	08	Feb	1860	04 Feb 1860	1y7w		WPT
Tillow, John	22	Feb	1862	15 Feb 1862	42		PTIMES
Tillow, Marie Louise	19	Nov	1864	17 Nov 1864	10y8m		PTIMES
Timanus, Jacob	17	Nov	1854				DET
Timanus, Jesse	10	Feb	1858				WPT
Timberman, Andrew	09	Apr	1864		87		PTIMES
Timmonds, Maria Lorenia	19	Apr	1854	17 Apr 1854	10m		DET
Tithe, William	19	Nov	1864				PTIMES
Tizzard, Samuel	30	May	1844	19 May 1844	57		TRIB
Tobin, Mary Ann	28	Nov	1859	26 Nov 1859	74		DET
Tobin, Mary Ann	30	Nov	1859	26 Nov 1859	74		WPT
Todleben, unk. (Gen.)	13	Aug	1855				DET
Toler, female	11	Feb	1860				DET
Tolley, Tho.	02	Jun	1854	31 May 1854			DET
Tolley, Thomas	02	Jun	1854	31 May 1854			PDD
Tomkins, Samuel	27	Jan	1843	04 Jan 1843			TRIB
Tomlinson, Hurd	17	Sep	1855	16 Sep 1855	7		DET
Tomlinson, L.E.	11	Jun	1856	05 Jun 1856			WPT
Tomlinson, unk. (Dr.)	21	May	1853	14 May 1853			PDD
	13	Jul	1853				
Tomlinson, unknown (Dr.)	25	May	1853	14 May 1853			PT&C
Tompkins, Harriet	15	Sep	1859				DET
Tompkins, Harriet	20	Sep	1859				PTIMES
Tompkins, Harriet	21	Sep	1859				WPT
Tompkins, J. Lewis	05	Nov	1860	05 Nov 1860	24		DET
Tompkins, male	10	Nov	1860	03 Nov 1860	24		PTIMES
Toner, male	21	Jun	1853	16 Jun 1853	6		PDD
Tope, John	07	Jun	1854	26 May 1854			DET
Torrey, James (Col.)	21	May	1853	26 Apr 1953			PDD
Touro, Judah	07	Feb	1854	18 Jan 1854			DET
Tracy, Charles Oscar	19	Oct	1855	19 Oct 1855	51		DET

Name	Notice Date			Death Date	Age	Comment	Paper
Tracy, Charles Oscar	19	Oct	1855	19 Oct 1855	51		OP
Tracy, Daniel	15	Jan	1855				DET
Tracy, Juliette	13	Apr	1859	24 Mar 1859	10		WPT
Tracy, male	29	Jun	1855	16 Jun 1855			DET
Tracy, Margaret	19	Aug	1854		14		DET
Tracy, Percus	23, 30	Jun	1852	17 Jun 1852	13		PT&C
Tracy, Persis	19	May	1857	03 May 1857	54		DET
Tracy, Persis	20	May	1857	03 May 1857	54		WPT
Tracy, V.D.L.	06	Aug	1860	04 Aug 1860	31		DET
Tracy, Van Der Lyn	11	Aug	1860	04 Aug 1860	31		PTIMES
Traverse, Arthur	14	Jan	1852		80		PT&C
Trayer, Andrew H.	24	Jan	1854	20 Jan 1854			PDD
Tressler, George	09	Jun	1860	06 Jun 1860	2y2m		PTIMES
Trice, John R.	15	Mar	1854				DET
Trigg, William (Major)	23	Jan	1838	11 Jan 1838			STRIB
Triggs, Catharine	10	May	1853	28 Apr 1853	10		PDD (S)
Trimble, Charles W. (Lieut.)	15	Nov	1862				PTIMES
Tripp, George	07	May	1864				PTIMES
Trueman, Jas.	09	Feb	1855	17 Jan 1855			DET
Trumball, John (Col.)	24	Nov	1843	10 Nov 1843	87		TRIB
Trumbo, Sarah Eugenia	14	Jan	1860	05 Jan 1860	2m22d		PTIMES
Tucker, Levi (Rev.)	26	Aug	1853	20 Aug 1853			DET
Tucker, unknown	08	Aug	1854		child		DET
Tuller, Achilles	03	May	1859	27 Apr 1859			PTIMES
Turley, John A.	20	May	1859	20 May 1859			DET
Turley, John A.	25	May	1859	20 May 1859	infant		WPT
Turley, unknown	24	May	1859	20 May 1859	infant		PTIMES
Turnball, male	07	Dec	1853	03 Dec 1853			PDD
Turner, Charles O.	25	Aug	1852	08 Jul 1852			PT&C
Turner, D.	30	Dec	1850				PI
Turner, James B., Sr.	29	Dec	1860	09 Dec 1860	70		PTIMES
Turner, John R.	19	Oct	1858	15 Oct 1858	71		PTIMES
Turner, John R.	27	Oct	1858				WPT
Turner, Vianna P.	14	Jul	1843	12 Jul 1843			TRIB
Turner, William M'Kendree	02	Sep	1825	31 Aug 1825	9		PG&LA
Turo, Juda	05	Jun	1854				DET
Tuttle, Libbins	11	Feb	1865				PTIMES
Tweedle, James	22	Dec	1852				PT&C
Tyler, Myrick	27	Jun	1860	25 Jun 1860		Slave	WPT
Tyler, unknown	03	Apr	1854		9		PDD
Tyler, unknown	03	Apr	1854				PDD
Tyler, unknown	03	Apr	1854				PDD
Tyler, unknown	03	Apr	1854				PDD

Name	Notice Date			Death Date	Age	Comment	Paper
Tyler, unknown	03	Apr	1854				PDD
Tyler, unknown	03	Apr	1854				PDD
Tyler, unknown	03	Apr	1854				PDD
Tyndale, unk. (Lieut.)	29	Oct	1864	Oct 1864			PTIMES
	20	May	1865				
Tyrrell, Hester Sarah	20	Jul	1855	16 Jul 1855	9m6d		DET
Ufford, Catharine	17	Sep	1855	11 Sep 1855	44	nee Burr	DET
Ujhazi, female	12	Nov	1851	11 Nov 1851			PT&C
Upshur, A.P. (Hon.)	08	Mar	1844	28 Feb 1844			TRIB
Utt, William	18	Oct	1862				PTIMES
Valdenar, Lycurgas C.	06	Feb	1864				PTIMES
Vallandigham, Rebecca	16	Jul	1864	09 Jul 1864			PTIMES
Van Allen, Anna	19	Jan	1859	14 Jan 1859	10		WPT
Van Buren, unk. (Capt.)	22	Aug	1854				PDD
Van Horn, unknown	15	Mar	1859		child		DET
Van Horn, unknown	16	Mar	1859				WPT
Van Krene, Maria	02	Oct	1855	25 Sep 1855			DET
Van Pelt, female	08	Aug	1853	05 Aug 1853			DET
Van Welsh, Susan	15, 17	Sep	1855	04 Sep 1855	26	nee Salter	DET
Vance, Elizabeth	22	Dec	1860	21 Dec 1860	20y1m20d	nee Shelleig	PTIMES
Vance, Elizabeth	26	Dec	1860	21 Dec 1860	20y1m20d	nee Shelleig	WPT
Vance, unknown	01	Sep	1852	24 Aug 1852		ex-Gov.	PT&C
Vanderberg, Jas.	31	Oct	1844	Oct 1844			TRIB
Vandwater, female	11	May	1853				PDD
Vanhorn, Bernard	10	Feb	1854	4 Feb 1854	87		DET
Vanmeter, female	04	Feb	1854				DET
Vann, David (Capt.)	31	Oct	1844	Oct 1844			TRIB
	07	Nov	1844				
Varner, C.M.	22	Sep	1843	18 Sep 1843			TRIB
Varner, Charles S.	28	Nov	1851	24 Nov 1851	8m		PI
Vaughan, male	04	Jul	1850	30 Jun 1850			PT&C
Vaustavoren, Wm.	23	Jul	1856	Jul 1856			WPT
Veach, Sylvester	26	Aug	1850	23 Aug 1850			PI
Verplanck, female	17	Nov	1852		15		PT&C
Vickery, male	12	Feb	1851				PT&C
Vigus, Benjamin F.	13	Apr	1860'	12 Apr 1860	38		DET
Vigus, Franklin	14	Apr	1860	11 Apr 1860			PTIMES
Vigus, George Oscar	22	Sep	1843	19 Sep 1843	1y5m		TRIB
Vigus, Rachel	12	Jan	1858	03 Jan 1858	30		PSOT
Vigus, Rachel	12	Jan	1858	03 Jan 1858	30		DET
Vigus, Sylvester Warren	11	Aug	1854	11 Aug 1854	18		DET
Vigus, Sylvester Warren	12	Aug	1854	11 Aug 1854	18		PDD
Vildabee, female	30	Aug	1854	27 Aug 1854			DET
Vildabee, unknown	30	Aug	1854	27 Aug 1854	child		DET

Name	Notice Date			Death Date	Age	Comment	Paper
Vildabee, unknown	30	Aug	1854	27 Aug 1854	child		DET
Vildabee, unknown	30	Aug	1854	27 Aug 1854	child		DET
Vildabee, unknown	30	Aug	1854	27 Aug 1854	child		DET
Voglesong, William (Dr.)	20	Jul	1854	19 Jul 1854	35		DET
Voglesong, Wm. (Dr.)	21	Jul	1854	19 Jul 1854	35		PDD
Voorhes, Abraham	10	Mar	1854		31		PDD
Voorhes, Eliza Ann	07	Jun	1853	4 Jun 1853			DET
Voorhes, Eliza Ann	08	Jun	1853	04 Jun 1853	28		PT&C (S)
Vorhees, Garrett	21	Dec	1861	14 Dec 1861			PTIMES
Wadleigh, male	23	Jul	1851	15 Jul 1851			PT&C
Wado, John W.	23	Feb	1853				PT&C
Wadsworth, Adna A.	24	Dec	1853	20 Dec 1853	59		DET
Wadsworth, unk. (Gen.)	14	May	1864				PTIMES
Waggaman, Geo. A. (Hon.)	14	Apr	1843	23 Mar 1843			TRIB
Waggener, Chas. P.	07	Jun	1853	03 Jun 1853	21		PDD
Waggoner, D.	09	Jun	1860	Jun 1860			PTIMES
Wainright, unk. (Bishop)	28	Sep	1854				PDD
Wainwright, (Bishop)	23	Sep	1854	21 Sep 1854	61		DET
Wait, Asa	12	Jul	1827	07 Jun 1827	80		WT
Wakeman, Margaret	20	Jul	1826	15 Jul 1826	24		WT
Walderen, B.	09	Aug	1855				DET
Wales, Jonathan	08	Feb	1859				PTIMES
Walke, Anthony (Hon.)	01	Apr	1865	20 Mar 1865	82		PTIMES
Walker, John W.	11	Feb	1860				PTIMES
Walker, Old Mother	09	Feb	1855				DET
Walker, Samuel	11	Jan	1832	04 Jan 1832			PC
Walker, William	01	Feb	1862	08 Jan 1862			PTIMES
Walker, William (Rev.)	18	Apr	1826	06 Apr 1826			WT
Wall, Alexander A.	21	Jun	1853				DET
Wall, Alexander A.	22	Jun	1853				PT&C
Wall, Wm. (Maj.)	10	Dec	1856	17 Nov 1856			WPT
Wallace (or Wallis), Philip	31	Oct	1844	Oct 1844			TRIB
	07	Nov	1844				
Wallace, John	17	Oct	1860		20		DET
Waller, William	27	Nov	1854				DET
Walsh, Mike	22	Mar	1859	Mar 1859			PTIMES
Walsham, unk. (Lieut.)	26	Oct	1854				DET
Walsham, unk. (Lieut.)	27	Oct	1854				PDD
Ward, Alex	30	Oct	1854				DET
Ward, female	30	Oct	1854				DET
Ward, Frank	26	Jan	1853	21 Jan 1853			PT&C
Ward, J.W.	02	Jul	1856				WPT
Ward, Nahum	16	Jun	1860	Jun 1860			PTIMES
Ward, unknown	18	Apr	1859	14 Apr 1859	child		DET

Name	Notice Date			Death Date	Age	Comment	Paper
Ward, unknown	27	Jun	1854	13 Jun 1854	2		PDD (S)
Ward, unknown	30	Oct	1854		child		DET
Ward, unknown	30	Oct	1854		child		DET
Ward, unknown	30	Oct	1854		child		DET
Ward, unknown	30	Oct	1854		child		DET
Ward, unknown	30	Oct	1854		child		DET
Ward, unknown	30	Oct	1854		child		DET
Ward, unknown	30	Oct	1854		child		DET
Ware, female	21	May	1853	11 May 1853			PDD
Ware, male	21	May	1853	11 May 1853			PDD
Warner, male	30	Jun	1854	17 Jun 1854			PDD
Warner, Nathaniel S.	15	Aug	1850	13 Aug 1850			PT&C
Warner, Nathaniel S.	19	Aug	1850	13 Aug 1850			PI
Warner, Robert Waylard	20	Sep	1854	17 Sep 1854	8m17d		DET
Warren, James	13	Oct	1852	05 Oct 1852			PT&C
Warren, Thaddeus	30	Nov	1853				DET
Warring, Mary	26	Jan	1861	21 Jan 1861	70		PTIMES
Washington, Hannah	11	Nov	1865	28 Oct 1865	42y3m1d		PTIMES
Washington, unk. (Col.)	24	Jan	1854				PDD
Waterman, Charles	14	Jan	1852	31 Dec 1851			PT&C
Waters, unknown	19	Oct	1858				PTIMES
Watkins, Ida	23	Mar	1855	22 Mar 1855	4		DET
Watkins, Nancy	05	Mar	1859	27 Feb 1859	88		DET
Watkins, Nancy	08	Mar	1859	27 Feb 1859	88		PTIMES
Watkins, Nancy	09	Mar	1859	27 Feb 1859	88		WPT
Watkins, Sarah	08	Sep	1851	3 Sep 1851	18		PI
Watkins, Sarah	10	Sep	1851	03 Sep 1851	18		PT&C
Watkins, Thomas	19	Nov	1864	15 Nov 1864	86		PTIMES
Watson, male	03	Sep	1857	29 Aug 1857			WPT
Watson, Rezin W.	05	Jul	1854				DET
Watt, female	20	Aug	1851				PT&C
Watt, Wm.	07	Nov	1844	Oct 1844			TRIB
Watterson, Charles	20	Jul	1854				DET
Watterson, Charles	21	Jul	1854				PDD
Watterson, female	20	Jul	1854				DET
Watterson, female	21	Jul	1854				PDD
Wayne, Isaac (Col.)	11	Nov	1852		83		PT&C
Ways, William	27	Dec	1854				DET
Wear, William	15	Jul	1850	11 Jul 1850	45		PI
Weatherwax, male	17	Nov	1859	17 Nov 1859	14		DET
Weatherwax, male	19	Nov	1859	17 Nov 1859	child		PTIMES
Weaver, George	13	Jun	1863				PTIMES
Weaver, Samuel	29	Dec	1843				TRIB
Webb, Charley	12	Mar	1851	06 Mar 1851			PT&C
Webb, male	23	Nov	1854				DET

Name	Notice Date			Death Date	Age	Comment	Paper
Webber, female	21	Apr	1859	16 Apr 1859			DET
Webber, Martin	21	Apr	1859	16 Apr 1859			DET
Weber, John H. (Capt.)	29	Mar	1859	07 Mar 1859	80		PTIMES
Webster, Daniel	03	Nov	1852				PT&C
Webster, female	04	Jun	1851	28 Feb 1851			PT&C
Webster, female	05, 12, 19	Mar	1851	28 Feb 1851			PT&C
Webster, Hannah	27	Dec	1862		18		PTIMES
Webster, Noah (L.L.D.)	09	Jun	1843	28 May 1843			TRIB
Webster, Peter	21	Jun	1854	16 Jun 1854			DET
Webster, Peter	22	Jun	1854		69		PDD
Webster, Simon C.	09	Mar	1854	21 Feb 1854	20		PDD
Wecks, Henry	16	Jun	1855				DET
Wecks, male	16	Jun	1855		10		DET
Weimer, Andrew	30	Jul	1851	23 Jul 1851			PT&C
Weize (or Wise, male)	28	Feb	1860		6		DET
Welch, D.A.	10	May	1853	06 May 1853			PDD
Welch, female	04	Feb	1854	25 Jan 1854			DET
Welch, male	10	Sep	1853	05 Sep 1853	8		DET
Welch, male	10	Sep	1853	05 Sep 1853	18		DET
Welch, Rufus (Gen.)	12	Jan	1854	31 Dec 1853			PDD
Welch, Thomas	10	Feb	1854	04 Feb 1854			PDD
Welde, female	22	Aug	1850	19 Aug 1850			PT&C
Welde, female	26	Aug	1850	19 Aug 1850			PI
Wells, Harriet	28	Oct	1865				PTIMES
Wells, Horace (Esq.)	21, 28	May	1851	16 May 1851			PT&C
Wells, Samuel	25	Feb	1860		104		PTIMES
Wells, William	25	Aug	1854	20 Aug 1854			PDD
Welsh, Ellen	05	Jan	1861				PTIMES
Welsh, J.	10	Jun	1854	07 Jun 1854			DET
Welsh, John	14	May	1853				PDD
Welty, Joseph	11	Nov	1852		16-18		PT&C
Wertz, Wm. Ambrose	14	Jul	1851	10 Jul 1851	11		PI
Wesley, Georgiana Harrison	17	Feb	1843	14 Feb 1843	1y10m12d		TRIB
West, Benjamin	18	May	1820	10 Mar 1820	82		STEL
Westfall, Wilson P.	12	Dec	1863	Nov 1863			PTIMES
Westland, Joseph M.	14	May	1851	07 May 1851			PT&C
Weston, Michael	15	Jun	1854	12 Jun 1854			DET
Westphell, Elizabeth	09	Jun	1860	Jun 1860			PTIMES
Westphell, G.C.	09	Jun	1860	Jun 1860			PTIMES
Westphell, unknown	09	Jun	1860	Jun 1860		child	PTIMES
Whaley, Luke	06	Apr	1855				DET
Wheat, male (Rev.)	02	Dec	1854				DET
Wheelan, Charles	08	Feb	1854				DET

Deaths

Name	Notice Date			Death Date	Age	Comment	Paper
Wheeler, Charles (Capt.)	23	Feb	1860	22 Feb 1860			DET
Wheeler, female	23	Jul	1851				PT&C
Wheeler, J.F.	29	Oct	1851	19 Oct 1851	28		PT&C
Wheeler, Levi	24	Nov	1852				PT&C
Wheeler, Lydia	09	Dec	1818		18	nee Stratton	PGAZ
Wheeler, Samuel	02	Dec	1831	08 Nov 1831	37		PC&WT
Wheeler, William	02	May	1850	26 Apr 1850			PT&C
Wheeler, William	29	Apr	1850	26 Apr 1850			PI
Wheeler, Wyatt C.	28	Oct	1850	18 Oct 1850			PI
Wheeler, Wyatt C.	31	Oct	1850	18 Oct 1850			PT&C
Whetstone, Pete	29	Dec	1843	05 Dec 1843	60		TRIB
Whipple, Amiel W. (Gen.)	30	May	1863		45		PTIMES
Whistler, Henry	22	Nov	1854	20 Nov 1854			DET
Whistler, Josiah	22	Nov	1854	20 Nov 1854			DET
Whitaker, male	15	Oct	1851				PT&C
Whitaker, Wm. H.	17	Apr	1855				DET
White, Anna	11	Nov	1865	06 Nov 1865	22		PTIMES
White, Ben T.	02	May	1860	24 Apr 1860			WPT
White, Ben T.	25	Apr	1860	24 Apr 1860			DET
White, Charles	08	Sep	1851	6 Sep 1851	20		PI
White, Charles	10	Sep	1851	06 Sep 1851	20		PT&C
White, female	09	Jul	1851	19 Jun 1851			PT&C
White, female	30	Oct	1854				DET
White, John	28	May	1864	May 1864			PTIMES
White, John, Sr.	08	Jan	1846	07 Jan 1846			TRIB
White, Margerite	13	Mar	1855	27 Jan 1855	82		DET (S)
White, Martha	24	Feb	1858				WPT
White, Mary E.	14	Sep	1860	04 Sep 1860	34		DET
White, Mary S.	02	Jun	1854		14m		PDD
White, Peyton	28	Aug	1854				PDD
White, Samuel (Esq.)	01	Aug	1844		32		TRIB
White, unknown	09	Jun	1860	Jun 1860	child		PTIMES
White, unknown	13	Mar	1855	22 Jan 1855	6		DET (S)
White, W.	07	Jan	1852				PT&C
Whiteman, Herman	09	Jun	1860	Jun 1860			PTIMES
Whiting, Susan	25	Jan	1859	17 Jan 1859			PTIMES
Whitman, Mahala	16	Mar	1858				DET
Whitney, Ruluff	13	Aug	1824	07 Aug 1824	21		PG&LA
Whittaker, J.T.	31	Dec	1851				PT&C
Whittemore, male	17	Nov	1852	11 Nov 1852			PT&C
Whittlesey, Elisha (Hon.)	17	Jan	1863	14 Jan 1863	80		PTIMES
Wibber, Starns	01	Dec	1853	15 Nov 1853			PDD
Wickham, female	07	Jun	1854				DET
Wickham, James	07	Jun	1854				DET

Name	Notice Date			Death Date	Age	Comment	Paper
Wickliffe, Margaret	26	Dec	1863	18 Dec 1863			PTIMES
Wicks, female	30	Aug	1854	27 Aug 1854			DET
Wighton, female	14	Jul	1843				TRIB
Wighton, unknown	14	Jul	1843	08 Jul 1843	child		TRIB
Wighton, unknown	14	Jul	1843	08 Jul 1843	child		TRIB
Wighton, unknown	14	Jul	1843	08 Jul 1843	child		TRIB
Wighton, unknown	14	Jul	1843	08 Jul 1843	child		TRIB
Wighton, unknown	14	Jul	1843	08 Jul 1843	child		TRIB
Wilbur, Augustus	02	Mar	1854		45		PDD
Wilbur, female	02	Mar	1854				PDD
Wilcox, Benjamin	22	Aug	1850				PT&C
Wilcox, female	22	Aug	1850				PT&C
Wilcox, Wm.	03	Jun	1854	31 May 1854			DET
Wilcoxin, Levi	31	Dec	1853	21 Dec 1853			DET
Wilcoxin, Resin	31	Dec	1853	23 Dec 1853			DET
Wilde, Andrew	03	Jun	1850	3 Jun 1850	18		PI
Wilde, Andrew	06	Jun	1850	03 Jun 1850	18		PT&C
Wilder, O.	30	Apr	1855				DET
Wiley, John	04	Jun	1864				PTIMES
Wilhite, male	11	Apr	1854		1		PDD
Wilkins, John R.	30	Jul	1864	20 Jul 1864			PTIMES
Wilkins, Maria	29	Jun	1853				PT&C
Wilkins, Mary	24	Jun	1853	19 Jun 1853			PDD
Wilkinson, H.L. (Esq.)	12	Nov	1851				PT&C
Will, Jacob	08	Feb	1854				PDD
Willard, female	08	Apr	1854	04 Apr 1854			PDD
Willard, J.O.	22	May	1855	19 May 1855			DET
Willett, John	03	Jun	1854	23 May 1854	85		DET
Willfong, George D.	01	Feb	1862	10 Dec 1861			PTIMES
Williams, Allen	30	May	1844	14 May 1844	5w		TRIB
Williams, Charles Oscar	26	Mar	1858	25 Mar 1858	2y20d		DET
Williams, Elisha	27	Jun	1854	14 Jun 1854	2		PDD (S)
Williams, Enoch (Capt.)	11	Aug	1852		30		PT&C
Williams, female	27	Jun	1860	25 Jun 1860			WPT
Williams, Isham	20	Jun	1854	29 May 1854			DET
Williams, J.H.	06	Jun	1863	16 May 1863			PTIMES
Williams, James	23	May	1859	19 May 1859			DET
Williams, James	24	Mar	1852	16 Mar 1852			PT&C
Williams, James	29	Dec	1843				TRIB
Williams, John	18	Nov	1865	13 Nov 1865			PTIMES
Williams, Joseph	19	Feb	1855				DET
Williams, male	31	Oct	1863	25 Oct 1863	child		PTIMES
Williams, Mary Elizabeth	08	Mar	1844	29 Feb 1844	8y11m2d		TRIB
Williams, Robert Alston	25	Sep	1858	21 Sep 1858	14m26d		DET
Williams, Thomas	30	Jun	1855	30 Jun 1855	16		DET

Deaths

Name	Notice Date			Death Date	Age	Comment	Paper
Williamson, Henry H. (Corp.)	18	Oct	1862				PTIMES
Williamson, James	03	Mar	1826		82		WT
Williamson, John Oliver	25	Feb	1865	23 Feb 1865	10		PTIMES
Willis, Mary E.	30	Aug	1854	26 Aug 1854	2y2m17d	da. of Welsh	DET
Willis, Wm. W.	12	Jan	1854	Nov 1853			PDD
Wilmarth, Thomas	24	Feb	1860		102		DET
Wilson, Benjamin	12	May	1858				WPT
Wilson, Clarinda	06	May	1853	27 Apr 1853	25		PDD
Wilson, Geo.	20	Apr	1853	02 Apr 1853			PT&C
Wilson, Harry	02	Nov	1860	02 Nov 1860	30		DET
Wilson, J.O.	23	Jul	1851				PT&C
Wilson, James	26	Jan	1854				PDD
Wilson, James	30	May	1863				PTIMES
Wilson, Jessie	03	Apr	1854	15 Mar 1854			PDD
Wilson, John	04	Jun	1851	13 May 1851			PT&C
Wilson, male	23	Nov	1854				DET
Wilson, male	30	Jun	1854	17 Jun 1854			PDD
Wilson, Mary	25	Aug	1858	24 Aug 1858	31		DET
Wilson, Patrick	10	Oct	1863				PTIMES
Wilson, Samuel	17	Aug	1854			Uncle Sam	PDD
Wilson, Samuel	19	Jan	1855	17 Jan 1855			DET
Wilson, Sarah	07	Mar	1854	28 Feb 1854	18		PDD (S)
Wilson, unknown	08	Apr	1854		child		PDD
Wilson, unknown	25	Aug	1858	24 Aug 1858	1d		DET
Wilson, William H.	14	Jan	1865	15 Aug 1864	25		PTIMES
Wiltshire, Frank	01	Jul	1854	27 Jun 1854	11		PDD
Wiltshire, Frank	24	Jun	1854	20 Jun 1854	11		DET
Winans, Thos. W.	01	Apr	1854				PDD
Winch, female	02	Jun	1852	21 May 1852	8		PT&C
Winchell, male	21	Feb	1863				PTIMES
Winfough, Alonzo	04	Jan	1856	22 Dec 1855	infant		DET
Wingate, female	22	Aug	1853				DET
Winn, unknown (Capt.)	26	Oct	1854				DET
Winn, unknown (Capt.)	27	Oct	1854				PDD
Winter, Edward M'Gee	28, 29	Sep	1854	26 Sep 1854	7		DET
Winters, Charles	21	Oct	1853				DET
Winters, O.	17	Aug	1854	03 Aug 1854	30		DET (S)
Wise (or Weize), male	03	Mar	1860		6		PTIMES
Wise, A.	27	Sep	1854	17 Sep 1854	30		DET (S)
Wise, A.	27	Sep	1854	17 Sep 1854	30		PDD (S)
Wisecup, female	21	Feb	1859				DET
Wisecup, Lydia	01	Mar	1859	Feb 1859			PTIMES
Wisner, female	25	Feb	1852				PT&C

Name	Notice Date			Death Date	Age	Comment	Paper
Witherow, Wm.	13	Mar	1855	13 Feb 1855	35		DET (S)
Withers, George	10	Jan	1854				PDD
Withers, unknown	06	Dec	1853	28 Nov 1853	2y		PDD (S)
Withers, unknown	11	Jan	1854	05 Jan 1854			DET
Witherspoon, Alexander S.	26	May	1854	04 May 1854			PDD
Wolfe, Adolf (Corporal)	04	Oct	1862	17 Sep 1862			PTIMES
Wolfe, Henry F. (Sergeant)	04	Oct	1862	21 Sep 1862	21		PTIMES
Wolfe, Wm. V.	07	May	1852	29 Apr 1852	30		PI
Wonderly, unknown	20	Feb	1856		child		DET
Wood, Benjamin	06	Aug	1824	31 Jul 1824	56		PG&LA
Wood, Emily	18	Jan	1855	18 Jan 1855	8		DET
Wood, French	05	Sep	1854				PDD
Wood, Gilbert J.	20	Oct	1843	22 Sep 1843	30		TRIB
Wood, Phineas T.	10	Nov	1860	03 Nov 1860			PTIMES
Wood, William	03	Aug	1820	14 Jun 1820	23		STEL
Wood, Wilson	01	Feb	1862	30 Nov 1861			PTIMES
Woodall, John R.	17	Nov	1858				WPT
Woodbridge, Dudley Henry	25	Jul	1844	15 Jul 1844	11y1m		TRIB
Woodbury, male	19	May	1854		6		PDD
Woodford, Seth	14	Apr	1860				DET
Woodhouse, female	10	Dec	1859			nee Orcutt	PTIMES
Woods, female	13	Aug	1855				DET
Woods, John	02	Aug	1855	30 Jul 1855			DET
Woods, unknown	13	Aug	1855		child		DET
Woods, unknown	13	Aug	1855		child		DET
Woods, unknown	13	Aug	1855		child		DET
Woods, unknown	13	Aug	1855		child		DET
Woolsey, female	17	Aug	1854	15 Aug 1854			DET
Worcester, Joseph	11	Nov	1865				PTIMES
Work, Charles D.	15	Aug	1853		3		PDD
Work, F.C.	30	Jun	1852	24 Jun 1852			PT&C
Work, Felicity C.	02	Jul	1852				PI
Work, unknown	23	Aug	1853	14 Aug 1853	27m		PDD
Workman, Mary A.	26	Jun	1854			nee Daily	DET
Worthington, female	06	Sep	1859	02 Sep 1859			DET
Worthington, James Chaytor	08	Sep	1857	29 Aug 1857	32		PSOT
Worthington, James Chaytor (M.D.)	09	Sep	1857	29 Aug 1857	32		WPT
Worthington, Thomas	12	Jul	1827	20 Jun 1827	45		WT
Worthington, unk. (Lieut.)	26	Oct	1854				DET
Worthington, unk. (Lieut.)	27	Oct	1854				PDD
Worthington, William D.	04	Nov	1850	28 Oct 1850			PI

Deaths

Name	Notice Date			Death Date	Age	Comment	Paper
Woster, Adam	07	Oct	1850	5 Oct 1850	32		PI
Wouge, unknown	13	Mar	1855	23 Jan 1855	9m		DET (S)
Wright, Agust J.	14	Jan	1852	31 Dec 1851			PT&C
Wright, male	19	Jan	1844	04 Jan 1844			TRIB
Wright, R. Jennings	26	Sep	1853	19 Sep 1853			DET
Wright, unknown	19	Jan	1844	04 Jan 1844	child		TRIB
Wright, unknown	19	Jan	1844	04 Jan 1844	child		TRIB
Wright, unknown (Dr.)	09	Feb	1859				WPT
Wroten, Nathan	08	Jul	1854	04 Jul 1854			PDD
Wyckoff, Cornelius	02	Aug	1854				DET
Wyckoff, Cornelius	03	Aug	1854	29 Jul 1854			PDD
Wyeth, Isabella	09	May	1863			nee Wait	PTIMES
Wymer, female	29	Jul	1850	27 Jul 1850			PI
Wynn, William H.	12	Jun	1855				DET
Yale, Benjamin (Dr.)	11	May	1853		102y10m3d		PT&C
Yates, R.W.	19	Nov	1864				PTIMES
Yaunot, Charles	01	Mar	1854	24 Feb 1854			PDD
Yeaman, Samuel Hempstead	04	Aug	1851	02 Aug 1851			PI
Yeaman, Samuel Hempstead	06	Aug	1851	02 Aug 1851			PT&C
Yellow Wolf	11	Apr	1863			Indian	PTIMES
Yerger, Peter	24	Aug	1853				DET
Yoakem, Catherine	10	May	1844	08 Apr 1844	67y6m4d	nee Harness	TRIB
Yoakley, Susan R.	16	Aug	1862	14 Aug 1862	34		PTIMES
Yokiam, Caroline	19	May	1855	26 Mar 1855	15		DET
Yokiam, Drucilla	19	May	1855	26 Mar 1855	11		DET
Yokiam, Harriet R.	19	May	1855	26 Mar 1855	2		DET
Yokiam, Nancy Ellen	19	May	1855	26 Mar 1855	4m		DET
Yokiam, Susanna	19	May	1855	26 Mar 1855	9		DET
Yost, unknown	13	Mar	1855	09 Feb 1855	2		DET (S)
Young, Alex. (Rev.)	23	Mar	1854	16 Mar 1854			PDD
Young, Daniel	31	Mar	1858	16 Mar 1858	19		WPT
Young, David	07	Dec	1858	15 Nov 1858			PTIMES
Young, female	17	Aug	1853	12 Aug 1853			DET
Young, female	20	Aug	1853				PDD
Young, Henderson (Hon.)	04	Aug	1854	23 Jul 1854			DET
Young, Jacob (Rev.)	04	Oct	1859	16 Sep 1859	83		PTIMES
Young, John George	21	Jun	1853				DET
Young, John George	22	Jun	1853				PT&C
Young, Johnston	30	Jul	1864	20 Jul 1864			PTIMES
Young, male	17	Aug	1853	12 Aug 1853	14		DET
Young, male	20	Aug	1853		14		PDD
Young, Mary	06	Aug	1851				PT&C
Young, Mary	16	Jul	1851				PT&C

Name	Notice Date			Death Date	Age	Comment	Paper
Young, Parker Y.	06	Aug	1851				PT&C
Young, Peter	01	Feb	1862	25 Dec 1861			PTIMES
Young, W. (Sir) (Capt.)	26	Oct	1854				DET
Young, W. (Sir) (Capt.)	27	Oct	1854				PDD
Yumbleston, Robert	09	May	1855	01 May 1855	4w		DET (S)
Zeigler, Peter	10	Nov	1860		15		PTIMES
Zeller, unknown (Capt.)	10	Jul	1854	07 Jul 1854			PDD

A RATIONAL REASON FOR MARRYING—"How could you do so imprudent a thing," said a curate to a very poor Taffy; "What reason could you have for marrying a girl so completely steeped in poverty as yourself, and both without the prospect of the slightest provision?" "Why, sir," replied the Benedict, "we had a very good reason. We had a blanket a piece, and as the cold winter weather was coming on, we thought that putting them together would be warmer."

—*Portsmouth Tribune & Clipper*
8 Jun 1853

Marriages (Grooms)

Name (Groom)	Name (Bride)	Notice Date	Marriage Date	Paper
Abbey, Selden	Russell, Katharine	08 Nov 1853	26 Oct 1853	DET
Abbott, Orrin H.	McManmes, Angeline	01 Oct 1852	29 Sep 1852	PI
Adair, Smilie R.	Whitcomb, Lucy C.	16 Sep 1850	02 Sep 1850	PI
Adair, Smilie R.	Whitcomb, Lucy C.	19 Sep 1850	02 Sep 1850	PT&C
Adams, Calvin	Moore, Letitia	16 Feb 1855	15 Feb 1855	DET
Adams, J.Q.	Nicholson, Carrie C.	06 Apr 1859		DET
Adams, John C.	Means, Mary A.	11 Jun 1853		DET
Adams, John C. (Esq.)	Means, Mary A.	15 Jun 1853	14 Jun 1853	PT&C
Albert, Rudolph	Smith, Cate	20 Aug 1856	06 Aug 1856	WPT
Aldrich, Asa, Jr.	Turner, Martha J.	04 Nov 1837	01 Nov 1837	STRIB
Alexander, J. W.	Drake, Angeline	11 Jun 1856	29 May 1856	WPT
Allemang, Erl	Gregory, Isabella	11 Nov 1865	06 Nov 1865	PTIMES
Allen, David	Fisher, Lucretia	15 Feb 1859	13 Feb 1859	PTIMES
Allen, Edward H.	Beecher, Agnes	19 Aug 1859	30 Jul 1859	DET
Allen, Edward H.	Beecher, Agnes	24 Aug 1859	30 Jul 1859	WPT
Allen, Isaac B.	Gaither, Eliza W.	17 Feb 1857	05 Feb 1857	PSOT
Allen, John	Cox, Mary	03 Dec 1856	01 Nov 1856	WPT
Allen, W.	Llocumb, P.S.(nee Wait)	10 Apr 1855	05 Apr 1855	DET
Altiff, Adam	Shatel, Mary	16 Nov 1855	14 Nov 1855	DET
Anderson, Abner	Haynes, Elizabeth	19 Nov 1855	17 Nov 1855	DET
Anderson, Abner	Haynes, Elizabeth	21 Nov 1855	17 Nov 1855	WPT
Anderson, Robert	Caughren, Louisa	21 Feb 1854	12 Feb 1854	PDD
Andrew, unk.(Rev.Bishop)	Childers, female (Mrs.)	23 Dec 1854	22 Nov 1854	DET
Andrews, William	Russell, Sarah B.	10 Jun 1852	03 Jun 1852	PI
Apple, Phillip	Bender, Catharine	09 May 1848	04 May 1848	DENQ
Appler, W.C. (Capt.)	Gilbert, Emma	21 Sep 1858		PSOT
Appler, Washington C. (Capt.)	Gilbert, Mary Emma	15 Sep 1858	13 Sep 1858	WPT
Archbold, David	Williams, Rebecca	13 May 1850	04 May 1850	PI
Archbold, David	Williams, Rebecca	09 May 1850	04 May 1850	PT&C
Arnold, Wart	Brazee, Mary	14 Feb 1854	09 Feb 1854	DET
Arthur, James S.	Richardson, Hester	03 Feb 1860	02 Feb 1860	DET
Arthur, James S.	Richardson, Hester	08 Feb 1860	02 Feb 1860	WPT
Ashton, Joseph	Yeamons, Elisa Ann	07 May 1855	30 Apr 1855	DET
Atkinson, James W.	Nixon, Rachel Ann	28 Nov 1853	17 Nov 1853	DET
Austill, George L.	Conally, Ellen	14 Jan 1854	11 Jan 1854	DET
Austin, Lycurgus C.	Worthington, Nancy	24 Jan 1854	12 Jan 1854	DET

Marriages (Grooms)

Name (Groom)	Name (Bride)	Notice Date	Marriage Date	Paper
Baesler, Frederick	Pelhene, Elizabeth	20 Jun 1855	19 Jun 1855	DET
Bail, J.T. (Rev.)	Baldwin, Minerva R.	02 Aug 1854	25 Jul 1854	DET
Baird, S.	Steece, M.J.	10 Oct 1851	01 Oct 1851	PI
Baird, S.	Steece, M.J.	08 Oct 1851	01 Oct 1851	PT&C
Baird, S.W.	Pond, Sarah E.	10 Dec 1864	06 Dec 1864	PTIMES
Baird, Zachariah J.	Easter, Catharine	17 Feb 1857	05 Feb 1857	PSOT
Baker, George	Martin, Nancy	28 Jan 1857	25 Dec 1856	WPT
Baker, John	Lane, Minerva	22 Oct 1856	25 Sep 1856	WPT
Baker, Robert	Wilson, Cornelia	02 Apr 1856	27 Mar 1856	WPT
Balcom, Henry	Reeve, Caddie	05 Jun 1860	04 Jun 1860	DET
Baldridge, Robert	Holt, Margaret	02 Sep 1850	24 Jul 1850	PI
Baldridge, Robert	Holt, Margaret	29 Aug 1850	24 Jun 1850	PT&C
Ball, Charles E. (Dr.)	O'Neal, Irena G.	25 Jun 1864	23 Jun 1864	PTIMES
Ball, George	Noel, Margaret	22 Apr 1858	21 Apr 1858	DET
Ball, George	Noel, Margaret	27 Apr 1858	21 Apr 1858	PSOT
Ball, George	Gillet, Jane	08 Jun 1853	02 Jun 1853	PT&C
Ball, Oscar	Nourse (or Nurse), Amanda	26 Dec 1855 08 Jan 1856	20 Dec 1855	DET
Ball, Oskar	Nurse (or Nourse), Amanda	26 Dec 1855 09 Jan 1856	20 Dec 1855	WPT
Banks, Joseph	Commander, Penelope	18 Mar 1820		STEL
Bannister, Byron L.	Herbert, Mary	13 Apr 1853	02 Apr 1853	PT&C
Barbee, Cornelius H.	Bowman, Eliza Jane	30 Jan 1864	20 Jan 1864	PTIMES
Barbee, Elias	Days, Elizabeth	26 Nov 1851	17 Nov 1851	PT&C
Barbee, Wesley	Ball, Lucy	23 Sep 1850	19 Sep 1850	PI
Barbee, Wesley	Ball, Lucy	26 Sep 1850	19 Sep 1850	PT&C
Barber, Wm. E.	Cole, Caroline	31 Dec 1851	25 Dec 1851	PT&C
Barnett, Andrew H.	Bowley, Hulda	15 Feb 1860	07 Feb 1860	DET
Barnett, Andrew H.	Bowley, Hulda	15 Feb 1860	07 Feb 1860	WPT
Barr, Andrew	Liggett, Jane	22 Mar 1844	13 Mar 1844	TRIB
Barr, Jos. C.	Grovin, Margaret J.	29 Aug 1850	27 Jul 1850	PT&C
Barr, Joseph C.	Grovin, Margaret J.	02 Sep 1850	27 Jul 1850	PI
Barr, Wm. H.	Dean, Cynthia M.	20 Apr 1853	17 Apr 1853	PT&C
Barrett, Henry, Jr.	Furry, Jane F.	03 Dec 1856		WPT
Barrick, Henry	Eifert, Mary A.	10 Dec 1851	05 Dec 1851	PT&C
Bartlett, M.R.	McCague, Mary	21 Apr 1843	20 Apr 1843	TRIB
Bartlett, Madison M.	Gray, Harriett E.	27 Nov 1855	17 Nov 1855	DET
Bartlett, Madison M.	Gray, Harriett E.	28 Nov 1855	17 Nov 1855	WPT
Barton, Charles A.	Madock, Mary J.	26 Feb 1858	25 Feb 1858	DET
Barton, Charles A.	Madock, Mary J.	03 Mar 1858	25 Feb 1858	WPT
Basey, John	Weaver, Elizabeth	26 Dec 1853	20 Dec 1853	PDD
Bateham, M.B.	Cushing, Josephine (Cowles)	03 Oct 1850		PT&C
Bateman, Clementious	Davis, Margaret	14 Jan 1854	02 Jan 1854	DET
Batterson, Addison	Oakes, Dorothy	26 Dec 1851	04 Dec 1851	PI

Name (Groom)	Name (Bride)	Notice Date	Marriage Date	Paper
Batterson, Addison	Sikes, Sarah	04 Nov 1850	27 Oct 1850	PI
Baty, L.T.	Larkins, Ana	07 Oct 1853	29 Sep 1853	PDD
Bayhan, Benjamin F.	Soward, Nannie F.	01 Sep 1851		PI
Beals, Asa G.	Black, Martha	20 Apr 1853	10 Apr 1853	PT&C
Bean, William	Greenfield, Sarah E.	12 Aug 1825	19 Jul 1825	PG&LA
Beatzhausen, Christian	Boechner, Phillpena	26 Jan 1844	26 Dec 1843	TRIB
Beck, George	Lory, Filinia	10 Oct 1854	10 Oct 1854	DET
Becket, J.	Cloniger, Mary Ann	16 Jun 1853	05 Jun 1853	DET
Becket, J.	Cloniger, Mary Ann	22 Jun 1853	05 Jun 1853	PT&C
Beerman, Louis	Patten, Lucy	12 Nov 1856	05 Nov 1856	WPT
Behmind, George	Rayner, Mary	20 Aug 1856	15 Aug 1856	WPT
Bellman, Joseph	Baker, Wilhelmina	09 Apr 1858	05 Apr 1858	DET
Bellman, Joseph	Baker, Wilhelmina	14 Apr 1858	05 Apr 1858	WPT
Bennet, Robert C.	Montgomery, Mary Ann	30 Nov 1826	23 Nov 1826	WT
Bennett, Madison	Johnson, Sarah	23 Mar 1853		PT&C
Bennett, Samuel	Hull, Jane	05 Jul 1827	07 Jun 1827	WT
Bentley, Morrison A.	Davis, Elizabeth	20 Feb 1856	14 Feb 1856	WPT
Bentley, Morrison A.	Davis, Elizabeth	16 Feb 1856	14 Feb 1856	DET
Berry, John H.	McCormick, Elizabeth	19 Aug 1854	15 Aug 1854	DET
Bertram, Henry	Venn, Aplona	18 Jun 1864	16 Jun 1864	PTIMES
Bescoe, John A.	Nagle, Philepena	17 Dec 1853	11 Dec 1853	DET
Bfofey, Daniel	Liback, Lydia	05 Jan 1853	01 Dec 1852	PT&C
Bibey, Abraham	Walker, Elizabeth	11 Jan 1853	06 Jan 1853	PI
Bickel, Charles B.	Kelley, Isabella	05 Jan 1853		PT&C
Biggs, Thomas N.	Humphreys, Ellen	14 Feb 1856	31 Jan 1856	DET
Bills, John	Banks, Louisa	07,09 Nov 1854		PDD
Bilton, Wm. H.	Dobbs, Matilda	21 May 1856	19 May 1856	WPT
Bindsey, William	Hamilton, Currence Ann	22 Aug 1853	17 Aug 1853	PDD
Bing, James P., (M.D.)	Powers, Minerva A.	14 Nov 1851	05 Nov 1851	PI
Bingham, Nathaniel	Many, Clementine	26 Nov 1856	19 Nov 1856	WPT
Black, Samuel	Mead, Martha Ann	05 Jan 1853	23 Dec 1852	PT&C
Blackford, Joseph	Courtney, Sarah	13 Feb 1855	30 Jan 1855	DET
Blackman, P.S.	Hurlburt, Julia	26 Oct 1854	15 Oct 1854	DET
Blackwell, Harry	Stone, Lucy	11 May 1855		DET
Blair, Charles W.	Medary, Kate	29 Dec 1858	25 Dec 1858	DET
Blair, Wm. H.	Craycraft, Sarah	16 Jul 1856	14 Jul 1856	WPT
Blake, Cincinnatus	Fuller, Gritia F.	04 May 1858	21 Apr 1858	PSOT
Blake, John	Swabia, Charlotte	20 Feb 1860	15 Feb 1860	DET
Blankenship, William	Hewlitt, Mildred	28, 31 Jan 1854	18 Jan 1854	DET
Bliss, Jonathan	Ellis, Anna	31 Jan 1829	25 Jan 1829	WT
Boal, William K.	Vanbibber, Elisa	14 Apr 1855	15 Mar 1855	DET
Bodkin, James	Cockerell, Mary Frances	19 Nov 1824		PG&LA
Bofey, Daniel	Liduke, Lydia	07 Jan 1853	21 Dec 1852	PI
Boile, Henry	Coryell, Malvina	29 Sep 1852	26 Sep 1852	PT&C
Boldman, John	Green, Mary	18 Mar 1820	09 Mar 1820	STEL

Marriages (Grooms)

Name (Groom)	Name (Bride)	Notice Date	Marriage Date	Paper
Bolinger, Jacob	Beniger, Francis	27 Mar 1855	09 Mar 1855	DET
Bonser, Isaac	Huddleston, Nancy Maria	14 Jan 1857	11 Jan 1857	WPT
Books, Samuel H.	Miller, Maria	17 Feb 1854	08 Feb 1854	DET
Bookwalter, Addison	Ross, Melissa	02 Dec 1850		PI
Bookwalter, J.N.	Pontious, Barbara	22 Nov 1853	15 Nov 1853	PDD
Booth, Levi	Feforgey, Levoria	06 Sep 1860	01 Sep 1860	DET
Booth, Levi	Feforgey, Levoria	12 Sep 1860	01 Sep 1860	WPT
Bordlleau, G.D.	Benton, Susan	12 Jun 1855		DET
Born, Victor	Hambibb, Hannah M.	15 Jun 1855	15 Jun 1855	DET
Boroff, Daniel	Fitzgerald, Janet	03 Aug 1820		STEL
Bosanpagh, Michael	Shred, Rosen	10 Mar 1854	07 Mar 1854	DET
Bosanpazk, Michael	Shred, Rosina	09 Mar 1854	07 Mar 1854	PDD
Boughner, V.E.	Morton, Mary R.	26 Aug 1865	22 Aug 1865	PTIMES
Bourshaw, Victor	Levery, Josephine	22 Oct 1856	16 Oct 1856	WPT
Bovey, George C.	Ryan, Clara C.	12 May 1854	09 May 1854	DET
Boyd, G.W.	Songer, Ann	19 Nov 1853	09 Nov 1853	DET
Boyd, William M.	Chandler, Elenor	17 Nov 1853	01 Nov 1853	PDD
Boyer, Thos. D.	Bliss, Hannah	06 Aug 1855	04 Aug 1855	DET
Boylston, John	Shupe, Abigail	15, 17 Sep 1855	13 Sep 1855	DET
Boynton, Asa, Jr.	Cadot, Madeline	09 Jan 1855	01 Jan 1855	DET
Boynton, Sumner	Flanders, Elizabeth	14 Oct 1855	12 Sep 1855	DET
Bradbury, George W.(Lieut.Col.)	Wright, Anna Rebecca	01 Dec 1843	22 Nov 1843	TRIB
Bradford, Samuel C.	Wilcoxin, Lovisa	07 Oct 1831	16 Sep 1831	PC&WT
Bradly, William	Browen, Sarah	21 Jan 1857	15 Jan 1857	WPT
Brady, Levi	Enslow, Emily	22 Jul 1825	14 Jul 1825	PG&LA
Brady, Levi, Jr.	Scofield, Adeline	30 Sep 1853	29 Sep 1853	DET
Branson, John C.	Griffis, Eliza E.	28 Nov 1853	20 Nov 1853	DET
Bratton, Allen T.	Sanford, Margaret	13 Mar 1854	01 Mar 1854	PDD
Bremigam, William	Williamson, Jemima	27 Aug 1855	16 Aug 1855	DET
Brenton, John	Brown, Rebecca	30 Dec 1853	29 Dec 1853	DET
Brenton, John	Brown, Rebecca	31 Dec 1853	29 Dec 1853	PDD
Breslin, John G. (Hon.)	Borland, Anna	04 May 1855	01 May 1855	DET
Briggs, Samuel C.	Timbrook, Rebecca	03 Mar 1826	29 Dec 1825	TA
Briggs, Wm.	Orms, Mary M.	31 Dec 1851	25 Dec 1851	PT&C
Bringham, Levi	Burton, Mandana	31 Aug 1858	05 Aug 1858	PSOT
Brisk, John	Howe, Amanda	02 Sep 1850	08 Aug 1850	PI
Brisk, John	Howe, Amanda	29 Aug 1850	08 Aug 1850	PT&C
Broadtree, Thomas S.	Perry, Bula	26 Jun 1854	17 Jun 1854	PDD
Brodess, Henry B.	Gibbs, Mary E.	01 Aug 1857	26 Jul 1857	DET
Brodess, Henry B.	Gibbs, Mary E.	05 Aug 1857	26 Jul 1857	WPT
Bronn, Leroy S.	Crozier, Eliza J.	12 Nov 1864	10 Nov 1864	PTIMES
Brooking, James H. (Rev.)	Craig, Sallie	16 Feb 1855	30 Jan 1855	DET
Brooks, Samuel	Miller, Maria	21 Feb 1854	08 Feb 1854	PDD
Brooks, W.C.	Hutton, Eliza	05 Jan 1858	31 Dec 1857	DET

Name (Groom)	Name (Bride)	Notice Date	Marriage Date	Paper
Brooks, W.C.	Hutton, Eliza A.	12 Jan 1858	31 Dec 1857	PSOT
Brown, David	Deacon, Hannah	26 Dec 1853	08 Dec 1853	PDD
Brown, Geo. W.	Wheellr, Narissa T.	30 Nov 1853	24 Nov 1853	PDD
Brown, George	White, Mary	18 May 1820		STEL
Brown, George W.	Wheeler, Narissa T.	28 Nov 1853	24 Nov 1853	DET
Brown, Henry	Duke, Sarah	06 Dec 1855	04 Dec 1855	DET
Brown, James	Smith, Elizabeth	05 Sep 1853	03 Sep 1853	DET
Brown, James	Smith, Elizabeth	06 Sep 1853	03 Sep 1853	PDD
Brown, John	Carter, Mary	13 Jan 1857	09 Jan 1857	PSOT
Brown, Sardine	Gibbons, Harriet M.	28 Jan 1854	18 Jan 1854	DET
Brown, Sardine	Gibbons, Harriet M.	14 Feb 1854	18 Jan 1854	DET
Brown, Stephen	Holmes, Melissa	18 Aug 1857	05 Jul 1857	PSOT
Brownell, A.W.	Farnandis, Martha B.	24 Aug 1854	23 Aug 1854	DET
Brubaker, John D.	Shute, Olive A.	20 Feb 1852	17 Feb 1852	PI
Brumfield, Bird F.	Hatten, Elizabeth F.	09, 14 Feb 1854	04 Feb 1854	DET
Buck, James	Sloat, Mary E.	07 Jul 1853	03 Jul 1853	DET
Buck, James	Sloat, Mary E.	09 Jul 1853	03 Jul 1853	PDD
Buck, James	Sloat_all, Mary E.	13 Jul 1853	03 Jul 1853	PT&C
Buckley, Samuel	Hall, Cynthia	11 Jan 1854	02 Dec 1853	DET
Buel, A.J.	Davey, Susan	06 Jan 1851	02 Jan 1851	PI
Bunker, Chang (siamese twin)	Lates (or Yeates), Adelaide	31 Oct 1850	13 Apr 1843	PT&C
Bunker, Eng (siamese twin)	Lates (or Yeates), Sarah	31 Oct 1850	13 Apr 1843	PT&C
Bunn, J. Harvey	Cavett, Elizabeth	22 Mar 1854	09 Mar 1854	DET
Burke, Joseph M.	Case, Martha E.	01 Apr 1854	16 Mar 1854	DET
Burks, Wm.	Simmons, Catherine	09 Jan 1855	28 Dec 1854	DET
Burt, Charles E.	Cook, Louisa	23 Apr 1858	22 Apr 1858	DET
Burt, Thomas	Buffington, Cornelia Ann	27 Apr 1826	23 Apr 1826	WT
Burt, Thomas T.	Ratcliff, Esther	11 Jul 1848	07 Jul 1848	DENQ
Bush, Seth R.	Wait, Melissa	22 Mar 1844	21 Mar 1844	TRIB
Busler, Solomon	Goff, Mahalah	30 Mar 1854	09 Mar 1854	DET
Butler, M.	Plumb, Christinia	02 May 1848	27 Apr 1848	DENQ
Butt, John	White, Eliza	20 Sep 1827		WT
Butterfield, John	Rankin, Ellen J.	27 Dec 1859	15 Dec 1859	DET
Byron, John	Corothers, Ellen	24 Oct 1844		TRIB
Cable, Jonathan	Price, Rebecca	23 Dec 1850	17 Dec 1850	PI
Cable, Jonathan	Price, Rebecca	19 Dec 1850	17 Dec 1850	PT&C
Cady, John M.	West, Emily	04 Jun 1856	01 Jun 1856	WPT
Cain, John	Monroe, Elizabeth	27 Dec 1853	08 Dec 1853	DET
Callihan (or Gallihan), Daniel	Hensley, Eliza Jane	12 Jan 1854	22 Dec 1853	PDD
Calvert, Frank W.	Allen, Mollie	02 Jan 1864	24 Dec 1863	PTIMES
Calvert, George	Reed, J.C. (Mrs.)	02 Feb 1859	02 Feb 1859	DET
Calvert, George	Reed, J.C. (Mrs.)	02, 09 Feb 1859	02 Feb 1859	WPT
Camden, W.P.	Bronn, Margaret A.	06 Jun 1848	04 Jun 1848	DENQ

Name (Groom)	Name (Bride)	Notice Date	Marriage Date	Paper
Campbell, Lancelot	Perry, Rachael Ann	04 Jan 1856	01 Jan 1856	DET
Campbell, Lancelot	Perry, Rachael Ann	09 Jan 1856	01 Jan 1856	WPT
Cane, Aquilla	Dunlap, Sarah Ann	04 Nov 1854	03 Nov 1854	DET
Cann, Arthur	Jones, Mary	12 Dec 1854	09 Dec 1854	DET
Canter, Milton	Woodruff, Nancy	28 Jan 1857	01 Jan 1857	WPT
Canterbury, John	Dixon, Nancy	24 Aug 1854		DET
Caps, Casper	Kaughman, Catharine	16 Feb 1847	09 Feb 1847	CLIPPER
Car_l, Frank, Jr.	Fisher, Amanda M.	02 Apr 1856	29 Jan 1856	WPT
Carnahan, James	Johnson, Mary	02 Sep 1825		PG&LA
Carner, A.W. (Capt.)	Kittle, Henrietta B.	14 Aug 1854	10 Aug 1854	DET
Carr, Cornelius	Ragan, Eliza F.	28 Oct 1865	23 Oct 1865	PTIMES
Carroll, Alexius	Burt, Eliza	16 Feb 1844	10 Feb 1844	TRIB
Carroll, John	Cutler, Fanny	31 Jan 1829	29 Jan 1829	WT
Carter, William S.	Boyd, A.A.	27 Sep 1855	26 Sep 1855	DET
Carthick, A. (Rev.)	Van Gundy, Jane	08 Apr 1854	04 Apr 1854	DET
Case, Stephen	Stratton, Salome	31 Mar 1843	02 Mar 1843	TRIB
Case, Stephen	Stratton, Salome	31 Mar 1843	02 Mar 1843	TRIB
Cassel, Allen	Goodrich, Angelina	29 Dec 1853	20 Dec 1853	DET
Cawford, John H.	Kibly, Nancy	16 Nov 1855	15 Nov 1855	DET
Chalfin, John	Lee, Susan D.	03 Dec 1853	26 Nov 1853	DET
Chamblin, T.H.B.	Jones, Hattie A.	25 Feb 1860	07 Feb 1860	PTIMES
Chaney, Benjamin F.	Pike, Margaret Amanda	23 May 1863	07 May 1863	PTIMES
Chaney, David	Pickerel, Jane	21 Jul 1851	16 Jul 1851	PI
Chaney, David	Pickerel, Jane	23 Jul 1851	17 Jul 1851	PT&C
Chang (see also, Bunker)	Yeates,or Lates, Adelaide	05 May 1843	13 Apr 1843	TRIB
Chapman, Martin	Shelton, Elizabeth A.	11 Aug 1854	09 Aug 1854	DET
Chapman, Martin	Shelten, Elizabeth A.	12 Aug 1854	08 Aug 1854	PDD
Chapman, Obediah	Burt, Amanda	07 Jan 1857	31 Dec 1856	WPT
Landon, Charles C.	Row, Mary C.	28 Sep 1858	15 Sep 1858	PSOT
Charlesworth, Henry	Lindsey, Orissa	19 Sep 1844	15 Sep 1844	TRIB
Charlesworth, James F.	Tallman, Laura A.	27 Jul 1855	04 Jul 1855	DET
Cheney, Duston	Giles, Ruth	18 Mar 1820		STEL
Chenoweth, Joel	McNutt, Harriet	06 Jan 1837	29 Dec 1836	STRIB
Chenoweth, Joel	Chenoweth, Mary	10 Sep 1856	02 Sep 1856	WPT
Chesney, David A.	Ous, Elizabeth J.	06 Aug 1851	04 Aug 1851	PT&C
Chick, Franklin	Stewart, Flora A.	02 Jun 1852	23 May 1852	PT&C
Chinn, A.N.	McCoy, Judith	09 Jan 1854	22 Dec 1853	DET
Chinn, Alford N.	McCoy, Judith	12 Jan 1854	29 Dec 1853	PDD
Chojur, Jacob	Cutsmeyer, M.	11 Jan 1853	02 Jan 1853	PI
Christian, William	Partlow, Julia Ann	16 Jun 1853	09 Jun 1853	DET
Christian, Wm.	Partlow, Julia Ann	22 Jun 1853	09 Jun 1853	PT&C
Church, E.F.	Carnes, Isabel M.	26 Jun 1860	14 Jun 1860	DET
Church, E.F.	Carnes, Isabel M.	27 Jun 1860	14 Jun 1860	WPT
Clark, Andrew J.	Anderson, Mary	13 Nov. 1838	08 Nov 1838	STRIB
Clark, Isaiah	Shuflin, Martha	08 Feb 1854	05 Feb 1854	PDD

Name (Groom)	Name (Bride)	Notice Date	Marriage Date	Paper
Clark, Josiah	Shuflin, Martha	07 Feb 1854	05 Feb 1854	DET
Clark, Lewis	Tinney, Lydia	05 Nov 1853	26 Oct 1853	DET
Clark, Lewis	Tenney, Lydia S.	10 Nov 1853	25 Oct 1853	DET
Clark, Orris A.	Woodruff, Jane Ann	31 Oct 1844	17 Oct 1844	TRIB
Clark, William	Moore, Mary	22 Jun 1826	11 Jun 1826	WT
Clarke, Abraham	Watrovs, Lydia Ann	01 Jun 1820		STEL
Clemens, Travis	Huddleston, Cynthia Ann	11 Jan 1854	05 Jan 1854	DET
Clemmer, Jacob	Harden, Ann	06 Jan 1855	06 Jan 1855	DET
Cline, Samuel	Russell, Rosanna	15 Jul 1850	10 Jul 1850	PI
Cline, Samuel	Russell, Rosanna	18 Jul 1850	10 Jul 1850	PT&C
Cline, Samuel	Russell, Rosanna	29 Aug 1850	10 Jul 1850	PT&C
Cline, W.H.	Johnson, E.	14 Nov 1851	13 Nov 1851	PI
Clingman, John M.	Lewis, Margaret	08 Jun 1826	30 May 1826	WT
Clough, G.W.A. (Dr.)	Steenbergen, Sarah M.	10 Mar 1843	02 Mar 1843	TRIB
Cochran, A.J.	Robinson, Ellen	18 Jul 1850	13 Jun 1850	PT&C
Coffee, Patrick	Davisson, Adaline	03 Oct 1850	29 Sep 1850	PT&C
Coffin, Constantine	Ellis, Rachel	28 Dec 1852	30 Dec 1852	PDD
Coffin, Constantine	Ellis, Rachel	07 Jan 1853	30 Dec 1852	PI
Coffman, Daniel	Edwards, Celia A.	30 Apr 1856	24 Apr 1856	WPT
Colburn, Frederick (Lieut.)	Davis, Lizzie	13 Feb 1864	10 Feb 1864	PTIMES
Cole, Amos B.	Orm, Martha E.	09 Jan 1851	02 Jan 1851	PT&C
Cole, Silas W.	Squires, Antionette	06 Feb 1864	27 Jan 1864	PTIMES
Colegrove Benjamin	Cole, Laura	21 Nov 1829		WT
Collett, A.M.	Howell, Sarah	28 Jul 1853	27 Jul 1853	DET
Collett, A.M.	Howell, Sarah	01 Aug 1853	27 Jul 1853	PDD
Collett, A.M.	Howell, Sarah	03 Aug 1853	27 Jul 1853	PT&C
Collier, Ambrose	Hall, Nancy	07 May 1856	23 Apr 1856	WPT
Collins, Gilbert H.	Huston, Cecilia Anna	31 Mar 1857	26 Mar 1857	PSOT
Collins, J. W.	Bell, Lucy M.	09 Jun 1853	07 Jun 1853	DET
Collins, J.W.	Bell, Lucy M.	10 Jun 1853	07 Jun 1853	PDD
Collins, J.W.	Bell, Lucy M.	15 Jun 1853	07 Jun 1853	PT&C
Collis, R.T. (Esq.)	Crull, (Mrs.) Julia	09 Jul 1856	01 Jul 1856	WPT
Colvin, Harrison	Bringham, Sarah Jane	23 Nov 1858	14 Oct 1858	PSOT
Colvin, Harrison	Bringham, Sarah Jane	23 Nov 1858	14 Oct 1858	PTIMES
Colvin, Jefferson	Porter, Louisa	30 Jul 1856	27 Jul 1856	WPT
Combs, John	Crawford, Lizzie	19 Nov 1853	14 Nov 1853	DET
Comer, Lawrence	Strowd, Margaret	06 Feb 1854	26 Jan 1854	DET
Comer, Lawrence	Strowd, Margaret	10 Feb 1854	26 Jan 1854	PDD
Conery, John	Call, Martha	24 Oct 1844	15 Sep 1844	TRIB
Connel, Wm.	Senegiger, Mary	07 Nov 1850	20 Oct 1850	PT&C
Conway, Kev. William, M.D.	E. Mary A.	10 Nov 1853	27 Oct 1853	DET
Cook, Edward	Leadbetter, Rhoda	16 Jul 1856	14 Jul 1856	WPT
Cook, Geo. W.	Evridge, Sintha	06 Sep 1855	06 Sep 1855	DET

Name (Groom)	Name (Bride)	Notice Date	Marriage Date	Paper
Cook, Henry	Neil, Lucy	29 Sep 1852	23 Sep 1852	PT&C
Cook, William A.	Sappington, Anna	25 Aug 1854	17 Aug 1854	DET
Cook, William L.	McCall, Calfurnia	04 Feb 1856	31 Jan 1856	DET
Cook, William T.	Gunn, Anna	15 Sep 1853	11 Sep 1853	PDD
Cooley, John	Mongomery, Mary	29 Apr 1853	28 Apr 1853	PDD
Cooley, John	Montgomery, Mary	04 May 1853	28 Apr 1853	PT&C
Coolman, Edward	Bemn, Margaret	13 Apr 1853	08 Apr 1853	PT&C
Coombs, Joseph J.	Leiby, Alice	23 May 1844	16 May 1844	TRIB
Copens, Samuel W.	Orcutt, Avis Amelia	19 Sep 1829		WT
Cornes, Wesley D.	Enslow, Hannah A.	05 Jul 1854	03 Jul 1854	DET
Corson, Joseph (M.D.)	Cutler, Martha H.	07 Jul 1843	29 Jun 1843	TRIB
Corwin, Daniel	Dorril, Eliza	06 Jul 1820	01 Jul 1820	STEL
Cosert, James	Dixon, Mary	17, 24 Dec 1853	12 Dec 1853	DET
Cosert, James	Dixon, Mary	19 Dec 1853	12 Dec 1853	PDD
Coverled, Martin	Haster, Corinea	09 May 1848	06 May 1848	DENQ
Craig, Thomas	Short, Elizabeth N.	08 Oct 1852	23 Sep 1852	PI
Craig, William S.	Parrs, Anna G.	09 Jul 1856	07 Jul 1856	WPT
Crain, Martin	Gibbs, Ellen	01 May 1854		DET
Crain, Martin	Gibbs, Ellen	02 May 1854	01 May 1854	PDD
Craine, Leonard	Smith, Nancy	05 Dec 1844	25 Nov 1844	TRIB
Crandal, Elias	Forsythe, Nancy F.	13 Jan 1857		PSOT
Crandall, Wesley	Glidden, Nancy Alice	10 Nov 1852	03 Nov 1852	PT&C
Crane, Adonijah	Morgan, Mary	18 Jan 1832		PC
Cranston, Benjamin E.	Henderson, Margaret J.	12 Nov 1855	08 Nov 1855	DET
Cranston, Edward (Capt.)	Whitcomb, Sally	14 Jan 1825	13 Jan 1825	PG&LA
Craudal, Elias	Forsythe, Nannie F.	07 Jan 1857		WPT
Crawford, D.H.	Girty, Margaret C.	28 Feb 1854	23 Feb 1854	PDD
Crichton, Andrew	Scott, H.M.	21 May 1852	13 May 1852	PI
Crichton, Andrew (Esq.)	McCoy, Virginia A.	30 May 1844	28 May 1844	TRIB
Criggs, Hezeriah	Patton, Ellen	30 Apr 1856	17 Apr 1856	WPT
Crighton, Nicholas D.	Garrett, Martha	28 Feb 1854	16 Feb 1854	PDD
Crooks, Henry H.	Prentice, Eliza Ann	05 Nov 1858	23 Oct 1858	SVREP
Cropper, Dyas P.	Malcolm, Luzzie	20 May 1857	13 May 1857	WPT
Cropper, V. (Major)	Johnson, Mary	18, 19, Jun 1855		DET
Cross, Wash.	Givens, Cynthia	15 Sep 1860	12 Sep 1860	DET
Crouse, C.F.	Cole, Elizabeth	11 Jan 1853	02 Dec 1852	PI
Crozier, Robert	Ward, Nancy	03 Oct 1848	25 Sep 1848	DENQ
Crull, David W.	Pool, Rhoda	07 Jul 1843	28 Jun 1843	TRIB
Crumpton, John	Porter, Elizabeth	28 Sep 1820		STEL
Cubinson, John	Kennard, Harriet	05 Jan 1854	24 Dec 1853	DET
Culbertson, H. (Dr.)	Safford, M. Louise	18 Nov 1854	15 Nov 1854	DET
Culbertson, W.W. (Capt.)	Means, Jeannie	04 Mar 1865	23 Feb 1865	PTIMES
Cummings, Jesse C.	Turnner, Harriet T.	24 Aug 1853	12 Aug 1853	PT&C
Cummings, Jesse O.	Turnner, Harriet T.	20 Aug 1853	12 Aug 1853	DET

Name (Groom)	Name (Bride)	Notice Date	Marriage Date	Paper
Cummings, Joseph D.	Willoughby, S. Marga-retta	03 Apr 1855	02 Apr 1855	DET
Cummings, Thomas B.	Hall, Axy F.	31 Jan 1829	29 Jan 1829	WT
Cumpson, Newton	Jones, Elizabeth	15 Jul 1857	14 Jul 1857	DET
Cumpson, Newton	Jones, Elizabeth	22 Jul 1857	14 Jul 1857	WPT
Cunning, Samuel W.	Scott, Adeline	23 Dec 1850		PI
Cunning, Samuel W.	Scott, Mary Adeline	26 Dec 1850	19 Dec 1850	PT&C
Custis, John	Smith, Elizabeth	31 May 1827	27 May 1827	WT
Cutler, Lyman D.	Hadley, Cynthia Ann	08 Jan 1846	01 Jan 1846	TRIB
Cutler, Pliny	Rankin, Nancy	31 Oct 1844	24 Oct 1844	TRIB
Cutler, Samuel N.	Reed, Ann M.	11 Nov 1853	08 Nov 1853	DET
Cutler, Samuel N.	Reed, Ann M.	15 Nov 1853	08 Nov 1853	PDD
Cutler, W.S. (Lieut.)	Fuller, Frances	22 Sep 1858	20 Sep 1858	WPT
Cutshaw, John	Dougerty, Ann	01 Jun 1853	18 May 1853	PDD
Dabney, S.W.	Webster, Harriet W.	16 Apr 1851	02 Apr 1851	PT&C
Dalabre, Michael	Vanbeek, Sena	30 Sep 1850	26 Sep 1850	PI
Dalabree, Michael	Vanbeek, Sena	03 Oct 1850	26 Sep 1850	PT&C
Damarin, Lewis C.	Catlin, Mary	31 Dec 1852	27 Dec 1852	PI
Daniels, S.H.	Lawson, Anastasia	11 Jan 1853	14 Jan 1853	PI
Daniels, S.W.	Dawson, Anastatio	19 Jan 1853	14 Jan 1853	PT&C
Dare, Henry	Collins, Emeline	09 Jul 1864	02 Jul 1864	PTIMES
Davenport, Whitle	Brown, Elizabeth	24 Sep 1852	19 Sep 1852	PI
Davey, P.	Varner, Mary J.	14 May 1853	12 May 1853	PDD
Davey, P.	Varner, Mary J.	18 May 1853	12 May 1853	PT&C
Davidson, Alfred D.	Stevenson, Harriet A.	03 Mar 1843	28 Feb 1843	TRIB
Davis, Alexander W.	Graves, Cynthia A.	09 Apr 1858	04 Apr 1858	DET
Davis, Alexander W.	Graves, Cynthia A.	14 Apr 1858	04 Apr 1858	WPT
Davis, Arthur	Leonard, Margaret	14 Jun 1828	11 Jun 1828	WT
Davis, D.T.	Jones, Sarah	29 Dec 1860	16 Dec 1860	PTIMES
Davis, David M.	Lewis, Catherine	07 Apr 1852	01 Apr 1852	PT&C
Davis, Henry	Fox, Catharine	28 Jan 1854	20 Jan 1854	DET
Davis, Henry	Fox, Catharine	31 Jan 1854	20 Jan 1854	DET
Davis, James	Lewis, Margaret	10 Sep 1853	09 Sep 1853	DET
Davis, James	Lewis, Margaret	12 Sep 1853	09 Sep 1853	PDD
Davis, James R.	Emory, Elizabeth J.	24 Mar 1860	14 Mar 1860	DET
Davis, James R.	Emory, Elizabeth J.	28 Mar 1860	14 Mar 1860	WPT
Davis, Joshua	Lewis, Kesiah	14 Jan 1854	05 Jan 1854	DET
Davis, P.W.	Mims, Mary A.	04 Jan 1856	27 Dec 1855	DET
Davis, P.W.	Mims, Mary A.	09 Jan 1856	27 Dec 1855	WPT
Davis, Thomas	Wymer, Martha E.	20 Oct 1857	16 Oct 1857	PSOT
Dawley, James	Goudy, Olivia E.	22 Jul 1850	18 Jul 1850	PI
Dawley, James	Goudy, Olivia E.	25 Jul 1850	18 Jul 1850	PT&C
Day, Alford C.	Easmon, Hester	05 Jan 1854	02 Jan 1854	PDD
Day, Alfred C.	Easmon, Hester	04 Jan 1854	02 Jan 1854	DET
Day, E.C.	Wheeler, E.J.	18 Jun 1852	14 Jun 1852	PI

Name (Groom)	Name (Bride)	Notice Date	Marriage Date	Paper
Deeliecks, Henry	Wolfard, Mary	10 Nov 1857	08 Nov 1857	DET
Deeliecks, Henry	Wolfard, Mary	11 Nov 1857	08 Nov 1857	WPT
Degrummom, William	Gessenger, Arrabella	15 Aug 1854	13 Aug 1854	PDD
DeGrummond, W.J.	Gesinger, Arabel B.	14 Aug 1854	13 Aug 1854	DET
Delany, Milton	Heslek, Sarah Sumantha	14 Jun 1858	03 Jun 1858	DET
Delany, Milton	Hesler, Sarah Sumantha	16 Jun 1858	03 Jun 1858	WPT
Delany, Samuel	Halterman, Mary	01 Oct 1844	15 Sep 1844	PDEM
Deming, Ezekiel	Stanley, Abigail	03 Aug 1820	25 Jul 1820	STEL
Denning, Newton B.	Williams, Mary A.	24 Jun 1853	19 Jun 1853	DET
Denning, Newton B.	Williams, Mary A.	29 Jun 1853	19 Jun 1853	PT&C
Densmore, Henry	Watkins, Rebecca Jane	16 Apr 1856	16 Apr 1856	WPT
Derby, N.	Coles, Martha A.	04 Mar 1865	23 Feb 1865	PTIMES
Dewy, James W.	Stinton, Mary E.	25 Jan 1854	19 Jan 1854	DET
Dillman, E.C.	Loomis, Lucy Jane	09 Apr 1852	17 Mar 1852	PI
Dillon, J.W. (Rev.)	Cox, Mary E.	16 Jan 1860	10 Jan 1860	DET
Dillon, J.W. (Rev.)	Cox, Mary E.	18 Jan 1860	10 Jan 1860	WPT
Doddridge, B.Z.B.	McCoy, Harriet	15 Nov 1853	08 Nov 1853	PDD
Doddridge, Henry C.	Griffith, Julia A.	14 Oct 1865	11 Oct 1865	PTIMES
Doggett, Walker W.	Parker, Lavisa F.	02 Jun 1851		PI
Dole, Edward P.	Lusk, Ella M.	27 Jan 1854	26 Jan 1854	DET
Dole, Edward P.	Lusk, Ella M.	30 Jan 1854	26 Jan 1854	PDD
Dole, Edward P.	Lusk, Ella M.	01 Feb 1854	26 Jun 1854	SVREP
Dole, John	Herman, Hannah	16 Jan 1856	15 Jan 1856	DET
Dole, Samuel	Hammill, Margaret	12 Nov 1824		PG&LA
Donley, Izaih	Calaen, Sophia	10 Oct 1853	29 Sep 1853	DET
Donohoo, Peter	Jeffords, Miranda	02 Sep 1850	26 Aug 1850	PI
Donohoo, Peter	Jeffords, Miranda	29 Aug 1850	26 Aug 1850	PT&C
Dorch, John	Greenslet, Susanna	03 Aug 1853	02 Aug 1853	DET
Dorch, John	Jones, Julia Ann	21 Nov 1854	16 Oct 1854	DET
Douglas, James	Stillwell, Mattie L.	12 Jul 1854	06 Jul 1854	DET
Douglas, Samuel	Lavery, Mary Ann	17 Nov 1853	27 Oct 1853	PDD
Douglass, H.G.	Turner, Margaret O.	30 Aug 1854	27 Aug 1854	DET
Down, Isaac F.	Reynolds, Eliza	27 Dec 1853	14 Dec 1853	DET
Downey, J.D.	Hastings, Catharine	09 May 1848	16 Apr 1848	DENQ
Downey, Nathaniel	Dewey, Eliza	09 Nov 1855	26 Oct 1855	OP
Drake, Samuel P.	Kelly, Sophia	16 Feb 1847		CLIPPER
Draper, William O.	Cavatt, Harriet	19 Aug 1854	15 Aug 1854	DET
Dresbach, Herr	Walter, Sallie	17 May 1854	27 Apr 1854	PDD
Dugan, Thomas	McCoy, Lavinia	09 May 1848	02 May 1848	DENQ
Duke, John S.	Hamilton, Rachel L.	20 Aug 1853		DET
Duke, John S.	Hamilton, Rachel L.	24 Aug 1853	16 Aug 1853	PT&C
Dukes, Wm. H.S.	Hyatt, Ella	02 Jan 1864	29 Dec 1863	PTIMES
Dumble, J.W.	Brice, Jennie E.	29 Dec 1860	17 Dec 1860	PTIMES
Dunkins, Alexander	Gammon, Elizabeth	13 Oct 1855	10 Oct 1855	DET
Dunkle, A.J.	Well, Susan F.	06 Feb 1854	02 Feb 1854	DET

Name (Groom)	Name (Bride)	Notice Date	Marriage Date	Paper
Dunkle, A.J.	Will, Susan E.	10 Feb 1854	02 Feb 1854	PDD
Earhart, Jacob S.	McQuality, Eliza	15 Oct 1852	13 Oct 1852	PI
Edgington, Francis	Vigus, Hannah C.	07 May 1864	02 May 1864	PTIMES
Edmundson, Nathan	Bradbury, Nancy	12 Aug 1854	02 Aug 1854	DET
Eichles, Joseph	Gahr, Charlotte	26 Oct 1853		PDD
Elden, Charles D.	Bowman, Mary C.	24 Sep 1853		DET
Elden, Charles D.	Bowman, Mary C.	26 Sep 1853	20 Sep 1853	PDD
Elden, William	Morrell, Jerush	08 Aug 1844	01 Aug 1844	TRIB
Elder, John S	Higgins, Laura	28 Jan 1865	24 Jan 1865	PTIMES
Ellion, James H.	Santy, Mary	12 Nov 1856	03 Nov 1856	WPT
Elliot, John A.	Fowler, Catharine	17 Feb 1854	11 Feb 1854	DET
Elliot, John Q.	Crumblet, Elizabeth R.	08 Apr 1854	02 Apr 1854	DET
Elliott, John	Fowler, Catharine	21 Feb 1854	11 Feb 1854	PDD
Ely, Seneca W.	Bell, Agatha Eustace	18 Jul 1850	11 Jul 1850	PT&C
Emmens, John	Jaynes, Sally Jane	20 May 1850	14 May 1850	PI
Emmens,John	Jaynes, Sally Jane	16 May 1850	14 May 1850	PT&C
Eng (see also, Bunker)	Yeates, or Lates, Sarah	05 May 1843	13 Apr 1843	TRIB
Engelbrecht, L.	Allman, Mary L.	27 Sep 1862	22 Sep 1862	PTIMES
England, J.H.	Brown, Anna M.	10 Aug 1858	29 Jul 1858	PSOT
Enslow, Revillo	Andre, Sophia	11 Jan 1853	23 Dec 1852	PI
Estill, William	Smith, Mary	04 Aug 1851	28 Jul 1851	PI
Estill, William	Smith, Mary	06 Aug 1851	28 Jul 1851	PT&C
Evans, D.R. (Rev.)	Dukes, Emily	26 Nov 1864	23 Nov 1864	PTIMES
Evans, Evan	Cartwright, Eliza Jane	05 Oct 1855	04 Oct 1855	DET
Evans, Evan, Jr.	Cherington, Sarah	19 Aug 1854	13 Aug 1854	DET
Evens, William	Hardin, Sarah	07 May 1852	01 May 1852	PI
Everit, Septer	Lauderbach, Louisa	18 Mar 1853	10 Dec 1852	PI
Ewing, Elmore	Folsom, Minerva	30 Sep 1865	21 Sep 1865	PTIMES
Ewing, James	Poe, Harriet	09 Feb 1854		DET
Ewing, James	Poe, Harriet	10 Feb 1854	07 Jan 1854	PDD
Fairchild, Aaron	Keating, Mary	17 Aug 1854	14 Aug 1854	DET
Farden, James A.	Thomas, Ellie	21 Sep 1857	15 Sep 1857	DET
Farden, James A.	Thomas, Ellie	23 Sep 1857	15 Sep 1857	WPT
Farrington, J.W.	Norris, Sarah	14 Mar 1854	12 Mar 1854	PDD
Farrington, James	Carter, Lucy E.	02 Sep 1850	17 Aug 1850	PI
Farrington, James W.	Norris, Sarah	14 Mar 1854	12 Mar 1854	DET
Farrington, Jas.	Carter, Lucy E.	29 Aug 1850	17 Aug 1850	PT&C
Fauble, George	Baker, Ella	10, 17 Feb 1854	07 Feb 1854	DET
Fauble, George	Baker, Ella	21 Feb 1854	07 Feb 1854	PDD
Faverty, Resin	Hood, Caroline	13 Apr 1854	09 Apr 1854	DET
Faverty, Rezin	Cisson, Frances	15 Jul 1850	01 Jul 1850	PI
Faverty, Rezin	Cisson, Frances	18 Jul 1850	01 Jul 1850	PT&C
Fawn, John	Lewis, Jane J.	15 Mar 1858	15 Mar 1858	DET
Fawn, John	Lewis, Jennie	16 Mar 1858	15 Mar 1858	PSOT
Fawn, John	Lewis, Jane J.	17 Mar 1858	15 Mar 1858	WPT

Name (Groom)	Name (Bride)	Notice Date	Marriage Date	Paper
Fehar, Lyman	Shepard, Eliza J.	02 Sep 1850	13 Aug 1850	PI
Fehar, Lyman	Shepard, Eliza J.	29 Aug 1850	13 Aug 1850	PT&C
Fenwick, David	Gregg, Eliza M.	28 Feb 1854	22 Feb 1854	PDD
Fergason, Hiram (Dr.)	Stewart, Elizabeth J.	01 Aug 1850	23 Jul 1850	PT&C
Ferguson, S. S.	Clemmins, Josephine	28 Mar 1856	27 Mar 1856	OP
Ferguson, S.S.	Clemens, Josephene	02 Apr 1856	27 Mar 1856	WPT
Ferrill, Daniel	Slocumb, Clarissa	08 Mar 1844	20 Jan 1844	TRIB
Fields, Jessee H.	Davis, Nancy	02 Apr 1856	06 Mar 1856	WPT
Finch, C.M. (Dr.)	Bruner, Mary Emma	23 Jun 1857	18 Jun 1857	PSOT
Finch, Morton B. (Dr.)	Barker, Mary E.	31 Dec 1853	30 Dec 1853	PDD
Finton, John J.	Orm, Emily A.	13 Dec 1859	11 Dec 1859	DET
Finton, John J.	Orm, Emily A.	14 Dec 1859	11 Dec 1859	WPT
Finton, Wm. H.H.	Stewart, Agnes	25 Nov 1865	16 Nov 1865	PTIMES
Firmstone, Joseph G.	March, Mary James	14 Nov 1844	04 Nov 1844	TRIB
Fisher, Andrew	Rockwell, Mary	05 Aug 1858	31 Jul 1858	DET
Fisher, Andrew	Rockwell, Mary	18 Aug 1858	31 Jul 1858	WPT
Fisher, David	Antram, Emma	09 Jul 1853	26 Jun 1853	DET
Fisher, Henry	Givens, Elizabeth	14 Apr 1854	09 Apr 1854	DET
Fisher, Jacob	Gebhardt, Jane A.	26 Mar 1856	06 Mar 1856	WPT
Fitch, Elias	Cutshall, Elizabeth	03 Oct 1851	27 Sep 1851	PI
Fitzgerald, Dr. Easton	Cissna, Hormeon	17 Feb 1854	09 Feb 1854	DET
Fitzgerald, Easom (Dr.)	Cissna, Harmeon	21 Feb 1854	09 Feb 1854	PDD
Flaugher, John	Johnson, Mary R.	02 Jul 1852	22 Jun 1852	PI
Flint, John T.	Feurt, Luna H.	31 Mar 1854		DET
Forbers, Arthur	Crawford, Martha	26 Nov 1856		WPT
Foster, Adam C.	Wormster, Sarah	30 Jan 1854	25 Jan 1854	DET*
Foster, Geo.	Hayward, Lora Ann	19 Dec 1853	08 Dec 1853	PDD
Foster, George	Hayward, Lora Ann	17 Dec 1853	08 Dec 1853	DET
Foster, J.J.	Ramsey, Ethalinda	06 Jan 1855	04 Jan 1855	DET
Foster, Joseph	Hamelton, Margaret	18 Mar 1853	21 Dec 1852	PI
Foulke, L.W. (M.D.)	McCoy, Elizabeth	11 Mar 1837	24 Feb 1837	STRIB
Fox, Benjamin	Smith, Nancy	02 Sep 1850	25 Jul 1850	PI
Fox, Benjamin	Smith, Nancy	29 Aug 1850	25 Jul 1850	PT&C
Foy, Randolf C.W.	Slack, Mary Ellen	08 Nov 1853	07 Nov 1853	DET
Foye, Winthrop	Finney, Roxana	01 Jun 1820	18 May 1820	STEL
Fraisor, John	Burk, Elisa	16 May 1854	11 May 1854	DET
Fraley, William C.	O'Neal, Martha	16 Sep 1850	08 Sep 1850	PI
Fraley, Wm.C.	O'Neil, Martha	19 Sep 1850	08 Sep 1850	PT&C
Frazer, William	Gappan, Hester A.	15 Jul 1850	11 Jul 1850	PI
Frazer, Wm.	Gappan, Hester A.	18 Jul 1850	11 Jul 1850	PT&C
Freeland, Middleton	McCann, Delilah	25 Oct 1853		PDD
Freelich, Jacob	Bey, Margaret	11 Jan 1853	13 Jan 1853	PI
Freelich, Jacob	Bey, Margaret	19 Jan 1853	13 Jan 1853	PT&C
Frost, John	Vickers, Margaret I.	17 Dec 1853	10 Dec 1853	DET
Frost, John	Vickers, Margaret J.	19 Dec 1853	10 Dec 1853	PDD

Name (Groom)	Name (Bride)	Notice Date	Marriage Date	Paper
Frost, Westley	Squires, Elizabeth	02 Jun 1854	01 Jun 1854	DET
Fullerton, Isaac	Mead, Elizabeth	21 Nov 1829		WT
Fulsom, Samuel	Cochran, Catharine	07 Oct 1850	30 Sep 1850	PI
Fultz, Andrew B.	Lewis, Emma H.	25 Mar 1858	18 Mar 1858	DET
Fultz, Andrew B.	Lewis, Emma H.	31 Mar 1858	18 Mar 1858	WPT
Funk, Jacob C.	Parnell, Hester	23 Sep 1850	27 Aug 1850	PI
Funk, Jacob C.	Parnell, Hester	26 Sep 1850	27 Aug 1850	PT&C
Furguson, William	Noel, Ellen	20 Dec 1849		PT&C
Gadburry, John	Lare, Minerva	28 Apr 1854	20 Apr 1854	DET
Gaffy, George B.	Jones, Isabella	13 Apr 1853	11 Apr 1853	PT&C
Gaffy, George H.	Gassoway, Annie L.	13 Aug 1864	11 Aug 1864	PTIMES
Garret, James	Hardy, Henrietta M.	27 Apr 1853	17 Apr 1853	PT&C
Garrett, Jno.	House, Louisa	13 May 1854		DET
Gartrell, Henry C.	Pogue, Lydia J.	19 Nov 1853	25 Oct 1853	DET
Gartrell, Henry C.	Pogue, Lida J.	08 Nov 1853	25 Oct 1853	DET
Garvin, Thomas	Allison, Mary	26 Jan 1844	18 Jan 1844	TRIB
Gates, Charles Valcalo	Cook, Mercy	12 May 1857	07 May 1857	PSOT
Gates, Erastus	Thompson, Maria L.	17 Mar 1854	16 Mar 1854	DET
Gates, Erastus	Thompson, Maria L.	20 Mar 1854	16 Mar 1854	PDD
Gates, Erastus	Thompson, Maria L.	22 Mar 1854	16 Mar 1854	SVREP
Gates, Wilson	Dodson, Julianna	21 Sep 1855	19 Sep 1855	DET
Gessert Jacob	Fortsib, Lissette	28 Jan 1857	22 Jan 1857	WPT
Gharky, G.H. (Capt.)	Oldfield, Martha	24 Sep 1852	20 Sep 1852	PI
Gibout, Peter	Smith, Sarah	18 Jun 1852		PI
Gilbert, Giles, Jr.	Currie, Mary	27 May 1857	27 May 1857	DET
Gilbert, Jos. C.	Varner, Sarah C.	31 Mar 1852	25 Mar 1852	PT&C
Gillianwottip, Leonard	White, Lucretia	16 Jun 1854	15 Jun 1854	DET
Gilliland, Nathan	Adams, Catherine	09 Feb 1844	18 Jan 1844	TRIB
Givens, Thomas J.	Laton, Elizabeth	28 May 1852	06 May 1852	PI
Glaze, Samuel W.	Coleman, Mary Jane	16 Apr 1851		PT&C
Glean, John	Neagle, Caroline	16 Feb 1853	10 Feb 1853	PT&C
Gleim, John	Neagle, Caroline	18 Feb 1853	10 Feb 1853	PI
Glenn, James	Franklin, Lizzie M.	06 Apr 1859	29 Mar 1859	WPT
Glidden, D.A.	Tomlinson, Josephene	16 Aug 1858	10 Aug 1858	DET
Glidden, D.A.	Tomlinson, Josephene	18 Aug 1858	10 Aug 1858	WPT
Glidden, J.M.	Young, Eliza E.	16 Feb 1844	06 Feb 1844	TRIB
Glidden, John J.	Bell, Mary E.	11 Oct 1862	08 Oct 1862	PTIMES
Glidden, Stephen S.	Garret, Sue M.	26 Dec 1855	20 Dec 1855	DET
Glidden, Stephen S.	Garret, Sue M.	26 Dec 1855	20 Dec 1855	WPT
Glover, Azel	Daring, Elizabeth	14 Jan 1825	30 Dec 1824	PG&LA
Goldenbury, Peter	Putrill, Cynthia	13, 14 Oct 1854	13 Oct 1854	DET
Goldsberry, Jacob	Martin, Mary (nee Pearl)	04 Jun 1851	18 May 1851	PT&C
Goldschmidt, Otto	Lind, Jenny	11 Feb 1852	05 Feb 1852	PT&C
Goligher, Samuel	Creely, Mary	10 Oct 1851	02 Oct 1851	PI
Goligher, Samuel	Creely, Mary	08 Oct 1851	02 Oct 1851	PT&C

Name (Groom)	Name (Bride)	Notice Date	Marriage Date	Paper
Goodin, Thomas	Carnes, Nancy	14 Jan 1854	05 Jan 1854	DET
Goodlor, R. Vivion	Blinn, Nettie	16 Jun 1855	05 Jun 1855	DET
Gordon, James Y.	Wetherbee, Cordelia	10 Apr 1855	09 Apr 1855	DET
Gould, Orrin B.	Willard, Lavenia S.	01 Feb 1859	26 Jan 1859	DET
Gould, Orrin B.	Willard, Lavinia Seeley	02 Feb 1859	26 Jan 1859	WPT
Graham, T.J. (Col.)	Toben, Eliza Mary	11 May 1855	10 May 1855	DET
Graham, William	Dunlap, Marcus	24 Dec 1853	17 Dec 1853	DET
Grant, George W.	Windgate, Rebecca	03 Dec 1853	27 Oct 1853	DET
Graves, William (Capt.)	Graves, Nancy	12 Aug 1825		PG&LA
Gray, David D.	Fields, Mary M.	08 Oct 1852	03 Oct 1852	PI
Gray, George	Warner, Susan	14 Nov 1853	13 Nov 1853	DET
Gray, George	Warner, Susan	16 Nov 1853	13 Nov 1853	PDD
Greathouse, W.C.	Allen, Maria	11 Jun 1855	07 Jun 1855	DET
Green, Gilbert T.	Green, Sarah E.	23 Jun 1857	09 Jun 1857	PSOT
Green, Samuel C.	Coleman, Mary	19 Oct 1854	12 Oct 1854	PDD
Gregmiles, James	Crisibles (?), Ellen	05 Apr 1855	29 Mar 1855	DET
Gregory, Moses	Tilton, Phebee	22 May 1838	13 May 1838	STRIB
Grimes, Will	Burriss, Hettie A.	27 Jun 1863	23 Jun 1863	PTIMES
Grinn, Henry	Powers, Catharine	16 Sep 1850		PI
Grinn, Henry	Powers, Catharine	12 Sep 1850		PT&C
Griswold, Dr. E.H.	Churchhill, Julia	11 Jun 1853	06 Jun 1853	DET
Griswold, E.H. (Dr.)	Churchhill, Julia	15 Jun 1853	06 Jun 1853	PT&C
Groniger, A.L.	Maynard, Amanda R.	12 Mar 1864	09 Mar 1864	PTIMES
Groniger, Leonard (Col.)	Darlinton, Mary B.	04 Jan 1856	27 Dec 1855	DET
Groniger, Leonard (Col.)	Darlinton, Mary B.	09 Jan 1856	27 Dec 1855	WPT
Grover, Isaiah	Malone, Hannah	20 Jul 1853	19 Jul 1853	DET
Gunn, Bela	Andrews, Almia	06 Sep 1828		WT
Gunn, Enos	McDonald, Nancy	04 Oct 1827	20 Sep 1827	WT
Gunn, Samuel	Moran, Margaret P.	06 Sep 1853	02 Sep 1853	PDD
Gunn, Samuel W.	Moran, Margaret P.	03 Sep 1853	02 Sep 1853	DET
Gunn, William	Cary, Nancy Jane	19 Dec 1851	16 Dec 1851	PI
Gunn, William	Cary, Nancy Jane	24 Dec 1851	16 Dec 1851	PT&C
Gurney, H.	Boyd, M.	11 Jul 1860	10 Jul 1860	DET
Guthrie, J.C.	Tracy, Emily A.	20 Jun 1863	11 Jun 1863	PTIMES
Gwynne, David (Maj.)	Claypool, Alice	17 Aug 1820	01 Aug 1820	STEL
Hacquard, Louis	Corns, Mary F.	02 Oct 1860	25 Sep 1860	DET
Hacquard, Louis	Corns, Mary F.	06 Oct 1860	25 Sep 1860	PTIMES
Hagan, J.D.	Hays, Margaret	07 Feb 1854	05 Feb 1854	PDD
Hall, H.L.	Fullerton, Lucy	02 Mar 1853	24 Feb 1853	PT&C
Hall, H.T.	Fullerton, Lucy	18 Mar 1853	24 Feb 1853	PI
Hall, O.J. (Dr.)	Boynton, Mary E.	17 May 1862	07 May 1862	PTIMES
Hall, Thomas F.S.	Rigdon, Sallie	25 May 1859	24 May 1859	DET
Hall, Thomas F.S.	Rigdon, Sallie	01 Jun 1859	27 May 1859	WPT
Hall, Wm. H.	Barbee, Sarah	23 Dec 1850	09 Dec 1850	PI
Hall, Wm. H.	Barbee, Sarah	19 Dec 1850	09 Dec 1850	PT&C

Name (Groom)	Name (Bride)	Notice Date	Marriage Date	Paper
Haller, Christian	Benning, Jael	13 Apr 1855		DET
Haller, William A.	Powers, Sarah Jane	19 May 1853	17 May 1853	PDD
Haller, Wm. A.	Powers, Sarah Jane	25 May 1853	17 May 1853	PT&C
Hamilton, J.A.	Rowland, Hattie A.	08 Oct 1859	06 Oct 1859	DET
Hamilton, J.A.	Rowland, Hattie A.	12 Oct 1859	06 Oct 1859	WPT
Hamilton, Robert	Rodgers, Rosa	16 Apr 1856	09 Apr 1856	WPT
Hamlin, Hannibal G.	Whitney, Mary	04 Feb 1825		PG&LA
Hammonds, Wyatt	Farney, Malinda G.	03 Jan 1855	25 Dec 1855	DET
Hard, Bethuel W.	Burke, Martha H.	12 Nov 1855	01 Nov 1855	DET
Hardy, Henry K. (Esq.)	Cade, Harriet (nee Sage)	03 Feb 1843	24 Jan 1843	TRIB
Harper, John J.	Jones, Emily	07 Feb 1856	06 Feb 1856	DET
Harper, John J.	Jones, Emily	08 Feb 1856	06 Feb 1856	OP
Harper, John L. (Capt.)	Abrams, Emma	01 Jun 1820	11 May 1820	STEL
Harris, Thomas L. (Hon.)	female	01 Dec 1855	24 Nov 1855	WPT
Harrison, Elizabeth	Cole, John	17 Jun 1853	07 Jun 1853	PDD
Harrison, Thomas B.	Voorhies, Mary E.	02 Jan 1864	23 Dec 1863	PTIMES
Hert, Erastus	Glove, Ann	22 Oct 1852	13 Oct 1852	PI
Hart, John W.	Collins, Harriette	13 Mar 1854	07 Mar 1854	DET
Hart, William	Howard, Mary Adeline	20 Aug 1856	14 Aug 1856	WPT
Harvey, James	Crain, Mary	18 Mar 1853	21 Jan 1853	PI
Hatch, John	Jones, _____ W.	23 Mar 1826	09 Mar 1826	TA
Hatch, Thomas	Ela, Sophia A.	14 Jan 1825	05 Aug 1824	PG&LA
Haule, H.	Stemshorn, Magdaline	28 Jan 1852	19 Jan 1852	PT&C
Havens, Howard J.	O'Briant, Sarah	06 Jun 1853	27 May 1853	PDD
Hawley, C.G.	Kelley, Mary	25 May 1858	19 May 1858	PSOT
Hawley, Josiah	Phillips, Azuba	18 Mar 1820		STEL
Hayes, John	Ormstead, Elizabeth	05 Jan 1853	04 Jan 1853	PT&C
Hays, Sylvester R.	Gilruth, Naomi M.	12 Mar 1846	05 Mar 1846	TRIB
Hayt, Benjamin	Rawley, Elizabeth	08 Mar 1844	23 Feb 1844	TRIB
Hayward, H.	Wait, O.	10 Apr 1855	22 Mar 1855	DET
Headley, George	Hitchcock, Rebecca	23 Dec 1850	11 Dec 1850	PI
Headley, George	Hitchcock, Rebecca	19 Dec 1850	11 Dec 1850	PT&C
Heakl, C.	Cilley, M.	11 Jan 1853	02 Jan 1853	PI
Hearn, W.T. Chatmers	Fuller, Frances H.	01 Dec 1855	23 Nov 1855	WPT
Hechinger, Anthony	Nugent, Mary	15 Oct 1851	09 Oct 1851	PT&C
Helphenstein, Geo. W.	Spry, Frances	31 Jan 1863	28 Jan 1863	PTIMES
Henry, William D.	Cloninger, Sarah V.	20 Jul 1858	08 Jul 1858	PSOT
Hernandez, Louis A.	Lodwick, Ellen	22 Nov 1859	14 Nov 1859	DET
Herron, John	Stokely, Mary	08 Sep 1855	07 Sep 1855	DET
Hervey, David E.	Glenn, Lizzie J.	11 Nov 1857	04 Nov 1857	WPT
Hewes, Edward	Robinson, Harriet A.	21 Apr 1854	20 Apr 1854	DET
Hewes, Edward	Robinson, Harriet	22 Apr 1854	20 Apr 1854	PDD
Hibbs, Van B. (Col.)	Vance, Electa	13 May 1865	27 Apr 1865	PTIMES
Hick, S.D.	Wheelock, S.J.	26 Jun 1855	25 Jun 1855	DET
Hickman, Adolphus	Hesler, Mary	24 Sep 1856	19 Sep 1856	WPT

Name (Groom)	Name (Bride)	Notice Date	Marriage Date	Paper
Hicks, William	Mault, Lucina	13 Dec 1855	09 Dec 1855	DET
Hicks, Williams	Tubbs, Susan	10 Nov 1853	27 Oct 1853	DET
Higgins, Robert B.	Simonson, Matilda	13 Apr 1853	07 Apr 1853	PT&C
Hildebrand, Charles	Martin, Lucina	27 May 1831	22 May 1831	PC&WT
Hill, John	Reddick, Eliza A.	20 Sep 1854	19 Sep 1854	DET
Hill, John	Reddick, Eliza A.S.	21 Sep 1854	19 Sep 1854	PDD
Hill, Perry	Hill, Catharine	03 Nov 1852	28 Oct 1852	PT&C
Hills, C. Elmer	Cowles, Sue B.	21 Jun 1862	10 Apr 1862	PTIMES
Hinkle, John	Stentemann, Barbara	21 Nov 1855	19 Nov 1855	DET
Hinkle, John	Stentzmann, Barbara	21 Nov 1855	19 Nov 1855	WPT
Hinman, John	Thurston, Lucy	10 Nov 1857	10 Nov 1857	DET
Hinman, John	Thurston, Lucy	11 Nov 1857	10 Nov 1857	WPT
Hise, Phillip	McClary, Nancy	26 Oct 1853		PDD
Hitchcock, Caleb	Rice, Sarah Anna	08 Jun 1853	19 May 1853	PT&C
Hitchcock, Lewis	Winkler, Mary Jane	23 Dec 1865	14 Dec 1865	PTIMES
Hobart, Jacob	Eck, Elizabeth	02 Jan 1852	30 Dec 1851	PI
Hobart, Jacob	Eck, Elizabeth	31 Dec 1851	30 Dec 1851	PT&C
Hobbins, James	Chambers, Harriet	27 Jul 1853		DET
Hobler, W.H.	Clary, Sarah Elizabeth	02 Jan 1864	27 Dec 1863	PTIMES
Hoe, H.	Handle, Ann	29 Apr 1853	23 Apr 1853	PDD
Hogan, John	Noel, Maria J.	09 Dec 1865	05 Dec 1865	PTIMES
Hogan, William	Reynolds, Martha Ann	24 Nov 1854	23 Nov 1854	DET
Holes, Tingeley	Holliday, Ann	23 Dec 1850	11 Dec 1850	PI
Holes, Tingeley	Holliday, Ann	19 Dec 1850	11 Dec 1850	PT&C
Holloday, John H.	Eakins, Temperance Jane	16 Apr 1856	06 Apr 1856	WPT
Hoover, Alaniah	Holcomb, Clarissa	28 Nov 1853	22 Nov 1853	DET
Hoover, Alaniah	Holcomb, Clarissa	30 Nov 1853	22 Nov 1853	PDD
Hoover, Andrew Jackson Lewis	Tucker, Caroline	10 Oct 1854	10 Oct 1854	DET
Hopkins, Joseph	Montgomery, Sarah	01 Oct 1856	25 Sep 1856	WPT
Hore, Philip H.	Wilhelms, Matilda C.	01 Oct 1856	Sep 1856	WPT
Horn, Jonathan	Smith, Eliza A.	14 Apr 1848	04 Apr 1848	DENQ
Horse, George	Appal, Mary	18 Jul 1854	17 Jul 1854	PDD
Hosward, Claburn	Brooks, Lucinda	11 Jun 1856	30 May 1856	WPT
Hott, Alfred M.	Reese, Rose E.	23 Oct 1858	20 Oct 1858	DET
Houston, William C.	Davis, Laura V.	04 Mar 1859	01 Mar 1859	DET
Houston, William C.	Davis, Laura V.	09 Mar 1859	01 Mar 1859	WPT
Hoy, Charles W., Esq.	Taylor, Caroline C.	16 Sep 1853	07 Sep 1853	DET
Hoyt, Alfred M.	Reese, Rose E.	27 Oct 1858	20 Oct 1858	WPT
Hubbard, Stephen	McGlone, Frances	23 Dec 1850	10 Oct 1850	PI
Hubbard, Stephen	McGlone, Frances	19 Dec 1850	20 Oct 1850	PT&C
Hubbell, Wake	Whitteker, Keith	17 Mar 1858	23 Feb 1858	WPT
Hughes, E.B.	Wigh__m, Lizzie	01 Feb 1856	31 Jan 1856	DET
Hughes, Edward (Capt.)	Holmes, Mary	07 Jul 1829		WT

Name (Groom)	Name (Bride)	Notice Date	Marriage Date	Paper
Hughes, Jacob B.	Stevenson, Annie Emeline	14 Apr 1855	09 Apr 1855	DET
Hull, Julius (Capt.)	Fuller, Jane M.	14 Jul 1854	12 Jul 1854	DET
Humph, Allen	Nail, Rachael	26 Jun 1854	17 Jun 1854	PDD
Humphries, G.W. (Sheriff)	Aldrich, Martha J. (nee Turner)	02 Jan 1845	28 Nov 1844	TRIB
Humphries, James	Lair, Frances	08 Mar 1844	02 Mar 1844	TRIB
Hunsuck, Nathan	Brown, Mary A.	09 Jan 1851	01 Jan 1851	PT&C
Hunt, Randall	McLean, female	14 Jul 1854	12 Jul 1854	PDD
Huodersheldt, Phillip	Smith, Jennet	10 Nov 1853	01 Nov 1853	DET
Hurdell, Wake	Whittaker, Keith	11 Mar 1858	23 Feb 1858	DET
Hutchins, Wells A. (Esq.)	Robinson, Cornelia M.	24 Feb 1843	23 Feb 1843	TRIB
Hutchinson, George	Loffland, Mary	30 Jan 1854	26 Jan 1854	DET
Hymanne, H.	Seeberger, Hannah	28 Jul 1860		DET
Hymanne, H.	Seeberger, Hannah	01 Aug 1860		WPT
Iams, Solomon	Gapin, Mary A.	09 Jan 1851	03 Jan 1851	PT&C
Ingles, Harrison	Hardin, Elizabeth	03 Oct 1848	15 Sep 1848	DENQ
Inman, William	Dixon, Clarissa	19 Dec 1850	12 Dec 1850	PT&C
Inman, William	Dixon, Clarissa	23 Dec 1850	12 Dec 1850	PI
Isaacs, Fielding	Wilson, Angeline	24 Dec 1853	19 Dec 1853	DET
Isinhart, Joseph	Neili, Barbary	23 Dec 1850	30 Nov 1850	PI
Isinhart, Joseph	Neili, Barbary	19 Dec 1850	30 Nov 1850	PT&C
Jack, William	M'Collister, Susan	03 Aug 1820		STEL
Jackson, Albert	Bleaks, Sarah	24 Feb 1851	18 Feb 1851	PI
Jackson, John	Faulkner, Eliza	09 Nov 1855	01 Nov 1855	DET
Jackson, William Jr.	Bennett, Eizabeth Jane	09 Jul 1856	15 Jun 1856	WPT
James, Alva H.	Skelton, Cynthia	06 Dec 1855	20 Nov 1855	DET
James, E.	Jurdan, Susannah	08 Feb 1854	22 Jan 1854	DET
Janney, L.	Wood, F.H.	21 Mar 1863	09 Mar 1863	PTIMES
Jarow, Anthony	Hannet, Mary	08 Jan 1856	29 Dec 1855	DET
Jarow, Anthony	Hanet, Mary	09 Jan 1856	29 Dec 1855	WPT
Jeffords, John	Rhodes, Emma	10 Oct 1851	01 Oct 1851	PI
Jeffords, John	Rhodes, Emma	08 Oct 1851	01 Oct 1851	PT&C
Jelly, Charles	Yearning, Sarah	01 May 1854	24 Apr 1854	DET
Jobes, Abraham	Miller, Ann E.	24 Feb 1851	18 Feb 1851	PI
Jobes, Abraham	Miller, Ann E.	19 Feb 1851	18 Feb 1851	PT&C
Johnson, Andrew	Reynolds, Lenas	31 Dec 1853	23 Dec 1853	DET
Johnson, Andrew	Reynolds, Lenas	05 Jan 1854	23 Dec 1853	PDD
Johnson, Benj. H.	Bailey, Mary Jane	15 Nov 1854	02 Nov 1854	DET
Johnson, Daniel	Johnson, Margaret T.	01 Dec 1853	20 Nov 1853	DET
Johnson, David	Johnson, Margaret T.	30 Nov 1853	02 Nov 1853	PDD
Johnson, Isaac	Yeager, Fanny L.	05 Mar 1864	26 Feb 1864	PTIMES
Johnson, J.H.	Davis, Mary Jane	13 Apr 1859	11 Apr 1859	WPT
Johnson, James A.	Payne, Bette F.	31 Mar 1854	29 Mar 1854	DET
Johnson, John (Esq.)	Gregg, female	28 Feb 1854	22 Feb 1854	PDD

Name (Groom)	Name (Bride)	Notice Date	Marriage Date	Paper
Johnson, Thomas	Vanmetre, Ann	17 Nov 1853	05 Nov 1853	PDD
Johnson, W.T.	Mathews Catharine	18 Mar 1853	12 Feb 1853	PI
Johnson, William S.	Mathews, Catharine	18 Feb 1853	12 Feb 1853	PI
Johnson, William S.	Mathews, Catharine	16 Feb 1853	12 Feb 1853	PT&C
Jones, Allen	M'Cleves, Mary Ann	20 Dec 1849	18 Dec 1849	PT&C
Jones, D.L.	Evans, Margaret E.	25 Oct 1853	22 Oct 1853	PDD
Jones, E. Glover	Young, Fanny Belle	03 May 1844	15 Apr 1844	TRIB
Jones, Elias	Swap, Delia (Mrs.)	11 Apr 1854	11 Feb 1854	PDD
Jones, Henry	Cameron, Nancy	25 Jul 1844	18 Jul 1844	TRIB
Jones, Isaac D.	Jones, Elizabeth	07 May 1856	06 May 1856	WPT
Jones, John Milton	Spence, Cynthia A.	17 Jun 1850	06 Jun 1850	PI
Jones, Nathan L., Jr.	Clare, Eliza	14 Feb 1856	13 Feb 1856	DET
Jones, William	Lewis, Sarah A.	11 Jun 1853	02 Jun 1853	DET
Jones, William	Lewis, Sarah A.	15 Jun 1853	02 Jun 1853	PT&C
Jones, William W.	Yemens, Susannah	07 Oct 1850	01 Oct 1850	PI
Jones, William W.	Yemens, Susannah	03 Oct 1850	01 Oct 1850	PT&C
Jordan, Edward W.	Ricker, Augusta	03 Nov 1852	27 Oct 1852	PT&C
Jordan, Edward W., Esq.	Ricker, Augusta	29 Oct 1852	27 Oct 1852	PI
Jordan, Robert C.	Clugsten, Mary E.	06 May 1850	30 Apr 1850	PI
Jordon, Thomas J.	Waring, Mary L.	29 Oct 1858	28 Oct 1858	DET
Jordon, Thomas J.	Waring, Mary L.	10 Nov 1858	28 Oct 1858	WPT
K_bler, C.H.	Brice, Mary E.	28 Feb 1854	24 Feb 1854	PDD
Karr, Abraham	Armstrong, Lettis	05 Nov 1858	21 Oct 1858	SVREP
Kaugh, Mathias	Clise, Catharine	30 Apr 1856	24 Apr 1856	WPT
Keagerice, Amos R.	Skimmer, Mary A.	27 Jun 1853	15 Jun 1853	DET
Keagerice, Amos R.	Skimmer, Mary A.	29 Jun 1853	15 Jun 1853	PT&C
Keeton, G.W.	Price, Maria	22 Jul 1854	08 Jul 1854	DET
Keeton, William	England, Melvina	27 Dec 1853	11 Dec 1853	DET
Kehoe, Chas. T.	Day, Eliza A.	01 Dec 1854	29 Nov 1854	DET
Kehoe, John	Wakeman, Jennie C.	15 May 1860	08 May 1860	DET
Kehoe, John	Wakeman, Jennie C.	16 May 1860	08 May 1860	WPT
Kellander, Wm. L.	Holbert, Nancy	16 Jul 1856	06 Jul 1856	WPT
Kelley, Henry	Call, Harriet E.	16 Dec 1854	06 Dec 1854	DET
Kelley, Thomas D.	Gilruth, Minerva	08 Jan 1856	01 Jan 1856	DET
Kelley, Thomas D.	Gilruth, Minerva	09 Jan 1856	01 Jan 1856	WPT
Kemp,. C.T.M.	Johnson, Adelia	11 Jun 1856	04 Jun 1856	WPT
Kendall, Henry	Barnett, Maria	15 Nov 1862	16 Oct 1862	PTIMES
Kendall, Stephen	Riggs, Rebecca	09 Aug 1839	06 Aug 1839	TRIB
Kendrick, Edward	Mulligan, Eliza	07 Feb 1863	01 Feb 1863	PTIMES
Kennedy, Milton	Hutchinson, Josephine B.	23 Dec 1850	20 Oct 1850	PI
Kennedy, Milton	Hutchinson, Josephine B.	19 Dec 1850	20 Oct 1850	PT&C
Kennedy, Peter	Timmons, Sarah	02 Jan 1852	28 Dec 1851	PI
Kennedy, Peter	Timmons, Sarah	31 Dec 1851	28 Dec 1851	PT&C
Kennedy, Rezin	Wite, Elizabeth	10 Mar 1855	08 Mar 1855	DET
Kennedy, Warren	Turner, Levina	19 Jan 1856	16 Jan 1856	DET

Name (Groom)	Name (Bride)	Notice Date	Marriage Date	Paper
Kent, Arod	Whitcomb, Narcissa	14 Jan 1825	21 Oct 1824	PG&LA
Kerr, J. Harry	Merritt, Libbie	09 Jul 1864	30 Jun 1864	PTIMES
Kiine (?), Henry	Hodge, Nancy	30 Jun 1854	29 Jun 1854	PDD
Killin, Joseph W.	Adams, Cornelia F.	03 Dec 1853	29 Nov 1853	DET
Killin, Joseph W.	Adams, Cornelia F.	04 Dec 1853	29 Nov 1853	PDD
Kilmer, Washington (Dr.)	Davey, Florence	22 Oct 1864	18 Oct 1864	PTIMES
Kimbro, William	Nookes, Rachel	20 May 1854	20 Apr 1854	DET
Kimbro, Wm.	Vorex, Rachael	06 May 1854	21 Apr 1854	PDD
Kinney, Alfred	Sill, Mary	28 Jan 1853	26 Jan 1853	PI
Kinney, Charles	Cox, Elizabeth	31 Oct 1848	09 Oct 1848	DENQ
Kinney, Eli	Lodwick, Martha	14 Oct 1837	10 Oct 1837	STRIB
Kinney, Henry	McNairn, Mary	10 Nov 1843	07 Nov 1843	TRIB
Kinney, John	Wright, Salina	12 Aug 1853	11 Aug 1853	PDD
Kinney, Philander C.	Clark, Marie Louisa	10 Jun 1850	04 Jun 1850	PI
Kinney, Philander C.	Clark, Maria Louisa	06 Jun 1850	04 Jun 1850	PT&C
Kirk, Thomas	Biggs, Nancy	30 Jul 1852	26 Jul 1852	PI
Kirkhouse, George	Smith, Elden	11 Jan 1853	25 Dec 1852	PI
Kittle, Jessee	Nurse, Lucy	04 Nov 1837	31 Oct 1837	STRIB
Kline, John	Wheeler, Susan	17 Aug 1854	16 Aug 1854	DET
Kline, John	Wheeler, Susan	19 Aug 1854	16 Aug 1854	PDD
Knobloch, Henry	Groves, Nancy	13 Apr 1853	03 Apr 1853	PT&C
Kramer, Adam	Reiss, Catharine	10 Aug 1854	06 Aug 1854	DET
Kringh, Charles W.	Doddridge, Ella Virginia	02 Dec 1859	24 Nov 1859	DET
Lackry, James	Sharp, Mary	24 Sep 1855	30 Aug 1855	DET
Lacy, Daniel	Boyd, Elizabeth	22 Dec 1855 08 Jan 1856	20 Dec 1855	DET
Lacy, Daniel	Boyd, Elizabeth	26 Dec 1855 09 Jan 1856	20 Dec 1855	WPT
Laird, David	Long, Nancy	20 Feb 1838	02 Feb 1838	STRIB
Lalendorf, Charles	Kidd, Sirena	23 Jul 1851	17 Jul 1851	PT&C
Lalendorff, Charles	Kidd, Serena	21 Jul 1851	17 Jul 1851	PI
Lamber, William	Andre, Rosina	19 May 1852	05 May 1852	PT&C
Landon, Charles	Row, C.	14 Sep 1858	13 Sep 1858	DET
Landon, Charles	Row, C.	15 Sep 1858	13 Sep 1858	WPT
Landon, Charles C.	Row, Mary C.	28 Sep 1858	15 Sep 1858	PTIMES
Lane, Wilson M.	Watson, Rhoda	10, 24 Feb 1854	04 Feb 1854	DET
Lantz, Francis	Russio, Alivno	22 Apr 1854	20 Apr 1854	PDD
Lawhead, Israel	Randall, Harriet J.	27 Feb 1854	16 Feb 1854	PDD
Lawrence, T.B. (Col.)	Chapman, female	24 Mar 1854		PDD
Lawson, Manasseh M.	Burr, Mollie	18 Jun 1864		PTIMES
Lawson, T.B.	Turley, Sarah C.	28 Oct 1865	24 Oct 1865	PTIMES
Lawyer, Alexander	Leasure, Mary Jane	06 Sep 1853	23 Aug 1853	DET
Leard, James	Fox, Catharine	15 Jul 1850	09 Jul 1850	PI
Leard, James	Fox, Catharine	11 Jul 1850	09 Jul 1850	PT&C
Lee, David W.	Walker, Hannah	08 Dec 1855	06 Dec 1855	DET

Name (Groom)	Name (Bride)	Notice Date	Marriage Date	Paper
Lehman, Joseph	Rishman, Hannah	06 May 1854	21 Apr 1854	PDD
Leonard, John	Cunningham, Hester	10 Jun 1850		PI
Lewis, Alexander	Cable, Melissa	06 Oct 1855	03 Oct 1855	DET
Lewis, Chas. B.	Wilson, Fanny E.	07 May 1856	01 May 1856	WPT
Lewis, Eli	Sweet, Susan	27 Apr 1853	21 Apr 1853	PT&C
Lewis, John	Baccus, Marilda	30 Jan 1858	21 Jan 1858	DET
Lewis, John	Baccus, Marilda	03 Feb 1858	21 Jan 1858	WPT
Lewis, John C.	Funk, Margaret Ann	28 Dec 1852	27 Dec 1852	PDD
Lewis, John C.	Funk, Margaret Ann	31 Dec 1852	27 Dec 1852	PI
Lewis, John C.	Funk, Margaret Ann	29 Dec 1852	27 Dec 1852	PT&C
Lewis, Josiah	Sweet, Eliza	01 Oct 1844	12 Sep 1844	PDEM
Lewis, Thomas C.	Malcom, Josefita Rais	18 Jul 1848	15 Jul 1848	DENQ
Lewis, W.	Pennington, Jane	16 Jun 1855	05 Jun 1855	DET
Lindsey, Peter	Wheeler, Abigail	18 May 1820	14 May 1820	STEL
Lindsey, William	Hamilton, Currance Ann	19 Aug 1853	17 Aug 1853	DET
Lindsey, William	Hamilton, Currence Ann	24 Aug 1853	17 Aug 1853	PT&C
Linly, James S.	Sly, Marthy Ann	05 Jan 1854	27 Dec 1853	DET
Little, William W.	Timmonds, M.A.J.	31 Jan 1854	29 Jan 1854	DET
Littlejohn, Daniel	Thompson, Elizabeth	14 Jan 1825	25 Dec 1824	PG&LA
Littlejohn, Henry	Smith, Caroline	07 Jan 1853	02 Jan 1853	PI
Littlejohn, Henry	Smith, Caroline	05 Jan 1853	02 Jan 1853	PT&C
Littlejohn, Joseph	Perry, Mary Ann	22 Oct 1856	29 Sep 1856	WPT
Littlejohn, Valentine	Griffith, Margaret	23 Dec 1850	12 Oct 1850	PI
Littlejohn, Valentine	Griffith, Margaret	19 Dec 1850	12 Oct 1850	PT&C
Lloyd, Charles P.	Bentley, Laura J.	28 Feb 1863	26 Feb 1863	PTIMES
Lloyd, Joseph S.	Meakley, Martha A.	28 Jun 1855	27 Jun 1855	DET
Lloyd, William	Price, Levina	28 Feb 1854	27 Feb 1854	DET
Lloyd, William	Price, Lavina E.	01 Mar 1854	26 Feb 1854	PDD
Lock, John F.	Glover, Sarah	21 May 1852	13 May 1852	PI
Locke, Hiram W.	Thomas, Mary Jane	29 Dec 1853	25 Dec 1853	DET
Lodwick, John K.	Thomas, E.M.	12 Sep 1850	09 Sep 1850	PT&C
Lodwick, Joseph F.(Capt.)	Thompson, Jane	18 Nov 1831	08 Nov 1831	PC&WT
Lodwick, Murty W.	Veach, Mary	16 Dec 1865	13 Dec 1865	PTIMES
Lolland, Jacob	Wazeily, Mary	12 Nov 1856		WPT
Long, James	Morrison, Emma	26 Nov 1858	23 Nov 1858	DET
Long, James	Morrison, Emma	01 Dec 1858	23 Nov 1858	WPT
Long, Joseph	Kerr, Ann Eliza	04 Oct 1862	01 Oct 1862	PTIMES
Long, William	Lawson, Nancy	14 Apr 1851	11 Apr 1851	PI
Long, William	Matison, Mary	31 Jan 1854	29 Jan 1854	PDD
Loomis, H.W.	Richart, Martha J.	28 Sep 1859	27 Sep 1859	DET
Loomis, H.W.	Richart, Martha J.	28 Sep 1859	27 Sep 1859	WPT
Loomsis, Thomas D.	Metcalf, Caroline	18 Mar 1853	13 Jan 1853	PI
Louderack, Phillip	Thompson, Ann	14 Oct 1855	25 Sep 1855	DET
Loughry, John C.	Brown, Sarah	07 Nov 1857	05 Nov 1857	DET
Louis, Wm.	Morrison, Philora	19 Nov 1856		WPT

Name (Groom)	Name (Bride)	Notice Date	Marriage Date	Paper
Lowe, Frederick	Chaffin, Mary	20 Feb 1860	15 Feb 1860	DET
Lowe, Frederick	Chaffin, Mary	22 Feb 1860	15 Feb 1860	WPT
Lowe, Peter T.	Butler, Julia A.	28 Apr 1843	20 Apr 1843	TRIB
Lowry, James P. (Esq.)	Pratling, Elizabeth	11 Feb 1857	29 Jan 1857	WPT
Lucas, John B.	Moore, Elizabeth F.	17 Mar 1854	14 Mar 1854	DET
Lucas, John B.	Moore, Elizabeth F.	20 Mar 1854	14 Mar 1854	PDD
Lucas, John B.	Moore, Elizabeth F.	22 Mar 1854	14 Mar 1854	SVREP
Ludlam, male	Baldwin, Lydia	13 Sep 1853	06 Sep 1853	PDD
Ludlam, male	Baldwin, Lydia	12 Sep 1853	06 Sep 1853	DET
Lusher, Louis W.	Chapman, Cynthia	12 Oct 1855	12 Oct 1855	DET
Lust, Philip	Winters, Christina	21 Jul 1853	19 Jul 1853	DET
Lust, Philip	Winters, Christina	27 Jul 1853	19 Jul 1853	PT&C
Luther, Lawrence	McGee, Effa	19 Apr 1844	28 Mar 1844	TRIB
Lutz, Lawrence	Luther, Margaret	20 Apr 1853	14 Apr 1853	PT&C
Lybrook, Henler	Ropp, Mary	25 Aug 1852	19 Aug 1852	PT&C
Lynn, John M.	Richardson, Alice	05 May 1854	04 May 1854	DET
Lyon, Stephen	Lamb, Rebecca	24 Feb 1855	01 Feb 1855	DET
Macatee, W.	Sulivan, Caroline	02 Mar 1854	28 Feb 1854	PDD
Mackey, Thos. R.	Morrison, Martha	04 Jun 1856	02 Jun 1856	WPT
Mackley, Davis	Hawk, Elisa	16 Oct 1858	05 Oct 1858	DET
MacKoy, H.C.	Timmons, Semantha	04 Oct 1853		DET
Mackoy, H.C.	Timmons, Semantha	05 Oct 1853	04 Oct 1853	PDD
MacKoy, J.L.	Pratt, Mary E.	24 Feb 1851	18 Feb 1851	PI
Macy, Joseph	Moore, Sarah	18 Aug 1852		PT&C
Maklem, R.S.	Boyd, Mary Jane	17 Nov 1852		PI
Malone, Thomas	Keough, Elizabeth Ann	06 Oct 1860	26 Sep 1860	PTIMES
Maloney, Wm. A.	Wilson, Rachel	29 Oct 1851	23 Oct 1851	PT&C
Mangen, Francis	Belica Anestatio	13 Jul 1854	12 Jul 1854	DET
Mangen, Francis	Belica, Anestatiio	15 Jul 1854	12 Jul 1854	PDD
Maratu, Washington	Sullivan, Caroline	01 Mar 1854	28 Feb 1854	DET
Marquart, Henry	Lidensmith, Christian	20 Dec 1849	14 Dec 1849	PT&C
Marsh, Wm. A.	Morgan, Eleanor	18 Jul 1850	26 Jun 1850	PT&C
Marshall, Clinton	Moore, Orpha	28 Sep 1858	12 Sep 1858	PSOT
Marshall, Clinton	Moore, female	28 Sep 1858	12 Sep 1858	PTIMES
Marshel, James	Noel, Sarah Ann	08 Apr 1854	04 Apr 1854	DET
Martin, John H.	Williams, Louisa	24 Mar 1854	19 Mar 1854	DET
Martin, Robert	Osborne, Sarah	22 Dec 1852	16 Dec 1852	PT&C
Martin, W.P.	Weatherbee, Mary J.	02 Apr 1856	31 Mar 1856	WPT
Masterson, James	Byers, Hannah	20 Apr 1853	13 Apr 1853	PT&C
Masterson, William N.	Williams, Ann G.	10 Nov 1853	01 Nov 1853	DET
Matthews, Rev. Joseph	Saunders, Mrs. Martha P.	17 Feb 1854	03 Feb 1854	DET
Maule, John	Washer, Olinda	26 Sep 1855	25 Sep 1855	DET
May, Hugh	Sworberry, Eliza	04 Jun 1858	03 Jun 1858	DET
May, Hugh	Sworberry, Eliza	09 Jun 1858	03 Jun 1858	WPT
May, Matthias	Och, Sophia	28 May 1852	29 Apr 1852	PI

Name (Groom)	Name (Bride)	Notice Date	Marriage Date	Paper
M'Call, Solomon	Moore, Maria	14 Nov 1851	06 Nov 1851	PI
McCann, Jennings	Vessall, Nancy	11 Aug 1852	07 Aug 1852	PT&C
McCarty, Michael	Robins, Mary Jane	09 Apr 1856	03 Apr 1856	WPT
McCauslen, A.W.	Armstrong, Ella E.	22 Mar 1855	15 Mar 1855	DET
McClean, Samuel	Kellough, Mary Jane	16 Feb 1854	12 Feb 1854	DET
McCloud, Uriah	Ruggles, Armena	25 Feb 1857	15 Feb 1857	WPT
McClure, Emmit	Stevenson, Sarah	28 Jan 1860	26 Jan 1860	DET
McCollister, Thomas J.	Shellieg, Maggie	15 Aug 1860	13 Aug 1860	DET
McCollister, Thomas J.	Shellieg, Maggie	22 Aug 1860	13 Aug 1860	WPT
McColm, William S.	Orm, Eliza Jane	02 Dec 1853	01 Dec 1853	DET
McConnell, Charles L.	Henderson, Belle R.	28 Oct 1853	28 Sep 1853	PDD
McConnell, John	Ord, Sophia	13 May 1825	08 May 1825	PG&LA
McConnell, Robert	Marford, Elizabeth	02 Apr 1856	27 Mar 1856	WPT
McCown, Monroe	Terry, Henrietta	29 Dec 1860	16 Dec 1860	PTIMES
McCracken, Ralph	McConnell, Caroline R.	02 Oct 1855	18 Sep 1855	DET
McCulcher, John	Hiett, Ruth	28 Feb 1854	22 Feb 1854	PDD
McDaniel, Horatio	Joice, Nercicia	03 Dec 1853	24 Nov 1853	DET
McDaniel, William	Helphinstine, Virginia E.	20 Jan 1854	12 Jan 1854	DET
McDaniel, Wm.	Helphinstine, Virginia E.	21 Jan 1854	12 Jan 1854	PDD
McDermit, A.J.	Allowase, Eliza C.	03 Dec 1858	02 Dec 1858	DET
McDermit, A.J.	Allowase, Eliza C.	08 Dec 1858	02 Dec 1858	WPT
McDivill, Daniel	Call, Malvina	24 Oct 1844	15 Sep 1844	TRIB
McDonald, W.D.	Moss, Sally Ann	25 Mar 1853	22 Mar 1853	PI
McDonald, W.D.	Moss, Sally Ann	30 Mar 1853	22 Mar 1853	PT&C
McDougal, James	Ball, Laura H.	06 Oct 1860	30 Sep 1860	PTIMES
McDougal, James O.	Ball, Laura H.	02 Oct 1860	30 Sep 1860	DET
McDowell, Joseph J.	Clover, Mary A.	23 Nov 1858	18 Nov 1858	DET
McDowell, Joseph J.	Clover, Mary A.	24 Nov 1858	18 Nov 1858	WPT
McDowell, Wm. (Esq.)	Breck, Bettie	30 Jan 1854	10 Jan 1854	PDD
McElhinney, John	Prescott, Harriet	09 Feb 1853	03 Feb 1853	PT&C
McElroy, J. Newton (Lt.Col.)	Sweetser, Della	21 Jun 1862	10 Apr 1862	PTIMES
McEntee, Thomas	Salladay, Marilda	22 Apr 1854	20 Apr 1854	DET
McFaun, A.J.	Anore, Nancy	11 Jan 1853	23 Dec 1852	PI
McGough, M.	Hester, Rebecca	20 Jul 1854	13 Jul 1854	DET
McIntire, Daniel	Jones, Mary	13 Nov 1838	06 Nov 1838	STRIB
McKey, Samuel	Huckworth, Hester	16, 17 Aug 1855	16 Aug 1855	DET
McLean, Samuey	Kellough, Mary Jane	17 Feb 1854	12 Feb 1854	PDD
M'Cloud, Samuel J.	Waterhouse, Elizabeth	09 Sep 1818	03 Sep 1818	PGAZ
M'Clure, Alexander	Rhineheart, Mary Ann	03 Apr 1838	01 Apr 1838	STRIB
McNamer, James	Wallace, Nancy A.	25 Nov 1865	16 Nov 1865	PTIMES
M'Colm, William L.	Orm, Eliza Jane	03 Dec 1853	01 Dec 1853	PDD
McQuillin, Samuel	Proctor, Elizabeth	03 Sep 1857	25 Aug 1857	WPT
M'Daniel, Horatio	Joice, Nercica	04 Dec 1853	24 Nov 1853	PDD
M'Dowel, John	Price, Elizabeth	13 Jan 1819		PGAZ

Name (Groom)	Name (Bride)	Notice Date	Marriage Date	Paper
M'Dowell, James S.	Smith, Mary W.	20 Aug 1851	14 Aug 1851	PT&C
M'Dowell, Jno., Jr.	Ackey, Mary E.	24 Sep 1852	21 Sep 1852	PI
M'Dowell, John	Jefferson, Mary W.	28 Sep 1820	19 Sep 1820	STEL
M'Dowell, William	Clingman, Eliza	07 Jan 1830	05 Jan 1830	WT
Meacham, Charles A.	Rush, Eliza	31 Dec 1853	22 Dec 1853	DET
Meacham, Chas. A.	Rush, Eliza	05 Jan 1854	22 Dec 1853	PDD
Meacham, James	Wollom, Margaret	25 Aug 1854	10 Aug 1854	DET
Medary, Samuel A.	Disney, Sallie	12 Apr 1858	07 Apr 1858	DET
Medary, Samuel A.	Disney, Sallie	14 Apr 1858	07 Apr 1858	WPT
Meek, William	Tomlinson, Julia	15 Jul 1850	11 Jul 1850	PI
Meek, William	Tomlinson, Julia	18 Jul 1850 29 Aug 1850	11 Jul 1850	PT&C
Merret, James A. (Dr.)	Brown, Antoinette (Rev.)	27 Oct 1854		DET
Merrill, John P.	Moore, Julia A.	03 Oct 1848	13 Sep 1848	DENQ
Messer, Charles	Cuppet, Nancy	13 Apr 1859	Apr 1859	WPT
Messing, Joseph	Hunt, Nancy	12 Jan 1856	03 Jan 1856	DET
Metcalf, F.J.	Duidwit, Caroline	02 May 1850	28 Apr 1850	PT&C
Metz, John	Rollins, Aletha	17 Mar 1852	02 Mar 1852	PT&C
Meyer, J.S.	Jordan, Mary E.	23 May 1850	21 May 1850	PT&C
M'Fadden, Charles	Harmon, Mary J.	19 Jun 1855	17 Jun 1855	DET
Mikel, A.E.	Paxton, C.W.	14 Aug 1854	09 Aug 1854	DET
Miles, Benjamin R.	Gilbert, Rosa	21 Sep 1857	21 Sep 1857	DET
Miller, A.P. (Dr.)	Dorman, Mary E.	07 Jun 1858	03 Jun 1858	DET
Miller, A.P. (Dr.)	Dorman, Mary E.	09 Jun 1858	03 Jun 1858	WPT
Miller, George W.	French, Eliza	19 Aug 1854	13 Aug 1854	DET
Miller, J.S.	Stains, Mary	26 Dec 1853	15 Dec 1853	PDD
Miller, John	Powers, Mary Margaret	02 Sep 1850	24 Aug 1850	PI
Miller, Samuel	Wilson, Mary L.	02 Mar 1854	21 Feb 1854	PDD
Miller, William H.	Duduit, L.	20 Jun 1859	19 Jun 1859	DET
Miller, William H.	Duduit, L.	22 Jun 1859	19 Jun 1859	WPT
Mills, James	Stevenson, Canzada	13, 20 Aug 1856	03 Aug 1856	WPT
Miner, Henry A.	McCohaha, Amanda	28 Apr 1854	23 Apr 1854	DET
Miner, John L.	Wright, Mary	04 Nov 1837	26 Oct 1837	STRIB
Minford, Robert J.	Greer, Elizabeth	09, 10, Nov 1854	08 Nov 1854	DET
Mitchel, R.A.	Miller, Sarah J.	15 Oct 1856	13 Oct 1856	WPT
Mitchell, David	Murphy, Harriet	07 Jun 1827	31 May 1827	WT
Mitchell, I.S.	Chandler, Annie E.	29 Jul 1857	21 Jul 1857	DET
Mitchell, William S.	M'Intosh, Jenny	02 Sep 1818	14 Jul 1818	PGAZ
M'Neel, Worthington	Delay, Catharine	01 May 1854	15 Apr 1854	DET
Montgomery, Elis	Chapman, Elizabeth	06 May 1853	04 May 1853	PDD
Montgomery, Homer	Willey, Lizzie	14 Oct 1865	11 Oct 1865	PTIMES
Montgomery, Robert	Long, Harriet	31 May 1827	27 May 1827	WT
Moore, Amanual	Dole, Lavina	16 Feb 1859	10 Feb 1859	WPT
Moore, Amanuel	Dole, Lavina	16 Feb 1859	10 Feb 1859	DET
Moore, Davis P.	Kendall, Elizabeth A.	23 Dec 1850	20 Oct 1850	PI

Marriages (Grooms)

Name (Groom)	Name (Bride)	Notice Date	Marriage Date	Paper
Moore, Davis P.	Kendall, Elizabeth A.	19 Dec 1850	22 Oct 1850	PT&C
Moore, Ebenezer F.	Rodgers, Martha Jane	31 Oct 1844	27 Oct 1844	TRIB
Moore, Joel	Saade, Sarah	17 Feb 1857	11 Feb 1857	PSOT
Moore, John	Wilhelm, Sarah D.	24 Sep 1852	20 Sep 1852	PI
Moore, John O.	__ott, Sarah Jane	02 Apr 1856	20 Mar 1856	WPT
Moore, Levi	Dickerson, Mary Emma	20 Apr 1860		DET
Moore, Loy N.	Dodds, Martha A.	14 Nov 1850	12 Nov 1850	PT&C
Moore, Oscar F. (Esq.)	Scott, Martha B.	22 Sep 1843	19 Sep 1843	TRIB
Moore, Samuel G.	Bradford, Mary E.	19 Sep 1863	16 Sep 1863	PTIMES
Moore, William R.	Oldfield, Caroline	24 Feb 1854	23 Feb 1854	DET
More, Philip	Smith, Catharine	24 Oct 1829	08 Oct 1829	WT
Moreman, Constantine (Esq.)	M'Allen, Mary V.	13, 20 Aug 1856	03 Aug 1856	WPT
Morford, W.C.	Finton, Josephine	04 Nov 1857	29 Oct 1857	DET
Morford, William C.	Finton, Celinda	20 Dec 1853	16 Nov 1853	DET
Morgan, Conrad	Turvey, Sarah	18 May 1854	09 May 1854	DET
Morgan, Ephraim	Farmer, Eliza	22 Dec 1855	20 Dec 1855	DET
Morgan, Ephraim	Farmer, Eliza	26 Dec 1855	20 Dec 1855	WPT
Morgan, Thomas	Williams, Mary	13 May 1850	24 Apr 1850	PI
Morgan, Thomas	Williams, Mary	09 May 1850	24 Apr 1850	PT&C
Morris, Thomas	Wood, Phoeba	19 Oct 1826	03 Oct 1826	WT
Morrison, William	Morrison, Jane	18 Mar 1853	06 Mar 1853	PI
Morrow, Stephen C.	Roberts, Ola	06 Dec 1858	06 Dec 1858	DET
Morrow, Stephen C.	Roberts, Ola	08 Dec 1858	06 Dec 1858	WPT
Morton, George W.	Higley, Nancy Alice	14 Jan 1854	26 Dec 1853	DET
Morton, Jonathan	Searl, Mary R.	21 Oct 1865	14 Oct 1865	PTIMES
Moss, George	Brouse, Letitia	26 Sep 1853		DET
Mott, Abanas	Loveland, Nancy	27 Jul 1853	26 Jul 1853	DET
Mott, Abanas	Loveland, Nancy	28 Jul 1853	29 Jul 1853	PDD
Mott, Abanas	Loveland, Nancy	03 Aug 1853	26 Jul 1853	PT&C
Mountjoy, John	Sprouse, Elizabeth	11 Aug 1855	09 Aug 1855	DET
Munk, George	Calf, Eliza	18 Mar 1853	14 Dec 1852	PI
Munns, David D.	Orrison, Sarah	28 Sep 1820	17 Sep 1820	STEL
Murdock, Drake	Story, Mahala	18 Aug 1852	05 Aug 1852	PT&C
Murdock, Harvey	Huff, Juliett	22 Feb 1854	16 Feb 1854	PDD
Murphey, Moses	Ferrell, Matilda	06 Aug 1844	27 Jul 1844	PDEM
Murphy, Andrew	Nixon, Rachel E.	17 Feb 1854	08 Feb 1854	DET
Murphy, Dave (Lieut.)	Ball, Jennie M.	23 Sep 1865	18 Sep 1865	PTIMES
Murphy, Michael	Ormsby, Adeline	30 Jan 1852	27 Jan 1852	PI
Murphy, Michael	Ormsby, Adaline	11 Feb 1852	27 Jan 1852	PT&C
Murphy, Reas	Tom, Susan	12 Dec 1853	24 Nov 1853	DET
Murphy, Reas	Tom, Susan	15 Dec 1853	24 Nov 1853	WPT
Murray, D.N.	White, Harriet	20 May 1850	14 May 1850	PI
Murray, D.N.	White, Harriet	16 May 1850	14 May 1850	PT&C
Murray, Newton (Capt.)	Updegraff, Eleanor	05 Jan 1844	25 Dec 1843	TRIB

Name (Groom)	Name (Bride)	Notice Date	Marriage Date	Paper
Murray, P.H.	Davey, Phillippa	22 Jul 1850	18 Jul 1850	PI
Murray, P.H.	Davey, Phillippa	25 Jul 1850	18 Jul 1850	PT&C
Murril, Asa	Holbrok, Artametia M.	14 Jan 1825	15 Sep 1824	PG&LA
Musser, James	Munn, Juliette	21 Oct 1865	05 Oct 1865	PTIMES
Musser, John	King, Mariah	08 Nov 1855	08 Nov 1855	DET
Musser, Joseph T.	Ockerman, Hester Ann	10 Oct 1851	25 Sep 1851	PI
Musser, Joseph T.	Ockerman, Hester Ann	15 Oct 1851	25 Sep 1851	PT&C
Musser, Wm.	Sturgeon, Sarah Jane	11, 18 Jun 1851	01 Jun 1851	PT&C
Myers, male	Dixon, Minerva	06 Feb 1854	07 Jan 1854	DET
Myers, A.N.	Montgomery, Sarah	29 Oct 1855	29 Oct 1855	DET
Myers, Allen	Calihan, India	20 Apr 1854		DET
Myers, Allen	Calihan, India	20 Apr 1854	17 Apr 1854	PDD
Myers, Joseph	Dixon, Minerva	10 Feb 1854	07 Jan 1854	PDD
Myers, Samuel	Fowler, Mary	01 Oct 1856	15 Sep 1856	WPT
Nall, Albert G.	Savage, Eliza J.	12 Jan 1856	02 Jan 1856	DET
Nall, John D.	Smith, Ellen O.	14 Apr 1855	10 Apr 1855	DET
Nash, William H.	Forsythe, Sue S.	13 Jan 1857	01 Jan 1857	PSOT
Nash, Wm. H.	Forsythe, Sue S.	07 Jan 1857		WPT
Neal, John C.	Farrane Fannie R.	17, 29 Dec 1853	07 Dec 1853	DET
Neal, John C.	Farrand, Fanny R.	19 Dec 1853	07 Dec 1853	PDD
Neel, Hudson	Ferrell, Ellen	22 Aug 1844	10 Aug 1844	TRIB
Nelson, Anderson	Mathews, Rebecca Jane	22 Jun 1855	21 Jun 1855	DET
Newell, L.W.	Vernon, Salena	24 Jun 1854	18 Jun 1854	DET
Newland, William	Lewis Susan	05 Nov 1859	29 Oct 1859	DET
Newland, William	Lewis, Susan	05 Nov 1859	29 Oct 1859	PTIMES
Newland, William	Lewis Susan	09 Nov 1859	29 Oct 1859	WPT
Newton, Jas. (Capt.)	Carel, Madeline	27 Jul 1856	01 Jul 1856	WPT
Nichol, S.P.	Gates, Polly	22 Dec 1852	14 Dec 1852	PT&C
Nichols, Gifford Gore	Devoss, Arietta	09 Sep 1858	02 Sep 1858	DET
Nichols, Gifford Gore	Devoss, Arietta	15 Sep 1858	02 Sep 1858	WPT
Nichols, J.B.	Merrill, Maria	17 Feb 1851	13 Feb 1851	PI
Nichols, J.B.	Merrill, Maria	19 Feb 1851	13 Feb 1851	PT&C
Nichols, Samuel P.	Gates, Dolly	17 Dec 1852	14 Dec 1852	PI
Nixon, male	Greenwood, female	14 Jul 1854	11 Jul 1854	PDD
Nixon, Samuel	Brooks, Mary	19 Jan 1828	16 Jan 1828	WT
Noel, Aaron T.	Stone, Sarah C.	23 Dec 1865	14 Dec 1865	PTIMES
Noel, David	Morgan, Nancy	19 Jan 1828		WT
Noel, Ezra H.	Barber, Louisa	15 Jan 1846	08 Jan 1846	TRIB
Noel, Francis Volney	Huston, Angelina	06 Jul 1859	03 Jul 1859	DET
Noel, Francis Volney	Huston, Angelina	27 Jul 1859	03 Jul 1859	WPT
Noel, John F.	Kelly, Olive	23 Feb 1853	16 Feb 1853	PT&C
Noel, John P.	Powers, Hannah V.	28 Jun 1860	24 Jun 1860	DET
Noel, John P.	Powers, Hannah V.	04 Jul 1860	24 Jun 1860	WPT
Noel, Josiah O.	Fuiton, Mary J.	07 Jan 1857	31 Dec 1856	WPT
Noel, N.M.	Miller, Margaret	19 Oct 1855	18 Oct 1855	DET

Name (Groom)	Name (Bride)	Notice Date	Marriage Date	Paper
Noel, William	Huston, Mary	31 Aug 1860	29 Aug 1860	DET
Norris, Amaziah	Smith, Lucinda	12 May 1857	04 May 1857	DET
Norris, Amaziah	Smith, Lucinda	13 May 1857	04 May 1857	WPT
Nurse, Lewis	Vance, Nancy	25 Jul 1859	20 Jul 1859	DET
Nurse, Lewis	Vance, Nancy	27 Jul 1859	20 Jul 1859	WPT
Nurse, Samuel R.	Burdick, Phoebe	25 Feb 1825	01 Feb 1825	PG&LA
Oakes, Francis J.	Tracy, Frances	25 Dec 1845	18 Dec 1845	TRIB
Oldfield, George S.	Baker, Eliza	19 Nov 1864	15 Nov 1864	PTIMES
Olds, Joseph	Scott, Eliza P.	12 Jan 1859	30 Dec 1858	DET
Olehy, William	Glaze, Mary	08 Jun 1826	23 May 1826	WT
O'Niel, Andrew	Duvall, Martha J.	06 Apr 1853	31 Mar 1853	PT&C
Orcutt, James W.	Collier, Mary Ann	01 Mar 1844	20 Feb 1844	TRIB
Ormsby, Jerome B.	Walker, P. Frances	24 Oct 1850	21 Oct 1850	PT&C
Ormsby, Jerome B.	Walker, P. Frances	28 Oct 1850	21 Oct 1850	PI
Ormsby, Jerome B.	Walker, Perilla F.	19 Dec 1850	20 Oct 1850	PT&C
Osborn, Michael W.	Parshley, Elizabeth	25, 27 Jul 1857	23 Jul 1857	DET
Osborne, Jacob	Flesher, Martha	25 Aug 1854	21 Aug 1854	DET
Ott, Valentine	Rhodes, Catharine	28 May 1852	16 May 1852	PI
Oviatt, Benjamin F.	Bennett, Mary F.	04 May 1858	25 Apr 1858	PSOT
Owens, Evan C. (Mayor)	Williams, Margaret	03 Jan 1855	25 Dec 1855	DET
Owns, Erasmus	Ranall, Mary	03 Aug 1853	28 Jul 1853	DET
Page, John C.	Kriser, Martha	03 Dec 1858		DET
Page, John C.	Keiser, Martha	08 Dec 1858		WPT
Painer, John	Urquhart, Jenette	20 Sep 1855	18 Sep 1855	DET
Palmer, Roswell E.	Cooper, Mary	06, 08 May 1854	06 May 1854	DET
Palmer, Rozwell E.	Cooper, Mary	09 May 1854	06 May 1854	PDD
Pancake, Harvey	Hulps, Jemima	10 Jun 1850	04 Jun 1850	PI
Pancake, Harvey	Hulps, Jemima	06 Jun 1850	04 Jun 1850	PT&C
Parker, H.H.	Bockwalter, Elizabeth D.	14 Nov 1850		PT&C
Parker, H.W.	Dole, Almira T.	08 Oct 1852	04 Oct 1852	PI
Parker, N.H.	Bookwalter, Elizabeth D.	18 Nov 1850	12 Nov 1850	PI
Parker, N.H.	Turner, S.E.	01 Oct 1852	30 Sep 1852	PI
Parkinson, William	Rodgers, Catharine Matilda	29 Dec 1843	21 Dec 1843	TRIB
Parl, Bazil	Heath, Julia A.	03 Mar 1852	22 Feb 1852	PT&C
Parman, Charles	Simley, Catharine	17 Oct 1854	17 Oct 1854	DET
Parsons, John K.	Leonard, Nettie Susan	20 Mar 1855	14 Feb 1855	DET
Partingale, James M.	Ball, Nancy C.	07 May 1864	28 Apr 1864	PTIMES
Patterson, Galbreth	Barber, Jane	18 Mar 1825	06 Mar 1825	PG&LA
Patterson, Joseph S.	Currie, Maggie A.	02 Jul 1856	01 Jul 1856	WPT
Patterson, Mores J.	McMeekin, Martha	22 Dec 1855	05 Dec 1855	DET
Patterson, Mores J.	McMeekin, Martha	26 Dec 1855	05Dec 1855	WPT
Patton, Abner	Hyette, Juliana	27 May 1831	19 May 1831	PC&WT
Patton, Joseph	Johnson, Eliza A.	07 Oct 1850	29 Sep 1850	PI
Patton, Samuel	Nichols, Catherine	24 Apr 1855	23 Apr 1855	DET

Name (Groom)	Name (Bride)	Notice Date	Marriage Date	Paper
Paul, H.H.	Featherstone, female	18 Aug 1854		PDD
Payne, Edymond	Martin, Margaret	13 Mar 1854	05 Mar 1854	PDD
Payne, Hiram	Eastham, Eliza Jane	12 Jan 1856	30 Dec 1855	DET
Pearce (or Pearch), Elgar B.	Knight, Bella Virginia	02 Dec 1857	26 Nov 1857	WPT
Pearce (or Pearon), Alex.	Ward, Amanda	04 Nov 1857	28 Oct 1857	WPT
Pearch, Elgar B.	Knight, Bella Virginia	01 Dec 1857	26 Nov 1857	DET
Pearon, Alex.	Ward, Amanda	02 Nov 1857	28 Oct 1857	DET
Pearson, (Dr.)	Royer, Elizabeth	08 Dec 1843	01 Dec 1843	TRIB
Peatling, Edward	Tyrrell, Mary Ann	13 Apr 1855	12 Apr 1855	DET
Peck, D.W.	Gillespie, Amanda	20 May 1854	14 May 1854	DET
Peck, W.V., Jr.	McCollister, Harriet C.	20 Apr 1858	19 Apr 1858	PSOT
Peebles, Joseph S.	Lodwick, Nancy	14 Apr 1851	08 Apr 1851	PI
Peebles, Richard R. (Dr.)	Groce, Mary Ann	12 May 1843	08 Mar 1843	TRIB
Peeples, William Harry	Manning, Mary E.	15 Sep 1851	08 Sep 1851	PI
Pepper, John D.	Glover, Martha J.	21 Jul 1843	16 Jul 1843	TRIB
Perry, Lindsey	Stimp, Celia	06 Feb 1855	04 Feb 1855	DET
Peters, John	Fuller, Mary C.	12 Jan 1844	21 Dec 1843	TRIB
Peters, Samuel	Gholson, Amanda	04 Feb 1854	01 Feb 1854	DET
Phelps, James E.	Mitchell, Angeline	15 Jun 1855	14 Jun 1855	DET
Phetteflace, Madison	Lott, Margaret	08 Apr 1854	16 Mar 1854	DET
Phillips, Rev. F.W.	Dungan, Lucy J.	10 Nov 1853	27 Oct 1853	DET
Phillips, Theophilus	Stepheson, Mary Ann	17 Jun 1854	14 Jun 1854	PDD
Piece, Samuel	Breese, Phoeba Ann	29 Dec 1853	08 Dec 1853	DET
Pilcher, George W.	Coulter, Rebecca E.	17 Jan 1854	05 Jan 1854	DET
Pilcher, J.M.	Shockey, Samantha	06 May 1865	28 Apr 1865	PTIMES
Pillow, Jonas	Scriptures, Sarah	16 Dec 1853		DET
Pinkerton, Wm. H.	Titus, Rebecca	27 Apr 1853	21 Apr 1853	PT&C
Plants, T.A. (Hon.)	Wheeler, Kate	05 Dec 1859	20 Nov 1859	WPT
Plotter, John O.	Smith, Sally	11 Jan 1853	22 Dec 1852	PI
Poage, Lindsey	M'Cormick, Ann	12 Nov 1824		PG&LA
Pogue, Henry E.	Wood, Fanny A.	08, 19 Nov 1853	03 Nov 1853	DET
Pollock, Andrew	Patrick, Sarah A.	11 Jan 1853	06 Jan 1853	PI
Pond, J. Evarts (Rev.)	Baird, Jeannie W.	19 Mar 1858	18 Mar 1858	DET
Pool, Aaron	Deerman, Eliza	17 Apr 1854	16 Apr 1854	DET
Porter, C.	Jones, Cornelia W.	22 Sep 1855	22 Sep 1855	DET
Porter, R.H.	Hannahs, R.S.	03 Mar 1852	23 Feb 1852	PT&C
Porter, William	Stapleton, Mary	13 May 1850	18 Apr 1850	PI
Porter, William	Stapleton, Mary	09 May 1850	18 Apr 1850	PT&C
Postlethwate, William H.S.	Heath, Elizabeth L.	31 Mar 1852	28 Mar 1852	PT&C
Postlewate, William H.S.	Heath, Elizabeth L.	02 Apr 1852	28 Mar 1852	PI
Pouch, Theophilus	Hare, Eleanor	19 Dec 1850	10 Sep 1850	PT&C
Powell, Silas D.	Farney, Amanda	19 Aug 1853	10 Aug 1853	DET
Powell, Silas D.	Farney, Amanda	16 Aug 1853	10 Aug 1853	PDD

Name (Groom)	Name (Bride)	Notice Date	Marriage Date	Paper
Powell, Silas D.	Farney, Amanda	24 Aug 1853	10 Aug 1853	PT&C
Powell, William Byrd	Mitchell, Sarah A.	11 Mar 1837	12 Feb 1837	STRIB
Powers, Archey	Hotman, Susan	03 Oct 1848	21 Sep 1848	DENQ
Pratt, E.P. (Rev.)	Loughry, Elizabeth	21 Oct 1853	18 Oct 1853	PDD
Pratt, Rev. E. P.	Loughry, Elizabeth	20 Oct 1853	18 Oct 1853	DET
Pressel, Daniel W.	Turner, Hester Ann	20 Jun 1844	19 Jun 1844	TRIB
Price, Isaac	Brown, Rebecca	22 Jun 1826	15 Jun 1826	WT
Price, Vinton	Bonner, Minerva	29 Mar 1854	26 Mar 1854	DET
Priggs, Isaac	Lisler, Epa_onia	19 May 1852	29 Apr 1852	PT&C
Pugh, George	Fowler, Sarah Ann	24 Apr 1854	15 Apr 1854	PDD
Pugh, George E. (Hon.)	Chalfant, Therese	26 Nov 1855	22 Nov 1855	DET
Pugh, George E. (Hon.)	Chalfant, Therese	28 Nov 1855	22 Nov 1855	WPT
Punch, Theophilus	Hare, Eleanor	23 Dec 1850	20 Sep 1850	PI
Purdham, Warner W.	M'Neil, Lydia	06 May 1850		PI
Purdom, W.W.	McNeal, Lydia	09 May 1850	01 May 1850	PT&C
Purdum, John W.	Powell, Sarah	10 Apr 1855	10 Apr 1855	DET
Purdum, W.W.	McNeal Lydia	13 May 1850	01 May 1850	PI
Pursell, James	Thompson, Amanda	17 Mar 1843	16 Mar 1843	TRIB
Pursell, Thomas J.	Spry, Thomasin H.	24 Mar 1857	17 Mar 1857	PSOT
Pursell, Thos. J.	Spry, Thomasin H.	18 Mar 1857	17 Mar 1857	WPT
Putland, Edward	Wheeler, Elizabeth	13 Apr 1858	21 Mar 1858	PSOT
Quant, Frank	Goudy, Sarah C.	15 Oct 1856	12 Oct 1856	WPT
Radcliff, Davis E.	Poor, Martha C.	06 Jun 1856	03 Jun 1856	OP
Rains, James A.	Durham, Martha	10 Nov 1853	30 Oct 1853	DET
Ramsey, David, Jr.	Gebhardt, Tena	06 Jan 1857	25 Dec 1856	PSOT
Randolf, Richard	Culbertson, Agnes	20 Apr 1858	30 Mar 1858	PSOT
Rank, Wm.	Stepleton, Nancy	23 Dec 1850	20 Nov 1850	PI
Rank, Wm.	Stepleton, Nancy	19 Dec 1850	20 Nov 1850	PT&C
Rankin, Benjamin	Black, Mary	09 Sep 1825	18 Aug 1825	PG&LA
Ransom, Jas.	Coughly (or Colghly), Matilda	01 Sep 1855	23 Aug 1855	DET
Ransom, Samuel	Clingman, Ann Eliza	30 Nov 1826	26 Nov 1826	WT
Rate, Jno. F.	Mackoy, Sallie E.	14 Mar 1860	05 Mar 1860	DET
Rate, Jno. F.	Mackoy, Sallie E.	14 Mar 1860	05 Mar 1860	WPT
Rate, Jno. F. (Elder)	Mackoy, Sally E.	10 Mar 1860	05 Mar 1860	PTIMES
Rathburn, Samuel B.	Vanden, Joanna	03 Feb 1843	22 Jan 1843	TRIB
Raymond, Philip	Menager, female (Mrs.)	14 Oct 1837	08 Oct 1837	STRIB
Rayner, William H.	Kendall, Rhoda O.	10 Sep 1855	09 Sep 1855	DET
Raynor, William	Kendall, Rhoda	14 Sep 1855	09 Sep 1855	OP
Raynor, Wm.	Munn, Mariah (nee Bonser)	06 May 1865	30 Apr 1865	PTIMES
Ream, Samuel K.	Ritchey, Marie (Bun)	10 Nov 1857	29 Oct 1857	PSOT
Red, James	Huskins, Emily J.	27 Jul 1856	13 Jul 1856	WPT
Reed, Calvin W.	Winkler, Adella	18 Feb 1857	12 Feb 1857	WPT
Reed, Elroy W.	Clark, Love J.	02 Jan 1864	28 Dec 1863	PTIMES

Name (Groom)	Name (Bride)	Notice Date	Marriage Date	Paper
Reed, Henry S.	Hawk, Ortensla S.	09 Jan 1854	29 Dec 1853	DET
Reed, Joseph G.	Newman, Annie M.	18 Nov 1865	16 Nov 1865	PTIMES
Reed, Marshall	Chase, Louisa M.	22 Oct 1856	16 Oct 1856	WPT
Reed, Rodney	Kelly, Jane	18 Mar 1853	13 Mar 1853	PI
Reed, Rodney	Kelly, Jane	16 Mar 1853	13 Mar 1853	PT&C
Reed, Samuel	Kinney, Ellen	26 Aug 1857	20 Aug 1857	WPT
Reed, Thompson J.	Kerr, Eliza Jane	20 Jun 1844	18 Jun 1844	TRIB
Reese, David	Gillet, Tennessee	03 Mar 1852	12 Feb 1852	PT&C
Reeves, N. (M.D.)	Daugherty, S.D.	04 Feb 1854	29 Jan 1854	DET
Regnler, Charles	Daniels, Editha K.	05 Nov 1858	11 Oct 1858	SVREP
Reid, Robert T.	Veach, Elizabeth	06 Oct 1843	24 Sep 1843	TRIB
Reilly, Hugh	McGuire, Elizabeth	11 May 1854	04 May 1854	DET
Reiniger, Charles F.	Ramsey, Mary Jane	13 May 1865	04 May 1865	PTIMES
Renolds, Robert	Topins, Matilda	01 Apr 1854	30 Mar 1854	PDD
Renshaw, John	Kinney, Sarah Ann	30 Jan 1852	29 Jan 1852	PI
Reynolds, Calvin	Chestnut, Nancy	01 Apr 1853	31 Mar 1853	PI
Reynolds, Calvin	Chesnut, Nancy	06 Apr 1853	31 Mar 1853	PT&C
Reynolds, Franklin	Miller, Elizabeth	31 May 1827	24 May 1827	WT
Reynolds, Robert	Topins Matilda	31 Mar 1854	30 Mar 1854	DET
Rfckard (?), F.M.	Henry, Lucy	19 Nov 1853	07 Nov 1853	DET
Rice, Jesse	Anderson, Mary	23 May 1854	18 May 1854	DET
Rice, Thos. H.	Allison, Mary	30 Jun 1854	29 Jun 1854	PDD
Richardson, B.F.	Bonsall, Laura A.	11 Nov 1865	19 Oct 1865	PTIMES
Richardson, James	Orm, Mary J.	05 Mar 1864	29 Feb 1864	PTIMES
Richart, William	Clingman, Ann Maria	11 May 1826	02 May 1826	WT
Richey, George B.	Clingan, M.L.(neeTerry)	19 Aug 1854	15 Aug 1854	DET
Richt, Henry	Bersteh, Louisa	17 Jul 1855	17 Jul 1855	DET
Ridgway, Tho. Jno.	Sweetser, Emma	07 May 1864	14 Apr 1864	PTIMES
Riggs, James W.	Taylor, Mary E.	21 Jul 1851	17 Jul 1851	PI
Riggs, James W.	Taylor, Mary E.	23 Jul 1851		PT&C
Riggs, Stephen B.	Withers, Evalne	13 Oct 1853	12 Oct 1853	DET
Riggs, Stephen B.	Withers, Evadne	14 Oct 1853	12 Oct 1853	PDD
Riley, Abraham	Walker, Elizabeth	18 Mar 1853	06 Mar 1853	PI
Rinehart, John	Bradford, Elizabeth	23 Dec 1850	17 Nov 1850	PI
Rinehart, John	Bradford, Elizabeth	19 Dec 1850	17 Nov 1850	PT&C
Ripley, William	Cassell, Josephine	14 Jan 1865	12 Jan 1865	PTIMES
Ritchie, W.F.	Mowatt, female (Mrs.)	16 Jun 1854		DET
Roach, William	Davidson, Sallie M.	26 Aug 1859	25 Aug 1859	DET
Roach, William	Davidson, Sallie M.	31 Aug 1859	25 Aug 1859	WPT
Robb, J. Cobe	Garland, Georgie A.	27 May 1865	24 May 1865	PTIMES
Robert, H.M. (Lieut)	Thresher, Helen M.	26 Dec 1859	17 Dec 1859	WPT
Robert, H.M. (Lieut.)	Thresher, Helen	29 Dec 1860	17 Dec 1860	PTIMES
Roberts, John W.	McCan, Mary Ann	25 Oct 1853	22 Oct 1853	PDD
Roberts, Julius W.	Sherfey, Caroline A.	30 Apr 1851	01 Apr 1851	PT&C
Robin, Horace	Oliver, Mary	13 Apr 1853	10 Apr 1853	PT&C

Name (Groom)	Name (Bride)	Notice Date	Marriage Date	Paper
Robinson, Andrew	Graham, Mahala	24 Feb 1851	20 Feb 1851	PI
Robinson, Joshua V.	Scott, Malvina	20 Oct 1843	17 Oct 1843	TRIB
Robinson, Joshua V., Jr.	Riggs, Martha B.	18 Mar 1853	10 Mar 1853	PI
Robuck, Thomas	Haines, Margaret	17 Feb 1857	05 Feb 1857	PSOT
Rochester, John C.	Cushing, Charlotte	30 Jan 1854	18 Jan 1854	DET
Roe, George E.	Howland, N.W.	12 Jan 1854	29 Dec 1853	PDD
Rolrins, Eli	Blagg, Sarah	18 Mar 1853	06 Mar 1853	PI
Ronaldson, Stephen	Rariden, Joanna	20 Jul 1854	17 Jul 1854	DET
Rose, Charles E.	Clugston, Eveline E.	20 Dec 1849	18 Dec 1849	PT&C
Rose, Edward	Ratcliff, Mary	08 Jan 1856	02 Jan 1856	DET
Rose, Edward	Ratcliff, Mary	09 Jan 1856	02 Jan 1856	WPT
Ross, James F.	Mick, Sally	11 Oct 1853		PDD
Ross, John (Cherokee Chief)	Stapler, Mary B.	19 Sep 1844	16 Sep 1844	TRIB
Ross, M.B.	Tracy, Elizabeth D.	30 Jun 1843	29 Jun 1843	TRIB
Rouch, Peter	Painer, Barbara	18 Feb 1853	12 Feb 1853	PI
Rouch, Peter	Painer, Barbara	16 Feb 1853	12 Feb 1853	PT&C
Rowley, Edward	Dever, Elizabeth Ann	28 Jan 1857	18 Jan 1857	WPT
Rowley, Jackson	Deavor, Emily	30 Apr 1856	24 Apr 1856	WPT
Royce, George	Wright, Dilla	17 Jun 1865	14 Jun 1865	PTIMES
Royer, Theodore	Rodgers, Elizabeth	08 Dec 1843	01 Dec 1843	TRIB
Ruggles, S.H.	Osborn, Kate R.	23 Feb 1859	05 Feb 1859	DET
Ruggles, S.H.	Osborn, Kate R.	02 Mar 1859	05 Feb 1859	WPT
Rundle, John	Furley, Sarah M.	22 Nov 1858	12 Nov 1858	DET
Rundle, John	Farley(or Furley),Sarah M.	24 Nov 1858	12 Nov 1858	WPT
Rupp, George H.	Mathews, Mary H.	31 Dec 1853	22 Dec 1853	DET
Rupp, George H.	Mathews, Mary H.	05 Jan 1854	22 Dec 1853	PDD
Rush, Jno.	Canter, Sarah	13 May 1854		DET
Russell, A.B. (Rev.)	Vollanvaider, Augustine	03 Nov 1852	28 Oct 1852	PT&C
Russell, Enoch J.	Hartman, Susan	04 Jan 1856	01 Jan 1856	DET
Russell, Enoch J.	Hartman, Susan	09 Jan 1856	01 Jan 1856	WPT
Russell, W.B.	Hibbs, Rebecca L.	06 Aug 1851	04 Aug 1851	PT&C
Safford, E.P.	Vinton, Romain M.	16 Oct 1854	09 Oct 1854	DET
Salladay, Obediah	Nurse, Phoeba	14 Oct 1855	27 Sep 1855	DET
Salleday, Calvin	Berry, Catherine	26 Mar 1856	20 Mar 1856	WPT
Salsbury, James	Kendall, Maria	20 Jan 1851	08 Jan 1851	PI
Salter, William, Jr.	Cook, Margaret	13 Feb 1852	05 Feb 1852	PI
Salter, Wm., Jr.	Cook, Margaret	11 Feb 1852	05 Feb 1852	PT&C
Sampson, George H.	Glenn, Catharine Isabella	27 Dec 1859	24 Dec 1859	DET
Sanders, L.D.	Bennett, Sarah	01 Oct 1856	28 Sep 1856	WPT
Sanford, Hiram	Kennedy, Jane Ann	13 Mar 1854	05 Mar 1854	PDD
Sanns, Peter A.	Hebard, Anna E.	03 Mar 1852	23 Feb 1852	PT&C
Santy, Francis	Russio, Aliono	21 Apr 1854	20 Apr 1854	DET
Sargent, John	Mead, Eleanor	29 Jul 1854	20 Jul 1854	DET
Scott, David H. (Dr.)	Allen, Effie	28 Oct 1865	18 Oct 1865	PTIMES

Name (Groom)	Name (Bride)	Notice Date	Marriage Date	Paper
Scott, James B.	M'Clintick, Catharine	11 Jun 1844	04 Jun 1844	TRIB
Scott, Perry	Bruner, Lucinda	12 Jan 1844	28 Dec 1843	TRIB
Scott, Uriah B.	Lionbarger, Clarinda	10 Oct 1851	01 Oct 1851	PI
Scott, Uriah B.	Lionbarger, Clarinda	08 Oct 1851	01 Oct 1851	PT&C
Seeberger, Henry	Stonhill, Sarah	14 Nov 1851	07 Nov 1851	PI
Seeberger, Henry	Stonhill, Sarah	12 Nov 1851	07 Nov 1851	PT&C
Selby, William	Smith, Agnes	20 Jan 1854	05 Jan 1854	DET
Selfridge, Chester W.	Miles, Lucy E.	22 Sep 1854	19 Sep 1854	DET
Sexton, John	Ray, Sarah	05 May 1852	25 Apr 1852	PT&C
Shafer, Samuel	Wingond, Elizabeth	09 Apr 1856	01 Apr 1856	WPT
Shannon, Charles	French, Mary A.	07 Nov 1850	03 Nov 1850	PT&C
Shannon, John	Fee, Mary E.	03 Feb 1854	31 Jan 1854	PDD
Shaw, James	Wise, Alma	25 Mar 1853	15 Mar 1853	PI
Shaw, James	Wise, Alma	23 Mar 1853	15 Mar 1853	PT&C
Shaw, John	Holt, Jerusia Adeline	05 Jul 1853	02 Jul 1853	DET
Shaw, John	Holt, Jerusia Adaline	06, 13 July 1853	02 Jul 1853	PT&C
Shedd, J.H. (Rev.)	Dawes, Jennie	05 Aug 1859	05 Aug 1859	DET
Sheeler, Michael	Wilson, Sardina	22 Aug 1855	21 Aug 1855	DET
Sheets, John	Parker, Isabella A.	31 May 1827	25 May 1827	WT
Shelpman, Cornelius (Esq.)	Kile, Mary	03 Mar 1852	26 Feb 1852	PT&C
Shephard, (or Shepherd), Alexander	Murphy(or Murphey), Maria	28 Nov 1850 19 Dec 1850	27 Nov 1850	PT&C
Shephard, Alexander	Murphy, Maria	02, 23 Dec 1850	27 Nov 1850	PI
Shephard, Charlton	Eicher, Margaret	02, 23 Dec 1850	27 Nov 1850	PI
Shephard, Charlton	Eicher, Margaret	28 Nov 1850 19 Dec 1850	27 Nov 1850	PT&C
Shepherd, L.E.	Johnston, Elizabeth A.	14 Apr 1855	03 Apr 1855	DET
Sherman, Alba	Swan, Mary	15 Aug 1854	10 Jun 1854	PDD
Shipman, William J.	Brasier, Catharine L.	09 Dec 1850	03 Dec 1850	PI
Shipman, Wm. J.	Brazier, Catharine L.	05 Dec 1850	03 Dec 1850	PT&C
Shiras, William	Rodgers, Elizabeth J.	09 Aug 1839	01 Aug 1839	TRIB
Shivengton, Barney	Henney, Mary	05 Nov 1856	02 Nov 1856	WPT
Shoemaker, Samuel	Taylor, Mary Jane	16 May 1854	03 May 1854	DET
Short, James H.	Crain, Mary	28 Jan 1853	21 Jan 1853	PI
Short, James Harvey	Crain, Mary	26 Jan 1853	22 Jan 1853	PT&C
Shoub, Henry A.	Springer, Calphurnia M.	10 Dec 1864	24 Nov 1864	PTIMES
Shriner, Daniel F.	Wiatt, Mary Jane	11 Jun 1856	30 May 1856	WPT
Shufflin, Edward G.	Barklow, Penelope	04 Mar 1857	25 Feb 1857	WPT
Shump, H.C. (Lieut.)	Basham, Ellen	27 May 1865	21 May 1865	PTIMES
Shute, J.G.	Kouns, Mary C.	11 Jun 1856	03 Jun 1856	WPT
Sillough, William	Evaley, Mary	09 Apr 1856	03 Apr 1856	WPT
Simcox, Wm.	Jones, Eliza Jane	22 Jul 1865	16 Jul 1865	PTIMES
Simmons, Augustus	McDaniel, Sue	01 Oct 1856	24 Sep 1856	WPT
Simmons, Francis	Lewis, Sarah Ann	14 Jan 1858	14 Jan 1858	DET

Marriages (Grooms)

Name (Groom)	Name (Bride)	Notice Date	Marriage Date	Paper
Simpson, C.W.	How, Susan	22 Oct 1856	13 Oct 1856	WPT
Sims, Robert	Crichton, Julia M.	10 Aug 1859	10 Aug 1859	DET
Slack, William J.	Feirel, Nancy C.	28 May 1852	06 May 1852	PI
Slaughter, Richard C.	Kelsey, Mary Jane	27 May 1831	22 May 1831	PC&WT
Slimp, Alfred	Chapman, Ann Adelaide	06 Jun 1856	28 May 1856	OP
Slimp, Alfred	Chapman, Ann Adelaide	11 Jun 1856	28 May 1856	WPT
Sloan, Geo. W.	Lambert, A.	24 Aug 1853		PT&C
Sloan, George W.	Lambert, A.	20 Aug 1853		DET
Sloan, Peter	Lambert, Melvina	23 Dec 1850	12 Sep 1850	PI
Sloan, Peter	Lambert, Melvina	19 Dec 1850	12 Sep 1850	PT&C
Sloat, John	Riggs, Mary	05 Jan 1853	23 Dec 1852	PT&C
Slone, P.P.	Lambert, Malvina A.	16 Sep 1850	12 Sep 1850	PI
Slone, P.P.	Lambert, Melvina A.	12 Sep 1850	12 Sep 1850	PT&C
Sly, Joseph	Nearl, Julia Ann	16 Apr 1856	13 Apr 1856	WPT
Sly, M.G. Tully Cicero	Shupe, Cynthia A.	27 Feb 1852	22 Feb 1852	PI
Sly, Samuel	Buckley, Mary F.	10 Dec 1851	30 Nov 1851	PT&C
Smallwood, Wm. (Rev.)	Douglass, Mary L.	12 Mar 1846	02 Mar 1846	TRIB
Smedley, Isaac F.	Storey, Hannah	08 Mar 1844	25 Feb 1844	TRIB
Smith, Charles	Dimner, Elizabeth	02 Sep 1850	18 Jul 1850	PI
Smith, Charles	Dimner, Elizabeth	29 Aug 1850	18 Jul 1850	PT&C
Smith, Charles S.	Ackerman, Mrs. C.W.	12 Jan 1854	05 Jan 1854	PDD
Smith, Charles S.	Locke, Mary G.	27 Oct 1843	20 Sep 1843	TRIB
Smith, Clarkson	Johnston, Hannah	01 Jun 1820		STEL
Smith, George	Howe, Minerva	24 Sep 1851	18 Sep 1851	PT&C
Smith, George W.	Olds, Mary	09 Mar 1860	07 Mar 1860	DET
Smith, George W.	Olds, Mary	14 Mar 1860	07 Mar 1860	WPT
Smith, J. H. (Capt.)	Haverty, Emma V.	19 Nov 1864	10 Nov 1864	PTIMES
Smith, J.W.	Paxton, Lottie H.	02 Nov 1859	31 Oct 1859	DET
Smith, J.W.	Paxton, Lottie H.	05 Nov 1859	31 Oct 1859	PTIMES
Smith, J.W.	Paxton, Lottie H.	02 Nov 1859	31 Oct 1859	WPT
Smith, John	Lloyd, Ann	14 Jan 1852	10 Jan 1852	PT&C
Smith, John D.	Wilcoxon, Drusilla W.	26 Jan 1828		WT
Smith, John M.	Coleman, Eulda	05 Jan 1853		PT&C
Smith, John O.	Vining, Sarabell	24 Dec 1864	14 Dec 1864	PTIMES
Smith, Nathaniel	Jeffords, Maria	23 Dec 1850	18 Dec 1850	PI
Smith, Nathaniel F.	Johnson, Rachel	30 May 1860	20 May 1860	DET
Smith, Nathaniel F.	Johnson, Rachel	30 May 1860	20 May 1860	WPT
Smith, Nelson	Burt, Julia	27 Jun 1844	20 Jun 1844	TRIB
Smith, P.C.	Osborn, Sarah	21 Dec 1858	14 Dec 1858	DET
Smith, P.C.	Osborn, Sarah	22 Dec 1858	14 Dec 1858	WPT
Smith, William E.	For_, Margaret	02 Apr 1856	27 Mar 1856	WPT
Snyder, Andrew I.	Johnson, Mary Ann	30 Jul 1852	27 Jul 1852	PI
Snyder, Isaac H.	Sage, Josanna	27 Dec 1853	08 Dec 1853	DET
Snyder, John	Chapman, Rosanna	07 Jan 1857	04 Jan 1857	WPT
Solitude, Abram	Sweet, Mary Ann	01 Sep 1843	12 Aug 1843	TRIB

Name (Groom)	Name (Bride)	Notice Date	Marriage Date	Paper
Souder, Samuel	Williams, Jane	09 Apr 1852	25 Mar 1852	PI
Southworth, J.H.	Henderson, Elizabeth W.	03 Oct 1855	01 Oct 1855	DET
Sowders, George	Sane, Eliza	21 Nov 1853	13 Nov 1853	DET
Spanady, James	McDonald, Martha	26 Apr 1854	24 Apr 1854	PDD
Spence, J.F.	Plyley, Artemesia	16 Oct 1854	10 Oct 1854	DET
Spencer, Horace G.	Ritchey, Elizabeth C.	17 Feb 1857	05 Feb 1857	PSOT
Spencer, John C.	Brunner, Maria	06 Nov 1858	04 Nov 1858	PSOT
Spencer, John C.	Brunner, Maria	16 Nov 1858	04 Nov 1858	PTIMES
Spherry, James	Rowley, Elizabeth	08 Jun 1826	11 May 1826	WT
Spongler, Michael	Mai, Theresa	23 Apr 1852	17 Apr 1852	PI
Spragg, Caleb	Dunlap, Mary Jane	17 Nov 1852	14 Nov 1852	PT&C
Sprago, Caleb	Dunlap, Mary Jane	19 Nov 1852	14 Nov 1852	PI
Spriggs, Benjamin F.	Dorch, Eliza	28 Oct 1859	27 Oct 1859	DET
Spry, John W.	Davey, Louisa	03 May 1855	02 May 1855	DET
Staley, Stephen	Gardner, Phelinda A.H.	16 Jun 1853	05 Jun 1853	DET
Staley, Stephen	Gardner, Phelinda A.H.	22 Jun 1853	05 Jun 1853	PT&C
Stallman, Frederick	Gilberthorpe, Priscilla	05 Dec 1859	27 Nov 1859	WPT
Starkum, Aaron	Tucker, Nancy C.	15 Aug 1853		DET
Starkum, Aaron	Tucker, Nancy	17 Aug 1853	15 Aug 1853	PDD
Starkum, Aaron	Tucker, Nancy C.	17 Aug 1853	15 Aug 1853	PT&C
Steen, James G.	Andre, Maria A.	08 Jan 1856	31 Dec 1855	DET
Steen, james G.	Andre, Maria A.	09 Jan 1856	31 Dec 1855	WPT
Stemshorn, Henry	Engelbrecht, Matilda	09 Jul 1864	04 Jul 1864	PTIMES
Stephenson, Joseph	Baker, Harriet (Mrs.)	21 Feb 1854	14 Feb 1854	PDD
Stepleton, Wm.	Goheen, Ann	23 Dec 1850	04 Dec 1850	PI
Stepleton, Wm.	Goheen, Ann	19 Dec 1850	04 Dec 1850	PT&C
Stevens, Calvin J.	Ripley, Cyntha Angeline	11 Jun 1844	03 Jun 1844	TRIB
Stevens, George H.	Brewer, Sarah	21 Nov 1853	10 Nov 1853	DET
Stewart, Arch V.	Marshall, Mollie A.	14 Jul 1858	14 Jul 1858	DET
Stewart, Hugh D.	Bradford, Wilhemna	29 Dec 1860	06 Dec 1860	PTIMES
Stewart, John	Williams, Elizabeth	19 Sep 1844	12 Sep 1844	TRIB
Stewart, John L.	McNeal, Mary Ann	16 Jun 1854	15 Jun 1854	DET
Stimpson, Rodney M.	Hurd, Juliaette B.	28 Jul 1851	23 Jul 1851	PI
Stiner, Peter	Adams, Ana	11 Nov 1853	09 Aug 1853	DET
Stockham, Aaron	Crawford, Mary Jane	16 Oct 1854	12 Oct 1854	DET
Stockham, Samuel	Lawson,Mary	28 Mar 1863	22 Mar 1863	PTIMES
Stone, Washington	Hannkins, Mary Ann	11 Jun 1856	29 May 1856	WPT
Stonebaker, Joseph A.	Cropper, Emily J.	18 May 1859	11 May 1859	WPT
Stonebraker, Joseph A.	Cropper, Emily J.	14 May 1859	11 May 1859	DET
Stoner, William	Maddock, Addban E.	08 May 1858	05 May 1858	DET
Storer, William	Bonser, Elinor	11 Jan 1853	28 Oct 1852	PI
Stout, Charles	Bean, Maggie	16 Feb 1854	07 Feb 1854	DET
Stout, Charles	Bean, Maggie	17 Feb 1854	07 Feb 1854	PDD
Strain, Samuel	Dawson, Irena	09 Apr 1852	25 Mar 1852	PI
Strother, Robert D.	Livingston, Mary E.	09 Jan 1854	01 Jan 1854	DET

Name (Groom)	Name (Bride)	Notice Date	Marriage Date	Paper
Stuart, John L.	McNeal, Mary Ann	17 Jun 1854	15 Jun 1854	PDD
Sturdy, George	Allords, Lydia	13 Apr 1853	06 Apr 1853	PT&C
Sullivan, Dennis	Gallagher, Mary	22 Apr 1854		PDD
Sutherlin, George H.	Tracy, Mary K.	02 Dec 1853	30 Nov 1853	DET
Sutherlin, George H.	Tracy, Mary K.	01 Dec 1853	30 Nov 1853	PDD
Swager, James	Snyder, Margaret	14 Nov 1851	09 Nov 1851	PI
Swager, James	Snyder, Margaret	12 Nov 1851	09 Nov 1851	PT&C
Swan, Joseph	McCartey, Julia Ann	20 Apr 1854	05 Apr 1854	DET
Sweet, Edward A.	Clark, Mary Ellen	23 Apr 1858	13 Apr 1858	DET
Sweet, Freeman	Cutler, Caroline	03 Mar 1852	26 Feb 1852	PT&C
Swift, Aurin R.	White, Mary J.	15 Sep 1858	09 Sep 1858	WPT
Swift, R.S.	Burke, Lizzie	31 Jul 1860	03 Jul 1860	DET
Swift, R.S.	Burke, Lizzie	01 Aug 1860	03 Jul 1860	WPT
Tanner, George	Tanner, Mary Ann	31 Jul 1857	31 Jul 1857	DET
Tanner, George	Tanner, Mary Ann	05 Aug 1857	31 Jul 1857	WPT
Taylor, Lorenzo D.	Halfhill, Sarah	12 Aug 1854	06 Aug 1854	DET
Taylor, Oliver C.	Sturgeon, Mary W.	12 Jan 1860	11 Jan 1860	DET
Taylor, Oliver C.	Sturgeon, Mary W.	25 Jan 1860	11 Jan 1860	WPT
Taylor, Stacy	Mulhena, Elizabeth	17 Nov 1853	12 Nov 1853	PDD
Temple, Henry	Ruble, Deleanah	28 Feb 1854	15 Feb 1854	PDD
Terry, Leroy G.	Scott, Ann Amelia	06 Jun 1848	01 Jun 1848	DENQ
Thomas, Isaiah	Glover, Mary Jane	18 Feb 1853	16 Feb 1853	PI
Thomas, Jonathan	Jones, Elizabeth	29 Dec 1860	16 Dec 1860	PTIMES
Thomas, Joseph W.	Cable, Sarah Ann	08 Feb 1856	07 Feb 1856	DET
Thomas, Joseph W.	Cable, Sarah Ann	13 Feb 1856	07 Feb 1856	WPT
Thompson, Dr. James	Gaines, Lucy	10 Nov 1853	25 Oct 1853	DET
Thompson, Nathan	Miller, Margaret	15 Dec 1854	08 Dec 1854	DET
Thompson, Samuel	Winning, Elizabeth	19 Aug 1854	15 Aug 1854	DET
Thompson, William	Ford, Maria	03 Dec 1856	25 Nov 1856	WPT
Thompson, William	Morris, Margaret	07 Feb 1855	17 Jan 1855	DET
Thornton, George W.	Pelhane, Dora	17 Feb 1860	16 Feb 1860	DET
Thrackmarton, Joseph	Ray, Lavina	03 Sep 1851	29 Aug 1851	PT&C
Thrall, William R.	Galigher, Hannah	16 Jul 1859	14 Jul 1859	DET
Thrall, William R. (Dr.)	Galigher, Hanah	20 Jul 1859	14 Jul 1859	WPT
Thurston, James D.	Hinman, Martha J.	21 Nov 1857	17 Nov 1857	DET
Timbrook, William	Hitchcock, Laura	17 Dec 1864	14 Dec 1864	PTIMES
Timmonds, John W.	Gebhardt, Caroline	13 Apr 1855	12 Apr 1855	DET
Timmonds, M.T.	Lawson, Mary J.	31 Mar 1852	25 Mar 1852	PT&C
Tomlinson, Alvin D.	Abbott, Mary A.	27 Feb 1854	19 Feb 1854	PDD
Tomlinson, Henry W.	Conway, E.E.	30 Jun 1854	28 Jun 1854	PDD
Tomlinson, William E.	Sweney, Elizabeth	28 Oct 1850	16 Oct 1850	PI
Towner, B.F.	Breedlove, Mahala	16 Dec 1853	15 Dec 1853	DET
Towner, B.W.	Breedlove, Mahala H.	26 Dec 1853	15 Dec 1853	PDD
Tracy, C.P.	McClain, Isabella	21 Dec 1858	20 Dec 1858	DET
Tracy, C.P.	McClain, Isabella	22 Dec 1858	20 Dec 1858	WPT

Name (Groom)	Name (Bride)	Notice Date	Marriage Date	Paper
Tracy, Charles O.	Kinney, Maria	20 Dec 1827	13 Dec 1827	WT
Tracy, Samuel M.	Thurston, Margaret	29 Oct 1851	27 Oct 1851	PT&C
Tracy, Uri	Lloyd, Harriet E.	10 Dec 1851	04 Dec 1851	PT&C
Tracy, V.D.L.	Davis, Annice B.	13 Apr 1854	12 Apr 1854	PDD
Tracy, V.D.L.	Davis, Annice B.	19 Apr 1854	13 Apr 1854	SVREP
Tracy, Van Der Lyn	Davis, Annice B.	13 Apr 1854	12 Apr 1854	DET
Trombo, Ambrose J.	Kelley, Martha A.	16 Mar 1858	03 Mar 1858	PSOT
Trotter, C.H.	Gallop, Eliza	29 Aug 1853		DET
Trotter, John C.	Lawrence, Eliza	08 Jul 1859	07 Jul 1859	DET
Trotter, John C.	Lawrence, (Mrs.) Eliza	13 Jul 1859	07 Jul 1859	WPT
Tucker, Lewis	Steene, Nancy	21 Oct 1850	17 Oct 1850	PI
Turley, John A.	Robinson, Charlotte E.	05 Jan 1844	02 Jan 1844	TRIB
Turner, David	Anderson, Mary	03 Aug 1855	02 Aug 1855	DET
Turner, James N.	Hagerman, Liza	20 Apr 1853	12 Apr 1853	PT&C
Tuxerty, Reason	Cisson, Frances	29 Aug 1850	01 Jul 1850	PT&C
Tyler, John (President)	Gardiner, Julia	04 Jul 1844	26 Jun 1844	TRIB
Umble, S.J.	Mott, Melissa F.	02 Jul 1856	30 Jun 1856	WPT
Upham, Edward S.	Gibbons, Lucy Ann	06 Nov 1838	02 Nov 1838	STRIB
Urquhart, George O.	McKenzie, Ann	15 May 1855	01 May 1855	DET
Van Garder, Green	Heran, Cynthia	03 Dec 1851	23 Nov 1851	PT&C
Vance, Jerome B.	Shelling, Elizabeth	07 Jul 1858	07 Jul 1858	DET
Vance, Jerome B.	Shellieg, Elizabeth	13 Jul 1858	07 Jul 1858	PSOT
Vance, Jerome B.	Shelling, Elizabeth	14 Jul 1858	07 Jul 1858	WPT
Vance, John	Sullivan, Ellen	30 Apr 1852	21 Apr 1852	PI
Vance, Miles W.	Ferree, Mary Jane	21 Nov 1853	16 Nov 1853	DET
Vance, Miles W.	Firree, Mary Jane	22 Nov 1853	16 Nov 1853	PDD
Vandwort, James	Fletcher, Julia A.	08 Oct 1856	30 Sep 1856	WPT
Vasmeter, Joseph	Fullerton, Margaret	12 Jun 1855	06 Jun 1855	DET
Vanscoy, Nelson	Selders, Cordella	25 Jan 1854	20 Jan 1854	DET
Varner, John	Noel, Caroline	22 Oct 1851	16 Oct 1851	PT&C
Vaughn, Wm.	Walterhouse, Agnes	04 Nov 1865	31 Oct 1865	PTIMES
Vaughters, John A.	Brouse, Ada Jane	21 Nov 1859	18 Nov 1859	WPT
Vaughters, Wm.	Bryson, Mary	05 Nov 1851		PT&C
Veach, Wm. (Esq.)	White, Sarah E.	21 Oct 1865	11 Oct 1865	PTIMES
Vermillion, Ratliff	Alexander, Elizabeth	18 May 1854	15 May 1854	DET
Vermillion, T.B.	Sinton, Artemisia	28 Sep 1858	14 Sep 1858	PSOT
Vermillion, T.B.	Sinton, Artemisia	28 Sep 1858	14 Sep 1858	PTIMES
Victor, Orsville J.	Fuller, Metta Victoria	09 Jul 1856	03 Jul 1856	WPT
Vincent, Joseph T.	Pratt, Lucy	29 Oct 1851	23 Oct 1851	PT&C
Violet, Sam'l. B. (Esq.)	Slattery, Jane C.	09 Jan 1856	20 Dec 1855	WPT
Violet, Samuel B.	Slattery, Jane C.	04 Jan 1856	20 Dec 1855	DET
Violet, Samuel B.(Esq.)	Slattery, Jane C.	09 Jan 1856	20 Dec 1855	WPT
Virgin, Kinsey	Young, Eliza	18 Mar 1831	13 Mar 1831	PC&WT
Voglesong, Wm. G. (M.D.)	Reynolds, Elizabeth	12 Mar 1846	05 Mar 1846	TRIB

Name (Groom)	Name (Bride)	Notice Date	Marriage Date	Paper
Wade, Jacob F.	Reynolds, Caroline J.	05 Nov 1853	31 Oct 1853	DET
Wainsley, John A.	Smolley, Nancy W.	15 Feb 1855	14 Feb 1855	DET
Waits, George	Louderback, Mary Jane	19 Nov 1856	16 Nov 1856	WPT
Waldo, Jehoil	Lewis, Polly	10 Oct 1851	08 Oct 1851	PI
Waldo, Jehoil	Lewis, Polty	15 Oct 1851	08 Oct 1851	PT&C
Walker, David M.	Cummings, Mary G.	07 Jan 1857	29 Dec 1856	WPT
Walker, Geo. Paul	Nichols, Hellen	22 Oct 1851	14 Oct 1851	PT&C
Walker, George P.	Nichols, Helen	17 Oct 1851	14 Oct 1851	PI
Walker, Thomas	Walker, Margaret	05 Nov 1853	31 Oct 1853	DET
Walker, Thomas D.	Suten, Malinda M.	25 Feb 1857	17 Feb 1857	WPT
Wallace, J.W.	Collins, Sarah A.	12 Jan 1853	02 Jan 1853	PT&C
Wallbright, Christian	Doty, Mary	02 Jan 1855	01 Jan 1855	DET
Waller, Robert	James, Eliza	17 Apr 1855	15 Apr 1855	DET
Walsh, Thomas V.	Salters, Susan	23 Dec 1850	15 Dec 1850	PI
Wamsley, William F. (Esq.)	Collins, Ellen J.	28 Oct 1865	19 Oct 1865	PTIMES
Ward, George	Stanly, Susan	18 Jan 1854		DET
Ware, Thornton W.	Richards, Maria	22 Mar 1862	13 Mar 1862	PTIMES
Ware, W.H.	Lancaster, Martha Ann	19 Oct 1854	12 Oct 1854	PDD
Warington, Nathaniel	Lynch, Elizabeth	09 Aug 1853	04 Aug 1853	DET
Warren, Beriah	Eagleson, Margaret J.	29 Jun 1855	21 Jun 1855	DET
Warring, James L.	Spanaler, Hannah S.	14 Feb 1856	24 Jan 1856	DET
Warwick, John B. (Dr.)	Moulten, Sallie B.	18 Feb 1860	14 Feb 1860	DET
Watkins, Thomas B.	Wiley, Mary Ann	04 Jan 1854	01 Jan 1854	DET
Watkins, Thomas B.	Wiley, Mary Ann	05 Jan 1854	01 Jan 1854	PDD
Watt, John Jr.	Fleming, Mary Julia C.	24 Jun 1854	15 Jun 1854	DET
Watt, M.H.	Tuttle, Jane S.	22 Nov 1853	17 Nov 1853	PDD
Watts, James M.	Collis, Nancy Jane	24 Jan 1860	18 Jan 1860	DET
Watts, James M.	Collis, Nancy Jane	25 Jan 1860	18 Jan 1860	WPT
Watts, W.W. (Dr.)	Rittle, Nancy	30 Apr 1856	29 Apr 1856	WPT
Wear, Marshall	West, Mary	11 Oct 1859	09 Oct 1859	DET
Wear, Marshall	West, Mary	12 Oct 1859	09 Oct 1859	WPT
Webster, Elizur G.	Thrall, Melissa H.	30 Jan 1858	28 Jan 1858	DET
Webster, Elizur G.	Thrall, Melissa H.	03 Feb 1858	28 Jan 1858	WPT
Weishch, John	Dott, Elizabeth	03 Jan 1855	02 Jan 1855	DET
Welch, Joshua	Baker, Mary	08 Mar 1844	23 Jan 1844	TRIB
Welsh, Joseph	Coway, Hannah	29 Sep 1852	27 Sep 1852	PT&C
Welty, Frank	Bish, Magdaline	16 Jul 1856	07 Jul 1856	WPT
West, John W.	Kearns, Mary	20 Aug 1855	19 Aug 1855	DET
West, N.A.	Long, Mary Jane	22 Oct 1856	08 Oct 1856	WPT
West, Pleasant (Esq.)	Combs, Elizabeth	11 Feb 1857	29 Jan 1857	WPT
West, Thomas	Cartwright, Hannah	28 Nov 1850 19 Dec 1850	27 Nov 1850	PT&C
West, Thomas W.	Cartwright, Hannah	02, 23 Dec 1850	27 Nov 1850	PI
Westwood, John I.	Gill, Mary Ann	12 Nov 1858	01 Nov 1858	DET

Name (Groom)	Name (Bride)	Notice Date	Marriage Date	Paper
Westwood, John I.	Gill, Mary Ann	17 Nov 1858	01 Nov 1858	WPT
Wheeler, Isaac	Burt, Elizabeth	26 Nov 1856	22 Nov 1856	WPT
Wheeler, John	Carter, Rebecca	20 Oct 1852	17 Oct 1852	PT&C
Wheeler, Joseph Franklin	Churchill, Melissa	17 Oct 1844	15 Oct 1844	TRIB
Wheeler, Samuel P.	Jones, Cornelia	23 Dec 1865	17 Dec 1865	PTIMES
Whitcher, Frederick P.	Throckmorton, Hannah	28 Mar 1832	22 Mar 1832	PC
Whitcomb, male	Pool, Eliza	01 Jul 1825		PG&LA
White, Anson	Bagley, Hannah	23 Nov 1858	21 Nov 1858	DET
White, Anson	Bagley, Hannah	24 Nov 1858	21 Nov 1858	WPT
White, Henry C.	Allen, Emily Jane	09, 10 Nov 1854	08 Nov 1854	DET
White, Homer	Cassidy, Sarah Jane	27 Jun 1855	27 Jun 1855	DET
White, Leonard	Hart, Margaret	10 Dec 1851	03 Dec 1851	PT&C
White, Samuel	Ransom, Mary	04 Jan 1856	20 Dec 1855	DET
White, Samuel	Ransom, Mary	09 Jan 1856	20 Dec 1855	WPT
Whitney, John	Kelley, Arena	29 Dec 1843	21 Dec 1843	TRIB
Whitney, Ruliff	Cassidy, Ellen	17 May 1862	26 Apr 1862	PTIMES
Wicks, Henry	Jones, Rachel	31 May 1853	19 May 1853	PDD
Wilhelm, John	Schwarzd, Wilhelm Sophia	09 Jun 1857	01 Jun 1857	PSOT
Willey, Henry	Glassford, Sarah	03 Sep 1852	30 Aug 1852	PI
Willey, Henry	Glossford, Sarah	01 Sep 1852	30 Aug 1852	PT&C
Williams, Abraham	Strait, Rebecca	28 Jun 1855	27 Jun 1855	DET
Williams, Daniel	Price, Mary J.	07 Mar 1855	01 Mar 1855	DET
Williams, E.	Crook, Julia	02 Oct 1855	17 Sep 1855	DET
Williams, George	Boynton, Lucy	16 Dec 1818		PGAZ
Williams, John	Page, Hannah A.	18 Mar 1853	04 Jan 1853	PI
Williams, John	Hibbs, Slona A.	11 Apr 1863	09 Apr 1863	PTIMES
Williams, Joseph	Sherman, Elizabeth	03 Dec 1855	01 Dec 1855	DET
Williams, Joseph	Sherman, Elizabeth	05 Dec 1855	01 Dec 1855	WPT
Williams, Matthew M.	Street, Minta M.	11 Apr 1863	05 Apr 1863	PTIMES
Williams, Samuel T.	Rives, Corrie	18 Aug 1858	02 Aug 1858	WPT
Williams, William	Powers, Martha Jane	15 Jun 1853	08 Jun 1853	PT&C
Williams, William E.	Bowers, Martha Jane	10 Jun 1853		DET
Williams, William E., Jr.	Powers, Mary Jane	11 Jun 1853	08 Jun 1853	PDD
Williamson, John	Page, Hannah A.	11 Jan 1853	04 Jan 1853	PI
Williamson, Peter	Shaffer, Rosanna	31 May 1827	24 May 1827	WT
Williamson, Thomas	Oard, Lucinda	11 Jan 1832	05 Jan 1832	PC
Willis, John	Rust, Rebecca	11 Jun 1856	28 May 1856	WPT
Wilson, Albert	Howe, Rebecca M.	29 Jul 1850	23 Jul 1850	PI
Wilson, Albert	Hone, Rebecca	29 Jul 1850	23 Jul 1850	PT&C
Wilson, Alexander	Brown, Maggie E.	05 Aug 1865	01 Aug 1865	PTIMES
Wilson, Charles	McKee, Melisla	31 Jan 1854	15 Jan 1854	DET
Wilson, Clarke	Swords, Sarah A.	27 Feb 1852	23 Feb 1852	PI
Wilson, Stephen	Gillen, Sarah	31 May 1827		WT
Winderly, Minrod	Strong, Annis	21 Jan 1857	11 Jan 1857	WPT

Name (Groom)	Name (Bride)	Notice Date	Marriage Date	Paper
Winkler, George C.(Capt.)	Lacroix, Mary J.	30 Sep 1865	21 Sep 1865	PTIMES
Winn, Thomas	Neve, Jane	28 Dec 1852	24 Dec 1852	PDD
Winn, Thomas	Neve, Jane	31 Dec 1852	24 Dec 1852	PI
Winn, Thomas	Neve, Jane	29 Dec 1852	24 Dec 1852	PT&C
Wirts, Caspar	Dortch, Rebecca	20 Jan 1851	16 Jan 1851	PI
Wishare, John B.	Bilker, Stacy	13 Jan 1851	07 Jan 1851	PI
Wisner, Samuel N.	Bagley, Martha J.	16 Jul 1856	11 Jul 1856	WPT
Wolcott, Henry	Richart, Elizabeth E.	30 Apr 1860	28 Apr 1860	DET
Womeldorff, Daniel L.	Mossmann, Sarah A.	05 Nov 1853	27 Oct 1853	DET
Wood, Robert	Peebles, Jane	31 May 1827	16 May 1827	WT
Woodside, Wm. J.	Kepler, Sarah A.	18 Jul 1860	18 Jul 1860	DET
Woodward, E.W.	Miller, Harriet	24 Feb 1855	20 Feb 1855	DET
Worcester, S.H.	Baylor, Elizabeth L.	22 Aug 1850	15 Aug 1850	PT&C
Worcester, Samuel H.	Baylor, Elizabeth L.	19 Aug 1850	15 Aug 1850	PI
Worley, Sylvester T.	Hicks, Elizabeth J.	10 Nov 1858	09 Nov 1858	DET
Worley, Sylvester T.	Hicks, Elizabeth J.	17 Nov 1858	09 Nov 1858	WPT
Worley, W.C.	Willet, Mary	26 Mar 1856		WPT
Worthington, Augustine (Dr.)	Frances, Catherine S.	15, 17 Sep 1855	12 Sep 1855	DET
Worthington, James	Fitzer, Elizabeth	13 Jul 1853	03 Jul 1853	PT&C
Worthington, James, Jr.	Fitzer, Elizabeth	07 Jul 1853	03 Jul 1853	DET
Wright, Charles H.	Williams, Caroline A.	15 Jul 1865	10 Jul 1865	PTIMES
Wright, John C.	Salsbury, Helen M.	27 Oct 1843	24 Oct 1843	TRIB
Wright, Presley	Reynolds, Lucinda	12 Dec 1853	01 Dec 1853	DET
Wright, Presley	Reynolds, Lucinda	15 Dec 1853	01 Dec 1853	WPT
Wyckoff, John	McGiffin, Jemimah J.	08 Nov 1853	30 Oct 1853	DET
Wyeth, Walter N.	Wait, Belle	09 May 1859	09 May 1859	DET
Wyeth, Walter N.	Wait, Belle	10 May 1859	09 May 1859	PTIMES
Wyeth, Walter N. (Rev.)	Wait, Belle	11 May 1859	09 May 1859	WPT
Wynn, Isaac C.	Towner, Eliza E.	04 Feb 1858	02 Feb 1858	DET
Wynn, Isaac C.	Towner, Eliza E.	09 Feb 1858	02 Feb 1858	PSOT
Yeager, Cornelius H.	Johnston, Fannie L.	07 Dec 1859	06 Dec 1859	DET
Yeley, James W.	Lionbarger, Emma	15 Oct 1858	14 Oct 1858	DET
Young, William	Newcomb, Susan	13 Jul 1853	11 Jul 1853	PDD
Zeek, Andrew	Loomis, Laura	27 Apr 1853	20 Apr 1853	PT&C
Zeigler, Henry D.	Norris, Mary M.	27 Jun 1844	27 Jun 1844	TRIB
Zollaes, Charles M.	McColm, Caroline	31 Aug 1853	31 Jul 1853	DET

*Listed under DIED by mistake in the paper.

Marriages (Brides)

Name (Bride)	Name (Groom)	Notice Date	Marriage Date	Paper
__ott, Sarah Jane	Moore, John O.	02 Apr 1856	20 Mar 1856	WPT
Abbott, Mary A.	Tomlinson, Alvin D.	27 Feb 1854	19 Feb 1854	PDD
Abrams, Emma	Harper, John L. (Capt.)	01 Jun 1820	11 May 1820	STEL
Ackerman, C.W. (Mrs.)	Smith, Charles S.	12 Jan 1854	05 Jan 1854	PDD
Ackey, Mary E.	M'Dowell, Jno., Jr.	24 Sep 1852	21 Sep 1852	PI
Adams, Ana	Stiner, Peter	11 Nov 1853	09 Aug 1853	DET
Adams, Catherine	Gilliland, Nathan	09 Feb 1844	18 Jan 1844	TRIB
Adams, Cornelia F.	Killin, Joseph W.	03 Dec 1853	29 Nov 1853	DET
Adams, Cornelia F.	Killin, Joseph W.	04 Dec 1853	29 Nov 1853	PDD
Aldrich, Martha J. (nee Turner)	Humphries, G.W. (Sheriff)	02 Jan 1845	23 Nov 1844	TRIB
Alexander, Elizabeth	Vermillion, Ratliff	18 May 1854	15 May 1854	DET
Allen, Effie	Scott, David H. (Dr.)	28 Oct 1865	18 Oct 1865	PTIMES
Allen, Emily Jane	White, Henry C.	09, 10 Nov 1854	08 Nov 1854	DET
Allen, Maria	Greathouse, W.C.	11 Jun 1855	07 Jun 1855	DET
Allen, Mollie	Calvert, Frank W.	02 Jan 1864	24 Dec 1863	PTIMES
Allison, Mary	Garvin, Thomas	26 Jan 1844	18 Jan 1844	TRIB
Allison, Mary	Rice, Thos. H.	30 Jun 1854	29 Jun 1854	PDD
Allman, Mary L.	Engelbrecht, L.	27 Sep 1862	22 Sep 1862	PTIMES
Allords, Lydia	Sturdy, George	13 Apr 1853	06 Apr 1853	PT&C
Allowase, Eliza C.	McDermit, A.J.	03 Dec 1858	02 Dec 1858	DET
Allowase, Eliza C.	McDermit, A.J.	08 Dec 1858	02 Dec 1858	WPT
Anderson, Mary	Clark, Andrew J.	13 Nov. 1838	08 Nov 1838	STRIB
Anderson, Mary	Rice, Jesse	23 May 1854	18 May 1854	DET
Anderson, Mary	Turner, David	03 Aug 1855	02 Aug 1855	DET
Andre, Maria A.	Steen, James G.	08 Jan 1856	31 Dec 1855	DET
Andre, Maria A.	Steen, James G.	09 Jan 1856	31 Dec 1855	WPT
Andre, Rosina	Lamber, William	19 May 1852	05 May 1852	PT&C
Andre, Sophia	Enslow, Revillo	11 Jan 1853	23 Dec 1852	PI
Andrews, Almia	Gunn, Bela	06 Sep 1828		WT
Anore, Nancy	McFaun, A.J.	11 Jan 1853	23 Dec 1852	PI
Antram, Emma	Fisher, David	09 Jul 1853	26 Jun 1853	DET
Appal, Mary	Horse, George	18 Jul 1854	17 Jul 1854	PDD
Armstrong, Ella E.	McCauslen, A.W.	22 Mar 1855	15 Mar 1855	DET
Armstrong, Lettis	Karr, Abraham	05 Nov 1858	21 Oct 1858	SVREP
Baccus, Marilda	Lewis, John	30 Jan 1858	21 Jan 1858	DET
Baccus, Marilda	Lewis, John	03 Feb 1858	21 Jan 1858	WPT

Marriages (Brides)

Name (Bride)	Name (Groom)	Notice Date	Marriage Date	Paper
Bagley, Hannah	White, Anson	23 Nov 1858	21 Nov 1858	DET
Bagley, Hannah	White, Anson	24 Nov 1858	21 Nov 1858	WPT
Bagley, Martha J.	Wisner, Samuel N.	16 Jul 1856	11 Jul 1856	WPT
Bailey, Mary Jane	Johnson, Benj. H.	15 Nov 1854	02 Nov 1854	DET
Baird, Jeannie W.	Pond, J. Evarts (Rev.)	19 Mar 1858	18 Mar 1858	DET
Baker, Eliza	Oldfield, George S.	19 Nov 1864	15 Nov 1864	PTIMES
Baker, Ella	Fauble, George	10, 17 Feb 1854	07 Feb 1854	DET
Baker, Ella	Fauble, George	21 Feb 1854	07 Feb 1854	PDD
Baker, Harriet (Mrs.)	Stephenson, Joseph	21 Feb 1854	14 Feb 1854	PDD
Baker, Mary	Welch, Joshua	08 Mar 1844	23 Jan 1844	TRIB
Baker, Wilhelmina	Bellman, Joseph	09 Apr 1858	05 Apr 1858	DET
Baker, Wilhelmina	Bellman, Joseph	14 Apr 1858	05 Apr 1858	WPT
Baldwin, Lydia	Ludlam, male	13 Sep 1853	06 Sep 1853	PDD
Baldwin, Lydia	Ludlam, male	12 Sep 1853	06 Sep 1853	DET
Baldwin, Minerva R.	Bail, J.T. (Rev.)	02 Aug 1854	25 Jul 1854	DET
Ball, Jennie M.	Murphy, Dave (Lieut.)	23 Sep 1865	18 Sep 1865	PTIMES
Ball, Laura H.	McDougal, James	06 Oct 1860	30 Sep 1860	PTIMES
Ball, Laura H.	McDougal, James O.	02 Oct 1860	30 Sep 1860	DET
Ball, Lucy	Barbee, Wesley	23 Sep 1850	19 Sep 1850	PI
Ball, Lucy	Barbee, Wesley	26 Sep 1850	19 Sep 1850	PT&C
Ball, Nancy C.	Partingale, James M.	07 May 1864	28 Apr 1864	PTIMES
Banks, Louisa	Bills, John	07,09 Nov 1854		PDD
Barbee, Sarah	Hall, Wm. H.	23 Dec 1850	09 Dec 1850	PI
Barbee, Sarah	Hall, Wm. H.	19 Dec 1850	09 Dec 1850	PT&C
Barber, Jane	Patterson, Galbreth	18 Mar 1825	06 Mar 1825	PG&LA
Barber, Louisa	Noel, Ezra H.	15 Jan 1846	08 Jan 1846	TRIB
Barker, Mary E.	Finch, Morton B. (Dr.)	31 Dec 1853	30 Dec 1853	PDD
Barklow, Penelope	Shufflin, Edward G.	04 Mar 1857	25 Feb 1857	WPT
Barnett, Maria	Kendall, Henry	15 Nov 1862	16 Oct 1862	PTIMES
Basham, Ellen	Shump, H.C. (Lieut.)	27 May 1865	21 May 1865	PTIMES
Baylor, Elizabeth L.	Worcester, S.H.	22 Aug 1850	15 Aug 1850	PT&C
Baylor, Elizabeth L.	Worcester, Samuel H.	19 Aug 1850	15 Aug 1850	PI
Bean, Maggie	Stout, Charles	16 Feb 1854	07 Feb 1854	DET
Bean, Maggie	Stout, Charles	17 Feb 1854	07 Feb 1854	PDD
Beecher, Agnes	Allen, Edward H.	19 Aug 1859	30 Jul 1859	DET
Beecher, Agnes	Allen, Edward H.	24 Aug 1859	30 Jul 1859	WPT
Belica Anestatio	Mangen, Francis	13 Jul 1854	12 Jul 1854	DET
Belica, Anestatiio	Mangen, Francis	15 Jul 1854	12 Jul 1854	PDD
Bell, Agatha Eustace	Ely, Seneca W.	18 Jul 1850	11 Jul 1850	PT&C
Bell, Lucy M.	Collins, J. W.	09 Jun 1853	07 Jun 1853	DET
Bell, Lucy M.	Collins, J.W.	10 Jun 1853	07 Jun 1853	PDD
Bell, Lucy M.	Collins, J.W.	15 Jun 1853	07 Jun 1853	PT&C
Bell, Mary E.	Glidden, John J.	11 Oct 1862	08 Oct 1862	PTIMES
Bemn, Margaret	Coolman, Edward	13 Apr 1853	08 Apr 1853	PT&C
Bender, Catharine	Apple, Phillip	09 May 1848	04 May 1848	DENQ

Name (Bride)	Name (Groom)	Notice Date	Marriage Date	Paper
Beniger, Francis	Bolinger, Jacob	27 Mar 1855	09 Mar 1855	DET
Bennett, Eizabeth Jane	Jackson, William Jr.	09 Jul 1856	15 Jun 1856	WPT
Bennett, Mary F.	Oviatt, Benjamin F.	04 May 1858	25 Apr 1858	PSOT
Bennett, Sarah	Sanders, L.D.	01 Oct 1856	28 Sep 1856	WPT
Benning, Jael	Haller, Christian	13 Apr 1855		DET
Bentley, Laura J.	Lloyd, Charles P.	28 Feb 1863	26 Feb 1863	PTIMES
Benton, Susan	Bordlleau, G.D.	12 Jun 1855		DET
Berry, Catherine	Salleday, Calvin	26 Mar 1856	20 Mar 1856	WPT
Bersteh, Louisa	Richt, Henry	17 Jul 1855	17 Jul 1855	DET
Bey, Margaret	Freelich, Jacob	11 Jan 1853	13 Jan 1853	PI
Bey, Margaret	Freelich, Jacob	19 Jan 1853	13 Jan 1853	PT&C
Biggs, Nancy	Kirk, Thomas	30 Jul 1852	26 Jul 1852	PI
Bilker, Stacy	Wishare, John B.	13 Jan 1851	07 Jan 1851	PI
Bish, Magdaline	Welty, Frank	16 Jul 1856	07 Jul 1856	WPT
Black, Martha	Beals, Asa G.	20 Apr 1853	10 Apr 1853	PT&C
Black, Mary	Rankin, Benjamin	09 Sep 1825	18 Aug 1825	PG&LA
Bleaks, Sarah	Jackson, Albert	24 Feb 1851	18 Feb 1851	PI
Blagg, Sarah	Rolrins, Eli	18 Mar 1853	06 Mar 1853	PI
Blinn, Nettie	Goodlor, R. Vivion	16 Jun 1855	05 Jun 1855	DET
Bliss, Hannah	Boyer, Thos. D.	06 Aug 1855	04 Aug 1855	DET
Bockwalter, Elizabeth D.	Parker, H.H.	14 Nov 1850		PT&C
Boechner, Phillpena	Beatzhausen, Christian	26 Jan 1844	26 Dec 1843	TRIB
Bonner, Minerva	Price, Vinton	29 Mar 1854	26 Mar 1854	DET
Bonsall, Laura A.	Richardson, B.F.	11 Nov 1865	19 Oct 1865	PTIMES
Bonser, Elinor	Storer, William	11 Jan 1853	28 Oct 1852	PI
Bookwalter, Elizabeth D.	Parker, N.H.	18 Nov 1850	12 Nov 1850	PI
Borland, Anna	Breslin, John G. (Hon.)	04 May 1855	01 May 1855	DET
Bowers, Martha Jane	Williams, William E.	10 Jun 1853		DET
Bowley, Hulda	Barnett, Andrew H.	15 Feb 1860	07 Feb 1860	DET
Bowley, Hulda	Barnett, Andrew H.	05 Feb 1860	07 Feb 1860	WPT
Bowman, Eliza Jane	Barbee, Cornelius H.	30 Jan 1864	20 Jan 1864	PTIMES
Bowman, Mary C.	Elden, Charles D.	24 Sep 1853		DET
Bowman, Mary C.	Elden, Charles D.	26 Sep 1853	20 Sep 1853	PDD
Boyd, A.A.	Carter, William S.	27 Sep 1855	26 Sep 1855	DET
Boyd, Elizabeth	Lacy, Daniel	22 Dec 1855	20 Dec 1855	DET
Boyd, Elizabeth	Lacy, Daniel	08 Jan 1856		DET
Boyd, Elizabeth	Lacy, Daniel	26 Dec 1855 09 Jan 1856	20 Dec 1855	WPT
Boyd, M.	Gurney, H.	11 Jul 1860	10 Jul 1860	DET
Boyd, Mary Jane	Maklem, R.S.	17 Nov 1852		PI
Boynton, Lucy	Williams, George	16 Dec 1818		PGAZ
Boynton, Mary E.	Hall, O.J. (Dr.)	17 May 1862	07 May 1862	PTIMES
Bradbury, Nancy	Edmundson, Nathan	12 Aug 1854	02 Aug 1854	DET
Bradford, Elizabeth	Rinehart, John	23 Dec 1850	17 Nov 1850	PI
Bradford, Elizabeth	Rinehart, John	19 Dec 1850	17 Nov 1850	PT&C

Name (Bride)	Name (Groom)	Notice Date	Marriage Date	Paper
Bradford, Mary E.	Moore, Samuel G.	19 Sep 1863	16 Sep 1863	PTIMES
Bradford, Wilhemna	Stewart, Hugh D.	29 Dec 1860	06 Dec 1860	PTIMES
Brasier, Catharine L.	Shipman, William J.	09 Dec 1850	03 Dec 1850	PI
Brazee, Mary	Arnold, Wart	14 Feb 1854	09 Feb 1854	DET
Brazier, Catharine L.	Shipman, Wm. J.	05 Dec 1850	03 Dec 1850	PT&C
Breck, Bettie	McDowell, Wm. (Esq.)	30 Jan 1854	10 Jan 1854	PDD
Breedlove, Mahala	Towner, B.F.	16 Dec 1853	15 Dec 1853	DET
Breedlove, Mahala H.	Towner, B.W.	26 Dec 1853	15 Dec 1853	PDD
Breese, Phoeba Ann	Piece, Samuel	29 Dec 1853	08 Dec 1853	DET
Brewer, Sarah	Stevens, George H.	21 Nov 1853	10 Nov 1853	DET
Brice, Jennie E.	Dumble, J.W.	29 Dec 1860	17 Dec 1860	PTIMES
Brice, Mary E.	K_bler, C.H.	28 Feb 1854	24 Feb 1854	PDD
Bringham, Sarah Jane	Colvin, Harrison	23 Nov 1858	14 Oct 1858	PSOT
Bringham, Sarah Jane	Colvin, Harrison	23 Nov 1858	14 Oct 1858	PTIMES
Bronn, Margaret A.	Camden, W.P.	06 Jun 1848	04 Jun 1848	DENQ
Brooks, Lucinda	Hosward, Claburn	11 Jun 1856	30 May 1856	WPT
Brooks, Mary	Nixon, Samuel	19 Jan 1828	16 Jan 1828	WT
Brouse, Ada Jane	Vaughters, John A.	21 Nov 1859	18 Nov 1859	WPT
Brouse, Letitia	Moss, George	26 Sep 1853		DET
Browen, Sarah	Bradly, William	21 Jan 1857	15 Jan 1857	WPT
Brown, Anna M.	England, J.H.	10 Aug 1858	29 Jul 1858	PSOT
Brown, Antoinette (Rev.)	Merret, James A. (Dr.)	27 Oct 1854		DET
Brown, Elizabeth	Davenport, Whitle	24 Sep 1852	19 Sep 1852	PI
Brown, Maggie E.	Wilson, Alexander	05 Aug 1865	01 Aug 1865	PTIMES
Brown, Mary A.	Hunsuck, Nathan	09 Jan 1851	01 Jan 1851	PT&C
Brown, Rebecca	Brenton, John	30 Dec 1853	29 Dec 1853	DET
Brown, Rebecca	Brenton, John	31 Dec 1853	29 Dec 1853	PDD
Brown, Rebecca	Price, Isaac	22 Jun 1826	15 Jun 1826	WT
Brown, Sarah	Loughry, John C.	07 Nov 1857	05 Nov 1857	DET
Bruner, Lucinda	Scott, Perry	12 Jan 1844	28 Dec 1843	TRIB
Bruner, Mary Emma	Finch, C.M. (Dr.)	23 Jun 1857	18 Jun 1857	PSOT
Brunner, Maria	Spencer, John C.	06 Nov 1858	04 Nov 1858	PSOT
Brunner, Maria	Spencer, John C.	16 Nov 1858	04 Nov 1858	PTIMES
Bryson, Mary	Vaughters, Wm.	05 Nov 1851		PT&C
Buckley, Mary F.	Sly, Samuel	10 Dec 1851	30 Nov 1851	PT&C
Buffington, Cornelia Ann	Burt, Thomas	27 Apr 1826	23 Apr 1826	WT
Burdick, Phoebe	Nurse, Samuel R.	25 Feb 1825	01 Feb 1825	PG&LA
Burk, Elisa	Fraisor, John	16 May 1854	11 May 1854	DET
Burke, Lizzie	Swift, R.S.	31 Jul 1860	03 Jul 1860	DET
Burke, Lizzie	Swift, R.S.	01 Aug 1860	03 Jul 1860	WPT
Burke, Martha H.	Hard, Bethuel W.	12 Nov 1855	01 Nov 1855	DET
Burr, Mollie	Lawson, Manasseh M.	18 Jun 1864		PTIMES
Burriss, Hettie A.	Grimes, Will	27 Jun 1863	23 Jun 1863	PTIMES
Burt, Amanda	Chapman, Obediah	07 Jan 1857	31 Dec 1856	WPT
Burt, Eliza	Carroll, Alexius	16 Feb 1844	10 Feb 1844	TRIB

Name (Bride)	Name (Groom)	Notice Date	Marriage Date	Paper
Burt, Elizabeth	Wheeler, Isaac	26 Nov 1856	22 Nov 1856	WPT
Burt, Julia	Smith, Nelson	27 Jun 1844	20 Jun 1844	TRIB
Burton, Mandana	Bringham, Levi	31 Aug 1858	05 Aug 1858	PSOT
Butler, Julia A.	Lowe, Peter T.	28 Apr 1843	20 Apr 1843	TRIB
Byers, Hannah	Masterson, James	20 Apr 1853	13 Apr 1853	PT&C
Cable, Melissa	Lewis, Alexander	06 Oct 1855	03 Oct 1855	DET
Cable, Sarah Ann	Thomas, Joseph W.	08 Feb 1856	07 Feb 1856	DET
Cable, Sarah Ann	Thomas, Joseph W.	13 Feb 1856	07 Feb 1856	WPT
Cade, Harriet (nee Sage)	Hardy, Henry K. (Esq.)	03 Feb 1843	24 Jan 1843	TRIB
Cadot, Madeline	Boynton, Asa, Jr.	09 Jan 1855	01 Jan 1855	DET
Calaen, Sophia	Donley, Izaih	10 Oct 1853	29 Sep 1853	DET
Calf, Eliza	Munk, George	18 Mar 1853	14 Dec 1852	PI
Calihan, India	Myers, Allen	20 Apr 1854		DET
Calihan, India	Myers, Allen	20 Apr 1854	17 Apr 1854	PDD
Call, Harriet E.	Kelley, Henry	16 Dec 1854	06 Dec 1854	DET
Call, Malvina	McDivill, Daniel	24 Oct 1844	15 Sep 1844	TRIB
Call, Martha	Conery, John	24 Oct 1844	15 Sep 1844	TRIB
Cameron, Nancy	Jones, Henry	25 Jul 1844	18 Jul 1844	TRIB
Canter, Sarah	Rush, Jno.	13 May 1854		DET
Carel, Madeline	Newton, Jas. (Capt.)	27 Jul 1856	01 Jul 1856	WPT
Carnes, Isabel M.	Church, E.F.	26 Jun 1860	14 Jun 1860	DET
Carnes, Isabel M.	Church, E.F.	27 Jun 1860	14 Jun 1860	WPT
Carnes, Nancy	Goodin, Thomas	14 Jan 1854	05 Jan 1854	DET
Carter, Lucy E.	Farrington, James	02 Sep 1850	17 Aug 1850	PI
Carter, Lucy E.	Farrington, Jas.	29 Aug 1850	17 Aug 1850	PT&C
Carter, Mary	Brown, John	13 Jan 1857	09 Jan 1857	PSOT
Carter, Rebecca	Wheeler, John	20 Oct 1852	17 Oct 1852	PT&C
Cartwright, Eliza Jane	Evans, Evan	05 Oct 1855	04 Oct 1855	DET
Cartwright, Hannah	West, Thomas W.	02, 23 Dec 1850	27 Nov 1850	PI
Cartwright, Hannah	West, Thomas	28 Nov 1850 19 Dec 1850	27 Nov 1850	PT&C
Cary, Nancy Jane	Gunn, William	19 Dec 1851	16 Dec 1851	PI
Cary, Nancy Jane	Gunn, William	24 Dec 1851	16 Dec 1851	PT&C
Case, Martha E.	Burke, Joseph M.	01 Apr 1854	16 Mar 1854	DET
Cassell, Josephine	Ripley, William	14 Jan 1865	12 Jan 1865	PTIMES
Cassidy, Ellen	Whitney, Ruliff	17 May 1862	26 Apr 1862	PTIMES
Cassidy, Sarah Jane	White, Homer	27 Jun 1855	27 Jun 1855	DET
Catlin, Mary	Damarin, Lewis C.	31 Dec 1852	27 Dec 1852	PI
Caughren, Louisa	Anderson, Robert	21 Feb 1854	12 Feb 1854	PDD
Cavatt, Harriet	Draper, William O.	19 Aug 1854	15 Aug 1854	DET
Cavett, Elizabeth	Bunn, J. Harvey	22 Mar 1854	09 Mar 1854	DET
Chalfant, Therese	Pugh, George E. (Hon.)	28 Nov 1855	22 Nov 1855	WPT
Chaffin, Mary	Lowe, Frederick	20 Feb 1860	15 Feb 1860	DET
Chaffin, Mary	Lowe, Frederick	22 Feb 1860	15 Feb 1860	WPT
Chalfant, Therese	Pugh, George E. (Hon.)	26 Nov 1855	22 Nov 1855	DET

Name (Bride)	Name (Groom)	Notice Date	Marriage Date	Paper
Chambers, Harriet	Hobbins, James	27 Jul 1853		DET
Chandler, Annie E.	Mitchell, I.S.	29 Jul 1857	21 Jul 1857	DET
Chandler, Elenor	Boyd, William M.	17 Nov 1853	01 Nov 1853	PDD
Chapman, female	Lawrence, T.B. (Col.)	24 Mar 1854		PDD
Chapman, Ann Adelaide	Slimp, Alfred	06 Jun 1856	28 May 1856	OP
Chapman, Ann Adelaide	Slimp, Alfred	11 Jun 1856	28 May 1856	WPT
Chapman, Cynthia	Lusher, Louis W.	12 Oct 1855	12 Oct 1855	DET
Chapman, Elizabeth	Montgomery, Elis	06 May 1853	04 May 1853	PDD
Chapman, Rosanna	Snyder, John	07 Jan 1857	04 Jan 1857	WPT
Chase, Louisa M.	Reed, Marshall	22 Oct 1856	16 Oct 1856	WPT
Chenoweth, Mary	Chenoweth, Joel	10 Sep 1856	02 Sep 1856	WPT
Cherington, Sarah	Evans, Evan, Jr.	19 Aug 1854	13 Aug 1854	DET
Chesnut, Nancy	Reynolds, Calvin	06 Apr 1853	31 Mar 1853	PT&C
Chestnut, Nancy	Reynolds, Calvin	01 Apr 1853	31 Mar 1853	PI
Childers, female (Mrs.)	Andrew, unk. (Rev.Bishop)	23 Dec 1854	22 Nov 1854	DET
Churchhill, Julia	Griswold, E.H. (Dr.)	11 Jun 1853	06 Jun 1853	DET
Churchhill, Julia	Griswold, E.H. (Dr.)	15 Jun 1853	06 Jun 1853	PT&C
Churchill, Melissa	Wheeler, Joseph Franklin	17 Oct 1844	15 Oct 1844	TRIB
Cilley, M.	Heakl, C.	11 Jan 1853	02 Jan 1853	PI
Cissna, Harmeon	Fitzgerald, Easom (Dr.)	21 Feb 1854	09 Feb 1854	PDD
Cissna, Hormeon	Fitzgerald, Dr. Easton	17 Feb 1854	09 Feb 1854	DET
Cisson, Frances	Faverty, Rezin	15 Jul 1850	01 Jul 1850	PI
Cisson, Frances	Faverty, Rezin	18 Jul 1850	01 Jul 1850	PT&C
Cisson, Frances	Tuxerty, Reason	29 Aug 1850	01 Jul 1850	PT&C
Clare, Eliza	Jones, Nathan L., Jr.	14 Feb 1856	13 Feb 1856	DET
Clark, Love J.	Reed, Elroy W.	02 Jan 1864	28 Dec 1863	PTIMES
Clark, Maria Louisa	Kinney, Philander C.	06 Jun 1850	04 Jun 1850	PT&C
Clark, Marie Louisa	Kinney, Philander C.	10 Jun 1850	04 Jun 1850	PI
Clark, Mary Ellen	Sweet, Edward A.	23 Apr 1858	13 Apr 1858	DET
Clary, Sarah Elizabeth	Hobler, W.H.	02 Jan 1864	27 Dec 1863	PTIMES
Claypool, Alice	Gwynne, David (Maj.)	17 Aug 1820	01 Aug 1820	STEL
Clemens, Josephene	Ferguson, S.S.	02 Apr 1856	27 Mar 1856	WPT
Clemmins, Josephine	Ferguson, S. S.	28 Mar 1856	27 Mar 1856	OP
Clingan, M.L.(neeTerry)	Richey, George B.	19 Aug 1854	15 Aug 1854	DET
Clingman, Ann Eliza	Ransom, Samuel	30 Nov 1826	26 Nov 1826	WT
Clingman, Ann Maria	Richart, William	11 May 1826	02 May 1826	WT
Clingman, Eliza	M'Dowell, William	07 Jan 1830	05 Jan 1830	WT
Clise, Catharine	Kaugh, Mathias	30 Apr 1856	24 Apr 1856	WPT
Cloniger, Mary Ann	Becket, J.	16 Jun 1853	05 Jun 1853	DET
Cloniger, Mary Ann	Becket, J.	22 Jun 1853	05 Jun 1853	PT&C
Cloninger, Sarah V.	Henry, William D.	20 Jul 1858	08 Jul 1858	PSOT
Clover, Mary A.	McDowell, Joseph J.	23 Nov 1858	18 Nov 1858	DET
Clover, Mary A.	McDowell, Joseph J.	24 Nov 1858	18 Nov 1858	WPT
Clugsten, Mary E.	Jordan, Robert C.	06 May 1850	30 Apr 1850	PI
Clugston, Eveline E.	Rose, Charles E.	20 Dec 1849	18 Dec 1849	PT&C

Name (Bride)	Name (Groom)	Notice Date	Marriage Date	Paper
Cochran, Catharine	Fulsom, Samuel	07 Oct 1850	30 Sep 1850	PI
Cockerell, Mary Frances	Bodkin, James	19 Nov 1824		PG&LA
Cole, Caroline	Barber, Wm. E.	31 Dec 1851	25 Dec 1851	PT&C
Cole, Elizabeth	Crouse, C.F.	11 Jan 1853	02 Dec 1852	PI
Cole, John	Harrison, Elizabeth	17 Jun 1853	07 Jun 1853	PDD
Cole, Laura	Colegrove Benjamin	21 Nov 1829		WT
Coleman, Eulda	Smith, John M.	05 Jan 1853		PT&C
Coleman, Mary	Green, Samuel C.	19 Oct 1854	12 Oct 1854	PDD
Coleman, Mary Jane	Glaze, Samuel W.	16 Apr 1851		PT&C
Coles, Martha A.	Derby, N.	04 Mar 1865	23 Feb 1865	PTIMES
Colghly, Matilda	Ransom, Jas.	01 Sep 1855	23 Aug 1855	DET
Collier, Mary Ann	Orcutt, James W.	01 Mar 1844	20 Feb 1844	TRIB
Collins, Ellen J.	Wamsley, William F.(Esq.)	28 Oct 1865	19 Oct 1865	PTIMES
Collins, Emeline	Dare, Henry	09 Jul 1864	02 Jul 1864	PTIMES
Collins, Harriette	Hert, John W.	13 Mar 1854	07 Mar 1854	DET
Collins, Sarah A.	Wallace, J.W.	12 Jan 1853	02 Jan 1853	PT&C
Collis, Nancy Jane	Watts, James M.	24 Jan 1860	18 Jan 1860	DET
Collis, Nancy Jane	Watts, James M.	25 Jan 1860	18 Jan 1860	WPT
Combs, Elizabeth	West, Pleasant (Esq.)	11 Feb 1857	29 Jan 1857	WPT
Commander, Penelope	Banks, Joseph	18 Mar 1820		STEL
Conally, Ellen	Austill, George L.	14 Jan 1854	11 Jan 1854	DET
Conway, E.E.	Tomlinson, Henry W.	30 Jun 1854	28 Jun 1854	PDD
Cook, Louisa	Burt, Charles E.	23 Apr 1858	22 Apr 1858	DET
Cook, Margaret	Salter, William, Jr.	13 Feb 1852	05 Feb 1852	PI
Cook, Margaret	Salter, Wm., Jr.	11 Feb 1852	05 Feb 1852	PT&C
Cook, Mercy	Gates, Charles Valcalo	12 May 1857	07 May 1857	PSOT
Cooper, Mary	Palmer, Roswell E.	06, 08 May 1854	06 May 1854	DET
Cooper, Mary	Palmer, Rozwell E.	09 May 1854	06 May 1854	PDD
Corns, Mary F.	Hacquard, Louis	02 Oct 1860	25 Sep 1860	DET
Corns, Mary F.	Hacquard, Louis	06 Oct 1860	25 Sep 1860	PTIMES
Corothers, Ellen	Byron, John	24 Oct 1844		TRIB
Coryell, Malvina	Boile, Henry	29 Sep 1852	26 Sep 1852	PT&C
Coughly, Matilda	Ransom, Jas.	01 Sep 1855	23 Aug 1855	DET
Coulter, Rebecca E.	Pilcher, George W.	17 Jan 1854	05 Jan 1854	DET
Courtney, Sarah	Blackford, Joseph	13 Feb 1855	30 Jan 1855	DET
Coway, Hannah	Welsh, Joseph	29 Sep 1852	27 Sep 1852	PT&C
Cowles, Sue B.	Hills, C. Elmer	21 Jun 1862	10 Apr 1862	PTIMES
Cox, Elizabeth	Kinney, Charles	31 Oct 1848	09 Oct 1848	DENQ
Cox, Mary	Allen, John	03 Dec 1856	01 Nov 1856	WPT
Cox, Mary E.	Dillon, J.W. (Rev.)	16 Jan 1860	10 Jan 1860	DET
Cox, Mary E.	Dillon, J.W. (Rev.)	18 Jan 1860	10 Jan 1860	WPT
Craig, Sallie	Brooking, James H. (Rev.)	16 Feb 1855	30 Jan 1855	DET
Crain, Mary	Harvey, James	18 Mar 1853	21 Jan 1853	PI
Crain, Mary	Short, James H.	28 Jan 1853	21 Jan 1853	PI
Crain, Mary	Short, James Harvey	26 Jan 1853	22 Jan 1853	PT&C

Marriages (Brides)

Name (Bride)	Name (Groom)	Notice Date	Marriage Date	Paper
Crawford, Lizzie	Combs, John	19 Nov 1853	14 Nov 1853	DET
Crawford, Martha	Forbers, Arthur	26 Nov 1856		WPT
Crawford, Mary Jane	Stockham, Aaron	16 Oct 1854	12 Oct 1854	DET
Craycraft, Sarah	Blair, Wm. H.	16 Jul 1856	14 Jul 1856	WPT
Creely, Mary	Goligher, Samuel	10 Oct 1851	02 Oct 1851	PI
Creely, Mary	Goligher, Samuel	08 Oct 1851	02 Oct 1851	PT&C
Crichton, Julia M.	Sims, Robert	10 Aug 1859	10 Aug 1859	DET
Crisibles (?), Ellen	Gregmiles, James	05 Apr 1855	29 Mar 1855	DET
Crook, Julia	Williams, E.	02 Oct 1855	17 Sep 1855	DET
Cropper, Emily J.	Stonebaker, Joseph A.	18 May 1859	11 May 1859	WPT
Cropper, Emily J.	Stonebraker, Joseph A.	14 May 1859	11 May 1859	DET
Crozier, Eliza J.	Bronn, Leroy S.	12 Nov 1864	10 Nov 1864	PTIMES
Crull, (Mrs.) Julia	Collis, R.T. (Esq.)	09 Jul 1856	01 Jul 1856	WPT
Crumblet, Elizabeth R.	Elliot, John Q.	08 Apr 1854	02 Apr 1854	DET
Culbertson, Agnes	Randolf, Richard	20 Apr 1858	30 Mar 1858	PSOT
Cummings, Mary G.	Walker, David M.	07 Jan 1857	29 Dec 1856	WPT
Cunningham, Hester	Leonard, John	10 Jun 1850		PI
Cuppet, Nancy	Messer, Charles	13 Apr 1859	Apr 1859	WPT
Currie, Maggie A.	Patterson, Joseph S.	02 Jul 1856	01 Jul 1856	WPT
Currie, Mary	Gilbert, Giles, Jr.	27 May 1857	27 May 1857	DET
Cushing, Charlotte	Rochester, John C.	30 Jan 1854	18 Jan 1854	DET
Cushing, Josephine (Cowles)	Bateham, M.B.	03 Oct 1850		PT&C
Cutler, Caroline	Sweet, Freeman	03 Mar 1852	26 Feb 1852	PT&C
Cutler, Fanny	Carroll, John	31 Jan 1829	29 Jan 1829	WT
Cutler, Martha H.	Corson, Joseph (M.D.)	07 Jul 1843	29 Jun 1843	TRIB
Cutshall, Elizabeth	Fitch, Elias	03 Oct 1851	27 Sep 1851	PI
Cutsmeyer, M.	Chojur, Jacob	11 Jan 1853	02 Jan 1853	PI
Daniels, Editha K.	Regnler, Charles	05 Nov 1858	11 Oct 1858	SVREP
Daring, Elizabeth	Glover, Azel	14 Jan 1825	30 Dec 1824	PG&LA
Darlinton, Mary B.	Groniger, Leonard (Col.)	04 Jan 1856	27 Dec 1855	DET
Darlinton, Mary B.	Groniger, Leonard (Col.)	09 Jan 1856	27 Dec 1855	WPT
Daugherty, S.D.	Reeves, N. (M.D.)	04 Feb 1854	29 Jan 1854	DET
Davey, Florence	Kilmer, Washington (Dr.)	22 Oct 1864	18 Oct 1864	PTIMES
Davey, Louisa	Spry, John W.	03 May 1855	02 May 1855	DET
Davey, Phillippa	Murray, P.H.	22 Jul 1850	18 Jul 1850	PI
Davey, Phillippa	Murray, P.H.	25 Jul 1850	18 Jul 1850	PT&C
Davey, Susan	Buel, A.J.	06 Jan 1851	02 Jan 1851	PI
Davidson, Sallie M.	Roach, William	26 Aug 1859	25 Aug 1859	DET
Davidson, Sallie M.	Roach, William	31 Aug 1859	25 Aug 1859	WPT
Davis, Annice B.	Tracy, V.D.L.	13 Apr 1854	12 Apr 1854	PDD
Davis, Annice B.	Tracy, V.D.L.	19 Apr 1854	13 Apr 1854	SVREP
Davis, Annice B.	Tracy, Van Der Lyn	13 Apr 1854	12 Apr 1854	DET
Davis, Elizabeth	Bentley, Morrison A.	20 Feb 1856	14 Feb 1856	WPT
Davis, Elizabeth	Bentley, Morrison A.	16 Feb 1856	14 Feb 1856	DET

Name (Bride)	Name (Groom)	Notice Date	Marriage Date	Paper
Davis, Laura V.	Houston, William C.	04 Mar 1859	01 Mar 1859	DET
Davis, Laura V.	Houston, William C.	09 Mar 1859	01 Mar 1859	WPT
Davis, Lizzie	Colburn, Frederick (Lieut.)	13 Feb 1864	10 Feb 1864	PTIMES
Davis, Margaret	Bateman, Clementious	14 Jan 1854	02 Jan 1854	DET
Davis, Mary Jane	Johnson, J.H.	13 Apr 1859	11 Apr 1859	WPT
Davis, Nancy	Fields, Jessee H.	02 Apr 1856	06 Mar 1856	WPT
Davisson, Adaline	Coffee, Patrick	03 Oct 1850	29 Sep 1850	PT&C
Dawes, Jennie	Shedd, J.H. (Rev.)	05 Aug 1859	05 Aug 1859	DET
Dawson, Anastatio	Daniels, S.W.	19 Jan 1853	14 Jan 1853	PT&C
Dawson, Irena	Strain, Samuel	09 Apr 1852	25 Mar 1852	PI
Day, Eliza A.	Kehoe, Charles T.	01 Dec 1854	29 Nov 1854	DET
Days, Elizabeth	Barbee, Elias	26 Nov 1851	17 Nov 1851	PT&C
Deacon, Hannah	Brown, David	26 Dec 1853	08 Dec 1853	PDD
Dean, Cynthia M.	Barr, Wm. H.	20 Apr 1853	17 Apr 1853	PT&C
Deavor, Emily	Rowley, Jackson	30 Apr 1856	24 Apr 1856	WPT
Deerman, Eliza	Pool, Aaron	17 Apr 1854	16 Apr 1854	DET
Delay, Catharine	M'Neel, Worthington	01 May 1854	15 Apr 1854	DET
Dever, Elizabeth Ann	Rowley, Edward	28 Jan 1857	18 Jan 1857	WPT
Devoss, Arietta	Nichols, Gifford Gore	09 Sep 1858	02 Sep 1858	DET
Devoss, Arietta	Nichols, Gifford Gore	15 Sep 1858	02 Sep 1858	WPT
Dewey, Eliza	Downey, Nathaniel	09 Nov 1855	26 Oct 1855	OP
Dickerson, Mary Emma	Moore, Levi	20 Apr 1860		DET
Dimner, Elizabeth	Smith, Charles	02 Sep 1850	18 Jul 1850	PI
Dimner, Elizabeth	Smith, Charles	29 Aug 1850	18 Jul 1850	PT&C
Disney, Sallie	Medary, Samuel A.	12 Apr 1858	07 Apr 1858	DET
Disney, Sallie	Medary, Samuel A.	14 Apr 1858	07 Apr 1858	WPT
Dixon, Clarissa	Inman, William	19 Dec 1850	12 Dec 1850	PT&C
Dixon, Clarrissa	Inman, William	23 Dec 1850	12 Dec 1850	PI
Dixon, Mary	Cosert, James	17, 24 Dec 1853	12 Dec 1853	DET
Dixon, Mary	Cosert, James	19 Dec 1853	12 Dec 1853	PDD
Dixon, Minerva	Myers, male	06 Feb 1854	07 Jan 1854	DET
Dixon, Minerva	Myers, Joseph	10 Feb 1854	07 Jan 1854	PDD
Dixon, Nancy	Canterbury, John	24 Aug 1854		DET
Dobbs, Matilda	Bilton, Wm. H.	21 May 1856	19 May 1856	WPT
Doddridge, Ella Virginia	Kringh, Charles W.	02 Dec 1859	24 Nov 1859	DET
Dodds, Martha A.	Moore, Loy N.	14 Nov 1850	12 Nov 1850	PT&C
Dodson, Julianna	Gates, Wilson	21 Sep 1855	19 Sep 1855	DET
Dole, Almira T.	Parker, H.W.	08 Oct 1852	04 Oct 1852	PI
Dole, Lavina	Moore, Amanual	16 Feb 1859	10 Feb 1859	WPT
Dole, Lavina	Moore, Amanuel	16 Feb 1859	10 Feb 1859	DET
Dorch, Eliza	Spriggs, Benjamin F.	28 Oct 1859	27 Oct 1859	DET
Dorman, Mary E.	Miller, A.P. (Dr.)	07 Jun 1858	03 Jun 1858	DET
Dorman, Mary E.	Miller, A.P. (Dr.)	09 Jun 1858	03 Jun 1858	WPT
Dorril, Eliza	Corwin, Daniel	06 Jul 1820	01 Jul 1820	STEL

Marriages (Brides)

Name (Bride)	Name (Groom)	Notice Date	Marriage Date	Paper
Dortch, Rebecca	Wirts, Caspar	20 Jan 1851	16 Jan 1851	PI
Dott, Elizabeth	Weishch, John	03 Jan 1855	02 Jan 1855	DET
Doty, Mary	Wallbright, Christian	02 Jan 1855	01 Jan 1855	DET
Dougerty, Ann	Cutshaw, John	01 Jun 1853	18 May 1853	PDD
Douglass, Mary L.	Smallwood, Wm. (Rev.)	12 Mar 1846	02 Mar 1846	TRIB
Drake, Angeline	Alexander, J. W.	11 Jun 1856	29 May 1856	WPT
Duduit, L.	Miller, William H.	20 Jun 1859	19 Jun 1859	DET
Duduit, L.	Miller, William H.	22 Jun 1859	19 Jun 1859	WPT
Duidwit, Caroline	Metcalf, F.J.	02 May 1850	28 Apr 1850	PT&C
Duke, Sarah	Brown, Henry	06 Dec 1855	04 Dec 1855	DET
Dukes, Emily	Evans, D.R. (Rev.)	26 Nov 1864	23 Nov 1864	PTIMES
Dungan, Lucy J.	Phillips, Rev. F.W.	10 Nov 1853	27 Oct 1853	DET
Dunlap, Marcus	Graham, William	24 Dec 1853	17 Dec 1853	DET
Dunlap, Mary Jane	Spragg, Caleb	17 Nov 1852	14 Nov 1852	PT&C
Dunlap, Mary Jane	Sprago, Caleb	19 Nov 1852	14 Nov 1852	PI
Dunlap, Sarah Ann	Cane, Aquilla	04 Nov 1854	03 Nov 1854	DET
Durham, Martha	Rains, James A.	10 Nov 1853	30 Oct 1853	DET
Duvall, Martha J.	O'Niel, Andrew	06 Apr 1853	31 Mar 1853	PT&C
E. Mary A.	Conway, Kev. William, M.D.	10 Nov 1853	27 Oct 1853	DET
Eagleson, Margaret J.	Warren, Beriah	29 Jun 1855	21 Jun 1855	DET
Eakins, Temperance Jane	Holloday, John H.	16 Apr 1856	06 Apr 1856	WPT
Easmon, Hester	Day, Alford C.	05 Jan 1854	02 Jan 1854	PDD
Easmon, Hester	Day, Alfred C.	04 Jan 1854	02 Jan 1854	DET
Easter, Catharine	Baird, Zachariah J.	17 Feb 1857	05 Feb 1857	PSOT
Eastham, Eliza Jane	Payne, Hiram	12 Jan 1856	30 Dec 1855	DET
Eck, Elizabeth	Hobart, Jacob	02 Jan 1852	30 Dec 1851	PI
Eck, Elizabeth	Hobart, Jacob	31 Dec 1851	30 Dec 1851	PT&C
Edwards, Celia A.	Coffman, Daniel	30 Apr 1856	24 Apr 1856	WPT
Eicher, Margaret	Shephard, Charlton	02, 23 Dec 1850	27 Nov 1850	PI
Eicher, Margaret	Shephard, Charlton	28 Nov 1850 19 Dec 1850	27 Nov 1850	PT&C
Eifert, Mary A.	Barrick, Henry	10 Dec 1851	05 Dec 1851	PT&C
Ela, Sophia A.	Hatch, Thomas	14 Jan 1825	05 Aug 1824	PG&LA
Ellis, Anna	Bliss, Jonathan	31 Jan 1829	25 Jan 1829	WT
Ellis, Rachel	Coffin, Constantine	28 Dec 1852	30 Dec 1852	PDD
Ellis, Rachel	Coffin, Constantine	07 Jan 1853	30 Dec 1852	PI
Emory, Elizabeth J.	Davis, James R.	24 Mar 1860	14 Mar 1860	DET
Emory, Elizabeth J.	Davis, James R.	28 Mar 1860	14 Mar 1860	WPT
Engelbrecht, Matilda	Stemshorn, Henry	09 Jul 1864	04 Jul 1864	PTIMES
England, Melvina	Keeton, William	27 Dec 1853	11 Dec 1853	DET
Enslow, Emily	Brady, Levi	22 Jul 1825	14 Jul 1825	PG&LA
Enslow, Hannah A.	Cornes, Wesley D.	05 Jul 1854	03 Jul 1854	DET
Evaley, Mary	Sillough, William	09 Apr 1856	03 Apr 1856	WPT

Name (Bride)	Name (Groom)	Notice Date	Marriage Date	Paper
Evans, Margaret E.	Jones, D.L.	25 Oct 1853	22 Oct 1853	PDD
Evridge, Sintha	Cook, Geo. W.	06 Sep 1855	06 Sep 1855	DET
Farley (or Furley), Sarah M.	Rundle, John	24 Nov 1858	12 Nov 1858	WPT
Farmer, Eliza	Morgan, Ephraim	22 Dec 1855	20 Dec 1855	DET
Farmer, Eliza	Morgan, Ephraim	26 Dec 1855	20 Dec 1855	WPT
Farnandis, Martha B.	Brownell, A.W.	24 Aug 1854	23 Aug 1854	DET
Farney, Amanda	Powell, Silas D.	19 Aug 1853	10 Aug 1853	DET
Farney, Amanda	Powell, Silas D.	16 Aug 1853	10 Aug 1853	PDD
Farney, Amanda	Powell, Silas D.	24 Aug 1853	10 Aug 1853	PT&C
Farney, Malinda G.	Hammonds, Wyatt	03 Jan 1855	25 Dec 1855	DET
Farrand, Fannie R.	Neal, John C.	17 Dec 1853	07 Dec 1853	DET
Farrand, Fanny R.	Neal, John C.	19 Dec 1853	07 Dec 1853	PDD
Farrane Fannie R.	Neal, John C.	29 Dec 1853	07 Dec 1853	DET
Faulkner, Eliza	Jackson, John	09 Nov 1855	01 Nov 1855	DET
Featherstone, female	Paul, H.H.	18 Aug 1854		PDD
Fee, Mary E.	Shannon, John	03 Feb 1854	31 Jan 1854	PDD
Feforgey, Levoria	Booth, Levi	06 Sep 1860	01 Sep 1860	DET
Feforgey, Levoria	Booth, Levi	12 Sep 1860	01 Sep 1860	WPT
Feirel, Nancy C.	Slack, William J.	28 May 1852	06 May 1852	PI
Ferree, Mary Jane	Vance, Miles W.	21 Nov 1853	16 Nov 1853	DET
Ferrell, Ellen	Neel, Hudson	22 Aug 1844	10 Aug 1844	TRIB
Ferrell, Matilda	Murphey, Moses	06 Aug 1844	27 Jul 1844	PDEM
Feurt, Luna H.	Flint, John T.	31 Mar 1854		DET
Fields, Mary M.	Gray, David D.	08 Oct 1852	03 Oct 1852	PI
Finney, Roxana	Foye, Winthrop	01 Jun 1820	18 May 1820	STEL
Finton, Celinda	Morford, William C.	20 Dec 1853	16 Nov 1853	DET
Finton, Josephine	Morford, W.C.	04 Nov 1857	29 Oct 1857	DET
Firree, Mary Jane	Vance, Miles W.	22 Nov 1853	16 Nov 1853	PDD
Fisher, Amanda M.	Car_l, Frank, Jr.	02 Apr 1856	29 Jan 1856	WPT
Fisher, Lucretia	Allen, David	15 Feb 1859	13 Feb 1859	PTIMES
Fitzer, Elizabeth	Worthington, James	13 Jul 1853	03 Jul 1853	PT&C
Fitzer, Elizabeth	Worthington, James, Jr.	07 Jul 1853	03 Jul 1853	DET
Fitzgerald, Janet	Boroff, Daniel	03 Aug 1820		STEL
Flanders, Elizabeth	Boynton, Sumner	14 Oct 1855	12 Sep 1855	DET
Fleming, Mary Julia C.	Watt, John Jr.	24 Jun 1854	15 Jun 1854	DET
Flesher, Martha	Osborne, Jacob	25 Aug 1854	21 Aug 1854	DET
Fletcher, Julia A.	Vandwort, James	08 Oct 1856	30 Sep 1856	WPT
Folsom, Minerva	Ewing, Elmore	30 Sep 1865	21 Sep 1865	PTIMES
For_, Margaret	Smith, William E.	02 Apr 1856	27 Mar 1856	WPT
Ford, Maria	Thompson, William	03 Dec 1856	25 Nov 1856	WPT
Forsythe, Nancy F.	Crandal, Elias	13 Jan 1857		PSOT
Forsythe, Nannie F.	Craudal, Elias	07 Jan 1857		WPT
Forsythe, Sue S.	Nash, William H.	13 Jan 1857	01 Jan 1857	PSOT
Forsythe, Sue S.	Nash, Wm. H.	07 Jan 1857		WPT

Name (Bride)	Name (Groom)	Notice Date	Marriage Date	Paper
Fortsib, Lissette	Gessert Jacob	28 Jan 1857	22 Jan 1857	WPT
Fowler, Catharine	Elliot, John A.	17 Feb 1854	11 Feb 1854	DET
Fowler, Catharine	Elliott, John	21 Feb 1854	11 Feb 1854	PDD
Fowler, Mary	Myers, Samuel	01 Oct 1856	15 Sep 1856	WPT
Fowler, Sarah Ann	Pugh, George	24 Apr 1854	15 Apr 1854	PDD
Fox, Catharine	Davis, Henry	28, 31 Jan 1854	20 Jan 1854	DET
Fox, Catharine	Leard, James	15 Jul 1850	09 Jul 1850	PI
Fox, Catharine	Leard, James	11 Jul 1850	09 Jul 1850	PT&C
Frances, Catherine S.	Worthington, Augustine (Dr.)	15, 17 Sep 1855	12 Sep 1855	DET
Franklin, Lizzie M.	Glenn, James	06 Apr 1859	29 Mar 1859	WPT
French, Eliza	Miller, George W.	19 Aug 1854	13 Aug 1854	DET
French, Mary A.	Shannon, Charles	07 Nov 1850	03 Nov 1850	PT&C
Fuiton, Mary J.	Noel, Josiah O.	07 Jan 1857	31 Dec 1856	WPT
Fuller, Frances	Cutler, W.S. (Lieut.)	22 Sep 1858	20 Sep 1858	WPT
Fuller, Frances H.	Hearn, W.T. Chatmers	01 Dec 1855	23 Nov 1855	WPT
Fuller, Gritia F.	Blake, Cincinnatus	04 May 1858	21 Apr 1858	PSOT
Fuller, Jane M.	Hull, Julius (Capt.)	14 Jul 1854	12 Jul 1854	DET
Fuller, Mary C.	Peters, John	12 Jan 1844	21 Dec 1843	TRIB
Fuller, Metta Victoria	Victor, Orsville J.	09 Jul 1856	03 Jul 1856	WPT
Fullerton, Lucy	Hall, H.L.	02 Mar 1853	24 Feb 1853	PT&C
Fullerton, Margaret	Vasmeter, Joseph	12 Jun 1855	06 Jun 1855	DET
Fulterton, Lucy	Hall, H.T.	18 Mar 1853	24 Feb 1853	PI
Funk, Margaret Ann	Lewis, John C.	28 Dec 1852	27 Dec 1852	PDD
Funk, Margaret Ann	Lewis, John C.	31 Dec 1852	27 Dec 1852	PI
Funk, Margaret Ann	Lewis, John C.	29 Dec 1852	27 Dec 1852	PT&C
Furley, Sarah M.	Rundle, John	22 Nov 1858	12 Nov 1858	DET
Furry, Jane F.	Barrett, Henry, Jr.	03 Dec 1856		WPT
Gahr, Charlotte	Eichles, Joseph	26 Oct 1853		PDD
Gaines, Lucy	Thompson, Dr. James	10 Nov 1853	25 Oct 1853	DET
Gaither, Eliza W.	Allen, Isaac B.	17 Feb 1857	05 Feb 1857	PSOT
Galigher, Hanah	Thrall, William R. (Dr.)	20 Jul 1859	14 Jul 1859	WPT
Galigher, Hannah	Thrall, William R.	16 Jul 1859	14 Jul 1859	DET
Gallagher, Mary	Sullivan, Dennis	22 Apr 1854		PDD
Gallop, Eliza	Trotter, C.H.	29 Aug 1853		DET
Gammon, Elizabeth	Dunkins, Alexander	13 Oct 1855	10 Oct 1855	DET
Gapin, Mary A.	Iams, Solomon	09 Jan 1851	03 Jan 1851	PT&C
Gappan, Hester A.	Frazer, William	15 Jul 1850	11 Jul 1850	PI
Gappan, Hester A.	Frazer, Wm.	18 Jul 1850	11 Jul 1850	PT&C
Gardiner, Julia	Tyler, John (President)	04 Jul 1844	26 Jun 1844	TRIB
Gardner, Phelinda A.H.	Staley, Stephen	16 Jun 1853	05 Jun 1853	DET
Gardner, Phelinda A.H.	Staley, Stephen	22 Jun 1853	05 Jun 1853	PT&C
Garland, Georgie A.	Robb, J. Cobe	27 May 1865	24 May 1865	PTIMES
Garret, Sue M.	Glidden, Stephen S.	26 Dec 1855	20 Dec 1855	DET
Garret, Sue M.	Glidden, Stephen S.	26 Dec 1855	20 Dec 1855	WPT

Name (Bride)	Name (Groom)	Notice Date	Marriage Date	Paper
Garrett, Martha	Crighton, Nicholas D.	28 Feb 1854	16 Feb 1854	PDD
Gassoway, Annie L.	Gaffy, George H.	13 Aug 1864	11 Aug 1864	PTIMES
Gates, Dolly	Nichols, Samuel P.	17 Dec 1852	14 Dec 1852	PI
Gates, Polly	Nichol, S.P.	22 Dec 1852	14 Dec 1852	PT&C
Gebhardt, Caroline	Timmonds, John W.	13 Apr 1855	12 Apr 1855	DET
Gebhardt, Jane A.	Fisher, Jacob	26 Mar 1856	06 Mar 1856	WPT
Gebhardt, Tena	Ramsey, David, Jr.	06 Jan 1857	25 Dec 1856	PSOT
Gesinger, Arabel B.	DeGrummond, W.J.	14 Aug 1854	13 Aug 1854	DET
Gessenger, Arrabella	Degrummom, William	15 Aug 1854	13 Aug 1854	PDD
Gholson, Amanda	Peters, Samuel	04 Feb 1854	01 Feb 1854	DET
Gibbons, Harriet M.	Brown, Sardine	28 Jan 1854	18 Jan 1854	DET
Gibbons, Harriet M.	Brown, Sardine	14 Feb 1854	18 Jan 1854	DET
Gibbons, Lucy Ann	Upham, Edward S.	06 Nov 1838	02 Nov 1838	STRIB
Gibbs, Ellen	Crain, Martin	01 May 1854		DET
Gibbs, Ellen	Crain, Martin	02 May 1854	01 May 1854	PDD
Gibbs, Mary E.	Brodess, Henry B.	01 Aug 1857	26 Jul 1857	DET
Gibbs, Mary E.	Brodess, Henry B.	05 Aug 1857	26 Jul 1857	WPT
Gilbert, Emma	Appler, W.C. (Capt.)	21 Sep 1858		PSOT
Gilbert, Mary Emma	Appler, Washington C. (Capt.)	15 Sep 1858	13 Sep 1858	WPT
Gilbert, Rosa	Miles, Benjamin R.	21 Sep 1857	21 Sep 1857	DET
Gilberthorpe, Priscilla	Stallman, Frederick	05 Dec 1859	27 Nov 1859	WPT
Giles, Ruth	Cheney, Duston	18 Mar 1820		STEL
Gill, Mary Ann	Westwood, John I.	12 Nov 1858	01 Nov 1858	DET
Gill, Mary Ann	Westwood, John I.	17 Nov 1858	01 Nov 1858	WPT
Gillen, Sarah	Wilson, Stephen	31 May 1827		WT
Gillespie, Amanda	Peck, D.W.	20 May 1854	14 May 1854	DET
Gillet, Jane	Ball, George	08 Jun 1853	02 Jun 1853	PT&C
Gillet, Tennessee	Reese, David	03 Mar 1852	12 Feb 1852	PT&C
Gilruth, Minerva	Kelley, Thomas D.	08 Jan 1856	01 Jan 1856	DET
Gilruth, Minerva	Kelley, Thomas D.	09 Jan 1856	01 Jan 1856	WPT
Gilruth, Naomi M.	Hays, Sylvester R.	12 Mar 1846	05 Mar 1846	TRIB
Girty, Margaret C.	Crawford, D.H.	28 Feb 1854	23 Feb 1854	PDD
Givens, Cynthia	Cross, Wash.	15 Sep 1860	12 Sep 1860	DET
Givens, Elizabeth	Fisher, Henry	14 Apr 1854	09 Apr 1854	DET
Glassford, Sarah	Willey, Henry	03 Sep 1852	30 Aug 1852	PI
Glaze, Mary	Olehy, William	08 Jun 1826	23 May 1826	WT
Glenn, Catharine Isabella	Sampson, George H.	27 Dec 1859	24 Dec 1859	DET
Glenn, Lizzie J.	Hervey, David E.	11 Nov 1857	04 Nov 1857	WPT
Glidden, Nancy Alice	Crandall, Wesley	10 Nov 1852	03 Nov 1852	PT&C
Glossford, Sarah	Willey, Henry	01 Sep 1852	30 Aug 1852	PT&C
Glove, Ann	Hart, Erastus	22 Oct 1852	13 Oct 1852	PI
Glover, Martha J.	Pepper, John D.	21 Jul 1843	16 Jul 1843	TRIB
Glover, Mary Jane	Thomas, Isaiah	18 Feb 1853	16 Feb 1853	PI
Glover, Sarah	Lock, John F.	21 May 1852	13 May 1852	PI

Name (Bride)	Name (Groom)	Notice Date	Marriage Date	Paper
Goff, Mahalah	Busler, Solomon	30 Mar 1854	09 Mar 1854	DET
Goheen, Ann	Stepleton, Wm.	23 Dec 1850	04 Dec 1850	PI
Goheen, Ann	Stepleton, Wm.	19 Dec 1850	04 Dec 1850	PT&C
Goodrich, Angelina	Cassel, Allen	29 Dec 1853	20 Dec 1853	DET
Goudy, Olivia E.	Dawley, James	22 Jul 1850	18 Jul 1850	PI
Goudy, Olivia E.	Dawley, James	25 Jul 1850	18 Jul 1850	PT&C
Goudy, Sarah C.	Quant, Frank	15 Oct 1856	12 Oct 1856	WPT
Graham, Mahala	Robinson, Andrew	24 Feb 1851	20 Feb 1851	PI
Graves, Cynthia A.	Davis, Alexander W.	09 Apr 1858	04 Apr 1858	DET
Graves, Cynthia A.	Davis, Alexander W.	14 Apr 1858	04 Apr 1858	WPT
Graves, Nancy	Graves, William (Capt.)	12 Aug 1825		PG&LA
Gray, Harriett E.	Bartlett, Madison M.	27 Nov 1855	17 Nov 1855	DET
Gray, Harriett E.	Bartlett, Madison M.	28 Nov 1855	17 Nov 1855	WPT
Green, Mary	Boldman, John	18 Mar 1820	09 Mar 1820	STEL
Green, Sarah E.	Green, Gilbert T.	23 Jun 1857	09 Jun 1857	PSOT
Greenfield, Sarah E.	Bean, William	12 Aug 1825	19 Jul 1825	PG&LA
Greenslet, Susanna	Dorch, John	03 Aug 1853	02 Aug 1853	DET
Greenwood, female	Nixon, male	14 Jul 1854	11 Jul 1854	PDD
Greer, Elizabeth	Minford, Robert J.	09, 10, Nov 1854	08 Nov 1854	DET
Gregg, female	Johnson, John (Esq.)	28 Feb 1854	22 Feb 1854	PDD
Gregg, Eliza M.	Fenwick, David	28 Feb 1854	22 Feb 1854	PDD
Gregory, Isabella	Allemang, Erl	11 Nov 1865	06 Nov 1865	PTIMES
Griffis, Eliza E.	Branson, John C.	28 Nov 1853	20 Nov 1853	DET
Griffith, Julia A.	Doddridge, Henry C.	14 Oct 1865	11 Oct 1865	PTIMES
Griffith, Margaret	Littlejohn, Valentine	23 Dec 1850	12 Oct 1850	PI
Griffith, Margaret	Littlejohn, Valentine	19 Dec 1850	12 Oct 1850	PT&C
Groce, Mary Ann	Peebles, Richard R. (Dr.)	12 May 1843	08 Mar 1843	TRIB
Groves, Nancy	Knobloch, Henry	13 Apr 1853	03 Apr 1853	PT&C
Grovin, Margaret J.	Barr, Jos. C.	29 Aug 1850	27 Jul 1850	PT&C
Grovin, Margaret J.	Barr, Joseph C.	02 Sep 1850	27 Jul 1850	PI
Gunn, Anna	Cook, William T.	15 Sep 1853	11 Sep 1853	PDD
Hadley, Cynthia Ann	Cutler, Lyman D.	08 Jan 1846	01 Jan 1846	TRIB
Hagerman, Liza	Turner, James N.	20 Apr 1853	12 Apr 1853	PT&C
Haines, Margaret	Robuck, Thomas	17 Feb 1857	05 Feb 1857	PSOT
Halfhill, Sarah	Taylor, Lorenzo D.	12 Aug 1854	06 Aug 1854	DET
Hall, Axy F.	Cummings, Thomas B.	31 Jan 1829	29 Jan 1829	WT
Hall, Cynthia	Buckley, Samuel	11 Jan 1854	02 Dec 1853	DET
Hall, Nancy	Collier, Ambrose	07 May 1856	23 Apr 1856	WPT
Halterman, Mary	Delany, Samuel	01 Oct 1844	15 Sep 1844	PDEM
Hambibb, Hannah M.	Born, Victor	15 Jun 1855	15 Jun 1855	DET
Hamelton, Margaret	Foster, Joseph	18 Mar 1853	21 Dec 1852	PI
Hamilton, Currance Ann	Lindsey, William	19 Aug 1853	17 Aug 1853	DET
Hamilton, Currence Ann	Bindsey, William	22 Aug 1853	17 Aug 1853	PDD
Hamilton, Currence Ann	Lindsey, William	24 Aug 1853	17 Aug 1853	PT&C
Hamilton, Rachel L.	Duke, John S.	20 Aug 1853		DET

Name (Bride)	Name (Groom)	Notice Date	Marriage Date	Paper
Hamilton, Rachel L.	Duke, John S.	24 Aug 1853	16 Aug 1853	PT&C
Hammill, Margaret	Dole, Samuel	12 Nov 1824		PG&LA
Handle, Ann	Hoe, H.	29 Apr 1853	23 Apr 1853	PDD
Hannet, Mary	Jarow, Anthony	09 Jan 1856	29 Dec 1855	WPT
Hannahs, R.S.	Porter, R.H.	03 Mar 1852	23 Feb 1852	PT&C
Hannet, Mary	Jarow, Anthony	08 Jan 1856	29 Dec 1855	DET
Hannkins, Mary Ann	Stone, Washington	11 Jun 1856	29 May 1856	WPT
Harden, Ann	Clemmer, Jacob	06 Jan 1855	06 Jan 1855	DET
Hardin, Elizabeth	Ingles, Harrison	03 Oct 1848	15 Sep 1848	DENQ
Hardin, Sarah	Evens, William	07 May 1852	01 May 1852	PI
Hardy, Henrietta M.	Garret, James	27 Apr 1853	17 Apr 1853	PT&C
Hare, Eleanor	Punch, Theophilus	23 Dec 1850	20 Sep 1850	PI
Hare, Eleanor	Pouch, Theophilus	19 Dec 1850	10 Sep 1850	PT&C
Harmon, Mary J.	M'Fadden, Charles	19 Jun 1855	17 Jun 1855	DET
Hart, Margaret	White, Leonard	10 Dec 1851	03 Dec 1851	PT&C
Hartman, Susan	Russell, Enoch J.	04 Jan 1856	01 Jan 1856	DET
Hartman, Susan	Russell, Enoch J.	09 Jan 1856	01 Jan 1856	WPT
Haster, Corinea	Coverled, Martin	09 May 1848	06 May 1848	DENQ
Hastings, Catharine	Downey, J.D.	09 May 1848	16 Apr 1848	DENQ
Hatten, Elizabeth F.	Brumfield, Bird F.	09, 14 Feb 1854	04 Feb 1854	DET
Haverty, Emma V.	Smith, J. H. (Capt.)	19 Nov 1864	10 Nov 1864	PTIMES
Hawk, Elisa	Mackley, Davis	16 Oct 1858	05 Oct 1858	DET
Hawk, Ortensla S.	Reed, Henry S.	09 Jan 1854	29 Dec 1853	DET
Haynes, Elizabeth	Anderson, Abner	19 Nov 1855	17 Nov 1855	DET
Hays, Margaret	Hagan, J.D.	07 Feb 1854	05 Feb 1854	PDD
Hayward, Lora Ann	Foster, Geo.	19 Dec 1853	08 Dec 1853	PDD
Hayward, Lora Ann	Foster, George	17 Dec 1853	08 Dec 1853	DET
Heath, Elizabeth L.	Postlethwate, William H.S.	31 Mar 1852	28 Mar 1852	PT&C
Heath, Elizabeth L.	Postlewate, William H.S.	02 Apr 1852	28 Mar 1852	PI
Heath, Julia A.	Parl, Bazil	03 Mar 1852	22 Feb 1852	PT&C
Hebard, Anna E.	Sanns, Peter A.	03 Mar 1852	23 Feb 1852	PT&C
Helphinstine, Virginia E.	McDaniel, Wm.	21 Jan 1854	12 Jan 1854	PDD
Helphinstine, Virginia E.	McDaniel, William	20 Jan 1854	12 Jan 1854	DET
Henderson, Belle R.	McConnell, Charles L.	28 Oct 1853	28 Sep 1853	PDD
Henderson, Elizabeth W.	Southworth, J.H.	03 Oct 1855	01 Oct 1855	DET
Henderson, Margaret J.	Cranston, Benjamin E.	12 Nov 1855	08 Nov 1855	DET
Henney, Mary	Shivengton, Barney	05 Nov 1856	02 Nov 1856	WPT
Henry, Lucy	Rfckard (?), F.M.	19 Nov 1853	07 Nov 1853	DET
Hensley, Eliza Jane	Callihan (or Gallihan), Daniel	12 Jan 1854	22 Dec 1853	PDD
Heran, Cynthia	Van Garder, Green	03 Dec 1851	23 Nov 1851	PT&C
Herbert, Mary	Bannister, Byron L.	13 Apr 1853	02 Apr 1853	PT&C
Herman, Hannah	Dole, John	16 Jan 1856	15 Jan 1856	DET
Heslek, Sarah Sumantha	Delany, Milton	14 Jun 1858	03 Jun 1858	DET

Marriages (Brides)

Name (Bride)	Name (Groom)	Notice Date	Marriage Date	Paper
Hesler, Mary	Hickman, Adolphus	24 Sep 1856	19 Sep 1856	WPT
Hesler, Sarah Sumantha	Delany, Milton	16 Jun 1858	03 Jun 1858	WPT
Hester, Rebecca	McGough, M.	20 Jul 1854	13 Jul 1854	DET
Hewlitt, Mildred	Blankenship, William	28, 31 Jan 1854	18 Jan 1854	DET
Hibbs, Rebecca L.	Russell, W.B.	06 Aug 1851	04 Aug 1851	PT&C
Hibbs, Slona A.	Williams, John	11 Apr 1863	09 Apr 1863	PTIMES
Hicks, Elizabeth J.	Worley, Sylvester T.	10 Nov 1858	09 Nov 1858	DET
Hicks, Elizabeth J.	Worley, Sylvester T.	17 Nov 1858	09 Nov 1858	WPT
Hiett, Ruth	McCulcher, John	28 Feb 1854	22 Feb 1854	PDD
Higgins, Laura	Elder, John S	28 Jan 1865	24 Jan 1865	PTIMES
Higley, Nancy Alice	Morton, George W.	14 Jan 1854	26 Dec 1853	DET
Hill, Catharine	Hill, Perry	03 Nov 1852	28 Oct 1852	PT&C
Hinman, Martha J.	Thurston, James D.	21 Nov 1857	17 Nov 1857	DET
Hitchcock, Laura	Timbrook, William	17 Dec 1864	14 Dec 1864	PTIMES
Hitchcock, Rebecca	Headley, George	23 Dec 1850	11 Dec 1850	PI
Hitchcock, Rebecca	Headley, George	19 Dec 1850	11 Dec 1850	PT&C
Hodge, Nancy	Kiine (?), Henry	30 Jun 1854	29 Jun 1854	PDD
Holbert, Nancy	Kellander, Wm. L.	16 Jul 1856	06 Jul 1856	WPT
Holbrok, Artametia M.	Murril, Asa	14 Jan 1825	15 Sep 1824	PG&LA
Holcomb, Clarissa	Hoover, Alaniah	28 Nov 1853	22 Nov 1853	DET
Holcomb, Clarissa	Hoover, Alaniah	30 Nov 1853	22 Nov 1853	PDD
Holliday, Ann	Holes, Tingeley	23 Dec 1850	11 Dec 1850	PI
Holliday, Ann	Holes, Tingeley	19 Dec 1850	11 Dec 1850	PT&C
Holmes, Mary	Hughes, Edward (Capt.)	07 Jul 1829		WT
Holmes, Melissa	Brown, Stephen	18 Aug 1857	05 Jul 1857	PSOT
Holt, Jerusia Adaline	Shaw, John	06, 13 July 1853	02 Jul 1853	PT&C
Holt, Jerusia Adeline	Shaw, John	05 Jul 1853	02 Jul 1853	DET
Holt, Margaret	Baldridge, Robert	02 Sep 1850	24 Jul 1850	PI
Holt, Margaret	Baldridge, Robert	29 Aug 1850	24 Jun 1850	PT&C
Hone, Rebecca	Wilson, Albert	29 Aug 1850	23 Jul 1850	PT&C
Hood, Caroline	Faverty, Resin	13 Apr 1854	09 Apr 1854	DET
Hotman, Susan	Powers, Archey	03 Oct 1848	21 Sep 1848	DENQ
House, Louisa	Garrett, Jno.	13 May 1854		DET
How, Susan	Simpson, C.W.	22 Oct 1856	13 Oct 1856	WPT
Howard, Mary Adeline	Hart, William	20 Aug 1856	14 Aug 1856	WPT
Howe, Amanda	Brisk, John	02 Sep 1850	08 Aug 1850	PI
Howe, Amanda	Brisk, John	29 Aug 1850	08 Aug 1850	PT&C
Howe, Minerva	Smith, George	24 Sep 1851	18 Sep 1851	PT&C
Howe, Rebecca M.	Wilson, Albert	29 Jul 1850	23 Jul 1850	PI
Howell, Sarah	Collett, A.M.	28 Jul 1853	27 Jul 1853	DET
Howell, Sarah	Collett, A.M.	01 Aug 1853	27 Jul 1853	PDD
Howell, Sarah	Collett, A.M.	03 Aug 1853	27 Jul 1853	PT&C
Howland, N.W.	Roe, George E.	12 Jan 1854	29 Dec 1853	PDD
Huckworth, Hester	McKey, Samuel	16, 17 Aug 1855	16 Aug 1855	DET
Huddleston, Cynthia Ann	Clemens, Travis	11 Jan 1854	05 Jan 1854	DET

Name (Bride)	Name (Groom)	Notice Date	Marriage Date	Paper
Huddleston, Nancy Maria	Bonser, Isaac	14 Jan 1857	11 Jan 1857	WPT
Huff, Juliett	Murdock, Harvey	22 Feb 1854	16 Feb 1854	PDD
Hull, Jane	Bennett, Samuel	05 Jul 1827	07 Jun 1827	WT
Hulps, Jemima	Pancake, Harvey	10 Jun 1850	04 Jun 1850	PI
Hulps, Jemima	Pancake, Harvey	06 Jun 1850	04 Jun 1850	PT&C
Humphreys, Ellen	Biggs, Thomas N.	14 Feb 1856	31 Jan 1856	DET
Hunt, Nancy	Messing, Joseph	12 Jan 1856	03 Jan 1856	DET
Hurd, Juliaette B.	Stimpson, Rodney M.	28 Jul 1851	23 Jul 1851	PI
Hurlburt, Julia	Blackman, P.S.	26 Oct 1854	15 Oct 1854	DET
Huskins, Emily J.	Red, James	27 Jul 1856	13 Jul 1856	WPT
Huston, Angelina	Noel, Francis Volney	06 Jul 1859	03 Jul 1859	DET
Huston, Angelina	Noel, Francis Volney	27 Jul 1859	03 Jul 1859	WPT
Huston, Cecilia Anna	Collins, Gilbert H.	31 Mar 1857	26 Mar 1857	PSOT
Huston, Mary	Noel, William	31 Aug 1860	29 Aug 1860	DET
Hutchinson, Josephine B.	Kennedy, Milton	23 Dec 1850	20 Oct 1850	PI
Hutchinson, Josephine B.	Kennedy, Milton	19 Dec 1850	20 Oct 1850	PT&C
Hutton, Eliza	Brooks, W.C.	05 Jan 1858	31 Dec 1857	DET
Hutton, Eliza A.	Brooks, W.C.	12 Jan 1858	31 Dec 1857	PSOT
Hyatt, Ella	Dukes, Wm. H.S.	02 Jan 1864	29 Dec 1863	PTIMES
Hyette, Juliana	Patton, Abner	27 May 1831	19 May 1831	PC&WT
James, Eliza	Waller, Robert	17 Apr 1855	15 Apr 1855	DET
Jaynes, Sally Jane	Emmens, John	20 May 1850	14 May 1850	PI
Jaynes, Sally Jane	Emmens,John	16 May 1850	14 May 1850	PT&C
Jefferson, Mary W.	M'Dowell, John	28 Sep 1820	19 Sep 1820	STEL
Jeffords, Maria	Smith, Nathaniel	23 Dec 1850	18 Dec 1850	PI
Jeffords, Miranda	Donohoo, Peter	02 Sep 1850	26 Aug 1850	PI
Jeffords, Miranda	Donohoo, Peter	29 Aug 1850	26 Aug 1850	PT&C
Johnson, Adelia	Kemp,. C.T.M.	11 Jun 1856	04 Jun 1856	WPT
Johnson, E.	Cline, W.H.	14 Nov 1851	13 Nov 1851	PI
Johnson, Eliza A.	Patton, Joseph	07 Oct 1850	29 Sep 1850	PI
Johnson, Margaret T.	Johnson, Daniel	01 Dec 1853	20 Nov 1853	DET
Johnson, Margaret T.	Johnson, David	30 Nov 1853	02 Nov 1853	PDD
Johnson, Mary	Carnahan, James	02 Sep 1825		PG&LA
Johnson, Mary	Cropper, V. (Major)	18, 19, Jun 1855		DET
Johnson, Mary Ann	Snyder, Andrew I.	30 Jul 1852	27 Jul 1852	PI
Johnson, Mary R.	Flaugher, John	02 Jul 1852	22 Jun 1852	PI
Johnson, Rachel	Smith, Nathaniel F.	30 May 1860	20 May 1860	DET
Johnson, Rachel	Smith, Nathaniel F.	30 May 1860	20 May 1860	WPT
Johnson, Sarah	Bennett, Madison	23 Mar 1853		PT&C
Johnston, Elizabeth A.	Shepherd, L.E.	14 Apr 1855	03 Apr 1855	DET
Johnston, Fannie L.	Yeager, Cornelius H.	07 Dec 1859	06 Dec 1859	DET
Johnston, Hannah	Smith, Clarkson	01 Jun 1820		STEL
Joice, Nercica	M'Daniel, Horatio	04 Dec 1853	24 Nov 1853	PDD
Joice, Nercicia	McDaniel, Horatio	03 Dec 1853	24 Nov 1853	DET
Jones, _____ W.	Hatch, John	23 Mar 1826	09 Mar 1826	TA

Marriages (Brides)

Name (Bride)	Name (Groom)	Notice Date	Marriage Date	Paper
Jones, Cornelia	Wheeler, Samuel P.	23 Dec 1865	17 Dec 1865	PTIMES
Jones, Cornelia W.	Porter, C.	22 Sep 1855	22 Sep 1855	DET
Jones, Eliza Jane	Simcox, Wm.	22 Jul 1865	16 Jul 1865	PTIMES
Jones, Elizabeth	Cumpson, Newton	15 Jul 1857	14 Jul 1857	DET
Jones, Elizabeth	Cumpson, Newton	22 Jul 1857	14 Jul 1857	WPT
Jones, Elizabeth	Jones, Isaac D.	07 May 1856	06 May 1856	WPT
Jones, Elizabeth	Thomas, Jonathan	29 Dec 1860	16 Dec 1860	PTIMES
Jones, Emily	Harper, John J.	07 Feb 1856	06 Feb 1856	DET
Jones, Emily	Harper, John J.	08 Feb 1856	06 Feb 1856	OP
Jones, Hattie A.	Chamblin, T.H.B.	25 Feb 1860	07 Feb 1860	PTIMES
Jones, Isabella	Gaffy, George B.	13 Apr 1853	11 Apr 1853	PT&C
Jones, Julia Ann	Dorch, John	21 Nov 1854	16 Oct 1854	DET
Jones, Mary	Cann, Arthur	12 Dec 1854	09 Dec 1854	DET
Jones, Mary	McIntire, Daniel	13 Nov 1838	06 Nov 1838	STRIB
Jones, Rachel	Wicks, Henry	31 May 1853	19 May 1853	PDD
Jones, Sarah	Davis, D.T.	29 Dec 1860	16 Dec 1860	PTIMES
Jordan, Mary E.	Meyer, J.S.	23 May 1850	21 May 1850	PT&C
Jurdan, Susannah	James, E.	08 Feb 1854	22 Jan 1854	DET
Kaughman, Catharine	Caps, Casper	16 Feb 1847	09 Feb 1847	CLIPPER
Kearns, Mary	West, John W.	20 Aug 1855	19 Aug 1855	DET
Keating, Mary	Fairchild, Aaron	17 Aug 1854	14 Aug 1854	DET
Keiser (or Kriser), Martha	Page, John C.	08 Dec 1858		WPT
Kelley, Arena	Whitney, John	29 Dec 1843	21 Dec 1843	TRIB
Kelley, Isabella	Bickel, Charles B.	05 Jan 1853		PT&C
Kelley, Martha A.	Trombo, Ambrose J.	16 Mar 1858	03 Mar 1858	PSOT
Kelley, Mary	Hawley, C.G.	25 May 1858	19 May 1858	PSOT
Kellough, Mary Jane	McClean, Samuel	16 Feb 1854	12 Feb 1854	DET
Kellough, Mary Jane	McLean, Samuey	17 Feb 1854	12 Feb 1854	PDD
Kelly, Jane	Reed, Rodney	18 Mar 1853	13 Mar 1853	PI
Kelly, Jane	Reed, Rodney	16 Mar 1853	13 Mar 1853	PT&C
Kelly, Olive	Noel, John F.	23 Feb 1853	16 Feb 1853	PT&C
Kelly, Sophia	Drake, Samuel P.	16 Feb 1847		CLIPPER
Kelsey, Mary Jane	Slaughter, Richard C.	27 May 1831	22 May 1831	PC&WT
Kendall, Elizabeth A.	Moore, Davis P.	23 Dec 1850	20 Oct 1850	PI
Kendall, Elizabeth A.	Moore, Davis P.	19 Dec 1850	22 Oct 1850	PT&C
Kendall, Maria	Salsbury, James	20 Jan 1851	08 Jan 1851	PI
Kendall, Rhoda	Raynor, William	14 Sep 1855	09 Sep 1855	OP
Kendall, Rhoda O.	Rayner, William H.	10 Sep 1855	09 Sep 1855	DET
Kennard, Harriet	Cubinson, John	05 Jan 1854	24 Dec 1853	DET
Kennedy, Jane Ann	Sanford, Hiram	13 Mar 1854	05 Mar 1854	PDD
Keough, Elizabeth Ann	Malone, Thomas	06 Oct 1860	26 Sep 1860	PTIMES
Kepler, Sarah A.	Woodside, Wm. J.	18 Jul 1860	18 Jul 1860	DET
Kerr, Ann Eliza	Long, Joseph	04 Oct 1862	01 Oct 1862	PTIMES
Kerr, Eliza Jane	Reed, Thompson J.	20 Jun 1844	18 Jun 1844	TRIB
Kibly, Nancy	Cawford, John H.	16 Nov 1855	15 Nov 1855	DET

Name (Bride)	Name (Groom)	Notice Date	Marriage Date	Paper
Kidd, Serena	Lalendorff, Charles	21 Jul 1851	17 Jul 1851	PI
Kidd, Sirena	Lalendorf, Charles	23 Jul 1851	17 Jul 1851	PT&C
Kile, Mary	Shelpman, Cornelius (Esq.)	03 Mar 1852	26 Feb 1852	PT&C
King, Mariah	Musser, John	08 Nov 1855	08 Nov 1855	DET
Kinney, Ellen	Reed, Samuel	26 Aug 1857	20 Aug 1857	WPT
Kinney, Maria	Tracy, Charles O.	20 Dec 1827	13 Dec 1827	WT
Kinney, Maria	Tracy, Charles O.	20 Dec 1827	13 Dec 1827	WT
Kinney, Sarah Ann	Renshaw, John	30 Jan 1852	29 Jan 1852	PI
Kittle, Henrietta B.	Carner, A.W. (Capt.)	14 Aug 1854	10 Aug 1854	DET
Knight, Bella Virginia	Pearce, Elgar B.	02 Dec 1857	26 Nov 1857	WPT
Knight, Bella Virginia	Pearch, Elgar B.	01 Dec 1857	26 Nov 1857	DET
Kouns, Mary C.	Shute, J.G.	11 Jun 1856	03 Jun 1856	WPT
Kriser, Martha	Page, John C.	03 Dec 1858		DET
Lacroix, Mary J.	Winkler, George C. (Capt.)	30 Sep 1865	21 Sep 1865	PTIMES
Lair, Frances	Humphries, James	08 Mar 1844	02 Mar 1844	TRIB
Lamb, Rebecca	Lyon, Stephen	24 Feb 1855	01 Feb 1855	DET
Lambert, A.	Sloan, Geo. W.	24 Aug 1853		PT&C
Lambert, A.	Sloan, George W.	20 Aug 1853		DET
Lambert, Malvina A.	Slone, P.P.	16 Sep 1850	12 Sep 1850	PI
Lambert, Melvina	Sloan, Peter	23 Dec 1850	12 Sep 1850	PI
Lambert, Melvina	Sloan, Peter	19 Dec 1850	12 Sep 1850	PT&C
Lambert, Melvina A.	Slone, P.P.	12 Sep 1850	12 Sep 1850	PT&C
Lancaster, Martha Ann	Ware, W.H.	19 Oct 1854	12 Oct 1854	PDD
Lane, Minerva	Baker, John	22 Oct 1856	25 Sep 1856	WPT
Lare, Minerva	Gadburry, John	28 Apr 1854	20 Apr 1854	DET
Larkins, Ana	Baty, L.T.	07 Oct 1853	29 Sep 1853	PDD
Lates, or Yeates, Adelaide	Bunker, Chang (siamese twin)	31 Oct 1850	13 Apr 1843	PT&C
Lates, or Yeates, Sarah	Bunker, Eng (siamese twin)	31 Oct 1850	13 Apr 1843	PT&C
Laton, Elizabeth	Givens, Thomas J.	28 May 1852	06 May 1852	PI
Lauderbach, Louisa	Everit, Septer	18 Mar 1853	10 Dec 1852	PI
Lavery, Mary Ann	Douglas, Samuel	17 Nov 1853	27 Oct 1853	PDD
Lawrence, (Mrs.) Eliza	Trotter, John C.	13 Jul 1859	07 Jul 1859	WPT
Lawrence, Eliza	Trotter, John C.	08 Jul 1859	07 Jul 1859	DET
Lawson, Anastasia	Daniels, S.H.	11 Jan 1853	14 Jan 1853	PI
Lawson, Mary J.	Timmonds, M.T.	31 Mar 1852	25 Mar 1852	PT&C
Lawson, Nancy	Long, William	14 Apr 1851	11 Apr 1851	PI
Lawson,Mary	Stockham, Samuel	28 Mar 1863	22 Mar 1863	PTIMES
Leadbetter, Rhoda	Cook, Edward	16 Jul 1856	14 Jul 1856	WPT
Leasure, Mary Jane	Lawyer, Alexander	06 Sep 1853	23 Aug 1853	DET
Lee, Susan D.	Chalfin, John	03 Dec 1853	26 Nov 1853	DET
Leiby, Alice	Coombs, Joseph J.	23 May 1844	16 May 1844	TRIB
Leonard, Margaret	Davis, Arthur	14 Jun 1828	11 Jun 1828	WT

Marriages (Brides)

Name (Bride)	Name (Groom)	Notice Date	Marriage Date	Paper
Leonard, Nettie Susan	Parsons, John K.	20 Mar 1855	14 Feb 1855	DET
Levery, Josephine	Bourshaw, Victor	22 Oct 1856	16 Oct 1856	WPT
Lewis Susan	Newland, William	05 Nov 1859	29 Oct 1859	DET
Lewis Susan	Newland, William	09 Nov 1859	29 Oct 1859	WPT
Lewis, Catherine	Davis, David M.	07 Apr 1852	01 Apr 1852	PT&C
Lewis, Emma H.	Fultz, Andrew B.	25 Mar 1858	18 Mar 1858	DET
Lewis, Emma H.	Fultz, Andrew B.	31 Mar 1858	18 Mar 1858	WPT
Lewis, Jane J.	Fawn, John	15 Mar 1858	15 Mar 1858	DET
Lewis, Jane J.	Fawn, John	17 Mar 1858	15 Mar 185	WPT
Lewis, Jennie	Fawn, John	16 Mar 1858	15 Mar 1858	PSOT
Lewis, Kesiah	Davis, Joshua	14 Jan 1854	05 Jan 1854	DET
Lewis, Margaret	Clingman, John M.	08 Jun 1826	30 May 1826	WT
Lewis, Margaret	Davis, James	10 Sep 1853	09 Sep 1853	DET
Lewis, Margaret	Davis, James	12 Sep 1853	09 Sep 1853	PDD
Lewis, Polly	Waldo, Jehoil	10 Oct 1851	08 Oct 1851	PI
Lewis, Polty	Waldo, Jehoil	15 Oct 1851	08 Oct 1851	PT&C
Lewis, Sarah A.	Jones, William	11 Jun 1853	02 Jun 1853	DET
Lewis, Sarah A.	Jones, William	15 Jun 1853	02 Jun 1853	PT&C
Lewis, Sarah Ann	Simmons, Francis	14 Jan 1858	14 Jan 1858	DET
Lewis, Susan	Newland, William	05 Nov 1859	29 Oct 1859	PTIMES
Liback, Lydia	Bfofey, Daniel	05 Jan 1853	01 Dec 1852	PT&C
Lidensmith, Christian	Marquart, Henry	20 Dec 1849	14 Dec 1849	PT&C
Liduke, Lydia	Bofey, Daniel	07 Jan 1853	21 Dec 1852	PI
Liggett, Jane	Barr, Andrew	22 Mar 1844	13 Mar 1844	TRIB
Lind, Jenny	Goldschmidt, Otto	11 Feb 1852	05 Feb 1852	PT&C
Lindsey, Orissa	Charlesworth, Henry	19 Sep 1844	15 Sep 1844	TRIB
Lionbarger, Clarinda	Scott, Uriah B.	10 Oct 1851	01 Oct 1851	PI
Lionbarger, Clarinda	Scott, Uriah B.	08 Oct 1851	01 Oct 1851	PT&C
Lionbarger, Emma	Yeley, James W.	15 Oct 1858	14 Oct 1858	DET
Lisler, Epa_onia	Priggs, Isaac	19 May 1852	29 Apr 1852	PT&C
Livingston, Mary E.	Strother, Robert D.	09 Jan 1854	01 Jan 1854	DET
Llocumb, P.S. (nee Wait)	Allen, W.	10 Apr 1855	05 Apr 1855	DET
Lloyd, Ann	Smith, John	14 Jan 1852	10 Jan 1852	PT&C
Lloyd, Harriet E.	Tracy, Uri	10 Dec 1851	04 Dec 1851	PT&C
Locke, Mary G.	Smith, Charles S.	27 Oct 1843	20 Sep 1843	TRIB
Lodwick, Ellen	Hernandez, Louis A.	22 Nov 1859	14 Nov 1859	DET
Lodwick, Martha	Kinney, Eli	14 Oct 1837	10 Oct 1837	STRIB
Lodwick, Nancy	Peebles, Joseph S.	14 Apr 1851	08 Apr 1851	PI
Loffland, Mary	Hutchinson, George	30 Jan 1854	26 Jan 1854	DET
Long, Harriet	Montgomery, Robert	31 May 1827	27 May 1827	WT
Long, Mary Jane	West, N.A.	22 Oct 1856	08 Oct 1856	WPT
Long, Nancy	Laird, David	20 Feb 1838	02 Feb 1838	STRIB
Loomis, Laura	Zeek, Andrew	27 Apr 1853	20 Apr 1853	PT&C
Loomis, Lucy Jane	Dillman, E.C.	09 Apr 1852	17 Mar 1852	PI
Lory, Filinia	Beck, George	10 Oct 1854	10 Oct 1854	DET

Name (Bride)	Name (Groom)	Notice Date	Marriage Date	Paper
Lott, Margaret	Phetteflace, Madison	08 Apr 1854	16 Mar 1854	DET
Louderback, Mary Jane	Waits, George	19 Nov 1856	16 Nov 1856	WPT
Loughry, Elizabeth	Pratt, E.P. (Rev.)	21 Oct 1853	18 Oct 1853	PDD
Loughry, Elizabeth	Pratt, Rev. E. P.	20 Oct 1853	18 Oct 1853	DET
Loveland, Nancy	Mott, Abanas	27 Jul 1853	26 Jul 1853	DET
Loveland, Nancy	Mott, Abanas	28 Jul 1853	29 Jul 1853	PDD
Loveland, Nancy	Mott, Abanas	03 Aug 1853	26 Jul 1853	PT&C
Lusk, Ella M.	Dole, Edward P.	27 Jan 1854	26 Jan 1854	DET
Lusk, Ella M.	Dole, Edward P.	30 Jan 1854	26 Jan 1854	PDD
Lusk, Ella M.	Dole, Edward P.	01 Feb 1854	26 Jun 1854	SVREP
Luther, Margaret	Lutz, Lawrence	20 Apr 1853	14 Apr 1853	PT&C
Lynch, Elizabeth	Warington, Nathaniel	09 Aug 1853	04 Aug 1853	DET
Mackoy, Sallie E.	Rate, Jno. F.	14 Mar 1860	05 Mar 1860	DET
Mackoy, Sallie E.	Rate, Jno. F.	14 Mar 1860	05 Mar 1860	WPT
Mackoy, Sally E.	Rate, Jno. F. (Elder)	10 Mar 1860	05 Mar 1860	PTIMES
Maddock, Addban E.	Stoner, William	08 May 1858	05 May 1858	DET
Madock, Mary J.	Barton, Charles A.	26 Feb 1858	25 Feb 1858	DET
Madock, Mary J.	Barton, Charles A.	03 Mar 1858	25 Feb 1858	WPT
Mai, Theresa	Spongler, Michael	23 Apr 1852	17 Apr 1852	PI
Malcolm, Luzzie	Cropper, Dyas P.	20 May 1857	13 May 1857	WPT
Malcom, Josefita Rais	Lewis, Thomas C.	18 Jul 1848	15 Jul 1848	DENQ
Malone, Hannah	Grover, Isaiah	20 Jul 1853	19 Jul 1853	DET
Manning, Mary E.	Peeples, William Harry	15 Sep 1851	08 Sep 1851	PI
Many, Clementine	Bingham, Nathaniel	26 Nov 1856	19 Nov 1856	WPT
March, Mary James	Firmstone, Joseph G.	14 Nov 1844	04 Nov 1844	TRIB
Marford, Elizabeth	McConnell, Robert	02 Apr 1856	27 Mar 1856	WPT
Marshall, Mollie A.	Stewart, Arch V.	14 Jul 1858	14 Jul 1858	DET
Martin, Lucina	Hildebrand, Charles	27 May 1831	22 May 1831	PC&WT
Martin, Margaret	Payne, Edymond	13 Mar 1854	05 Mar 1854	PDD
Martin, Mary (nee Pearl)	Goldsberry, Jacob	04 Jun 1851	18 May 1851	PT&C
Martin, Nancy	Baker, George	28 Jan 1857	25 Dec 1856	WPT
Mathews Catharine	Johnson, W.T.	18 Mar 1853	12 Feb 1853	PI
Mathews, Catharine	Johnson, William S.	18 Feb 1853	12 Feb 1853	PI
Mathews, Catharine	Johnson, William S.	16 Feb 1853	12 Feb 1853	PT&C
Mathews, Mary H.	Rupp, George H.	31 Dec 1853	22 Dec 1853	DET
Mathews, Mary H.	Rupp, George H.	05 Jan 1854	22 Dec 1853	PDD
Mathews, Rebecca Jane	Nelson, Anderson	22 Jun 1855	21 Jun 1855	DET
Matison, Mary	Long, William	31 Jan 1854	29 Jan 1854	PDD
Mault, Lucina	Hicks, William	13 Dec 1855	09 Dec 1855	DET
Maynard, Amanda R.	Groniger, A.L.	12 Mar 1864	09 Mar 1864	PTIMES
McCague, Mary	Bartlett, M.R.	21 Apr 1843	20 Apr 1843	TRIB
McCall, Calfurnia	Cook, William L.	04 Feb 1856	31 Jan 1856	DET
McCan, Mary Ann	Roberts, John W.	25 Oct 1853	22 Oct 1853	PDD
McCann, Delilah	Freeland, Middleton	25 Oct 1853		PDD
McCartey, Julia Ann	Swan, Joseph	20 Apr 1854	05 Apr 1854	DET

Name (Bride)	Name (Groom)	Notice Date	Marriage Date	Paper
McClain, Isabella	Tracy, C.P.	21 Dec 1858	20 Dec 1858	DET
McClain, Isabella	Tracy, C.P.	22 Dec 1858	20 Dec 1858	WPT
McClary, Nancy	Hise, Phillip	26 Oct 1853		PDD
McCohaha, Amanda	Miner, Henry A.	28 Apr 1854	23 Apr 1854	DET
McCollister, Harriet C.	Peck, W.V., Jr.	20 Apr 1858	19 Apr 1858	PSOT
McColm, Caroline	Zollaes, Charles M.	31 Aug 1853	31 Jul 1853	DET
McConnell, Caroline R.	McCracken, Ralph	02 Oct 1855	18 Sep 1855	DET
McCormick, Elizabeth	Berry, John H.	19 Aug 1854	15 Aug 1854	DET
McCoy, Elizabeth	Foulke, L.W. (M.D.)	11 Mar 1837	24 Feb 1837	STRIB
McCoy, Harriet	Doddridge, B.Z.B.	15 Nov 1853	08 Nov 1853	PDD
McCoy, Judith	Chinn, A.N.	09 Jan 1854	22 Dec 1853	DET
McCoy, Judith	Chinn, Alford N.	12 Jan 1854	29 Dec 1853	PDD
McCoy, Lavinia	Dugan, Thomas	09 May 1848	02 May 1848	DENQ
McCoy, Virginia A.	Crichton, Andrew (Esq.)	30 May 1844	28 May 1844	TRIB
McDaniel, Sue	Simmons, Augustus	01 Oct 1856	24 Sep 1856	WPT
McDonald, Martha	Spanady, James	26 Apr 1854	24 Apr 1854	PDD
McDonald, Nancy	Gunn, Enos	04 Oct 1827	20 Sep 1827	WT
McGee, Effa	Luther, Lawrence	19 Apr 1844	28 Mar 1844	TRIB
McGiffin, Jemimah J.	Wyckoff, John	08 Nov 1853	30 Oct 1853	DET
McGlone, Frances	Hubbard, Stephen	23 Dec 1850	10 Oct 1850	PI
McGlone, Frances	Hubbard, Stephen	19 Dec 1850	20 Oct 1850	PT&C
McGuire, Elizabeth	Reilly, Hugh	11 May 1854	04 May 1854	DET
McKee, Melisla	Wilson, Charles	31 Jan 1854	15 Jan 1854	DET
McKenzie, Ann	Urquhart, George O.	15 May 1855	01 May 1855	DET
McLean, female	Hunt, Randall	14 Jul 1854	12 Jul 1854	PDD
McManmes, Angeline	Abbott, Orrin H.	01 Oct 1852	29 Sep 1852	PI
McMeekin, Martha	Patterson, Mores J.	22 Dec 1855	05 Dec 1855	DET
McMeekin, Martha	Patterson, Mores J.	26 Dec 1855	05Dec 1855	WPT
McNairn, Mary	Kinney, Henry	10 Nov 1843	07 Nov 1843	TRIB
McNeal Lydia	Purdum, W.W.	13 May 1850	01 May 1850	PI
McNeal, Lydia	Purdom, W.W.	09 May 1850	01 May 1850	PT&C
McNeal, Mary Ann	Stewart, John L.	16 Jun 1854	15 Jun 1854	DET
McNeal, Mary Ann	Stuart, John L.	17 Jun 1854	15 Jun 1854	PDD
McNutt, Harriet	Chenoweth, Joel	06 Jan 1837	29 Dec 1836	STRIB
McQuality, Eliza	Earhart, Jacob S.	15 Oct 1852	13 Oct 1852	PI
Mead, Eleanor	Sargent, John	29 Jul 1854	20 Jul 1854	DET
Mead, Elizabeth	Fullerton, Isaac	21 Nov 1829		WT
Mead, Martha Ann	Black, Samuel	05 Jan 1853	23 Dec 1852	PT&C
Meakley, Martha A.	Lloyd, Joseph S.	28 Jun 1855	27 Jun 1855	DET
Means, Jeannie	Culbertson, W.W. (Capt.)	04 Mar 1865	23 Feb 1865	PTIMES
Means, Mary A.	Adams, John C.	11 Jun 1853		DET
Means, Mary A.	Adams, John C. (Esq.)	15 Jun 1853	14 Jun 1853	PT&C
Medary, Kate	Blair, Charles W.	29 Dec 1858	25 Dec 1858	DET
Menager, female (Mrs.)	Raymond, Philip	14 Oct 1837	08 Oct 1837	STRIB
Merrill, Maria	Nichols, J.B.	17 Feb 1851	13 Feb 1851	PI

Name (Bride)	Name (Groom)	Notice Date	Marriage Date	Paper
Merrill, Maria	Nichols, J.B.	19 Feb 1851	13 Feb 1851	PT&C
Merritt, Libbie	Kerr, J. Harry	09 Jul 1864	30 Jun 1864	PTIMES
Metcalf, Caroline	Loomsis, Thomas D.	18 Mar 1853	13 Jan 1853	PI
Mick, Sally	Ross, James F.	11 Oct 1853		PDD
Miles, Lucy E.	Selfridge, Chester W.	22 Sep 1854	19 Sep 1854	DET
Miller, Ann E.	Jobes, Abraham	24 Feb 1851	18 Feb 1851	PI
Miller, Ann E.	Jobes, Abraham	19 Feb 1851	18 Feb 1851	PT&C
Miller, Elizabeth	Reynolds, Franklin	31 May 1827	24 May 1827	WT
Miller, Harriet	Woodward, E.W.	24 Feb 1855	20 Feb 1855	DET
Miller, Margaret	Noel, N.M.	19 Oct 1855	18 Oct 1855	DET
Miller, Margaret	Thompson, Nathan	15 Dec 1854	08 Dec 1854	DET
Miller, Maria	Books, Samuel H.	17 Feb 1854	08 Feb 1854	DET
Miller, Maria	Brooks, Samuel	21 Feb 1854	08 Feb 1854	PDD
Miller, Sarah J.	Mitchel, R.A.	15 Oct 1856	13 Oct 1856	WPT
Mims, Mary A.	Davis, P.W.	04 Jan 1856	27 Dec 1855	DET
Mims, Mary A.	Davis, P.W.	09 Jan 1856	27 Dec 1855	WPT
Mitchell, Angeline	Phelps, James E.	15 Jun 1855	14 Jun 1855	DET
Mitchell, Sarah A.	Powell, William Byrd	11 Mar 1837	12 Feb 1837	STRIB
Mongomery, Mary	Cooley, John	29 Apr 1853	28 Apr 1853	PDD
Monroe, Elizabeth	Cain, John	27 Dec 1853	08 Dec 1853	DET
Montgomery, Mary	Cooley, John	04 May 1853	28 Apr 1853	PT&C
Montgomery, Mary Ann	Bennet, Robert C.	30 Nov 1826	23 Nov 1826	WT
Montgomery, Sarah	Hopkins, Joseph	01 Oct 1856	25 Sep 1856	WPT
Montgomery, Sarah	Myers, A.N.	29 Oct 1855	29 Oct 1855	DET
Moore, female	Marshall, Clinton	28 Sep 1858	12 Sep 1858	PTIMES
Moore, Elizabeth F.	Lucas, John B.	17 Mar 1854	14 Mar 1854	DET
Moore, Elizabeth F.	Lucas, John B.	20 Mar 1854	14 Mar 1854	PDD
Moore, Elizabeth F.	Lucas, John B.	22 Mar 1854	14 Mar 1854	SVREP
Moore, Julia A.	Merrill, John P.	03 Oct 1848	13 Sep 1848	DENQ
Moore, Letitia	Adams, Calvin	16 Feb 1855	15 Feb 1855	DET
Moore, Maria	M'Call, Solomon	14 Nov 1851	06 Nov 1851	PI
Moore, Mary	Clark, William	22 Jun 1826	11 Jun 1826	WT
Moore, Orpha	Marshall, Clinton	28 Sep 1858	12 Sep 1858	PSOT
Moore, Sarah	Macy, Joseph	18 Aug 1852		PT&C
Moran, Margaret P.	Gunn, Samuel	06 Sep 1853	02 Sep 1853	PDD
Moran, Margaret P.	Gunn, Samuel W.	03 Sep 1853	02 Sep 1853	DET
Morgan, Eleanor	Marsh, Wm. A.	18 Jul 1850	26 Jun 1850	PT&C
Morgan, Mary	Crane, Adonijah	18 Jan 1832		PC
Morgan, Nancy	Noel, David	19 Jan 1828		WT
Morrell, Jerush	Elden, William	08 Aug 1844	01 Aug 1844	TRIB
Morris, Margaret	Thompson, William	07 Feb 1855	17 Jan 1855	DET
Morrison, Emma	Long, James	26 Nov 1858	23 Nov 1858	DET
Morrison, Emma	Long, James	01 Dec 1858	23 Nov 1858	WPT
Morrison, Jane	Morrison, William	18 Mar 1853	06 Mar 1853	PI
Morrison, Martha	Mackey, Thos. R.	04 Jun 1856	02 Jun 1856	WPT

Name (Bride)	Name (Groom)	Notice Date	Marriage Date	Paper
Morrison, Philora	Louis, Wm.	19 Nov 1856		WPT
Morton, Mary R.	Boughner, V.E.	26 Aug 1865	22 Aug 1865	PTIMES
Moss, Sally Ann	McDonald, W.D.	25 Mar 1853	22 Mar 1853	PI
Moss, Sally Ann	McDonald, W.D.	30 Mar 1853	22 Mar 1853	PT&C
Mossmann, Sarah A.	Womeldorff, Daniel L.	05 Nov 1853	27 Oct 1853	DET
Mott, Melissa F.	Umble, S.J.	02 Jul 1856	30 Jun 1856	WPT
Moulten, Sallie B.	Warwick, John B. (Dr.)	18 Feb 1860	14 Feb 1860	DET
Mowatt, female (Mrs.)	Ritchie, W.F.	16 Jun 1854		DET
Mulhena, Elizabeth	Taylor, Stacy	17 Nov 1853	12 Nov 1853	PDD
Mulligan, Eliza	Kendrick, Edward	07 Feb 1863	01 Feb 1863	PTIMES
Munn, Juliette	Musser, James	21 Oct 1865	05 Oct 1865	PTIMES
Munn, Mariah (nee Bonser)	Raynor, Wm.	06 May 1865	30 Apr 1865	PTIMES
Murphy, Harriet	Mitchell, David	07 Jun 1827	31 May 1827	WT
Murphy, Maria	Shephard, (or Shepherd) Alexander	28 Nov 1850 19 Dec 1850	27 Nov 1850	PT&C
Murphy (or Murphey), Maria	Shephard (or Shepherd), Alexander	02, 23 Dec 1850	27 Nov 1850	PI
M'Allen, Mary V.	Moreman, Constantine (Esq.)	13, 20 Aug 1856	03 Aug 1856	WPT
M'Cleves, Mary Ann	Jones, Allen	20 Dec 1849	18 Dec 1849	PT&C
M'Clintick, Catharine	Scott, James B.	11 Jun 1844	04 Jun 1844	TRIB
M'Collister, Susan	Jack, William	03 Aug 1820		STEL
M'Cormick, Ann	Poage, Lindsey	12 Nov 1824		PG&LA
M'Intosh, Jenny	Mitchell, William S.	02 Sep 1818	14 Jul 1818	PGAZ
M'Neil, Lydia	Purdham, Warner W.	06 May 1850		PI
Nagle, Philepena	Bescoe, John A.	17 Dec 1853	11 Dec 1853	DET
Nail, Rachael	Humph, Allen	26 Jun 1854	17 Jun 1854	PDD
Neagle, Caroline	Glean, John	16 Feb 1853	10 Feb 1853	PT&C
Neagle, Caroline	Gleim, John	18 Feb 1853	10 Feb 1853	PI
Nearl, Julia Ann	Sly, Joseph	16 Apr 1856	13 Apr 1856	WPT
Neil, Lucy	Cook, Henry	29 Sep 1852	23 Sep 1852	PT&C
Neili, Barbary	Isinhart, Joseph	23 Dec 1850	30 Nov. 1850	PI
Neili, Barbary	Isinhart, Joseph	19 Dec 1850	30 Nov 1850	PT&C
Neve, Jane	Winn, Thomas	28 Dec 1852	24 Dec 1852	PDD
Neve, Jane	Winn, Thomas	31 Dec 1852	24 Dec 1852	PI
Neve, Jane	Winn, Thomas	29 Dec 1852	24 Dec 1852	PT&C
Newcomb, Susan	Young, William	13 Jul 1853	11 Jul 1853	PDD
Newman, Annie M.	Reed, Joseph G.	18 Nov 1865	16 Nov 1865	PTIMES
Nichols, Catherine	Patton, Samuel	24 Apr 1855	23 Apr 1855	DET
Nichols, Helen	Walker, George P.	17 Oct 1851	14 Oct 1851	PI
Nichols, Hellen	Walker, Geo. Paul	22 Oct 1851	14 Oct 1851	PT&C
Nicholson, Carrie C.	Adams, J.Q.	06 Apr 1859		DET
Nixon, Rachel Ann	Atkinson, James W.	28 Nov 1853	17 Nov 1853	DET
Nixon, Rachel E.	Murphy, Andrew	17 Feb 1854	08 Feb 1854	DET
Noel, Caroline	Varner, John	22 Oct 1851	16 Oct 1851	PT&C

Name (Bride)	Name (Groom)	Notice Date	Marriage Date	Paper
Noel, Ellen	Furguson, William	20 Dec 1849		PT&C
Noel, Margaret	Ball, George	22 Apr 1858	21 Apr 1858	DET
Noel, Margaret	Ball, George	27 Apr 1858	21 Apr 1858	PSOT
Noel, Maria J.	Hogan, John	09 Dec 1865	05 Dec 1865	PTIMES
Noel, Sarah Ann	Marshel, James	08 Apr 1854	04 Apr 1854	DET
Nookes, Rachel	Kimbro, William	20 May 1854	20 Apr 1854	DET
Norris, Mary M.	Zeigler, Henry D.	27 Jun 1844	27 Jun 1844	TRIB
Norris, Sarah	Farrington, J.W.	14 Mar 1854	12 Mar 1854	PDD
Norris, Sarah	Farrington, James W.	14 Mar 1854	12 Mar 1854	DET
Nourse, Amanda	Ball, Oscar	08 Jan 1856		DET
Nourse, Amanda	Ball, Oscar	09 Jan 1856		WPT
Nugent, Mary	Hechinger, Anthony	15 Oct 1851	09 Oct 1851	PT&C
Nurse, Amanda	Ball, Oskar	26 Dec 1855	20 Dec 1855	DET
Nurse, Amanda	Ball, Oskar	26 Dec 1855	20 Dec 1855	WPT
Nurse, Lucy	Kittle, Jessee	04 Nov 1837	31 Oct 1837	STRIB
Nurse, Phoeba	Salladay, Obediah	14 Oct 1855	27 Sep 1855	DET
Oakes, Dorothy	Batterson, Addison	26 Dec 1851	04 Dec 1851	PI
Oard, Lucinda	Williamson, Thomas	11 Jan 1832	05 Jan 1832	PC
Och, Sophia	May, Matthias	28 May 1852	29 Apr 1852	PI
Ockerman, Hester Ann	Musser, Joseph T.	10 Oct 1851	25 Sep 1851	PI
Ockerman, Hester Ann	Musser, Joseph T.	15 Oct 1851	25 Sep 1851	PT&C
Oldfield, Caroline	Moore, William R.	24 Feb 1854	23 Feb 1854	DET
Oldfield, Martha	Gharky, G.H. (Capt.)	24 Sep 1852	20 Sep 1852	PI
Olds, Mary	Smith, George W.	09 Mar 1860	07 Mar 1860	DET
Olds, Mary	Smith, George W.	14 Mar 1860	07 Mar 1860	WPT
Oliver, Mary	Robin, Horace	13 Apr 1853	10 Apr 1853	PT&C
Orcutt, Avis Amelia	Copens, Samuel W.	19 Sep 1829		WT
Ord, Sophia	McConnell, John	13 May 1825	08 May 1825	PG&LA
Orm, Eliza Jane	McColm, William S.	02 Dec 1853	01 Dec 1853	DET
Orm, Eliza Jane	M'Colm, William L.	03 Dec 1853	01 Dec 1853	PDD
Orm, Emily A.	Finton, John J.	13 Dec 1859	11 Dec 1859	DET
Orm, Emily A.	Finton, John J.	14 Dec 1859	11 Dec 1859	WPT
Orm, Martha E.	Cole, Amos B.	09 Jan 1851	02 Jan 1851	PT&C
Orm, Mary J.	Richardson, James	05 Mar 1864	29 Feb 1864	PTIMES
Orms, Mary M.	Briggs, Wm.	31 Dec 1851	25 Dec 1851	PT&C
Ormsby, Adaline	Murphy, Michael	11 Feb 1852	27 Jan 1852	PT&C
Ormsby, Adeline	Murphy, Michael	30 Jan 1852	27 Jan 1852	PI
Ormstead, Elizabeth	Hayes, John	05 Jan 1853	04 Jan 1853	PT&C
Orrison, Sarah	Munns, David D.	28 Sep 1820	17 Sep 1820	STEL
Osborn, Kate R.	Ruggles, S.H.	23 Feb 1859	05 Feb 1859	DET
Osborn, Kate R.	Ruggles, S.H.	02 Mar 1859	05 Feb 1859	WPT
Osborn, Sarah	Smith, P.C.	21 Dec 1858	14 Dec 1858	DET
Osborn, Sarah	Smith, P.C.	22 Dec 1858	14 Dec 1858	WPT
Osborne, Sarah	Martin, Robert	22 Dec 1852	16 Dec 1852	PT&C
Ous, Elizabeth J.	Chesney, David A.	06 Aug 1851	04 Aug 1851	PT&C

Name (Bride)	Name (Groom)	Notice Date	Marriage Date	Paper
O'Briant, Sarah	Havens, Howard J.	06 Jun 1853	27 May 1853	PDD
O'Neal, Irena G.	Ball, Charles E. (Dr.)	25 Jun 1864	23 Jun 1864	PTIMES
O'Neal, Martha	Fraley, William C.	16 Sep 1850	08 Sep 1850	PI
O'Neil, Martha	Fraley, Wm.C.	19 Sep 1850	08 Sep 1850	PT&C
Page, Hannah A.	Williams, John	18 Mar 1853	04 Jan 1853	PI
Page, Hannah A.	Williamson, John	11 Jan 1853	04 Jan 1853	PI
Painer, Barbara	Rouch, Peter	18 Feb 1853	12 Feb 1853	PI
Painer, Barbara	Rouch, Peter	16 Feb 1853	12 Feb 1853	PT&C
Parker, Isabella A.	Sheets, John	31 May 1827	25 May 1827	WT
Parker, Lavisa F.	Doggett, Walker W.	02 Jun 1851		PI
Parnell, Hester	Funk, Jacob C.	23 Sep 1850	27 Aug 1850	PI
Parnell, Hester	Funk, Jacob C.	26 Sep 1850	27 Aug 1850	PT&C
Parrs, Anna G.	Craig, William S.	09 Jul 1856	07 Jul 1856	WPT
Parshley, Elizabeth	Osborn, Michael W.	25, 27 Jul 1857	23 Jul 1857	DET
Partlow, Julia Ann	Christian, William	16 Jun 1853	09 Jun 1853	DET
Partlow, Julia Ann	Christian, Wm.	22 Jun 1853	09 Jun 1853	PT&C
Patrick, Sarah A.	Pollock, Andrew	11 Jan 1853	06 Jan 1853	PI
Patten, Lucy	Beerman, Louis	12 Nov 1856	05 Nov 1856	WPT
Patton, Ellen	Criggs, Hezeriah	30 Apr 1856	17 Apr 1856	WPT
Paxton, C.W.	Mikel, A.E.	14 Aug 1854	09 Aug 1854	DET
Paxton, Lottie H.	Smith, J.W.	02 Nov 1859	31 Oct 1859	DET
Paxton, Lottie H.	Smith, J.W.	05 Nov 1859	31 Oct 1859	PTIMES
Paxton, Lottie H.	Smith, J.W.	02 Nov 1859	31 Oct 1859	WPT
Payne, Bette F.	Johnson, James A.	31 Mar 1854	29 Mar 1854	DET
Peebles, Jane	Wood, Robert	31 May 1827	16 May 1827	WT
Pelhane, Dora	Thornton, George W.	17 Feb 1860	16 Feb 1860	DET
Pelhene, Elizabeth	Baesler, Frederick	20 Jun 1855	19 Jun 1855	DET
Pennington, Jane	Lewis, W.	16 Jun 1855	05 Jun 1855	DET
Perry, Bula	Broadtree, Thomas S.	26 Jun 1854	17 Jun 1854	PDD
Perry, Mary Ann	Littlejohn, Joseph	22 Oct 1856	29 Sep 1856	WPT
Perry, Rachael Ann	Campbell, Lancelot	04 Jan 1856	01 Jan 1856	DET
Perry, Rachael Ann	Campbell, Lancelot	09 Jan 1856	01 Jan 1856	WPT
Phillips, Azuba	Hawley, Josiah	18 Mar 1820		STEL
Pickerel, Jane	Chaney, David	21 Jul 1851	16 Jul 1851	PI
Pickerel, Jane	Chaney, David	23 Jul 1851	17 Jul 1851	PT&C
Pike, Margaret Amanda	Chaney, Benjamin F.	23 May 1863	07 May 1863	PTIMES
Plumb, Christinia	Butler, M.	02 May 1848	27 Apr 1848	DENQ
Plyley, Artemesia	Spence, J.F.	16 Oct 1854	10 Oct 1854	DET
Poe, Harriet	Ewing, James	09 Feb 1854		DET
Poe, Harriet	Ewing, James	10 Feb 1854	07 Jan 1854	PDD
Pogue, Lida J.	Gartrell, Henry C.	08 Nov 1853	25 Oct 1853	DET
Pogue, Lydia J.	Gartrell, Henry C.	19 Nov 1853	25 Oct 1853	DET
Pond, Sarah E.	Baird, S.W.	10 Dec 1864	06 Dec 1864	PTIMES
Pontious, Barbara	Bookwalter, J.N.	22 Nov 1853	15 Nov 1853	PDD
Pool, Eliza	Whitcomb,	01 Jul 1825		PG&LA

Name (Bride)	Name (Groom)	Notice Date	Marriage Date	Paper
Pool, Rhoda	Crull, David W.	07 Jul 1843	28 Jun 1843	TRIB
Poor, Martha C.	Radcliff, Davis E.	06 Jun 1856	03 Jun 1856	OP
Porter, Elizabeth	Crumpton, John	28 Sep 1820		STEL
Porter, Louisa	Colvin, Jefferson	30 Jul 1856	27 Jul 1856	WPT
Powell, Sarah	Purdum, John W.	10 Apr 1855	10 Apr 1855	DET
Powers, Catharine	Grinn, Henry	16 Sep 1850		PI
Powers, Catharine	Grinn, Henry	12 Sep 1850		PT&C
Powers, Hannah V.	Noel, John P.	28 Jun 1860	24 Jun 1860	DET
Powers, Hannah V.	Noel, John P.	04 Jul 1860	24 Jun 1860	WPT
Powers, Martha Jane	Williams, William	15 Jun 1853	08 Jun 1853	PT&C
Powers, Mary Jane	Williams, William E., Jr.	11 Jun 1853	08 Jun 1853	PDD
Powers, Mary Margaret	Miller, John	02 Sep 1850	24 Aug 1850	PI
Powers, Minerva A.	Bing, James P., (M.D.)	14 Nov 1851	05 Nov 1851	PI
Powers, Sarah Jane	Haller, William A.	19 May 1853	17 May 1853	PDD
Powers, Sarah Jane	Haller, Wm. A.	25 May 1853	17 May 1853	PT&C
Pratling, Elizabeth	Lowry, James P. (Esq.)	11 Feb 1857	29 Jan 1857	WPT
Pratt, Lucy	Vincent, Joseph T.	29 Oct 1851	23 Oct 1851	PT&C
Pratt, Mary E.	MacKoy, J.L.	24 Feb 1851	18 Feb 1851	PI
Prentice, Eliza Ann	Crooks, Henry H.	05 Nov 1858	23 Oct 1858	SVREP
Prescott, Harriet	McElhinney, John	09 Feb 1853	03 Feb 1853	PT&C
Price, Maria	Keeton, G.W.	22 Jul 1854	08 Jul 1854	DET
Price, Elizabeth	M'Dowel, John	13 Jan 1819		PGAZ
Price, Lavina E.	Lloyd, William	01 Mar 1854	26 Feb 1854	PDD
Price, Levina	Lloyd, William	28 Feb 1854	27 Feb 1854	DET
Price, Mary J.	Williams, Daniel	07 Mar 1855	01 Mar 1855	DET
Price, Rebecca	Cable, Jonathan	23 Dec 1850	17 Dec 1850	PI
Price, Rebecca	Cable, Jonathan	19 Dec 1850	17 Dec 1850	PT&C
Proctor, Elizabeth	McQuillin, Samuel	03 Sep 1857	25 Aug 1857	WPT
Putrill, Cynthia	Goldenbury, Peter	13, 14 Oct 1854	13 Oct 1854	DET
Ragan, Eliza F.	Carr, Cornelius	28 Oct 1865	23 Oct 1865	PTIMES
Ramsey, Ethalinda	Foster, J.J.	06 Jan 1855	04 Jan 1855	DET
Ramsey, Mary Jane	Reiniger, Charles F.	13 May 1865	04 May 1865	PTIMES
Ranall, Mary	Owns, Erasmus	03 Aug 1853	28 Jul 1853	DET
Randall, Harriet J.	Lawhead, Israel	27 Feb 1854	16 Feb 1854	PDD
Rankin, Ellen J.	Butterfield, John	27 Dec 1859	15 Dec 1859	DET
Rankin, Nancy	Cutler, Pliny	31 Oct 1844	24 Oct 1844	TRIB
Ransom, Mary	White, Samuel	04 Jan 1856	20 Dec 1855	DET
Ransom, Mary	White, Samuel	09 Jan 1856	20 Dec 1855	WPT
Rariden, Joanna	Ronaldson, Stephen	20 Jul 1854	17 Jul 1854	DET
Ratcliff, Esther	Burt, Thomas T.	11 Jul 1848	07 Jul 1848	DENQ
Ratcliff, Mary	Rose, Edward	08 Jan 1856	02 Jan 1856	DET
Ratcliff, Mary	Rose, Edward	09 Jan 1856	02 Jan 1856	WPT
Rawley, Elizabeth	Hayt, Benjamin	08 Mar 1844	23 Feb 1844	TRIB
Ray, Lavina	Thrackmarton, Joseph	03 Sep 1851	29 Aug 1851	PT&C
Ray, Sarah	Sexton, John	05 May 1852	25 Apr 1852	PT&C

Marriages (Brides)

Name (Bride)	Name (Groom)	Notice Date	Marriage Date	Paper
Rayner, Mary	Behmind, George	20 Aug 1856	15 Aug 1856	WPT
Reddick, Eliza A.	Hill, John	20 Sep 1854	19 Sep 1854	DET
Reddick, Eliza A.S.	Hill, John	21 Sep 1854	19 Sep 1854	PDD
Reed, Ann M.	Cutler, Samuel N.	11 Nov 1853	08 Nov 1853	DET
Reed, Ann M.	Cutler, Samuel N.	15 Nov 1853	08 Nov 1853	PDD
Reed, J.C. (Mrs.)	Calvert, George	09 Feb 1859	02 Feb 1859	DET
Reed, J.C. (Mrs.)	Calvert, George	02, 09 Feb 1859	02 Feb 1859	WPT
Reese, Rose E.	Hott, Alfred M.	23 Oct 1858	20 Oct 1858	DET
Reese, Rose E.	Hoyt, Alfred M.	27 Oct 1858	20 Oct 1858	WPT
Reeve, Caddie	Balcom, Henry	05 Jun 1860	04 Jun 1860	DET
Reiss, Catharine	Kramer, Adam	10 Aug 1854	06 Aug 1854	DET
Reynolds, Caroline J.	Wade, Jacob F.	05 Nov 1853	31 Oct 1853	DET
Reynolds, Eliza	Down, Isaac F.	27 Dec 1853	14 Dec 1853	DET
Reynolds, Elizabeth	Voglesong, Wm. G. (M.D.)	12 Mar 1846	05 Mar 1846	TRIB
Reynolds, Lenas	Johnson, Andrew	31 Dec 1853	23 Dec 1853	DET
Reynolds, Lenas	Johnson, Andrew	05 Jan 1854	23 Dec 1853	PDD
Reynolds, Lucinda	Wright, Presley	12 Dec 1853	01 Dec 1853	DET
Reynolds, Lucinda	Wright, Presley	15 Dec 1853	01 Dec 1853	WPT
Reynolds, Martha Ann	Hogan, William	24 Nov 1854	23 Nov 1854	DET
Rhineheart, Mary Ann	M'Clure, Alexander	03 Apr 1838	01 Apr 1838	STRIB
Rhodes, Catharine	Ott, Valentine	28 May 1852	16 May 1852	PI
Rhodes, Emma	Jeffords, John	10 Oct 1851	01 Oct 1851	PI
Rhodes, Emma	Jeffords, John	08 Oct 1851	01 Oct 1851	PT&C
Rice, Sarah Anna	Hitchcock, Caleb	08 Jun 1853	19 May 1853	PT&C
Richards, Maria	Ware, Thornton W.	22 Mar 1862	13 Mar 1862	PTIMES
Richardson, Alice	Lynn, John M.	05 May 1854	04 May 1854	DET
Richardson, Hester	Arthur, James S.	03 Feb 1860	02 Feb 1860	DET
Richardson, Hester	Arthur, James S.	08 Feb 1860	02 Feb 1860	WPT
Richart, Elizabeth E.	Wolcott, Henry	30 Apr 1860	28 Apr 1860	DET
Richart, Martha J.	Loomis, H.W.	28 Sep 1859	27 Sep 1859	DET
Richart, Martha J.	Loomis, H.W.	28 Sep 1859	27 Sep 1859	WPT
Ricker, Augusta	Jordan, Edward W.	03 Nov 1852	27 Oct 1852	PT&C
Ricker, Augusta	Jordan, Edward W., Esq.	29 Oct 1852	27 Oct 1852	PI
Rigdon, Sallie	Hall, Thomas F.S.	25 May 1859	24 May 1859	DET
Rigdon, Sallie	Hall, Thomas F.S.	01 Jun 1859	27 May 1859	WPT
Riggs, Martha B.	Robinson, Joshua V., Jr.	18 Mar 1853	10 Mar 1853	PI
Riggs, Mary	Sloat, John	05 Jan 1853	23 Dec 1852	PT&C
Riggs, Rebecca	Kendall, Stephen	09 Aug 1839	06 Aug 1839	TRIB
Ripley, Cyntha Angeline	Stevens, Calvin J.	11 Jun 1844	03 Jun 1844	TRIB
Rishman, Hannah	Lehman, Joseph	06 May 1854	21 Apr 1854	PDD
Ritchey, Elizabeth C.	Spencer, Horace G.	17 Feb 1857	05 Feb 1857	PSOT
Ritchey, Marie (Bun)	Ream, Samuel K.	10 Nov 1857	29 Oct 1857	PSOT
Rittle, Nancy	Watts, W.W. (Dr.)	30 Apr 1856	29 Apr 1856	WPT
Rives, Corrie	Williams, Samuel T.	18 Aug 1858	02 Aug 1858	WPT
Roberts, Ola	Morrow, Stephen C.	06 Dec 1858	06 Dec 1858	DET

Name (Bride)	Name (Groom)	Notice Date	Marriage Date	Paper
Roberts, Ola	Morrow, Stephen C.	08 Dec 1858	06 Dec 1858	WPT
Robins, Mary Jane	McCarty, Michael	09 Apr 1856	03 Apr 1856	WPT
Robinson, Charlotte E.	Turley, John A.	05 Jan 1844	02 Jan 1844	TRIB
Robinson, Cornelia M.	Hutchins, Wells A. (Esq.)	24 Feb 1843	23 Feb 1843	TRIB
Robinson, Ellen	Cochran, A.J.	18 Jul 1850	13 Jun 1850	PT&C
Robinson, Harriet	Hewes, Edward	22 Apr 1854	20 Apr 1854	PDD
Robinson, Harriet A.	Hewes, Edward	21 Apr 1854	20 Apr 1854	DET
Rockwell, Mary	Fisher, Andrew	05 Aug 1858	31 Jul 1858	DET
Rockwell, Mary	Fisher, Andrew	18 Aug 1858	31 Jul 1858	WPT
Rodgers, Elizabeth	Royer, Theodore	08 Dec 1843	01 Dec 1843	TRIB
Rodgers, Elizabeth J.	Shiras, William	09 Aug 1839	01 Aug 1839	TRIB
Rodgers, Martha Jane	Moore, Ebenezer F.	31 Oct 1844	27 Oct 1844	TRIB
Rodgers, Catharine Matilda	Parkinson, William	29 Dec 1843	21 Dec 1843	TRIB
Rodgers, Rosa	Hamilton, Robert	16 Apr 1856	09 Apr 1856	WPT
Rollins, Aletha	Metz, John	17 Mar 1852	02 Mar 1852	PT&C
Ropp, Mary	Lybrook, Henler	25 Aug 1852	19 Aug 1852	PT&C
Ross, Melissa	Bookwalter, Addison	02 Dec 1850		PI
Row, C.	Landon, Charles	14 Sep 1858	13 Sep 1858	DET
Row, C.	Landon, Charles	15 Sep 1858	13 Sep 1858	WPT
Row, Mary C.	Landon, Charles C.	28 Sep 1858	15 Sep 1858	PSOT
Row, Mary C.	Landon, Charles C.	28 Sep 1858	15 Sep 1858	PTIMES
Rowland, Hattie A.	Hamilton, J.A.	08 Oct 1859	06 Oct 1859	DET
Rowland, Hattie A.	Hamilton, J.A.	12 Oct 1859	06 Oct 1859	WPT
Rowley, Elizabeth	Spherry, James	08 Jun 1826	11 May 1826	WT
Royer, Elizabeth	Pearson, (Dr.)	08 Dec 1843	01 Dec 1843	TRIB
Ruble, Deleanah	Temple, Henry	28 Feb 1854	15 Feb 1854	PDD
Ruggles, Armena	McCloud, Uriah	25 Feb 1857	15 Feb 1857	WPT
Rush, Eliza	Meacham, Charles A.	31 Dec 1853	22 Dec 1853	DET
Rush, Eliza	Meacham, Chas. A.	05 Jan 1854	22 Dec 1853	PDD
Russell, Katharine	Abbey, Selden	08 Nov 1853	26 Oct 1853	DET
Russell, Rosanna	Cline, Samuel	15 Jul 1850	10 Jul 1850	PI
Russell, Rosanna	Cline, Samuel	18 Jul 1850	10 Jul 1850	PT&C
Russell, Rosanna	Cline, Samuel	29 Aug 1850	10 Jul 1850	PT&C
Russell, Sarah B.	Andrews, William	10 Jun 1852	03 Jun 1852	PI
Russio, Aliono	Santy, Francis	21 Apr 1854	20 Apr 1854	DET
Russio, Alivno	Lantz, Francis	22 Apr 1854	20 Apr 1854	PDD
Rust, Rebecca	Willis, John	11 Jun 1856	28 May 1856	WPT
Ryan, Clara C.	Bovey, George C.	12 May 1854	09 May 1854	DET
Saade, Sarah	Moore, Joel	17 Feb 1857	11 Feb 1857	PSOT
Safford, M. Louise	Culbertson, H. (Dr.)	18 Nov 1854	15 Nov 1854	DET
Sage, Josanna	Snyder, Isaac H.	27 Dec 1853	08 Dec 1853	DET
Salladay, Marilda	McEntee, Thomas	22 Apr 1854	20 Apr 1854	DET
Salsbury, Helen M.	Wright, John C.	27 Oct 1843	24 Oct 1843	TRIB
Salters, Susan	Walsh, Thomas V.	23 Dec 1850	15 Dec 1850	PI

Name (Bride)	Name (Groom)	Notice Date	Marriage Date	Paper
Sane, Eliza	Sowders, George	21 Nov 1853	13 Nov 1853	DET
Sanford, Margaret	Bratton, Allen T.	13 Mar 1854	01 Mar 1854	PDD
Santy, Mary	Ellion, James H.	12 Nov 1856	03 Nov 1856	WPT
Sappington, Anna	Cook, William A.	25 Aug 1854	17 Aug 1854	DET
Saunders, Mrs. Martha P.	Matthews, Rev. Joseph	17 Feb 1854	03 Feb 1854	DET
Savage, Eliza J.	Nall, Albert G.	12 Jan 1856	02 Jan 1856	DET
Schwarzd, Wilhelm Sophia	Wilhelm, John	09 Jun 1857	01 Jun 1857	PSOT
Scofield, Adeline	Brady, Levi, Jr.	30 Sep 1853	29 Sep 1853	DET
Scott, Adeline	Cunning, Samuel W.	23 Dec 1850		PI
Scott, Ann Amelia	Terry, Leroy G.	06 Jun 1848	01 Jun 1848	DENQ
Scott, Eliza P.	Olds, Joseph	12 Jan 1859	30 Dec 1858	DET
Scott, H.M.	Crichton, Andrew	21 May 1852	13 May 1852	PI
Scott, Malvina	Robinson, Joshua V.	20 Oct 1843	17 Oct 1843	TRIB
Scott, Martha B.	Moore, Oscar F. (Esq.)	22 Sep 1843	19 Sep 1843	TRIB
Scott, Mary Adeline	Cunning, Samuel W.	26 Dec 1850	19 Dec 1850	PT&C
Scriptures, Sarah	Pillow, Jonas	16 Dec 1853		DET
Searl, Mary R.	Morton, Jonathan	21 Oct 1865	14 Oct 1865	PTIMES
Seeberger, Hannah	Hymanne, H.	28 Jul 1860		DET
Seeberger, hannah	Hymanne, H.	01 Aug 1860		WPT
Selders, Cordella	Vanscoy, Nelson	25 Jan 1854	20 Jan 1854	DET
Senegiger, Mary	Connel, Wm.	07 Nov 1850	20 Oct 1850	PT&C
Shaffer, Rosanna	Williamson, Peter	31 May 1827	24 May 1827	WT
Sharp, Mary	Lackry, James	24 Sep 1855	30 Aug 1855	DET
Shatel, Mary	Altiff, Adam	16 Nov 1855	14 Nov 1855	DET
Shellieg, Maggie	McCollister, Thomas J.	15 Aug 1860	13 Aug 1860	DET
Shellieg, Maggie	McCollister, Thomas J.	22 Aug 1860	13 Aug 1860	WPT
Shellieg, Elizabeth	Vance, Jerome B.	13 Jul 1858	07 Jul 1858	PSOT
Shelling, Elizabeth	Vance, Jerome B.	07 Jul 1858	07 Jul 1858	DET
Shelling, Elizabeth	Vance, Jerome B.	14 Jul 1858	07 Jul 1858	WPT
Shelten, Elizabeth A.	Chapman, Martin	12 Aug 1854	08 Aug 1854	PDD
Shelton, Elizabeth A.	Chapman, Martin	11 Aug 1854	09 Aug 1854	DET
Shepard, Eliza J.	Fehar, Lyman	02 Sep 1850	13 Aug 1850	PI
Shepard, Eliza J.	Fehar, Lyman	29 Aug 1850	13 Aug 1850	PT&C
Sherfey, Caroline A.	Roberts, Julius W.	30 Apr 1851	01 Apr 1851	PT&C
Sherman, Elizabeth	Williams, Joseph	03 Dec 1855	01 Dec 1855	DET
Sherman, Elizabeth	Williams, Joseph	05 Dec 1855	01 Dec 1855	WPT
Shockey, Samantha	Pilcher, J.M.	06 May 1865	28 Apr 1865	PTIMES
Short, Elizabeth N.	Craig, Thomas	08 Oct 1852	23 Sep 1852	PI
Shred, Rosen	Bosanpagh, Michael	10 Mar 1854	07 Mar 1854	DET
Shred, Rosina	Bosanpazk, Michael	09 Mar 1854	07 Mar 1854	PDD
Shuflin, Martha	Clark, Isaiah	08 Feb 1854	05 Feb 1854	PDD
Shuflin, Martha	Clark, Josiah	07 Feb 1854	05 Feb 1854	DET
Shupe, Abigail	Boylston, John	15, 17 Sep 1855	13 Sep 1855	DET
Shupe, Cynthia A.	Sly, M.G. Tully Cicero	27 Feb 1852	22 Feb 1852	PI

Name (Bride)	Name (Groom)	Notice Date	Marriage Date	Paper
Shute, Olive A.	Brubaker, John D.	20 Feb 1852	17 Feb 1852	PI
Sikes, Sarah	Batterson, Addison	04 Nov 1850	27 Oct 1850	PI
Sill, Mary	Kinney, Alfred	28 Jan 1853	26 Jan 1853	PI
Simley, Catharine	Parman, Charles	17 Oct 1854	17 Oct 1854	DET
Simmons, Catherine	Burks, Wm.	09 Jan 1855	28 Dec 1854	DET
Simonson, Matilda	Higgins, Robert B.	13 Apr 1853	07 Apr 1853	PT&C
Sinton, Artemisia	Vermillion, T.B.	28 Sep 1858	14 Sep 1858	PSOT
Sinton, Artemisia	Vermillion, T.B.	28 Sep 1858	14 Sep 1858	PTIMES
Skelton, Cynthia	James, Alva H.	06 Dec 1855	20 Nov 1855	DET
Skimmer, Mary A.	Keagerice, Amos R.	27 Jun 1853	15 Jun 1853	DET
Skimmer, Mary A.	Keagerice, Amos R.	29 Jun 1853	15 Jun 1853	PT&C
Slack, Mary Ellen	Foy, Randolf C.W.	08 Nov 1853	07 Nov 1853	DET
Slattery, Jane C.	Violet, Sam'l. B. (Esq.)	09 Jan 1856	20 Dec 1855	WPT
Slattery, Jane C.	Violet, Samuel B.	04 Jan 1856	20 Dec 1855	DET
Slattery, Jane C.	Violet, Samuel B. (Esq.)	09 Jan 1856	20 Dec 1855	WPT
Sloat, Mary E.	Buck, James	07 Jul 1853	03 Jul 1853	DET
Sloat, Mary E.	Buck, James	09 Jul 1853	03 Jul 1853	PDD
Sloat_all, Mary E.	Buck, James	13 Jul 1853	03 Jul 1853	PT&C
Slocumb, Clarissa	Ferrill, Daniel	08 Mar 1844	20 Jan 1844	TRIB
Sly, Marthy Ann	Linly, James S.	05 Jan 1854	27 Dec 1853	DET
Smith, Agnes	Selby, William	20 Jan 1854	05 Jan 1854	DET
Smith, Caroline	Littlejohn, Henry	07 Jan 1853	02 Jan 1853	PI
Smith, Caroline	Littlejohn, Henry	05 Jan 1853	02 Jan 1853	PT&C
Smith, Cate	Albert, Rudolph	20 Aug 1856	06 Aug 1856	WPT
Smith, Catharine	More, Philip	24 Oct 1829	08 Oct 1829	WT
Smith, Elden	Kirkhouse, George	11 Jan 1853	25 Dec 1852	PI
Smith, Eliza A.	Horn, Jonathan	14 Apr 1848	04 Apr 1848	DENQ
Smith, Elizabeth	Brown, James	05 Sep 1853	03 Sep 1853	DET
Smith, Elizabeth	Brown, James	06 Sep 1853	03 Sep 1853	PDD
Smith, Elizabeth	Custis, John	31 May 1827	27 May 1827	WT
Smith, Ellen O.	Nall, John D.	14 Apr 1855	10 Apr 1855	DET
Smith, Jennet	Huodersheldt, Phillip	10 Nov 1853	01 Nov 1853	DET
Smith, Lucinda	Norris, Amaziah	12 May 1857	04 May 1857	DET
Smith, Lucinda	Norris, Amaziah	13 May 1857	04 May 1857	WPT
Smith, Mary	Estill, William	04 Aug 1851	28 Jul 1851	PI
Smith, Mary	Estill, William	06 Aug 1851	28 Jul 1851	PT&C
Smith, Mary W.	M'Dowell, James S.	20 Aug 1851	14 Aug 1851	PT&C
Smith, Nancy	Craine, Leonard	05 Dec 1844	25 Nov 1844	TRIB
Smith, Nancy	Fox, Benjamin	02 Sep 1850	25 Jul 1850	PI
Smith, Nancy	Fox, Benjamin	29 Aug 1850	25 Jul 1850	PT&C
Smith, Sally	Plotter, John O.	11 Jan 1853	22 Dec 1852	PI
Smith, Sarah	Gibout, Peter	18 Jun 1852		PI
Smolley, Nancy W.	Wainsley, John A.	15 Feb 1855	14 Feb 1855	DET
Snyder, Margaret	Swager, James	14 Nov 1851	09 Nov 1851	PI
Snyder, Margaret	Swager, James	12 Nov 1851	09 Nov 1851	PT&C

Name (Bride)	Name (Groom)	Notice Date	Marriage Date	Paper
Songer, Ann	Boyd, G.W.	19 Nov 1853	09 Nov 1853	DET
Soward, Nannie F.	Bayhan, Benjamin F.	01 Sep 1851		PI
Spanaler, Hannah S.	Warring, James L.	14 Feb 1856	24 Jan 1856	DET
Spence, Cynthia A.	Jones, John Milton	17 Jun 1850	06 Jun 1850	PI
Springer, Calphurnia M.	Shoub, Henry A.	10 Dec 1864	24 Nov 1864	PTIMES
Sprouse, Elizabeth	Mountjoy, John	11 Aug 1855	09 Aug 1855	DET
Spry, Frances	Helphenstein, Geo. W.	31 Jan 1863	28 Jan 1863	PTIMES
Spry, Thomasin H.	Pursell, Thos. J.	18 Mar 1857	17 Mar 1857	WPT
Spry, Thomasin H.	Pursell, Thomas J.	24 Mar 1857	17 Mar 1857	PSOT
Squires, Antionette	Cole, Silas W.	06 Feb 1864	27 Jan 1864	PTIMES
Squires, Elizabeth	Frost, Westley	02 Jun 1854	01 Jun 1854	DET
Stains, Mary	Miller, J.S.	26 Dec 1853	15 Dec 1853	PDD
Stanley, Abigail	Deming, Ezekiel	03 Aug 1820	25 Jul 1820	STEL
Stanly, Susan	Ward, George	18 Jan 1854		DET
Stapler, Mary B.	Ross, John (Cherokee Chief)	19 Sep 1844	16 Sep 1844	TRIB
Stapleton, Mary	Porter, William	13 May 1850	18 Apr 1850	PI
Stapleton, Mary	Porter, William	09 May 1850	18 Apr 1850	PT&C
Steece, M.J.	Baird, S.	10 Oct 1851	01 Oct 1851	PI
Steece, M.J.	Baird, S.	08 Oct 1851	01 Oct 1851	PT&C
Steenbergen, Sarah M.	Clough, G.W.A. (Dr.)	10 Mar 1843	02 Mar 1843	TRIB
Steene, Nancy	Tucker, Lewis	21 Oct 1850	17 Oct 1850	PI
Stemshorn, Magdaline	Haule, H.	28 Jan 1852	19 Jan 1852	PT&C
Stentemann, Barbara	Hinkle, John	21 Nov 1855	19 Nov 1855	DET
Stentzmann, Barbara	Hinkle, John	21 Nov 1855	19 Nov 1855	WPT
Stepheson, Mary Ann	Phillips, Theophilus	17 Jun 1854	14 Jun 1854	PDD
Stepleton, Nancy	Rank, Wm.	23 Dec 1850	20 Nov 1850	PI
Stepleton, Nancy	Rank, Wm.	19 Dec 1850	20 Nov 1850	PT&C
Stevenson, Annie Emeline	Hughes, Jacob B.	14 Apr 1855	09 Apr 1855	DET
Stevenson, Canzada	Mills, James	13, 20 Aug 1856	03 Aug 1856	WPT
Stevenson, Harriet A.	Davidson, Alfred D.	03 Mar 1843	28 Feb 1843	TRIB
Stevenson, Sarah	McClure, Emmit	28 Jan 1860	26 Jan 1860	DET
Stewart, Agnes	Finton, Wm. H.H.	25 Nov 1865	16 Nov 1865	PTIMES
Stewart, Elizabeth J.	Fergason, Hiram (Dr.)	01 Aug 1850	23 Jul 1850	PT&C
Stewart, Flora A.	Chick, Franklin	02 Jun 1852	23 May 1852	PT&C
Stillwell, Mattie L.	Douglas, James	12 Jul 1854	06 Jul 1854	DET
Stimp, Celia	Perry, Lindsey	06 Feb 1855	04 Feb 1855	DET
Stinton, Mary E.	Dewy, James W.	25 Jan 1854	19 Jan 1854	DET
Stokely, Mary	Herron, John	08 Sep 1855	07 Sep 1855	DET
Stone, Lucy	Blackwell, Harry	11 May 1855		DET
Stone, Sarah C.	Noel, Aaron T.	23 Dec 1865	14 Dec 1865	PTIMES
Stonhill, Sarah	Seeberger, Henry	14 Nov 1851	07 Nov 1851	PI
Stonhill, Sarah	Seeberger, Henry	12 Nov 1851	07 Nov 1851	PT&C
Storey, Hannah	Smedley, Isaac F.	08 Mar 1844	25 Feb 1844	TRIB

Name (Bride)	Name (Groom)	Notice Date	Marriage Date	Paper
Story, Mahala	Murdock, Drake	18 Aug 1852	05 Aug 1852	PT&C
Strait, Rebecca	Williams, Abraham	28 Jun 1855	27 Jun 1855	DET
Stratton, Salome	Case, Stephen	31 Mar 1843	02 Mar 1843	TRIB
Street, Minta M.	Williams, Matthew M.	11 Apr 1863	05 Apr 1863	PTIMES
Strong, Annis	Winderly, Minrod	21 Jan 1857	11 Jan 1857	WPT
Strowd, Margaret	Comer, Lawrence	06 Feb 1854	26 Jan 1854	DET
Strowd, Margaret	Comer, Lawrence	10 Feb 1854	26 Jan 1854	PDD
Sturgeon, Mary W.	Taylor, Oliver C.	12 Jan 1860	11 Jan 1860	DET
Sturgeon, Mary W.	Taylor, Oliver C.	25 Jan 1860	11 Jan 1860	WPT
Sturgeon, Sarah Jane	Musser, Wm.	11, 18 Jun 1851	01 Jun 1851	PT&C
Sulivan, Caroline	Macatee, W.	02 Mar 1854	28 Feb 1854	PDD
Sullivan, Caroline	Maratu, Washington	01 Mar 1854	28 Feb 1854	DET
Sullivan, Ellen	Vance, John	30 Apr 1852	21 Apr 1852	PI
Suten, Malinda M.	Walker, Thomas D.	25 Feb 1857	17 Feb 1857	WPT
Swabia, Charlotte	Blake, John	20 Feb 1860	15 Feb 1860	DET
Swan, Mary	Sherman, Alba	15 Aug 1854	10 Jun 1854	PDD
Swap, Delia (Mrs.)	Jones, Elias	11 Apr 1854	11 Feb 1854	PDD
Sweet, Eliza	Lewis, Josiah	01 Oct 1844	12 Sep 1844	PDEM
Sweet, Mary Ann	Solitude, Abram	01 Sep 1843	12 Aug 1843	TRIB
Sweet, Susan	Lewis, Eli	27 Apr 1853	21 Apr 1853	PT&C
Sweetser, Della	McElroy, J. Newton (Lt.Col.)	21 Jun 1862	10 Apr 1862	PTIMES
Sweetser, Emma	Ridgway, Tho. Jno.	07 May 1864	14 Apr 1864	PTIMES
Sweney, Elizabeth	Tomlinson, William E.	28 Oct 1850	16 Oct 1850	PI
Sworberry, Eliza	May, Hugh	04 Jun 1858	03 Jun 1858	DET
Sworberry, Eliza	May, Hugh	09 Jun 1858	03 Jun 1858	WPT
Swords, Sarah A.	Wilson, Clarke	27 Feb 1852	23 Feb 1852	PI
Tallman, Laura A.	Charlesworth, James F.	27 Jul 1855	04 Jul 1855	DET
Tanner, Mary Ann	Tanner, George	31 Jul 1857	31 Jul 1857	DET
Tanner, Mary Ann	Tanner, George	05 Aug 1857	31 Jul 1857	WPT
Taylor, Caroline C.	Hoy, Charles W., Esq.	16 Sep 1853	07 Sep 1853	DET
Taylor, Mary E.	Riggs, James W.	21 Jul 1851	17 Jul 1851	PI
Taylor, Mary E.	Riggs, James W.	23 Jul 1851		PT&C
Taylor, Mary Jane	Shoemaker, Samuel	16 May 1854	03 May 1854	DET
Tenney, Lydia S.	Clark, Lewis	10 Nov 1853	25 Oct 1853	DET
Terry, Henrietta	McCown, Monroe	29 Dec 1860	16 Dec 1860	PTIMES
Thomas, E.M.	Lodwick, John K.	12 Sep 1850	09 Sep 1850	PT&C
Thomas, Ellie	Farden, James A.	21 Sep 1857	15 Sep 1857	DET
Thomas, Ellie	Farden, James A.	23 Sep 1857	15 Sep 1857	WPT
Thomas, Mary Jane	Locke, Hiram W.	29 Dec 1853	25 Dec 1853	DET
Thompson, Amanda	Pursell, James	17 Mar 1843	16 Mar 1843	TRIB
Thompson, Ann	Louderack, Phillip	14 Oct 1855	25 Sep 1855	DET
Thompson, Elizabeth	Littlejohn, Daniel	14 Jan 1825	25 Dec 1824	PG&LA
Thompson, Jane	Lodwick, Joseph F. (Capt.)	18 Nov 1831	08 Nov 1831	PC&WT

Marriages (Brides)

Name (Bride)	Name (Groom)	Notice Date	Marriage Date	Paper
Thompson, Maria L.	Gates, Erastus	17 Mar 1854	16 Mar 1854	DET
Thompson, Maria L.	Gates, Erastus	20 Mar 1854	16 Mar 1854	PDD
Thompson, Maria L.	Gates, Erastus	22 Mar 1854	16 Mar 1854	SVREP
Thrall, Melissa H.	Webster, Elizur G.	30 Jan 1858	28 Jan 1858	DET
Thrall, Melissa H.	Webster, Elizur G.	03 Feb 1858	28 Jan 1858	WPT
Thresher, Helen	Robert, H.M. (Lieut.)	29 Dec 1860	17 Dec 1860	PTIMES
Thresher, Helen M.	Robert, H.M. (Lieut)	26 Dec 1859	17 Dec 1859	WPT
Throckmorton, Hannah	Whitcher, Frederick P.	28 Mar 1832	22 Mar 1832	PC
Thurston, Lucy	Hinman, John	10 Nov 1857	10 Nov 1857	DET
Thurston, Lucy	Hinman, John	11 Nov 1857	10 Nov 1857	WPT
Thurston, Margaret	Tracy, Samuel M.	29 Oct 1851	27 Oct 1851	PT&C
Tilton, Phebee	Gregory, Moses	22 May 1838	13 May 1838	STRIB
Timbrook, Rebecca	Briggs, Samuel C.	03 Mar 1826	29 Dec 1825	TA
Timmonds, M.A.J.	Little, William W.	31 Jan 1854	29 Jan 1854	DET
Timmons, Sarah	Kennedy, Peter	02 Jan 1852	28 Dec 1851	PI
Timmons, Sarah	Kennedy, Peter	31 Dec 1851	28 Dec 1851	PT&C
Timmons, Semantha	MacKoy, H.C.	04 Oct 1853		DET
Timmons, Semantha	Mackoy, H.C.	05 Oct 1853	04 Oct 1853	PDD
Tinney, Lydia	Clark, Lewis	05 Nov 1853	26 Oct 1853	DET
Titus, Rebecca	Pinkerton, Wm. H.	27 Apr 1853	21 Apr 1853	PT&C
Toben, Eliza Mary	Graham, T.J. (Col.)	11 May 1855	10 May 1855	DET
Tom, Susan	Murphy, Reas	12 Dec 1853	24 Nov 1853	DET
Tom, Susan	Murphy, Reas	15 Dec 1853	24 Nov 1853	WPT
Tomlinson, Josephene	Glidden, D.A.	16 Aug 1858	10 Aug 1858	DET
Tomlinson, Josephene	Glidden, D.A.	18 Aug 1858	10 Aug 1858	WPT
Tomlinson, Julia	Meek, William	15 Jul 1850	11 Jul 1850	PI
Tomlinson, Julia	Meek, Wm.	18 Jul 1850 29 Aug 1850	11 Jul 1850	PT&C
Topins Matilda	Reynolds, Robert	31 Mar 1854	30 Mar 1854	DET
Topins, Matilda	Renolds, Robert	01 Apr 1854	30 Mar 1854	PDD
Towner, Eliza E.	Wynn, Isaac C.	04 Feb 1858	02 Feb 1858	DET
Towner, Eliza E.	Wynn, Isaac C.	09 Feb 1858	02 Feb 1858	PSOT
Tracy, Elizabeth D.	Ross, M.B.	30 Jun 1843	29 Jun 1843	TRIB
Tracy, Emily A.	Guthrie, J.C.	20 Jun 1863	11 Jun 1863	PTIMES
Tracy, Frances	Oakes, Francis J.	25 Dec 1845	18 Dec 1845	TRIB
Tracy, Mary K.	Sutherlin, George H.	02 Dec 1853	30 Nov 1853	DET
Tracy, Mary K.	Sutherlin, George H.	01 Dec 1853	30 Nov 1853	PDD
Tubbs, Susan	Hicks, William	10 Nov 1853	27 Oct 1853	DET
Tucker, Caroline	Hoover, Andrew Jackson Lewis	10 Oct 1854	10 Oct 1854	DET
Tucker, Nancy	Starkum, Aaron	17 Aug 1853	15 Aug 1853	PDD
Tucker, Nancy C.	Starkum, Aaron	15 Aug 1853		DET
Tucker, Nancy C.	Starkum, Aaron	17 Aug 1853	15 Aug 1853	PT&C
Turley, Sarah C.	Lawson, T.B.	28 Oct 1865	24 Oct 1865	PTIMES
Turnner, Harriet T.	Cummings, Jesse O.	20 Aug 1853	12 Aug 1853	DET

Name (Bride)	Name (Groom)	Notice Date	Marriage Date	Paper
Turner, Hester Ann	Pressel, Daniel W.	20 Jun 1844	19 Jun 1844	TRIB
Turner, Levina	Kennedy, Warren	19 Jan 1856	16 Jan 1856	DET
Turner, Margaret O.	Douglass, H.G.	30 Aug 1854	27 Aug 1854	DET
Turner, Martha J.	Aldrich, Asa, Jr.	04 Nov 1837	01 Nov 1837	STRIB
Turner, S.E.	Parker, N.H.	01 Oct 1852	30 Sep 1852	PI
Turnner, Harriet T.	Cummings, Jesse C.	24 Aug 1853	12 Aug 1853	PT&C
Turvey, Sarah	Morgan, Conrad	18 May 1854	09 May 1854	DET
Tuttle, Jane S.	Watt, M.H.	22 Nov 1853	17 Nov 1853	PDD
Tyrrell, Mary Ann	Peatling, Edward	13 Apr 1855	12 Apr 1855	DET
female	Harris, Thomas L. (Hon.)	01 Dec 1855	24 Nov 1855	WPT
Updegraff, Eleanor	Murray, Newton (Capt.)	05 Jan 1844	25 Dec 1843	TRIB
Urquhart, Jenette	Painer, John	20 Sep 1855	18 Sep 1855	DET
Van Gundy, Jane	Carthick, A. (Rev.)	08 Apr 1854	04 Apr 1854	DET
Vanbeek, Sena	Dalabre, Michael	30 Sep 1850	26 Sep 1850	PI
Vanbeek, Sena	Dalabree, Michael	03 Oct 1850	26 Sep 1850	PT&C
Vanbibber, Elisa	Boal, William K.	14 Apr 1855	15 Mar 1855	DET
Vance, Electa	Hibbs, Van B. (Col.)	13 May 1865	27 Apr 1865	PTIMES
Vance, Nancy	Nurse, Lewis	25 Jul 1859	20 Jul 1859	DET
Vance, Nancy	Nurse, Lewis	27 Jul 1859	20 Jul 1859	WPT
Vanden, Joanna	Rathburn, Samuel B.	03 Feb 1843	22 Jan 1843	TRIB
Vanmetre, Ann	Johnson, Thomas	17 Nov 1853	05 Nov 1853	PDD
Varner, Mary J.	Davey, P.	14 May 1853	12 May 1853	PDD
Varner, Mary J.	Davey, P.	18 May 1853	12 May 1853	PT&C
Varner, Sarah C.	Gilbert, Jos. C.	31 Mar 1852	25 Mar 1852	PT&C
Veach, Elizabeth	Reid, Robert T.	06 Oct 1843	24 Sep 1843	TRIB
Veach, Mary	Lodwick, Murty W.	16 Dec 1865	13 Dec 1865	PTIMES
Venn, Aplona	Bertram, Henry	18 Jun 1864	16 Jun 1864	PTIMES
Vernon, Salena	Newell, L.W.	24 Jun 1854	18 Jun 1854	DET
Vessall, Nancy	McCann, Jennings	11 Aug 1852	07 Aug 1852	PT&C
Vickers, Margaret I.	Frost, John	17 Dec 1853	10 Dec 1853	DET
Vickers, Margaret J.	Frost, John	19 Dec 1853	10 Dec 1853	PDD
Vigus, Hannah C.	Edgington, Francis	07 May 1864	02 May 1864	PTIMES
Vining, Sarabell	Smith, John O.	24 Dec 1864	14 Dec 1864	PTIMES
Vinton, Romain M.	Safford, E.P.	16 Oct 1854	09 Oct 1854	DET
Vollanvaider, Augustine	Russell, A.B. (Rev.)	03 Nov 1852	28 Oct 1852	PT&C
Voorhies, Mary E.	Harrison, Thomas B.	02 Jan 1864	23 Dec 1863	PTIMES
Vorex, Rachael	Kimbro, Wm.	06 May 1854	21 Apr 1854	PDD
Wait, Belle	Wyeth, Walter N.	09 May 1859	09 May 1859	DET
Wait, Belle	Wyeth, Walter N.	10 May 1859	09 May 1859	PTIMES
Wait, Belle	Wyeth, Walter N. (Rev.)	11 May 1859	09 May 1859	WPT
Wait, Melissa	Bush, Seth R.	22 Mar 1844	21 Mar 1844	TRIB
Wait, O.	Hayward, H.	10 Apr 1855	22 Mar 1855	DET
Wakeman, Jennie C.	Kehoe, John	15 May 1860	08 May 1860	DET
Wakeman, Jennie C.	Kehoe, John	16 May 1860	08 May 1860	WPT
Walker, Elizabeth	Bibey, Abraham	11 Jan 1853	06 Jan 1853	PI

Marriages (Brides)

Name (Bride)	Name (Groom)	Notice Date	Marriage Date	Paper
Walker, Elizabeth	Riley, Abraham	18 Mar 1853	06 Mar 1853	PI
Walker, Hannah	Lee, David W.	08 Dec 1855	06 Dec 1855	DET
Walker, Margaret	Walker, Thomas	05 Nov 1853	31 Oct 1853	DET
Walker, P. Frances	Ormsby, Jerome B.	24 Oct 1850	21 Oct 1850	PT&C
Walker, P. Frances	Ormsby, Jerome B.	28 Oct 1850	21 Oct 1850	PI
Walker, Perilla F.	Ormsby, Jerome B.	19 Dec 1850	20 Oct 1850	PT&C
Wallace, Nancy A.	McNamer, James	25 Nov 1865	16 Nov 1865	PTIMES
Walter, Sallie	Dresbach, Herr	17 May 1854	27 Apr 1854	PDD
Walterhouse, Agnes	Vaughn, Wm.	04 Nov 1865	31 Oct 1865	PTIMES
Ward, Amanda	Pearce (or Pearon), Alex.	04 Nov 1857	28 Oct 1857	WPT
Ward, Amanda	Pearon, Alex.	02 Nov 1857	28 Oct 1857	DET
Ward, Nancy	Crozier, Robert	03 Oct 1848	25 Sep 1848	DENQ
Waring, Mary L.	Jordon, Thomas J.	29 Oct 1858	28 Oct 1858	DET
Waring, Mary L.	Jordon, Thomas J.	10 Nov 1858	28 Oct 1858	WPT
Warner, Susan	Gray, George	14 Nov 1853	13 Nov 1853	DET
Warner, Susan	Gray, George	16 Nov 1853	13 Nov 1853	PDD
Washer, Olinda	Maule, John	26 Sep 1855	25 Sep 1855	DET
Waterhouse, Elizabeth	M'Cloud, Samuel J.	09 Sep 1818	03 Sep 1818	PGAZ
Watkins, Rebecca Jane	Densmore, Henry	16 Apr 1856	16 Apr 1856	WPT
Watrovs, Lydia Ann	Clarke, Abraham	01 Jun 1820		STEL
Watson, Rhoda	Lane, Wilson M.	24 Feb 1854	04 Feb 1854	DET
Watson, Rhoda	Lane, Wilson M.	10 Feb 1854	04 Feb 1854	DET
Wazeily, Mary	Lolland, Jacob	12 Nov 1856		WPT
Weatherbee, Mary J.	Martin, W.P.	02 Apr 1856	31 Mar 1856	WPT
Weaver, Elizabeth	Basey, John	26 Dec 1853	20 Dec 1853	PDD
Webster, Harriet W.	Dabney, S.W.	16 Apr 1851	02 Apr 1851	PT&C
Well, Susan F.	Dunkle, A.J.	06 Feb 1854	02 Feb 1854	DET
West, Emily	Cady, John M.	04 Jun 1856	01 Jun 1856	WPT
West, Mary	Wear, Marshall	11 Oct 1859	09 Oct 1859	DET
West, Mary	Wear, Marshall	12 Oct 1859	09 Oct 1859	WPT
Wetherbee, Cordelia	Gordon, James Y.	10 Apr 1855	09 Apr 1855	DET
Wheeler, Abigail	Lindsey, Peter	18 May 1820	14 May 1820	STEL
Wheeler, E.J.	Day, E.C.	18 Jun 1852	14 Jun 1852	PI
Wheeler, Elizabeth	Putland, Edward	13 Apr 1858	21 Mar 1858	PSOT
Wheeler, Kate	Plants, T.A. (Hon.)	05 Dec 1859	20 Nov 1859	WPT
Wheeler, Narissa T.	Brown, George W.	28 Nov 1853	24 Nov 1853	DET
Wheeler, Susan	Kline, John	17 Aug 1854	16 Aug 1854	DET
Wheeler, Susan	Kline, John	19 Aug 1854	16 Aug 1854	PDD
Wheellr, Narissa T.	Brown, Geo. W.	30 Nov 1853	24 Nov 1853	PDD
Wheelock, S.J.	Hick, S.D.	26 Jun 1855	25 Jun 1855	DET
Whitcomb, Lucy C.	Adair, Smilie R.	16 Sep 1850	02 Sep 1850	PI
Whitcomb, Lucy C.	Adair, Smilie R.	19 Sep 1850	02 Sep 1850	PT&C
Whitcomb, Narcissa	Kent, Arod	14 Jan 1825	21 Oct 1824	PG&LA
Whitcomb, Sally	Cranston, Edward (Capt.)	14 Jan 1825	13 Jan 1825	PG&LA
White, Eliza	Butt, John	20 Sep 1827		WT

Name (Bride)	Name (Groom)	Notice Date	Marriage Date	Paper
White, Harriet	Murray, D.N.	20 May 1850	14 May 1850	PI
White, Harriet	Murray, D.N.	16 May 1850	14 May 1850	PT&C
White, Lucretia	Gillianwottip, Leonard	16 Jun 1854	15 Jun 1854	DET
White, Mary	Brown, George	18 May 1820		STEL
White, Mary J.	Swift, Aurin R.	15 Sep 1858	09 Sep 1858	WPT
White, Sarah E.	Veach, Wm. (Esq.)	21 Oct 1865	11 Oct 1865	PTIMES
Whitney, Mary	Hamlin, Hannibal G.	04 Feb 1825		PG&LA
Whittaker, Keith	Hubbell, Wake	11 Mar 1858	23 Feb 1858	DET
Whitteker, Keith	Hubbell, Wake	17 Mar 1858	23 Feb 1858	WPT
Wiatt, Mary Jane	Shriner, Daniel F.	11 Jun 1856	30 May 1856	WPT
Wigh__m, Lizzie	Hughes, E.B.	01 Feb 1856	31 Jan 1856	DET
Wilcoxin, Lovisa	Bradford, Samuel C.	07 Oct 1831	16 Sep 1831	PC&WT
Wilcoxon, Drusilla W.	Smith, John D.	26 Jan 1828		WT
Wiley, Mary Ann	Watkins, Thomas B.	04 Jan 1854	01 Jan 1854	DET
Wiley, Mary Ann	Watkins, Thomas B.	05 Jan 1854	01 Jan 1854	PDD
Wilhelm, Sarah D.	Moore, John	24 Sep 1852	20 Sep 1852	PI
Wilhelms, Matilda C.	Hore, Philip H.	01 Oct 1856	Sep 1856	WPT
Will, Susan E.	Dunkle, A.J.	10 Feb 1854	02 Feb 1854	PDD
Willard, Lavenia S.	Gould, Orrin B.	01 Feb 1859	26 Jan 1859	DET
Willard, Lavinia Seeley	Gould, Orrin B.	02 Feb 1859	26 Jan 1859	WPT
Willet, Mary	Worley, W.C.	26 Mar 1856		WPT
Willey, Lizzie	Montgomery, Homer	14 Oct 1865	11 Oct 1865	PTIMES
Williams, Ann G.	Masterson, William N.	10 Nov 1853	01 Nov 1853	DET
Williams, Caroline A.	Wright, Charles H.	15 Jul 1865	10 Jul 1865	PTIMES
Williams, Elizabeth	Stewart, John	19 Sep 1844	12 Sep 1844	TRIB
Williams, Jane	Souder, Samuel	09 Apr 1852	25 Mar 1852	PI
Williams, Louisa	Martin, John H.	24 Mar 1854	19 Mar 1854	DET
Williams, Margaret	Owens, Evan C. (Mayor)	03 Jan 1855	25 Dec 1855	DET
Williams, Mary	Morgan, Thomas	13 May 1850	24 Apr 1850	PI
Williams, Mary	Morgan, Thomas	09 May 1850	24 Apr 1850	PT&C
Williams, Mary A.	Denning, Newton B.	24 Jun 1853	19 Jun 1853	DET
Williams, Mary A.	Denning, Newton B.	29 Jun 1853	19 Jun 1853	PT&C
Williams, Rebecca	Archbold, David	13 May 1850	04 May 1850	PI
Williams, Rebecca	Archbold, David	09 May 1850	04 May 1850	PT&C
Williamson, Jemima	Bremigam, William	27 Aug 1855	16 Aug 1855	DET
Willoughby, S. Marga-retta	Cummings, Joseph D.	03 Apr 1855	02 Apr 1855	DET
Wilson, Angeline	Isaacs, Fielding	24 Dec 1853	19 Dec 1853	DET
Wilson, Cornelia	Baker, Robert	02 Apr 1856	27 Mar 1856	WPT
Wilson, Fanny E.	Lewis, Chas. B.	07 May 1856	01 May 1856	WPT
Wilson, Mary L.	Miller, Samuel	02 Mar 1854	21 Feb 1854	PDD
Wilson, Rachel	Maloney, Wm. A.	29 Oct 1851	23 Oct 1851	PT&C
Wilson, Sardina	Sheeler, Michael	22 Aug 1855	21 Aug 1855	DET
Windgate, Rebecca	Grant, George W.	03 Dec 1853	27 Oct 1853	DET
Wingond, Elizabeth	Shafer, Samuel	09 Apr 1856	01 Apr 1856	WPT

Marriages (Brides)

Name (Bride)	Name (Groom)	Notice Date	Marriage Date	Paper
Winkler, Adella	Reed, Calvin W.	18 Feb 1857	12 Feb 1857	WPT
Winkler, Mary Jane	Hitchcock, Lewis	23 Dec 1865	14 Dec 1865	PTIMES
Winning, Elizabeth	Thompson, Samuel	19 Aug 1854	15 Aug 1854	DET
Winters, Christina	Lust, Philip	21 Jul 1853	19 Jul 1853	DET
Winters, Christina	Lust, Philip	27 Jul 1853	19 Jul 1853	PT&C
Wise, Alma	Shaw, James	25 Mar 1853	15 Mar 1853	PI
Wise, Alma	Shaw, James	23 Mar 1853	15 Mar 1853	PT&C
Wite, Elizabeth	Kennedy, Rezin	10 Mar 1855	08 Mar 1855	DET
Withers, Evadne	Riggs, Stephen B.	14 Oct 1853	12 Oct 1853	PDD
Withers, Evalne	Riggs, Stephen B.	13 Oct 1853	12 Oct 1853	DET
Wolfard, Mary	Deeliecks, Henry	10 Nov 1857	08 Nov 1857	DET
Wolfard, Mary	Deeliecks, Henry	11 Nov 1857	08 Nov 1857	WPT
Wollom, Margaret	Meacham, James	25 Aug 1854	10 Aug 1854	DET
Wood, F.H.	Janney, L.	21 Mar 1863	09 Mar 1863	PTIMES
Wood, Fanny A.	Pogue, Henry E.	08, 19 Nov 1853	03 Nov 1853	DET
Wood, Phoeba	Morris, Thomas	19 Oct 1826	03 Oct 1826	WT
Woodruff, Jane Ann	Clark, Orris A.	31 Oct 1844	17 Oct 1844	TRIB
Woodruff, Nancy	Canter, Milton	28 Jan 1857	01 Jan 1857	WPT
Wormster, Sarah	Foster, Adam C.	30 Jan 1854	25 Jan 1854	DET*
Worthington, Nancy	Austin, Lycurgus C.	24 Jan 1854	12 Jan 1854	DET
Wright, Anna Rebecca	Bradbury, George W.(Lieut.Col.)	01 Dec 1843	22 Nov 1843	TRIB
Wright, Dilla	Royce, George	17 Jun 1865	14 Jun 1865	PTIMES
Wright, Mary	Miner, John L.	04 Nov 1837	26 Oct 1837	STRIB
Wright, Salina	Kinney, John	12 Aug 1853	11 Aug 1853	PDD
Wymer, Martha E.	Davis, Thomas	20 Oct 1857	16 Oct 1857	PSOT
Yeager, Fanny L.	Johnson, Isaac	05 Mar 1864	26 Feb 1864	PTIMES
Yeamons, Elisa Ann	Ashton, Joseph	07 May 1855	30 Apr 1855	DET
Yearning, Sarah	Jelly, Charles	01 May 1854	24 Apr 1854	DET
Yeates, or Lates, Adelaide	Chang (see also, Bunker)	05 May 1843	13 Apr 1843	TRIB
Yeates, or Lates, Sarah	Eng (see also, Bunker)	05 May 1843	13 Apr 1843	TRIB
Yemens, Susannah	Jones, William W.	03 Oct 1850	01 Oct 1850	PT&C
Yemens, Susannah	Jones, William W.	07 Oct 1850	01 Oct 1850	PI
Young, Eliza	Virgin, Kinsey	18 Mar 1831	13 Mar 1831	PC&WT
Young, Eliza E.	Glidden, J.M.	16 Feb 1844	06 Feb 1844	TRIB
Young, Fanny Belle	Jones, E. Glover	03 May 1844	15 Apr 1844	TRIB

*Listed under DIED by mistake in the paper.

Appendix A
Newspaper Repositories

The following citations representing newspapers researched for Portsmouth, Scioto County, Ohio, are located in 1) The Ohio Historical Society Library Archives (OHS), in Columbus, Ohio; 2) The Ohio University Library (OU); and 3) The Portsmouth Public Library (PPL).

In the table below, the abbreviations used to identify papers researched for this book follow the title of the paper under which it is filed in the libraries. The location and/or roll numbers are listed for convenience in requesting the roll or bound copies while visiting the library. In some cases, the name of the paper changed during the course of ownership without a break in publication. As a result, a paper with one name could be filed with that of a different name. Such information is provided in "hints" that are included in parentheses after the location information in the following table.

The information provided below is accurate for the time period that research was conducted for this index. However, changes may occur if the libraries add to their collections or make more microfilmed copies available. It is always a good idea to check with the libraries for current listings.

Library Titles (Actual Newspaper Abbreviations)	Dates	Repository	Location/Roll No.
Clipper (CLIPPER)	02 Sep 1845 - 04 May 1847	OHS	22697
Courier (PC, PC&WT)	01 Jan 1831 - 18 Sep 1833	OHS	Vault
Courier (PC)	21 Mar 1832 - 23 Aug 1836	OHS	Vault
Courier (PC)	02 Jul 1836 - 23 Aug 1836	OHS	Vault
Daily Evening Tribune (DET)	Jun 1853 - Feb 1856, Apr 1857 - Nov 1860	OHS	B4171-4176
Daily Evening Tribune (DET)	07 Jun 1853 - 12 Apr 1860 Apr 1859 - 12 Apr 1860	OU	"Evening Tribune"
Democrat (PDEM)	03 Jul 1844 - 22 Oct 1844	OHS	22697
Democratic Enquirer (DENQ)	06 Apr 1848 - 27 Mar 1849	OHS	39819
Dispatch (PDD)	28 Dec 1852 - 01 Jan 1853	OHS	N129 Vol. 4a
Dispatch (PDD)	26 Apr 1853 - 28 Nov 1853	OHS	N129 Vol. 4
Dispatch (PDD)	29 Nov 1853 - 31 May 1854	OHS	N129 Vol. 5
Dispatch (PDD)	01 Jun 1854 - 14 Nov 1854	OHS	N129 Vol. 6

Library Titles (Actual Newspaper Abbreviations)	Dates	Repository	Location/Roll No.
Gazette & Lawrence Advertiser (PGLA)	05 Nov 1824 - 02 Dec 1825	OHS	21715
Gazette (PG&LA)	30 Jul 1824 - 28 Oct 1825	OHS	Vault
Gazette (PG&LA)	05 Nov 1824 - 02 Dec 1825	OHS	Vault
Gazette (PGAZ)	05 Nov 1824 - 02 Dec 1825	OHS	21715
Gazette (PGAZ)	05 Aug 1818 - 17 Mar 1819	OHS	Vault
Inquirer (PI)	Apr 1850 - Mar 1853, Dec 1854 - Jul 1855	OHS	B29925
Inquirer (PI)	08 Apr 1850 - 01 Apr 1853, 01 Dec 1854 - 13 Jul 1855	OHS	39670
Ohio Pennant (OP)	24 Aug 1855 - 13 Jan 1856	OHS	39819
Portsmouth Evening Tribune (DET)	07 Jun 1853 - 22 Oct 1853 03 Nov 1853 - 24 Jul 1854 25 Jul 1854 - 01 Sep 1854 15 Sep 1854 - 22 May 1855 07 Jun 1855 - 10 Sep 1855 11 Sep 1855 - 06 Mar 1856 21 Apr 1857 - 07 Aug 1857 15 Sep 1857 - 02 Jan 1858 04 Jan 1858 - 19 Feb 1859 21 Feb 1859 - 12 Apr 1860 13 Apr 1860 - 10 Nov 1860	PPL	"Portsmouth Evening Tribune"
Portsmouth Inquirer (PI)	08 Apr 1850 - 01 Apr 1853 01 Dec 1854 - 13 Jul 1855	PPL	"Portsmouth Inquirer"
Portsmouth Times (PTIMES)	28 Sep 1858 - 30 Jun 1860 23 Nov 1861 - 30 Sep 1865	PPL	"Portsmouth Times"
Portsmouth Times (PTIMES)	28 Sep 1858 - 26 Dec 1914	OU	"Portsmouth Times"
Scioto Telegraph (STEL)	04 Mar 1820 - 01 Sep 1821	OHS	Vault
Scioto Tribune (TRIB)	02 Aug 1839 - 09 Aug 1839	OHS	Vault (see next entry)
Scioto Tribune (STRIB, TRIB)	06 Jan 1837 - 18 Dec 1838, 02-09 Aug 1839	OHS	Vault (hint: filed with Portsmouth Courier)
Scioto Valley Post (SVPOST)	09 Jun 1840 - 24 Oct 1843	OHS	39811
Scioto Valley Republican (SVREP)	07 Jan 1854 - 19 Apr 1854, 05 Nov 1858, 14 Jan 1860, 02 Apr 1864 - 16 Apr 1864	OHS	22697
Spirit of the Times (PSOT)	06 Jan 1857 - 04 May 1858	OHS	N297 Vol. 4
Temporary Advertiser (TA)	24 Feb 1826 - 06 Apr 1826	OHS	Vault (hint: filed with The Western Times)
The Union and The Times	28 Jul 1860 - 09 Mar 1861	PPL	"The Union & The Times"
Times (PTIMES)	11 May 1858 - 28 Dec 1858	OHS	N297 Vol. 4a
Times (PTIMES)	04 Jan 1859 - 30 Jun 1860	OHS	N297 Vol. 5
Times (PTIMES)	25 Jul 1863 - 08 Jun 1867	OHS	N297 Vol. 9
Tribune (PT&C)	28 Feb 1850 - 03 Mar 1852	OHS	N287 Vol. 28
Tribune (PT&C)	10 Mar 1852 - 15 Dec 1853	OHS	N287 Vol. 29
Tribune (DET)	14 Aug 1853 - 31 May 1854	OHS	N287 Vol. 30
Tribune (DET)	01 Jun 1854 - 26 Sep 1854	OHS	N287 Vol. 31

Library Titles (Actual Newspaper Abbreviations)	Dates	Repository	Location/Roll No.
Tribune (DET)	01 Jun 1854 - 26 Sep 1854	OHS	N287 Vol. 31
Tribune (DET)	27 Sep 1854 - 28 Feb 1855	OHS	N287 Vol. 32
Tribune (DET)	01 Mar 1855 - 29 Oct 1855	OHS	N287 Vol. 33
Tribune (TRIB)	17 Sep 1841 - 17 Sep 1841	OHS	N287 Vol. 14
Tribune (TRIB)	24 Mar 1843 - 25 Jun 1846	OHS	N287 Vol. 14a
Tribune (TRIB)	20 Jan 1843 - 09 Jan 1845	OHS	N287 Vol. 15
Tribune (WPT)	14 Nov 1855 - 03 Dec 1856	OHS	N287 Vol. 34
Tribune (WPT)	10 Dec 1856 - 29 Dec 1858	OHS	N287 Vol. 35
Tribune (WPT)	19 Jan 1859 - 26 Dec 1860	OHS	N287 Vol. 36
Tribune and Clipper (PT&C)	20 Dec 1849	OHS	22697
Western Times (WT)	Jul 1826 - Dec 1827	OHS	B13759
Western Times (WT)	29 Jun 1826 - 13 Dec 1827	OU	"Western Times"
Western Times (WT)	29 Jun 1826 - 13 Dec 1827	PPL	"Western Times"
Western Times (WT)	18 Apr 1826 - 11 Nov 1830	OHS	Vault

MARRIED.—In South Carolina on the first inst., Mr. Stephen Lyon and Miss Rebecca Lamb.

The happy time at length's arrived.
In scripture day foretold,
When Lamb and Lyon both unite,
Embrace and keep one fold.
Now Join'd in matrimonial tether,
The Lamb and Lyon lie together,
And at the appointed time in troth,
"A little child shall lead them both."

—Daily Evening Tribune
24 Feb 1855

Appendix B
Community Name Changes

The following table, although not totally inclusive, represents many of the name changes that occurred to Scioto County, Ohio, towns, communities, and post office addresses. (NLE = Community name no longer exists on current maps.)

Former Name	Current Name and Location
Abashai	NLE. N. of Sciotoville
Alexandria	NLE. Washington Twp. w. of old mouth of the Scioto River, near present-day Carey's Run.
Andre	NLE. Andre Station, Lyra
Basham	NLE. W. of Sciotoville along Ohio River.
Bertha	West Portsmouth
Bloom Furnace	NLE. Bloom Twp., s.e. of S. Webster.
Bloom Switch	NLE. Bloom Twp. e. of S. Webster.
Bloomfield	South Webster
Bradford	Friendship area
Brookside	NLE. Union Twp. near Arion.
Burrsburg	Haverhill
Camp Eureka	NLE. Rush Twp., along SR104 n. of SR 73.
Chaffins Mill	Lyra
Concord	Wheelersburg
Cooney	NLE. S. of Vernon Twp., s. of Lyra.
Crawford	NLE. S. of Lyra in Vernon Twp.
Crone	NLE. S.E. of Lucasville.
Diffen	NLE. Jefferson Twp., intersection of Flatwood-Fallen Timber and Miller's Run-Fallen Timber Roads.
Edmunds	Frederick
Edwardsville	Sciotoville
Feurt's Flats	Lombardsville
Freeman	Otway
Freestone	Buena Vista

Former Name	Current Name and Location
French	NLE. Rush Twp., crossroads of SR 73 and Pond Creek Road.
Galena	Rarden
Gervais	NLE. S. of Franklin Furnace.
Harrisonville	Minford
Henly	NLE. Washington Twp.
Holmesville	NLE. E. of Bloom Twp.
Iron Furnace	South Webster
Lois	N.W. of Wallace Mills
Lower Delaware Town	NLE. E. of Scioto River near Portsmouth.
Lower Shawnee Town	NLE. See Alexandria.
Madland	NLE. Bloom Twp., s.e. of S. Webster.
Massie	NLE. Madison Twp. near Warren Hill Road and George Allen Road.
Moccasin	Rarden
Moss Mills	West Portsmouth
Myrtle	NLE. Madison Twp.
Nairn	NLE. Madison Twp.
Nauvoo	West Portsmouth
Old Lower Town	NLE. See Alexandria.
Pink	NLE. Brush Creek Twp., SR125 and Rocky Fork Road.
Pioneer Station	Hales Creek
Purdy Corner	Muletown
Ryon	NLE. Madison Twp., s.w. of Massie.
Stony Hill	Lombardsville
Stringtown	NLE. Valley Twp., Pike County border.
Tempervale	NLE. Nile or Washington Twp. n. of former Alexandria.
Twin Oaks Mills	NLE. Porter Twp., s. of Wheelersburg.
Union Mills	West Portsmouth
Vera	NLE. Clay Twp., area of Rosemount.
Waits Station	Slocum
Webster	South Webster
Wharton	NLE. N.E. Washington Twp.
Wyandot Town	NLE. Location unknown. Former Native American village.
Yno	NLE. Jefferson Twp. on Miller's Run-Fallen Timber Road.

Bibliography

American Heritage Dictionary, 3rd ed., s.v. "Gretna Green."

Bullock, Edward I., James M. Nesbitt, and George W. Craddock, compilers. *The General Statutes of Kentucky*, 1883. Frankfort: Major, Johnston & Barrett, 1883.

Chase, Salmon P., editor. *The Statutes of Ohio and of the Northwestern Territory, from 1788 to 1833 inclusive*. Cincinnati: Corey & Fairbank, 1883.

Deming, Sister Mary Caritas, "Portsmouth, Ohio: The First Hundred Years of its Economic Development, 1800-1900." Master's thesis, Catholic University of America, 1952. Ohio Historical Society Archives.

Downs, Randolph Chandler. *Evolution of Ohio County Boundaries*. Reprint. Columbus, Ohio: Ohio Historical Society. 1970.

Encyclopaedia Britannica, 15th ed., s.v. "Gretna Green."

Evans, Nelson W. *A History of Scioto County, Ohio, together with a Pioneer Record of Southern Ohio*. Portsmouth, Ohio: 1903.

Getty Thesaurus of Geographic Names (TGN) [online]. Los Angeles (Calif.): Getty Information Institute, 1997- [cited 11 December 1998]. Available from World Wide Web <http://www.ahip.getty.edu/tgn_browser/index.html>.

Hansen, James L. Research in Newspapers. Chap. 12 in *The Source: A Guidebook of American Genealogy*, edited by Loretto Dennis Szucs and Sandra Hargreaves Luebking. Revised. ed. Salt Lake City, Utah: Ancestry Incorporated. 1997.

Littell, William., compiler. *The Statute Law of Kentucky*, 1814. Frankfort: William Hunter, 1814.

Scioto County Department of Engineering. n.d. *Scioto County in Facts and Figures*. 4th ed. By Harlan Danner. Portsmouth, Ohio.

Shamhart, Carl, and Elizabeth Shamhart. *History of Scioto County Post Offices 1805-1991*. Portsmouth, Ohio. Originally published as a series in the *Scioto Voice* newspaper (1996). Portsmouth Public Library.

Swan, Joseph R., collator. *Revised Statutes of the State of Ohio, of a General Nature, in Force 1 August 1860*. Cincinnati: Robert Clarke & Co., 1870.

Sword, Elmer Bernard. *The Story of Portsmouth, Ohio*. Sesquicentennial ed. Portsmouth, Ohio: 1965.

Vastine, Roy E. *Scioto, A County History.* Portsmouth, Ohio: 1986.

Wilson, Bernice, and W. Waltrip *Ohio Cities & Towns, Including Defunct Locations* [online]. Place of publication unknown: OHGenWeb, 1998- [cited 11 December 1998]. Available from World Wide Web <http://www.rootsweb.com/~ohdefunc/index.html>.

World Book Encylopedia. 1960. s.v. "Gretna Green."

Index

Ballou, Ruth 18
Bankin, Alfred Giles 18
Banks (see Grieve, Hanna) 53
Banks, Joseph 120, 163
Banks, Louisa 121, 158
Bannister, Byron L. 120, 171
Bannon, Edward 18
Bannon, Hugh 18
Barbee, Cornelius H. 120, 159
Barbee, Elias 120, 165
Barbee, Joseph 18
Barbee, Mary E. 18
Barbee, Sarah 132, 158
Barbee, Wesley 120, 158
Barber, Catharine 18
Barber, Jane 144, 158
Barber, Louisa 143, 158
Barber, Wm. E. 120, 163
Barbour, male 18
Bard, Margaret Ann 18
Barker, John 18
Barker, Joseph (Judge) 18
Barker, Mary E. 130, 158
Barklow, Penelope 149, 158
Barlow, unknown 18
Barnard, Robert 18
Barnard, Wm. 18
Barnes (see Martin, Sarah) 72
Barnes, female 18
Barnes, male 18
Barnes, Wm. (Major General) 18
Barnett, Andrew H. 120, 159
Barnett, Maria 136, 158
Barnham, female 18
Barns, Gasper 18
Barnum, unknown 18
Barr, Andrew 120, 176
Barr, female 18
Barr, George Griswold 18
Barr, John 18
Barr, Jos. C. 120, 170
Barr, Joseph C. 120, 170
Barr, Oliver 18
Barr, William 18
Barr, Wm. H. 120, 165
Barrett, Henry, Jr. 120, 168
Barrett, Lyman 19
Barrick, Henry 120, 166
Barron, Edward (Rev.) 19
Barsdale, female 19
Bartlett, Josiah (Dr.) 19
Bartlett, M.R. 120, 177
Bartlett, Madison M. 120, 170
Bartley (see Thomson, female) 105
Barton, Charles A. 120, 177
Barton, F. 19
Barton, female 19
Barton, John 19

Barton, Willim (Maj.) 19
Basey, John 120, 192
Basham, Augustus 19
Basham, Ellen 149, 158
Bass, B. 19
Bass, Wm. 19
Bassett, Thos. 19
Bateham, M.B. 120, 164
Bateman, Clementious 120, 165
Bates, Wm. H. 19
Batlow, female 19
Batterson, Addison 19, 120, 121, 181, 187
Baty, L.T. 121, 175
Bayhan, Benjamin F. 121, 188
Bayles, Jehn (Private) 19
Baylor, Elizabeth L. 156, 158
Baymiller, Mary A. 19
Bays, Wm. 19
Beach, D. 19
Beach, Walter H. 19
Beall, female 19
Beall, Reasin (Gen.) 19
Beals, Asa G. 121, 159
Beaman, male 19
Bean, Maggie 151, 158
Bean, William 121, 170
Bear, Jennie 19
Beasley, James 19
Beatty, Samuel 19
Beaty, unknown 19
Beatzhausen, Christian 121, 159
Beaver, unknown 19
Beck, Anna 19
Beck, George 121, 177
Beck, L.C. (Prof.) 19
Becket, J. 121, 162
Beckman, Fountain 19
Beebe, C.F. 19
Beebe, Cyrus F. (Officer) 19
Beecher, Agnes 119, 158
Beecher, George (Rev.) 19
Beecher, male (twin) 19
Beerman, Louis 121, 182
Beery, Nicholas 19
Beeson, Martha S. 19
Beggs, James 19
Behmind, George 121, 184
Behrens, John 19
Belica Anestatio 139, 158
Belica, Anestatiio 139, 158
Belknap, Daniel 19
Belknap, female 19
Bell (see Newton, Nancy G.) 83
Bell, Agatha Eustace 129, 158
Bell, Isaac 19
Bell, John L. 20
Bell, Lucy M. 125, 158
Bell, male 20

Bleaks, Sarah 135, 159
Blennernassett, Herman 21
Blentlinger, Andrew J. 21
Blessing, John R. (Maj.) 21
Bligger, Stephen 21
Blinn, male 21
Blinn, Nettie 132, 159
Bliss, Esther 21
Bliss, Hannah 122, 159
Bliss, Jonathan 121, 166
Blocksom, William (Judge) 21
Blynn, female 21
Boal, William K. 121, 191
Bocker, John 22
Bockwalter (see Parker, Elizabeth D.) 85
Bockwalter, Elizabeth D. 144, 159
Bodkin, James 121, 163
Bodman, unknown 22
Boechner, Phillpena 121, 159
Bofey, Daniel 121, 176
Boggs, Andrew 22
Boile, Henry 121, 163
Boker, John G. 22
Boldman, John 121, 170
Bolinger, Andrew 22
Bolinger, Jacob 122, 159
Bolinger, Michael 22
Bond (see McBrayer, female) 73
Bond, James 22
Bond, William Key 22
Bonnear, Charles 22
Bonnell, male 22
Bonnell, unknown 22
Bonner, Minerva 146, 159
Bonsall, Joseph 22
Bonsall, Laura A. 147, 159
Bonsall, S.N. (Capt.-A.Q.M.) 22
Bonser 151, 159
Bonser (see Munn, Mariah)) 146
Bonser, Elinor 151, 159
Bonser, Isaac 122, 173
Bonser, Jacob 22
Books, Samuel H. 122, 179
Bookwalter, Addison 122, 185
Bookwalter, Elizabeth D. 144, 159
Bookwalter, Henry 22
Bookwalter, J.N. 122, 182
Boon, Daniel 22
Boone, Daniel 22
Booth, J.B. 22
Booth, John Wilkes 22
Booth, Levi 122, 167
Boothe, Thos. G. 22
Bordlleau, G.D. 122, 159
Borick 22
Borick, Henry 22
Borland, Anna 122, 159
Born, Victor 122, 170

Boroff, Daniel 122, 167
Bosanpagh, Michael 122, 186
Bosanpazk, Michael 122, 186
Bossier, male 22
Boston, Catharine 22
Bostwick, Charles 22
Boswell, John L. 22
Bothel Loammi (Priv.) 22
Boughner, V.E. 122, 180
Bourbon, James 22
Bourne, unknown 22
Bourshaw, Victor 122, 176
Boursholt, Lewis 22
Bouts, George 22
Bovey, George C. 122, 185
Bowden, G.F. (Rev.) 22
Bowen, female 22
Bowen, male 22
Bowen, unknown 22
Bowers, Martha Jane 155, 159
Bowles, male 22
Bowley, Hulda 120, 159
Bowman, Eliza Jane 120, 159
Bowman, Geo. 22
Bowman, George 22
Bowman, Mary C. 129, 159
Bowman, Rosan 22
Bowman, Ruth 22
Boyd, A.A. 124, 159
Boyd, Elizabeth 137, 159
Boyd, female 22
Boyd, G.W. 122, 188
Boyd, John L. 22
Boyd, Lynn 22
Boyd, M. 132, 159
Boyd, male 23
Boyd, Mary Jane 139, 159
Boyd, William M. 122, 162
Boyer, Alexander 23
Boyer, Thos. D. 122, 159
Boylston, John 122, 186
Boynton, Asa, Jr. 122, 161
Boynton, Lucy 155, 159
Boynton, Mary E. 132, 159
Boynton, Sumner 122, 167
Bradbury, George W.(Lieut.Col.) 122, 194
Bradbury, Nancy 129, 159
Bradfield, Wm. 23
Bradford, C.W. 23
Bradford, Elizabeth 147, 159
Bradford, Mary E. 142, 160
Bradford, Samuel C. 122, 193
Bradford, Wilhemna 151, 160
Bradly, female 23
Bradly, James 23
Bradly, William 122, 160
Brady, female 23
Brady, James 23

Brown, Walter L. (Corp.) 25
Brown, William 25
Brown, William H. 25
Brown,Lewis 24
Browne, L.M. 25
Brownell, A.W. 123, 167
Browning, Arthur 25
Browning, William 25
Brubaker, John D. 123, 187
Brumfield, Bird F. 123, 171
Brunel, Isambard Kingdom 25
Bruner, Lucinda 149, 160
Bruner, Mary Emma 130, 160
Bruner, Samuel 25
Brunner, Anna Lucy 25
Brunner, Frederick 25
Brunner, Maria 151, 160
Brunner, Melinda 25
Brunson, male 25
Bryan, Henry C. 25
Bryan, John L. 25
Bryson, male 25
Bryson, Mary 153, 160
Buchanan (see Pottenger, Mary) 88
Buchanan, (Dr.) 25
Buchanan, Alexander 25
Buchanan, Elizabeth (nee Belt) 25
Buchanan, John 25
Buchanan, Margaret B. 25
Buchanan, Thomas J. (Esq.) 25
Buck, D. 25
Buck, James 123, 187
Buckley, Mary F. 150, 160
Buckley, Samuel 123, 170
Bucknick, male 25
Buel, A.J. 123, 164
Buffington, Cornelia Ann 123, 160
Buhoup, Sarah 25
Bulkingen, Michael 25
Bullinger, male 25
Bunch, F.M. (Dr.) 25
Bundrant, male 25
Bunker (see Chang) 124
Bunker, Chang (siamese twin) 123, 175
Bunker, Eng (siamese twin) 123, 175
Bunkry (Capt.) (see Johnson, Joseph) 62
Bunn, J. Harvey 123, 161
Burch, female 25
Burdick, Phoebe 144, 160
Burgess, James 25
Burgos, Luis (Joaquin) 25
Burk, Ann Marie 26
Burk, Elisa 130, 160
Burke, John 26
Burke, Joseph M. 123, 161
Burke, Lizzie 152, 160
Burke, male 26
Burke, Martha H. 133, 160

Burke, Robert 26
Burke, Wm. 26
Burks, Wm. 123, 187
Burnet, Jacob (Judge) 26
Burnet, Judge 26
Burnet, Robert (Maj.) 26
Burnett, Emily M. 26
Burns, Arthur 26
Burns, Charles Raymond 26
Burns, female 26
Burns, Robert 26
Burns, unknown 26
Burr (see Ufford, Catharine) 108
Burr, Anna Howard 26
Burr, Mollie 137, 160
Burriss, Hettie A. 132, 160
Burt, Alice 26
Burt, Amanda 124, 160
Burt, Charles E. 123, 163
Burt, Eliza 124, 160
Burt, Elizabeth 155, 161
Burt, Francis 26
Burt, Francis (Gov.) 26
Burt, Julia 150, 161
Burt, Thomas 123, 160
Burt, Thomas T. 123, 183
Burton, female 26
Burton, Mandana 122, 161
Burtwell, James (Col.) 26
Busey, John P. 26
Bush, Llewellyn 26
Bush, Seth R. 123, 191
Buskirk, Charles Tracy 26
Busler, Solomon 123, 170
Bussey, Demsey 26
Butaff, Augustus 26
Butler, female 26
Butler, Julia A. 139, 161
Butler, M. 123, 182
Butler, unknown 26
Butler, unknown (Lieut.) 26
Butler, William A. (Esq.) 26
Butler, Wm. (Col.) 26
Butler, Wm. H. (Barney) 26
Butler, Wm. H.G. (Prof.) 26
Butt, Eliza 26
Butt, John 123, 193
Butterfield, John 123, 183
Byers, Elizabeth R. 26
Byers, Hannah 139, 161
Byers, James E. 26
Bynum, Junius A. 26
Byrne, Luke 26
Byrnes, Robert 26
Byron, John 123, 163

C

Cabel, Samuel 27
Cable, Jonathan 123, 183
Cable, Martha 27
Cable, Melissa 138, 161
Cable, Sarah Ann 152, 161
Cade, Harriet (nee Sage) 133, 161
Cadot, Madeline 122, 161
Cady, John M. 123, 192
Caflin, male 27
Cahill, Wm. 27
Cain, Daniel 27
Cain, John 123, 179
Calaen, Sophia 128, 161
Calb, Madaline 27
Caldwell, Charles (Prof.) 27
Caldwell, Hugh (Capt.) 27
Caldwell, Jacob (Capt.) 27
Caldwell, James D. 27
Caldwell, John 27
Calf, Eliza 142, 161
Calhoun, John 27
Calhoun, male 27
Calhoun, unknown 27
Calihan, India 143, 161
Call, Harriet E. 136, 161
Call, Malvina 140, 161
Call, Martha 125, 161
Callaway, John W. 27
Callaway, male 27
Callihan (or Gallihan), Daniel 123, 171
Calloway, female 27
Calvert, Frank W. 123, 157
Calvert, George 123, 184
Camden, female 27
Camden, Margaret A. 27
Camden, Nanny E. 27
Camden, W.P. 123, 160
Camden, William P. 27
Cameon, William 27
Cameron, Daniel 27
Cameron, Nancy 136, 161
Camerone, Robert 27
Camp, James M. 27
Campbell, Emeline 27
Campbell, female 27
Campbell, Geo. 27
Campbell, George 27
Campbell, Hugh 27
Campbell, J.W. (Dr.) 27
Campbell, James 27
Campbell, James M. 27
Campbell, Joseph 27
Campbell, Lancelot 124, 182
Campbell, Lebens 27
Campbell, male 27
Campbell, Robert 27
Campbell, unknown 28

Campbell, unknown (Capt.) 28
Campbill, Darius S. 28
Campcell, M.W. 28
Campfield, David 28
Cane, Aquilla 124, 166
Canfield, Augustus (Capt.) 28
Canfield, Horace 28
Canfield, unknown 28
Canfield, unknown (Capt.) 28
Cann, Arthur 124, 174
Cannon, Dennis 28
Canter, Levi 28
Canter, Milton 124, 194
Canter, Sarah 148, 161
Canter, William 28
Canterbury, John 124, 165
Caperton, Woods 28
Caps, Casper 124, 174
Car_l, Frank, Jr. 124, 167
Carawan (or Caraman), Geo. W. 28
Carel, Joseph 28
Carel, Madeline 143, 161
Carel, Sarah 28
Carey, Archibald (Esq.) 28
Carlisle (see Eckhart, Eleanor Ann) 42
Carmine, David C. 28
Carmine, Tuman M. 28
Carnahan, James 124, 173
Carner, A.W. (Capt.) 124, 175
Carnes, Isabel M. 124, 161
Carnes, Nancy 132, 161
Carpenter, male 28
Carr, Benton 28
Carr, Cornelius 124, 183
Carr, E.W. 28
Carre, William J. 28
Carrick (see Backus, Isabella Graham) 17
Carrico, Thomas 28
Carrigan, male 28
Carroll, Alexius 124, 160
Carroll, John 124, 164
Carroll, male 28
Carroll, Wm. (Hon.)(ex-Gov./Tenn.) 28
Carskadon, John 28
Carter, Francis M. 28
Carter, Joseph 28
Carter, Lucy E. 129, 161
Carter, Mary 123, 161
Carter, Rebecca 155, 161
Carter, Richard 28
Carter, William S. 124, 159
Carthick, A. (Rev.) 124, 191
Cartner, female 28
Cartner, John 28
Cartner, unknown 28
Cartwright, Eliza Jane 129, 161
Cartwright, Hannah 154, 161
Carty, unknown 28

Cummings, Joseph D. 127, 193
Cummings, Mary G. 154, 164
Cummings, Rebecca 35
Cummings, Thomas B. 127, 170
Cummings, unknown 35
Cummins, George 35
Cummins, S.P. (Rev.) 4
Cumpson, Newton 127, 174
Cunning, Samuel W. 127, 186
Cunningham, E.L. 36
Cunningham, Hester 138, 164
Cunningham, James 36
Cuppet, Nancy 141, 164
Curles, Wm. L. 36
Curran, Hannah 36
Currie, female 36
Currie, Maggie A. 144, 164
Currie, Mary 131, 164
Currie, Samuel A. (Capt.) 36
Curry, Otway 36
Curtis, (see Darst, female) 37
Curtis, Caroline 36
Curtis, W.B. 36
Curtiss, L.G. 36
Curvis, Caroline 36
Cushing, Charlotte 148, 164
Cushing, Josephine (Cowles) 120, 164
Cushing, Luther C. 36
Cushing, William V.H. 36
Cushman, Diodate 36
Custis, John 127, 187
Cutler, Caroline 152, 164
Cutler, Ephraim (Judge) 36
Cutler, Ephram 36
Cutler, Fanny 124, 164
Cutler, Henry M. 36
Cutler, Jonathan B. 36
Cutler, Laura Jane 36
Cutler, Lydia Ann 36
Cutler, Lyman 36
Cutler, Lyman D. 127, 170
Cutler, Martha H. 126, 164
Cutler, Pliny 127, 183
Cutler, Rhoda B. 36
Cutler, Rusina D. 36
Cutler, Samuel N. 127, 184
Cutler, W.S. (Lieut.) 127, 168
Cutshall, Elizabeth 130, 164
Cutshaw, John 127, 166
Cutsmeyer, M. 124, 164
Cypress, Catherine 36
Cysley, Mary J. 36

D

Dabney, S.W. 127, 192
Dahrley, John 36
Dailey, unknown 36

Daily (see Workman, Mary A.) 115
Dalabre, Michael 127, 191
Dalabree, Michael 127, 191
Dallam, unknown (Major) 36
Dallas, Alexander J. (Commander) 36
Dallas, George M. (ex-V.President) 36
Dalton (see Stewart, Mildred E.) 102
Dalton, William 36
Damarin, Charles A.M. 36
Damarin, female 36
Damarin, Lewis C. 127, 161
Damarin, Louis Augustus 36
Damarin, Pauline 36
Damarin, Pauline Hariette M. 36
Damarin, William Virgie 36
Dan, Samuel 36
Dana, John (Dr.) 37
Dandridge, Nathaniel 37
Daniels, Editha K. 147, 164
Daniels, S.H. 127, 175
Daniels, S.W. 127, 165
Daniels, William 37
Dann (or Dunn), I.T. 37
Danon, Emanuel 37
Darbor, William D. 37
Darby, Sanders 37
Dare, Henry 127, 163
Daring, Elizabeth 131, 164
Darlington, Joseph (Gen) 37
Darlinton, Mary B. 132, 164
Darst, female 37
Darst, Jacob 37
Daugherty, John James 37
Daugherty, S.D. 147, 164
Daughters, James 37
Davenport, Whitle 127, 160
Davey, Alfred Ingalls 37
Davey, Florence 137, 164
Davey, Louisa 151, 164
Davey, P. 127, 191
Davey, Phillippa 143, 164
Davey, Susan 123, 164
David, B. 37
Davidson, Alfred D. 127, 188
Davidson, Morris W. 37
Davidson, Nancy 37
Davidson, Sallie M. 147, 164
Davies, R. 37
Davies, Sam W. (Col.) 37
Davies, Thomas E. 37
Davis (see Hamilton, Genevieve) 55
Davis, A. 37
Davis, Alexander W. 127, 170
Davis, Amelia 37
Davis, Annice B. 153, 164
Davis, Arthur 127, 175
Davis, Arthur C. 37
Davis, Charles 37

Dillon, John 39
Dillon, Mary 39
Dillon, Missouri Alice 39
Dimmock, D.W. 39
Dimner, Elizabeth 150, 165
Dinton, female 39
Disney, Sallie 141, 165
Diver, Joseph A. 39
Divis, B.S. 39
Dixon, Clarissa 135, 165
Dixon, Clarrissa 135, 165
Dixon, Mary 126, 165
Dixon, Meredith 39
Dixon, Minerva 143, 165
Dixon, Nancy 124, 165
Doane, Catharine W. 39
Doane, Charles Edward 39
Doane, female 39
Doane, George Washington (D.D.L.L.D.) 39
Dobbins, John W. 39
Dobbs, Matilda 121, 165
Dobyn, male 39
Dobyns, Luther 39
Dobyns, Mary 39
Doddridge, B.Z.B. 128, 178
Doddridge, Ella Virginia 137, 165
Doddridge, Ellen S. 39
Doddridge, Henry C. 128, 170
Doddridge, Julian B. 39
Doddridge, Juliana 40
Doddridge, Phillip B. (Capt.) 40
Dodds, Martha A. 142, 165
Dodds, T.B. 40
Dodge, Ellen 40
Dodge, male 40
Dodson, Julianna 131, 165
Doggett, Walker W. 128, 182
Dois, Fred (Lt.) 40
Dole, Almira T. 144, 165
Dole, Edward P. 128, 177
Dole, Elizabeth Emily 40
Dole, John 128, 171
Dole, Lavina 141, 165
Dole, Samuel 40, 128, 171
Doley, unknown 40
Donahoe, John 40
Donahoe, Samuel Wilson 40
Donaldson, Israel 40
Donelly, Robert 40
Donelly, Thos. 40
Donley, Dan 40
Donley, Izaih 128, 161
Donnavan, Gilbert 40
Donne, Charles 40
Donohey, John 40
Donohoo, Peter 128, 173
Donovan, Timothy 40
Door, male 40

Dopp, Jacob 40
Doran, Jno. 40
Doras, James 40
Dorch, Eliza 151, 165
Dorch, John 128, 170, 174
Dorer, unknown 40
Dorman, Mary E. 141, 165
Dorman, Rufus 40
Dorne, unknown 40
Dorr, female 40
Dorr, male 40
Dorr, Thomas W. 40
Dorries, unknown (Lieut.) 40
Dorril, Eliza 126, 165
Dortch, Rebecca 156, 166
Dott, Elizabeth 154, 166
Doty, Abner 40
Doty, Mary 154, 166
Doucett, male 40
Dougerty, Ann 127, 166
Dougherty, Charles 40
Dougherty, male 40
Douglas, James 128, 188
Douglas, John W. 40
Douglas, male 40
Douglas, Mary 40
Douglas, Samuel 128, 175
Douglas, W. (Lieut.) 40
Douglass, H.G. 128, 191
Douglass, Mary L. 150, 166
Douglass, Richard (Esq.) 40
Douglass, Thomas 41
Dowd, Philander W. 41
Dowdal, unknown (Capt.) 41
Dowling, Edward 41
Down, Isaac F. 128, 184
Downey, Eliza 41
Downey, J.D. 128, 171
Downey, Lake Erie 41
Downey, M. (Corporal) 41
Downey, Nathaniel 128, 165
Downing, William 41
Downs, J.F.J. 41
Downy, Lake Erie 41
Drake, Angeline 119, 166
Drake, Harriet 41
Drake, Paul P. 41
Drake, Paul P. (or B.) 41
Drake, Ruth Francenia 41
Drake, Samuel P. 128, 174
Drake, Thomas M. (Dr.) 41
Drake, unknown (Dr.) 41
Draper, William O. 128, 161
Dray, male 41
Drayer, male 41
Dresbach, David 41
Dresbach, Herr 128, 192
Drescher, Nancy 41

Elder, John S 129, 172
Elkins, male 43
Ellafield, unknown 43
Ellery, William 43
Ellington, James 43
Ellion, James H. 129, 186
Elliot, John A. 129, 168
Elliot, John Q. 129, 164
Elliott, John 43, 129, 168
Ellis, Anna 121, 166
Ellis, F.M. 43
Ellis, male 43
Ellis, Rachel 125, 166
Ellis, unknown 43
Ellis, unknown (Major) 43
Ellison, Felix 43
Ellison, George 43
Ellison, William 43
Ellison, Wm. A. 43
Ellston, Jonathan 43
Ely, D.L. (Dr.) 43
Ely, Sarah Wilson 44
Ely, Seneca W. 129, 158
Emery, Samuel (Rev.) 44
Emig, male 44
Emmens, John 129, 173
Emmens,John 129, 173
Emory, Elizabeth J. 127, 166
Emrich, Jacob 44
Endicott, Daniel 44
Eng (see also, Bunker) 129, 194
Engelbrecht, F.W. 44
Engelbrecht, L. 129, 157
Engelbrecht, Matilda 151, 166
England, J.H. 129, 160
England, Melvina 136, 166
Englebrecht, Charlotte Barbara 44
Englison, female 44
Englison, male 44
Ennis, Susan 44
Enochs, male 44
Enslow, Emily 122, 166
Enslow, Hannah A. 126, 166
Enslow, Mary 44
Enslow, Resin 44
Enslow, Revillo 129, 157
Enslow, Rezin 44
Ereeman (or Freeman), James 44
Estill, Eliphaz 44
Estill, unknown (Judge) 44
Estill, William 129, 187
Eustis, unk. (Brig. Gen.) 44
Eustis, William 44
Evaley, Mary 149, 166
Evans, D.R. (Rev.) 129, 166
Evans, David 44
Evans, Elijah 44
Evans, Evan 129, 161

Evans, Evan, Jr. 129, 162
Evans, female 44
Evans, James (Corp.) 44
Evans, John 44
Evans, male 44
Evans, Margaret E. 136, 167
Evans, Mary 44
Evans, unknown (Capt.) 44
Evans, William 44
Evens, William 129, 171
Everett, Edward 44
Everit, Septer 129, 175
Evridge, Sintha 125, 167
Ewing, Elmore 129, 167
Ewing, female 44
Ewing, James 129, 182
Ewing, Presley 44
Exline, Daniel 44

F

Fagan, Ann 44
Fairchild, Aaron 129, 174
Falls, Bellows 44
Fanning, male 44
Fanshaw, Daniel 45
Farden, Ella 45
Farden, James A. 129, 189
Farenbaugh, Cephas 45
Farley (or Furley), Sarah M. 148, 167
Farmer, Eliza 142, 167
Farmer, John W. 45
Farnandis, Martha B. 123, 167
Farney, Amanda 145, 146, 167
Farney, Malinda G. 133, 167
Farney, Mary 45
Farrand, Fannie R. 167
Farrand, Fanny R. 143, 167
Farrane Fannie R. 143, 167
Farrar, Nancy 45
Farrer, male 45
Farril, Edward 45
Farrington, J.W. 129, 181
Farrington, James 129, 161
Farrington, James W. 129, 181
Farrington, Jas. 129, 161
Farris, William 45
Farwell, O.K. 45
Fasgan, Ann 45
Fauble, George 129, 158
Faulkner, Eliza 135, 167
Faulkner, Neil 45
Faverty, Resin 129, 172
Faverty, Rezin 129, 162
Fawn, John 129, 176
Featherstone, female 145, 167
Fee, Mary E. 149, 167
Fee, Nancy 45

Haggerty, Patrick 54
Haines, Margaret 148, 170
Hale, Foster 54
Haley, female 54
Halfhill, Sarah 152, 170
Hall, Albert McFarland 54
Hall, Axy F. 127, 170
Hall, Cornelia 54
Hall, Cynthia 123, 170
Hall, Edwin 54
Hall, Faneuil 54
Hall, Faneuil 54
Hall, H.L. 132, 168
Hall, H.T. 132, 168 ·
Hall, J.A. 54
Hall, James 54
Hall, Joshua 54
Hall, male 54
Hall, Margaret Kinney 54
Hall, Nancy 125, 170
Hall, Nancy Dickson 54
Hall, O.J. (Dr.) 132, 159
Hall, O.V. 54
Hall, Thomas F.S. 132, 184
Hall, unknown 54
Hall, Vilena 54
Hall, Wm. 54
Hall, Wm. H. 132, 158
Haller, Christian 133, 159
Haller, Elizabeth 54
Haller, William A. 133, 183
Haller, Wm. A. 133, 183
Halley, Henry 54
Halsey, Fanny Dean 54
Halsey, S.W. 54
Halterman, John 54
Halterman, Mary 128, 170
Halton, A.B. 54
Ham, male 54
Hambibb, Hannah M. 122, 170
Hamblin, Isaac 54
Hamblin, Isaac, Sr. 55
Hamelton, Margaret 130, 170
Hamer, Thomas M. 55
Hamilton (see Davis, Genevieve Hamilton) 37
Hamilton (see Holly, female) 59
Hamilton, (see Dillon, Mary) 39
Hamilton, Currance Ann 138, 170
Hamilton, Currence Ann 121, 138, 170
Hamilton, Genevieve 55
Hamilton, J.A. 133, 185
Hamilton, J.K. 55
Hamilton, Rachel L. 128, 170, 171
Hamilton, Robert 133, 185
Hamilton, unknown 55
Hamilton, Wm. 55
Hamlin, Hannibal G. 133, 193
Hamlin, James G. (M.D.) 55

Hammer, Hiram 55
Hammill, Margaret 128, 171
Hammit, S. 55
Hammond (see Scott, Nancy) 96
Hammonds, Wyatt 133, 167
Hampson, Jno. 55
Hancok, Denis 55
Handle, Ann 5, 134, 171
Handley, female 55
Handy, B.S. 55
Hanel, Casper 55
Hanet, Mary 135
Haney, male 55
Hanna, Charles Edward 55
Hanna, female 55
Hanna, Harriet Maria 55
Hanna, Samuel 55
Hannah, Shadrach 55
Hannahs, R.S. 145, 171
Hannahs, Susannah 55
Hannet, Mary 135, 171
Hannkins, Mary Ann 151, 171
Hans, male 55
Haraden, John 55
Harbor, J. 55
Harcum, male 55
Hard, Bethuel W. 133, 160
Harden, Ann 125, 171
Hardin, Elizabeth 135, 171
Hardin, Sarah 129, 171
Hardwick, male 55
Hardy, Henrietta M. 131, 171
Hardy, Henry K. (Esq.) 133, 161
Hare, Eleanor 145, 146, 171
Harge, George 55
Harley, female 55
Harley, unknown 55
Harman, Henry 55
Harmon, John 55
Harmon, Mary J. 141, 171
Harness (see Yoakem, Catherine) 116
Harover, Milburn 55
Harper, John J. 133, 174
Harper, John L. (Capt.) 133, 157
Harper, Robert Goodloe (Gen.) 55
Harr, Thomas 55
Harrington, female 55
Harrington, Jonathan 55
Harrington, Solon 55
Harris, Elijah L. 55
Harris, Elisha W. 55
Harris, F.F. (Dr.) 55
Harris, female 55, 56
Harris, Prentice 56
Harris, Thomas L. (Hon.) 133, 191
Harrison (see Taylor, female) 104
Harrison, Elizabeth 133, 163
Harrison, Henry 56

Holmes, Melissa 123, 172
Holmes, W.R. 59
Holt, James 59
Holt, Jerusia Adaline 149, 172
Holt, Jerusia Adeline 149, 172
Holt, Margaret 120, 172
Hone, Rebecca 155, 172
Hood (see Birkhimer, Temperance) 21
Hood, Caroline 129, 172
Hood, Charles Francis 59
Hooft, A. 59
Hooper, Thomas W. 59
Hoover, Alaniah 134, 172
Hoover, Andrew Jackson Lewis 134, 190
Hoover, Garrett 59
Hopkins, George 59
Hopkins, J.W. 59
Hopkins, Joseph 134, 179
Hopkins, S.H. 59
Hore, Philip H. 134, 193
Horn, Jonathan 134, 187
Horse, George 134, 157
Horton, female 59
Horton, John 59
Horton, unknown 59, 60
Hosward, Claburn 134, 160
Hotman, Susan 146, 172
Hott, Alfred M. 134, 184
House, female 60
House, Louisa 131, 172
Housman, female 60
Housman, unknown 60
Houston, William C. 134, 165
Houtchins, Christopher 60
Hover, unknown 60
Hovey, Alfred 60
How, Susan 150, 172
Howard, Clarence S. 60
Howard, H.B. 60
Howard, Henry 60
Howard, Mary Adeline 133, 172
Howard, Tilghman A. (Hon.) 60
Howard, unknown (Col.) 60
Howe, Abel 60
Howe, Amanda 122, 172
Howe, Joseph 60
Howe, Minerva 150, 172
Howe, Pulaski 60
Howe, Rebecca M. 155, 172
Howell, A. 60
Howell, Hester 60
Howell, Sarah 125, 172
Howells, Seth (Rev.) 60
Howland, N.W. 148, 172
Howland, Sylvia Ann 60
Howland, Wm. 60
Hoy, C.W. 60
Hoy, Charles W., Esq. 134, 189

Hoylan, Robert 60
Hoyt, A.B. 60
Hoyt, Alfred M. 134, 184
Hubbard, C.D. 60
Hubbard, Stephen 134, 178
Hubbell, Wake 134, 193
Huckworth, Hester 140, 172
Huddleston, Cynthia Ann 125, 172
Huddleston, Nancy Maria 122, 173
Hudson, Mary Emma 60
Huff, Juliett 142, 173
Huffman, Joseph 60
Hughes, Amanda Pursell 60
Hughes, E.B. 134, 193
Hughes, Edward (Capt.) 134, 172
Hughes, Hannah 60
Hughes, Jacob B. 135, 188
Hughes, Joseph 60
Hughes, male 60
Hughes, Thomas 60
Hughes, Tom (Col.) 60
Hull (see Gill, Eliza) 50
Hull, Isaac (Commodore) 60
Hull, Jane 121, 173
Hull, Julius (Capt.) 135, 168
Hulps, Jemima 144, 173
Humph 135, 180
Humph, Allen 135, 180
Humphreys, Ellen 121, 173
Humphreys, George Ella 60
Humphries, G.W. 4
Humphries, G.W. (Sheriff) 135, 157
Humphries, James 135, 175
Hunsuck, Nathan 135, 160
Hunt, Nancy 141, 173
Hunt, Randall 135, 178
Huntemuler, H.F.D. 60
Hunter, Charles 60
Hunter, John 60
Huntington, Elijah (Esq.) 60
Huodersheldt, Phillip 135, 187
Hurd, John R. 60
Hurd, Juliaette B. 151, 173
Hurd, Mary 61
Hurdell, Wake 135
Hurlburt, Julia 121, 173
Hurley, John 61
Huskins, Emily J. 146, 173
Huston 144, 173
Huston, Andrew 61
Huston, Angelina 143, 173
Huston, Benj. Franklin 61
Huston, Cecilia Anna 125, 173
Huston, Giles 61
Huston, James L.O. 61
Huston, Mary 144, 173
Hutchins, unknown 61
Hutchins, Wells A. (Esq.) 135, 185

Kehoe, Caroline C. 64
Kehoe, Charles T. 165
Kehoe, Chas. T. 136
Kehoe, female 64
Kehoe, John 136, 191
Kehoe, M.E. 64
Kehrer, Caroline Sophia 64
Keiningham, unknown 64
Keiser (or Kriser), Martha 174
Keiser, Martha 144
Kellander, Wm. L. 136, 172
Keller, Thomas 64
Kelley (see Jaynes, Betsy Ann) 62
Kelley, Arena 155, 174
Kelley, female 64
Kelley, G.W. 64
Kelley, G.W. (aka Wash) 64
Kelley, George T. 64
Kelley, Harriet 64
Kelley, Henry 136, 161
Kelley, Isabella 121, 174
Kelley, James 64
Kelley, John 64
Kelley, Martha A. 153, 174
Kelley, Mary 133, 174
Kelley, Michael 64
Kelley, Thomas D. 136, 169
Kelley, unknown 64
Kelley, William S. 64
Kellogg, William W. 65
Kellough, Mary Jane 140, 174
Kelly, Alfred 65
Kelly, J.F. 65
Kelly, Jane 147, 174
Kelly, John 65
Kelly, John (Rev.) 65
Kelly, Mary J. 65
Kelly, Olive 143, 174
Kelly, Patrick 65
Kelly, Sophia 128, 174
Kelly, Whitfeld 65
Kelsey, Mary Jane 150, 174
Kemp,. C.T.M. 136, 173
Kendall (see Overturf, Rhoda) 84
Kendall, Elizabeth A. 141, 142, 174
Kendall, Henry 136, 158
Kendall, Ida E. 65
Kendall, Maria 148, 174
Kendall, Milton 65
Kendall, Rhoda 146, 174
Kendall, Rhoda O. 146, 174
Kendall, Stephen 136, 184
Kendrick, Edward 136, 180
Kennard, Harriet 126, 174
Kennedy, Charles 65
Kennedy, female 65
Kennedy, Jane 65
Kennedy, Jane Ann 148, 174

Kennedy, male 65
Kennedy, Milton 136, 173
Kennedy, Nancy 65
Kennedy, Peter 136, 190
Kennedy, Rezin 136, 194
Kennedy, Samuel 65
Kennedy, Thomas Henry 65
Kennedy, Warren 136, 191
Kennon, unknown (Commodore) 65
Kent, Arod 137, 192
Keogh, James 65
Keough, Elizabeth Ann 139, 174
Kephart, Charles Fenelon 65
Kepler, Mitchel 65
Kepler, Sarah A. 156, 174
Kerley, Sidney 65
Kerne, R.H. 65
Kerne, R.H. (Capt.) 65
Kerr (see Scott, Elizabeth) 96
Kerr, Ann Eliza 138, 174
Kerr, Eliza Jane 147, 174
Kerr, female 65
Kerr, Franklin C. 65
Kerr, J. Harry 137, 179
Kerr, Mary 65
Kerr, William R., Jr. 65
Ketcham, John 65
Key, male 65
Key, Philip Barton 65
Keyes, Catharine 65
Keys, John 65
Keys, male 65
Kibly, Nancy 124, 174
Kidd, Margaret J. 66
Kidd, Serena 137, 175
Kidd, Sirena 137, 175
Kiel, female 66
Kierman, John 66
Kiine (?), Henry 137, 172
Kile, Mary 149, 175
Killen, Robert L. 66
Killin, Joseph W. 137, 157
Kilmer, Washington (Dr.) 137, 164
Kilpatrick, Hugh 66
Kimball, female 66
Kimberly, Wollaston 66
Kimbro, William 137, 181
Kimbro, Wm. 137, 191
King 66
King, male 66
King, Mariah 143, 175
King, Nathaniel, Jr. 66
King, Preston (Hon.) 66
King, William R. 66
Kingsbury, Cornelia 66
Kingsbury, Francis 66
Kingsbury, Lewis B. 66
Kinney, Alfred 137, 187

Latimer, male 68
Laton, Elizabeth 131, 175
Lattimore, John 68
Lauderbach, Louisa 129, 175
Laughlin, Catharine 68
Laughlin, female 68
Laughlin, Robert 68
Laughlin, unknown 68
Laughlin, William 68
Laughlin, Wm. C. 68
Laur, George 68
Lavering, John 68
Lavery, Mary Ann 128, 175
Lawhead, Israel 137, 183
Lawrence, (Mrs.) Eliza 153, 175
Lawrence, Eliza 153, 175
Lawrence, T.B. (Col.) 137, 162
Lawson, A.W. 68
Lawson, Anastasia 127, 175
Lawson, Franklin 68
Lawson, John 68
Lawson, Manasseh M. 137, 160
Lawson, Mary J. 152, 175
Lawson, Nancy 138, 175
Lawson, T.B. 137, 190
Lawson, Thomas E. 68
Lawson, William 68
Lawson,Mary 151, 175
Lawyer, Alexander 137, 175
Lazell, female 68
Leadbetter, Rhoda 125, 175
Leak, Cordelia M. 68
Leard, James 137, 168
Leary, Dennis 68
Leasure, Mary Jane 137, 175
Lebaum, female 68
Ledbetter, Georgiana 68
Leddy, female 68
Lee, Ann 68
Lee, David W. 137, 192
Lee, Eleanor 68
Lee, male 68
Lee, Susan D. 124, 175
Lee, Thomas 68
Leet, female 68
Leet, Frank Herndon 68
Leet, M. Frank 68
Leete, Uriah 68
Legare, Davidson 68
Lehman, Joseph 138, 184
Lehmann, Caroline 68
Leiby, Alice 126, 175
Leichner, Conrad 68
Leister, Peter 68
Lene, male 68
Lenox, Lawrence 68
Leonard (see Spencer, Cordelia) 101
Leonard, Elizabeth 68

Leonard, John 138, 164
Leonard, Margaret 127, 175
Leonard, Nettie Susan 144, 176
Lester, J.J. 68
Letcher, Robert P. 68
Letz, Frederick 68
Levery, Josephine 122, 176
Levi, Joseph 69
Lewellyn, male 69
Lewis Susan 143, 176
Lewis, Alexander 138, 161
Lewis, Catherine 127, 176
Lewis, Charles 69
Lewis, Chas. B. 138, 193
Lewis, Eli 138, 189
Lewis, Emma H. 131, 176
Lewis, Francis Cotton 69
Lewis, James 69
Lewis, Jane J. 129, 176
Lewis, Jennie 129, 176
Lewis, John 69, 138, 157
Lewis, John C. 138, 168
Lewis, Josiah 138, 189
Lewis, Kesiah 127, 176
Lewis, male 69
Lewis, Margaret 125, 127, 176
Lewis, Maria 69
Lewis, Polly 154, 176
Lewis, Polty 154, 176
Lewis, Rachel 69
Lewis, Robert 69
Lewis, Samuel (Hon.) 69
Lewis, Sarah A. 136, 176
Lewis, Sarah Ann 149, 176
Lewis, Sherrod 69
Lewis, Susan 143, 176
Lewis, Thomas C. 138, 177
Lewis, W. 138, 182
Lewis, William 69
Liback, Lydia 121, 176
Lidensmith, Christian 139, 176
Liduke, Lydia 121, 176
Liggett, Jane 120, 176
Liggett, John 69
Lilly, Mary 69
Lincoln, Abraham (President) 69
Lind, Jenny 131, 176
Lindermood, George 69
Lindley, Angeline 69
Lindley, unknown 69
Lindsey, Abagail 69
Lindsey, Crissa 176
Lindsey, Orissa 124
Lindsey, Peter 138, 192
Lindsey, William 138, 170
Linly, James S. 138, 187
Linn (see Tewksbury, Sarah) 105
Linn, Ann Elizabeth 69

Lutz, Lawrence 139, 177
Lutz, Marcus 71
Lybrook, Henler 139, 185
Lyle, William 71
Lynch, Elizabeth 154, 177
Lynch, Ellen 71
Lynch, female 71
Lynch, James 71
Lynch, John 71
Lynn, Anna Neill 71
Lynn, John M. 139, 184
Lyon, Stephen 139, 175
Lyons, James 71
Lyons, Joseph 71
Lytle, Andrew, Jr. 71
Lytle, Elizabeth 71

M

M'Allen, Mary V. 142, 180
M'Call, Solomon 140, 179
M'Cartney, female 81
M'Cleves, Mary Ann 136, 180
M'Clintick, Catharine 149, 180
M'Cloud, Samuel J. 140, 192
M'Clure, Alexander 140, 184
M'Collister, Martha 81
M'Collister, Susan 135, 180
M'Colm, William L. 140, 181
M'Cormick, Ann 145, 180
M'Cormick, Ellis C. 81
M'Coy, B.F. (Dr.) 82
M'Daniel, Horatio 140, 173
M'Donald, Nathaniel W. 82
M'Donnel, Patrick 82
M'Dowel, John 140, 183
M'Dowell, James S. 141, 187
M'Dowell, Jno., Jr. 141, 157
M'Dowell, John 141, 173
M'Dowell, William 141, 162
M'Dugal, Nancy 82
M'Erlain, Mary 82
M'Fadden, Charles 141, 171
M'Farland, A.B. 82
M'Farlin, unknown 82
M'Gire, Kate 82
M'Guigan, Sarah 82
M'Guire, Jno. 82
M'Inteer, Elizah 82
M'Intosh, Jenny 141, 180
M'Intyre, Jas. 82
M'Lean, Wm. (Capt.) 9
M'Lewis, Jacob 82
M'Neel, Worthington 141, 165
M'Neil, Lydia 146, 180
M'Querk, Catherine 82
M'Vean, Chas. 82
Mabee, Edmund (Rev.) 71

Macatee, W. 139, 189
Macdonald, William 71
Mace, John (Col.) 71
Mack, Thomas B. 71
Mack, unknown 71
Mackay, male 71
Mackey, Thos. R. 139, 179
Mackley, Davis 139, 171
MacKoy, H.C. 139, 190
Mackoy, H.C. 139, 190
Mackoy, Harriet Levernia 71
MacKoy, J.L. 139, 183
Mackoy, Sallie E. 146, 177
Mackoy, Sally E. 146, 177
Macracon, John 71
Macy, Joseph 139, 179
Macy, Virgil (Hon.) 71
Maddock, Addban E. 151, 177
Maddock, Ella H. 71
Maddox, William 71
Madock, Mary J. 120, 177
Maffit, John Newland (Rev.) 71
Magee, female 71
Maguire, Thomas 71
Mahon, William 71
Mahon, Wm. 71
Mahoney, Honora 71
Mai, Theresa 151, 177
Maklem, R.S. 139, 159
Malcolm, Luzzie 126, 177
Malcom, Josefita Rais 138, 177
Mallen, Mary Ann 71
Mallin, Isabella 71
Mallin, Joseph D. 71
Mallin, Rosa 71
Mallory, William 71
Mallory, Wm. 71
Malone, Hannah 132, 177
Malone, Thomas 139, 174
Maloney, Wm. A. 139, 193
Mangen, Francis 139, 158
Manley, Geo. W. 71
Mann, Alvah (Col.) 71
Manning, Mary E. 145, 177
Manring, G.W. 71
Mansfield, male 72
Mantle, John 72
Many, Clementine 121, 177
Manypenny, Robert L. 72
Maratta, Robert Franklin 72
Maratu, Washington 139, 189
March, Mary James 130, 177
Marcy, unknown (Capt.) 72
Mardlow, unknown (Lieut.) 72
Marford, Elizabeth 140, 177
Marion, Elizabeth 72
Marker, female 72
Markham, male 72

Markin, Samuel 72
Marklin, unknown 72
Marquart, Henry 139, 176
Marsell, female 72
Marsh, David 72
Marsh, Rhoda Francis 72
Marsh, Wm. A. 139, 179
Marshall, Clinton 139, 179
Marshall, female 72
Marshall, Joseph G. (Hon.) 72
Marshall, Mollie A. 151, 177
Marshall, Thomas (Gen.) 72
Marshall, W.C. 72
Marshall, W.G. 72
Marshel, James 139, 181
Martin, female 72
Martin, Frank 72
Martin, John H. 139, 193
Martin, Lucina 134, 177
Martin, Lucy Lorette 72
Martin, Luther (Hon.) 72
Martin, M. 72
Martin, Margaret 145, 177
Martin, Mary (nee Pearl) 177
Martin, Mrs. Mary (nee Pearl) 131
Martin, Nancy 120, 177
Martin, Robert 139, 181
Martin, Sarah (nee Barnes) 72
Martin, unknown 72
Martin, W.P. 139, 192
Martz, male 72
Mason (see Kiel, female) 66
Mason, female 72
Mason, J. M. 72
Mason, John Y. 72
Mason, Stevens Thompsen 72
Massie, female 72
Massie, Henry 72
Masterson, James 139, 161
Masterson, William N. 139, 193
Mather, George 72
Mather, Wm. W. (Prof.) 72
Mathews Catharine 136, 177
Mathews, Catharine 136, 177
Mathews, Hugh H. 72
Mathews, Mary H. 148, 177
Mathews, Rebecca Jane 143, 177
Mathias, Benjamin 73
Matison, Mary 138, 177
Matlock, male 73
Matney, Thomas 73
Matson, Wm. 73
Matthews, male 73
Matthews, Phineas 73
Matthews, Rev. Joseph 139, 186
Matthews, unknown 73
Mauk, John 73
Maule, John 139, 192

Maule, Magdalene Stemshorn 73
Maule, Margaret 73
Mault, Lucina 134, 177
Maupin, Mary Eugenia 73
Maury, unknown (ex-Mayor) 73
May, Hugh 139, 189
May, male 73
May, Matthias 139, 181
Mayberry, male 73
Mayer, Judge (slave) 73
Maynard, Amanda R. 132, 177
Mayo, Edward C. 73
McAdams, Robert 73
McAndrew, Thomas 73
McArthur, Allen C. 73
McAuley, William 73
McBeth, female 73
McBrayer, female (nee Bond) 73
McBride, Edward 73
McBride, male 73
McBride, unknown 73
McCague, Mary 120, 177
McCall, Calfurnia 126, 177
McCan, Mary Ann 147, 177
McCann, Delilah 130, 177
McCann, Jennings 140, 191
McCann, Mike 73
McCarrell, James Wallace 73
McCarrell, Mary Isabelle 73
McCartey, Julia Ann 152, 177
McCarthy, Peter 73
McCarthy, Thomas 73
McCarty, Michael 140, 185
McCarty, Richard 73
McCaulsen, A. Wray 73
McCauly, Catharine 73
McCauly, Margaret 73
McCauslen, A.W. 140, 157
McCerren, Robt. (Capt.) 73
McChesney, Richard J. 73
McClain, Isabella 152, 178
McClain, James (Esq.) 73
McClary, Nancy 134, 178
McClean, Samuel 140, 174
McClellen, unknown (Capt.) 73
McClinteck, Jacob 73
McClintick, James (Sheriff) 74
McClosky, male 74
McCloud, Marie Lutisia 74
McCloud, Samuel J. 74
McCloud, Uriah 140, 185
McCloud, Vianna 74
McClure, Emmit 140, 188
McClurg, James 74
McClusky, Patrick 74
McCohaha, Amanda 141, 178
McCollister, Dorinda 74
McCollister, Harriet C. 145, 178

McCollister, Henry 74
McCollister, John Milton 74
McCollister, Maggie 74
McCollister, Thomas J. 140, 186
McColm, Caroline 156, 178
McColm, James A. 74
McColm, William 74
McColm, William S. 140, 181
McComas, J. Parker 74
McComas, Parker 74
McComb, Julia Ann 74
McComb, William 74
McConnell, Caroline R. 140, 178
McConnell, Charles L. 140, 171
McConnell, John 140, 181
McConnell, Robert 140, 177
McConnell, Thomas (Hon.) 74
McCook, Dan (Col.) 74
McCook, Daniel (Maj.) 74
McCormick, Elizabeth 121, 178
McCormick, John 74
McCowan, H.H. 74
McCown, Monroe 140, 189
McCoy, Elizabeth 130, 178
McCoy, Harriet 128, 178
McCoy, Judith 124, 178
McCoy, Lavinia 128, 178
McCoy, Virginia A. 126, 178
McCoy, William 74
McCoy, Wm. 74
McCracken, Ralph 140, 178
McCreary, James (Rev.) 74
McCulcher, John 140, 172
McCullough, unknown 74
McCullum, male 74
McCutcheon, John 74
McDaniel, Horatio 140, 173
McDaniel, Sue 149, 178
McDaniel, William 140, 171
McDaniel, Wm. 140, 171
McDermit, A.J. 140, 157
McDermott, Thos. 74
McDivill, Daniel 140, 161
McDonal, James 74
McDonald, female 74
McDonald, Martha 151, 178
McDonald, Nancy 132, 178
McDonald, W.D. 140, 180
McDonald, Wm. 74
McDonnold, Solomon 74
McDonough, John 74
McDougal, James 140, 158
McDougal, James O. 140, 158
McDougal, male 74
McDowell, Eliza 74
McDowell, Joseph J. 140, 162
McDowell, Wm. 74
McDowell, Wm. (Esq.) 140, 160

McDuffie, George (Gen.) 75
McElhinney, John 140, 183
McElroy, J. Newton (Lt.Col.) 140, 189
McElroy, Mary Ann 75
McElroy, R.A. 75
McElroy, Thomas 75
McElvaine, Joseph 75
McEntee, Thomas 140, 185
McFann, Andrew J., Jr. 75
McFarland, A.B. 75
McFarland, Rachel 75
McFarlin, James S. 75
McFaun, A.J. 140, 157
McGee, Effa 139, 178
McGilligan, Hannah 75
McGinnis, John 75
McGintey, Martin 75
McGinty, Martin 75
McGlone, Frances 134, 178
McGough, M. 140, 172
McGowan, Jno. 75
McGrady, I.V. 75
McGraw, Archibald 75
McGuire, Elizabeth 147, 178
McHale, female 75
McIntire, Daniel 140, 174
McIntire, Davis 75
McIntire, James 75
McIntire, Samuel 75
McIntosh, male 75
McIntyre, Henry (Lieut.) 75
McKay, Alexander 75
McKay, Daniel 75
McKay, James J. 75
McKean, Andrew 75
McKean, Wm. (Capt.) 75
McKee, Amos 75
McKee, Arthur 75
McKee, David 75
McKee, Melisla 155, 178
McKenzie, Ann 153, 178
McKenzie, male 75
McKey, Samuel 140, 172
McKinney, L. B. 75
McKinney, male 75
McKinney, William 75
McKinney, William J. 75
McLaughlin, John 75
McLaughlin, Levi 75
McLean, female 135, 178
McLean, male 75
McLean, Samuey 140, 174
McLeland, male 75
McLellan, Andrew 75
McLellan, Moses (Capt.) 75
McLure, D.A. 75
McMahon, James 75
McManmes, Angeline 119, 178

McManus, Edward 76
McMeekin, Martha 144, 178
McMelan, Wm. 76
McMicken, unknown (Col.) 76
McMullen, Jane 76
McMullen, male 76
McMullen, unknown 76
McNabb, Robt. (Rev.) 76
McNairin, Joseph 76
McNairn 137, 178
McNairn, Eliza R. 76
McNairn, Mary 137, 178
McNally, Thomas (Dr.) 76
McNamer, James 140, 192
McNeal Lydia 146, 178
McNeal, A., Jr. 76
McNeal, Lydia 146, 178
McNeal, Mary Ann 151, 152, 178
McNeal, Washington 76
McNeil, Elizabeth 76
McNulty, female 76
McNulty, female (nee Arnold) 76
McNulty, John 76
McNutt, Harriet 124, 178
McQuality, Eliza 129, 178
McQuillin, Samuel 140, 183
McRoberts, Samuel (Hon.) 76
McVey, Jane Andrews 76
McVey, Nathaniel W. 76
McVey, William (Col.) 76
McWhirt, George 76
Meach, Robert 76
Meacham, Charles A. 141, 185
Meacham, Chas. A. 141, 185
Meacham, Eliza 76
Meacham, James 141, 194
Mead, Eleanor 148, 178
Mead, Elizabeth 131, 178
Mead, Martha Ann 121, 178
Meakley, Martha A. 138, 178
Meaney, Margaret 76
Means, Esther E. 76
Means, female 76
Means, James W. 76
Means, Jeannie 126, 178
Means, Mary A. 119, 178
Medary, Kate 121, 178
Medary, Samuel (ex-Gov.) 76
Medary, Samuel A. 141, 165
Medill, William (ex-Gov.) 76
Meek, William 141, 190
Meek, Wm. 141, 190
Meeker, Jacob 76
Meeker, male 76
Meigs (see Forsythe, Clara) 46
Meigs, Jno. R. (Lieut.) 76
Melcher, George Henry 76
Melcher, James Johnson 76

Melcher, Joseph C. 76
Menager, female (Mrs.) 146, 178
Menager, Mary 76
Mercer, Henry 76
Merret, James A. (Dr.) 141, 160
Merrill, Addison 77
Merrill, Adison 77
Merrill, John 77
Merrill, John B. 77
Merrill, John P. 141, 179
Merrill, Maria 143, 178, 179
Merriman 77
Merriman, Henry 77
Merrit, F. 77
Merritt, Elizabeth 77
Merritt, Enos 77
Merritt, Libbie 137, 179
Merritt, Tom 77
Mershon, Henry Sr. 77
Mershon, Henry, Sr. 77
Messenger, Henry C. (Capt.) 77
Messenger, W. 77
Messer, Charles 141, 164
Messing, Joseph 141, 173
Metcalf, Benjamin (Hon.) 77
Metcalf, Caroline 138, 179
Metcalf, F.J. 141, 166
Metcalf, Frances Adelia 77
Metcalf, J.F. 77
Metcalf, male 77
Metcalf, unknown (ex-Gov.) 77
Metz, John 141, 185
Meyer, J.S. 141, 174
Meyer, Rosa 77
Meyle, Augustus 77
Meyle, unknown 77
Meynter, male 77
Michaels, female 77
Mick, Sally 148, 179
Middleton, male 77
Mikel, A.E. 141, 182
Milam, unknown (Col.) 77
Miles, Benjamin R. 141, 169
Miles, John 77
Miles, Lucy E. 149, 179
Miles, Sally 77
Milford, William 77
Miller, A.P. (Dr.) 141, 165
Miller, Abraham 77
Miller, Abraham M. 77
Miller, Ann E. 135, 179
Miller, Carlton 77
Miller, Charles S. 77
Miller, child 77
Miller, Elizabeth 147, 179
Miller, female 77
Miller, Francis 77
Miller, George W. 77, 141, 168

Miller, Harriet 156, 179
Miller, Harvey 77
Miller, Horace 77
Miller, Horace (Capt.) 78
Miller, J.S. 141, 188
Miller, Jesse 78
Miller, John 78, 141, 183
Miller, John G. 78
Miller, John W. 78
Miller, Lydia 78
Miller, Margaret 143, 152, 179
Miller, Maria 122, 179
Miller, Michael 78
Miller, Parmelia Ann 78
Miller, Peter 78
Miller, Samuel 141, 193
Miller, Sarah J. 141, 179
Miller, William A. 78
Miller, William H. 141, 166
Miller, Wm. 78
Millham, John S. 78
Mills, Edward H. 78
Mills, James 141, 188
Mills, male 78
Millson, Eli 78
Milton, unknown 78
Mims, Mary A. 127, 179
Miner, Henry A. 141, 178
Miner, John L. 141, 194
Minford, Mary 78
Minford, Robert J. 141, 170
Mink, John 78
Misner, Eliza Jane 78
Mitchel (see Fitzgerald, female) 46
Mitchel, John 78
Mitchel, R.A. 141, 179
Mitchell, Amasia 78
Mitchell, Angeline 145, 179
Mitchell, David 141, 180
Mitchell, Desire 78
Mitchell, Edmund 78
Mitchell, Henry 78
Mitchell, I.S. 141, 162
Mitchell, John 78
Mitchell, John W. 78
Mitchell, Misa 78
Mitchell, Sarah A. 146, 179
Mitchell, Susan 78
Mitchell, unknown 78
Mitchell, unknown (Gen.) 78
Mitchell, William S. 141, 180
Molen, unknown (Capt.) 78
Mollier, female 78
Molma, Don Felipe 78
Monahan, William 78
Monck, unknown (Capt. 78
Mongomery, Mary 126, 179
Monk, male 78

Monroe, Daniel B. 78
Monroe, Elizabeth 123, 179
Monroe, G.B. 79
Montague, unknown (Lieut.) 79
Montgomery (see Myers, Sarah E.) 81
Montgomery, C.P. (Cath. Priest) 79
Montgomery, Elis 141, 162
Montgomery, Homer 141, 193
Montgomery, Joseph S. 79
Montgomery, male 79
Montgomery, Mary 126, 179
Montgomery, Mary Ann 121, 179
Montgomery, Rebecca 79
Montgomery, Robert 141, 176
Montgomery, Sarah 134, 143, 179
Moodie, Jackson 79
Moodie, Nicholas 79
Moody, Nancy 79
Moor, David 79
Moore (see _____, female) 15
Moore, Amanual 141, 165
Moore, Amanuel 141, 165
Moore, Anna Laura 79
Moore, Davis P. 141, 142, 174
Moore, Ebenezer F. 142, 185
Moore, Elizabeth F. 139, 179
Moore, Emma 79
Moore, female 139, 179
Moore, H. 79
Moore, H.A. 79
Moore, Hannah 79
Moore, James H. (Dr.) 79
Moore, Joel 142, 185
Moore, John 79, 142, 193
Moore, John O. 142, 157
Moore, Joseph W. 79
Moore, Julia A. 141, 179
Moore, Letitia 119, 179
Moore, Levi 79, 142, 165
Moore, Levina 79
Moore, Loy N. 142, 165
Moore, Maria 140, 179
Moore, Mary 125, 179
Moore, Milton 79
Moore, Orpha 139, 179
Moore, Oscar F. (Esq.) 142
Moore, Oscar F.(Esq.) 186
Moore, Samuel 79
Moore, Samuel G. 142, 160
Moore, Sarah 139, 179
Moore, Thomas 79
Moore, William 79
Moore, William R. 142, 181
Moran, J. 79
Moran, James 79
Moran, Jas. 79
Moran, Margaret P. 132, 179
More, Philip 142, 187

Murphy, Patrick 81
Murphy, Reas 142, 190
Murphy, unknown (Gen.) 81
Murray 143, 164
Murray, D.N. 142, 193
Murray, female 81
Murray, Harriett Ardelia 81
Murray, Harriett Ardella 81
Murray, John 81
Murray, John E. 81
Murray, Newton (Capt.) 142, 191
Murray, P.H. 143, 164
Murrell, John A. 81
Murrey, (slave of, Tom) 81
Murril, Asa 143, 172
Musser, James 143, 180
Musser, John 143, 175
Musser, Joseph T. 143, 181
Musser, Patience 81
Musser, Wm. 143, 189
Mussey, Frank 81
Mussey, Mary Lucretia 81
Myers, A.N. 143, 179
Myers, Allen 143, 161
Myers, Bartley J. 81
Myers, Bartly J. 81
Myers, John 81
Myers, Joseph 143, 165
Myers, male 81, 143, 165
Myers, Samuel 143, 168
Myers, Sarah E. 81
Myers, unknown 81
Myres, female 81

N

Nagle, Philepena 121, 180
Nagler, Leonard 82
Nail, H. 82
Nail, Rachael 135, 180
Nall, Albert G. 143, 186
Nall, John D. 143, 187
Nash, William H. 143, 167
Nash, Wm. H. 143, 167
Nathaway, unknown 82
Natthews, unknown 82
Neagle, Caroline 131, 180
Neal, John C. 143, 167
Nearl, Julia Ann 150, 180
Neel, Hudson 143, 167
Neil, Lucy 126, 180
Neili, Barbary 135, 180
Neill, William 82
Nelson 82
Nelson, Anderson 143, 177
Nelson, Emily 82
Nelson, John 82
Nelson, Joseph Washington 82

Nelson, Raleigh 82
Nelson, Simon 82
Nesbit, male 82
Neuanburger, Mary 82
Neudoerfer, Margaret 82
Neve 156, 180
Neve, Jane 156, 180
Newcomb, Susan 156, 180
Newell, L.W. 143, 191
Newland, (Rev.) 82
Newland, William 143, 176
Newman, Annie M. 147, 180
Newman, Catherine 82
Newman, Henry Carpenter 82
Newman, male 82
Newson, Robert 82
Newton, Cynthia 82
Newton, Isaac 82
Newton, Jas. (Capt.) 143, 161
Newton, Nancy G. (nee Bell) 83
Nibit, Soloman 83
Nichol, S.P. 143, 169
Nicholr, Samuel 83
Nichols, Catherine 144, 180
Nichols, female 83
Nichols, Gifford Gore 143, 165
Nichols, H.M. 83
Nichols, Helen 154, 180
Nichols, Hellen 154, 180
Nichols, J.B. 143, 178, 179
Nichols, Samuel P. 143, 169
Nichols, Thomas 83
Nichols, unknown 83
Nicholson, Carrie C. 119, 180
Nickells, Clara 83
Nickols, Clarence Ivey 83
Nigh, Michael 83
Nigh, Reese 83
Nixon, male 143, 170
Nixon, Rachel Ann 119, 180
Nixon, Rachel E. 142, 180
Nixon, Samuel 143, 160
Noble, (ex-Gov.) 83
Noel, Aaron T. 143, 188
Noel, Caroline 153, 180
Noel, Catherine Ann 83
Noel, David 143, 179
Noel, Ellen 131, 181
Noel, Ezra H. 143, 158
Noel, Francis Volney 143, 173
Noel, Harriet (nee Oldfield) 83
Noel, Jacob 83
Noel, John 83
Noel, John F. 143, 174
Noel, John P. 143, 183
Noel, John W. (Hon.) 83
Noel, Josiah O. 143, 168
Noel, male 83

Ous, Elizabeth J. 124, 181
Ovaton, male 84
Overturf, Rhoda 84
Oviatt, Benjamin F. 144, 159
Owen, Eliziannah 84
Owen, Mary 84
Owen, Samuel 84
Owens, Evan C. (Mayor) 144, 193
Owens, John 85
Owens, Richard 85
Owns, Erasmus 144, 183
Owster, James 85

P

Paden, Angeline C. 85
Page, Hannah A. 155, 182
Page, John C. 144, 174, 175
Page, T.N. (Major) 85
Paige, Barney R. 85
Paine, unknown 85
Paine, Wm. V. (Dr.) 85
Painer, Barbara 148, 182
Painer, John 144, 191
Palmer, male 85
Palmer, Roswell E. 144, 163
Palmer, Rozwell E. 144, 163
Pancake, Harvey 144, 173
Parish, female 85
Parish, Orris 85
Parke (see Cartner, female) 28
Parke, John B. 85
Parker, Elizabeth D. 85
Parker, Elizabeth D. (nee Bockwalter) 85
Parker, H.H. 144, 159
Parker, H.W. 144, 165
Parker, Isabella A. 149, 182
Parker, Lavisa F. 128, 182
Parker, male 85
Parker, N.H. 144, 159, 191
Parker, Richard 85
Parker, Samuel C. (Rev.) 85
Parker, Tamar 85
Parker, Theodore (Rev.) 85
Parker, unknown 85
Parker, Walker 85
Parker, Willie 85
Parkinson, William 144, 185
Parks, Beverly 85
Parl, Bazil 144, 171
Parman, Charles 144, 187
Parnell, Hester 131, 182
Parnell, John W. 85
Parratt, Alfred A. 85
Parrs, Anna G. 126, 182
Parshley, Elizabeth 144, 182
Parsons, John K. 144, 176
Parsons, male 85

Parsons, unknown (Dr.) 85
Partingale, James M. 144, 158
Partloe, George 85
Partlow, Julia Ann 124, 182
Partridge, Alden (Capt.) 86
Patch, female 86
Paterson, female 86
Paterson, unknown 86
Paton, James Downey 86
Patrick, Sarah A. 145, 182
Patten, female 86
Patten, Lucy 121, 182
Patterson, Augusta 86
Patterson, Caroline 86
Patterson, Galbreth 144, 158
Patterson, Horace 86
Patterson, Joseph S. 144, 164
Patterson, Linton A. 86
Patterson, Mores J. 144, 178
Patterson, R. (Col.) 86
Patton, Abner 144, 173
Patton, Catharine 86
Patton, Ellen 126, 182
Patton, John 86
Patton, Joseph 144, 173
Patton, Samuel 144, 180
Paul, H.H. 145, 167
Paxton, C.W. 141, 182
Paxton, Lottie H. 150, 182
Paxton, Michael 86
Payne, Bette F. 135, 182
Payne, Edmond 145, 177
Payne, Hiram 145, 166
Payne, John (Gen.) 86
Payne, Joshua (Rev.) 86
Payne, male (ex-Gov.) 86
Payne, Woodford 86
Peabody, Charles H. 86
Pearce (or Pearch), Elgar B. 145
Pearce (or Pearon), Alex. 145, 192
Pearce, Elgar B. 86, 175
Pearce, unknown 86
Pearch (see Pearce, Elgar B.) 145
Pearch, Elgar B. 145, 175
Pearl (see Martin, Mary) 131, 177
Pearon, (or Pearce), Alex. 192
Pearon, Alex. 145, 192
Pearson, (Dr.) 145, 185
Pearson, male 86
Peatling, Edward 145, 191
Peatling, Edward C. 86
Peck, D.W. 145, 169
Peck, George 86
Peck, Margaret 86
Peck, Mary Cotlin 86
Peck, Mary Emma 86
Peck, Myron H. 86
Peck, W.V., Jr. 145, 178

Powell, Sarah 146, 183
Powell, Silas D. 145, 146, 167
Powell, William Byrd 146, 179
Powers, Archey 146, 172
Powers, Catharine 132, 183
Powers, Hannah V. 143, 183
Powers, L.G. 88
Powers, Martha Jane 155, 183
Powers, Mary Jane 155, 183
Powers, Mary Margaret 141, 183
Powers, Minerva A. 121, 183
Powers, Sarah Jane 133, 183
Powlhill, unknown (Lieut.) 88
Poynter, James Lucien 88
Pratent, Adaline 88
Prather, Alice 88
Prather, Ann Oleivia 88
Prather, female 88
Prather, Mary O. 88
Prather, Silas D. (Corp.) 88
Prather, Thomas 88
Prather, unknown 88
Prather, Wilson 88
Pratling, Elizabeth 139, 183
Pratt, E.P. (Rev.) 146, 177
Pratt, Lucy 153, 183
Pratt, Mary E. 139, 183
Pratt, Rev. E. P. 146, 177
Prentice 88
Prentice, Eliza Ann 126, 183
Prentice, unknown 88
Prescott, female 88
Prescott, Harriet 140, 183
Prescott, O.G. (Dr.) 88
Prescott, Wm. H. 88
Pressel, Daniel W. 146, 191
Pretchard, unknown 88
Prettyman, William Jameson 88
Price 88
Price, David 88
Price, Elizabeth 88, 140, 183
Price, Isaac 146, 160
Price, John (Judge) 88
Price, Lavina E. 138, 183
Price, Levina 138, 183
Price, Maria 136, 183
Price, Mary J. 155, 183
Price, Rebecca 123, 183
Price, Sam'l 88
Price, unknown (Col.) 88
Price, Vinton 146, 159
Price, Willie 88
Priggs, Isaac 146, 176
Pritchard, male 89
Proctor, Elizabeth 140, 183
Pry, Daniel (Priv.) 89
Pry, Henry 89
Puffet, William 89

Pugh, George 146, 168
Pugh, George E. (Hon.) 146, 161
Pugh, male 89
Punch, Theophilus 146, 171
Purdam, E. 89
Purdham, Warner W. 146, 180
Purdom, Eliza 89
Purdom, W.W. 146, 178
Purdum, Eliza 89
Purdum, John W. 146, 183
Purdum, W.W. 146, 178
Pursell, Emma Loretta 89
Pursell, James 89, 146, 189
Pursell, Thomas J. 146, 188
Pursell, Thos. J. 146, 188
Putland, Edward 146, 192
Putrill, Cynthia 131, 183
Pye, female 89
Pyles, Peter 89

Q

Quant, Frank 146, 170
Quartz, S.B. 89
Querry, female 89
Quick, Jacob 89
Quigley, Ann Eliza 89
Quigley, Catherine 89
Quinn, Francis 89
Quirk, James 89

R

Rabbe, John Augustus 89
Rachel, female 89
Rachel, male 89
Rachel, unknown 89
Radcliff (see Purdom, Eliza) 89
Radcliff, Davis E. 146, 183
Radcliff, Isham Perry 89
Radcliff, Thomas Jefferson 89
Radcliff, unknown (Lieut.) 89
Radcliffe, Wm. 89
Rader, Wm. 89
Rader, Wm. S. 89
Radford, Isaac 89
Ragan, Eliza F. 124, 183
Ragin, J.M. 89
Raglan, (Field Marshal) (Lord) 89
Railman, Elizabeth 89
Rainey, George T. 89
Rainey, John C. 89
Rains, female 89
Rains, James A. 146, 166
Ralston, male 89
Ralston, unknown 89
Ramsey, David, Jr. 146, 169
Ramsey, Ethalinda 130, 183
Ramsey, Mary Jane 147, 183

Scott, Nancy 96
Scott, Perry 149, 160
Scott, Samuel (Col.) 96
Scott, Thomas Winter 96
Scott, unknown 96
Scott, Uriah B. 149, 176
Scott, William C. (Judge) 96
Scott, Winfield 96
Scriptures, Sarah 145, 186
Seal, George 96
Seal, unknown 96
Seaman, Margaret 96
Searl, Mary R. 142, 186
Sears, male 96
Seavens, Joel 96
Seaver, male 96
Secoy, unknown 97
Secrist, female 97
Sedgwick, unknown (Maj.Gen.) 97
Seeberger, Hannah 135, 186
Seeberger, hannah 186
Seeberger, Henry 149, 188
Seele, male 97
Seeley (see Willard, Lavinia S.) 4
Seeley (see Willard, Lavinia) 132, 193
Seeley, Uri (Esq.) 4
Seidenbach, L. 97
Seifurt, Adam 97
Selby, William 149, 187
Selders, Cordella 153, 186
Selfridge, Chester W. 149, 179
Selfridge, E.C. 97
Sellers, George 97
Senate, male 97
Senegiger, Mary 125, 186
Sergeant, John (Hon.) 97
Seward, female 97
Sexton, John 149, 183
Seymour, J.W. 97
Shackleford, Daniel 97
Shackleford, Hattie 97
Shackleford, John 97
Shackleford, male 97
Shackleford, Sam. 97
Shackleford, Wm. 97
Shafer, Samuel 149, 193
Shaffels, Jas. 97
Shaffer, Joseph 97
Shaffer, Rosanna 155, 186
Shaffer, unknown 97
Shakes, John 97
Shambert, I. 97
Shane, George 97
Shannon, Charles 149, 168
Shannon, Hugh 97
Shannon, John 149, 167
Shannon, Patrick 97
Shannon, Thomas (Hon.) 97

Shape, John 97
Sharp, female 97
Sharp, G. 97
Sharp, George W. 97
Sharp, Mary 137, 186
Shatel, Mary 119, 186
Shaw, Emily 97
Shaw, George W. (Capt.) 97
Shaw, Hannah 97
Shaw, James 149, 194
Shaw, John 149, 172
Shaw, Tristam 97
Shawley, William 97
Shawney, male 97
Shea, Patrick 97
Shearer, P.S. 97
Sheckler, male 98
Shed, John 98
Shedd, J.H. (Rev.) 149, 165
Sheeler, Michael 149, 193
Sheeley, Jacob 98
Sheely, Elizabeth 98
Sheets, John 149, 182
Shelby, Isaac (Hon.) 98
Sheldon, Thomas C. 98
Sheldon, unknown 98
Shelleig (see Vance, Elizabeth) 108
Shellieg (see McCollister, Maggie) 74
Shellieg, Elizabeth 153, 186
Shellieg, Maggie 140, 186
Shellieg, Mary Jane 98
Shellige, Mary 98
Shelling, Elizabeth 153, 186
Shelly, Isaac 98
Shelpman, Cornelius (Esq.) 149, 175
Shelten, Elizabeth A. 124, 186
Shelton, Elizabeth A. 124, 186
Shelton, Thomas 7, 8
Shenk, Andrew J. 98
Shepard, Charles C. 98
Shepard, Eliza J. 130, 186
Shepard, Hezekiah 98
Shephard 180
Shephard, (or Shepherd) Alexander 180
Shephard, (or Shepherd), Alexander 149
Shephard, Alexander 149, 180
Shephard, Charlton 149, 166
Shepherd, female 98
Shepherd, L.E. 149, 173
Shepherd, William 98
Sheppard, unknown 98
Sheppard, Wm. B. 98
Sherer, Joseph 98
Sherfey, Caroline A. 147, 186
Sheridan, David (Rev.) 98
Sheridan, John 98
Sherman, Alba 149, 189
Sherman, Elizabeth 155, 186

Sherman, unknown 98
Sherman, unknown (Capt.) 98
Sherman, unknown (Col.) 98
Sherrard, James 98
Shewell, Edward 98
Shiddell, male 98
Shields, Jno. 98
Shields, Laura 98
Shields, Michael 98
Shields, Theodore F. 98
Shinn, Charles Samuel 98
Shinn, F. 98
Shinn, Francis 98
Shinn, Francis A.G. 98
Shinn, George 98
Shipman, Hannah 98
Shipman, William J. 149, 160
Shipman, Wm. J. 149, 160
Shipp, female 98
Shiras, William 149, 185
Shirley, unknown 98
Shivengton, Barney 149, 171
Shockey, Samantha 145, 186
Shoemaker, Samuel 149, 189
Shoenberger, Peter (Dr.) 98
Short, Daniel 98
Short, Elizabeth N. 126, 186
Short, James H. 149, 163
Short; James Harvey 149, 163
Short, Josiah M. 98
Short, male 98, 99
Shoub, Henry A. 149, 188
Shoubertz, Peter 99
Shoup, female 99
Shred, Rosen 122, 186
Shred, Rosina 122, 186
Shriner, Daniel F. 149, 193
Shrivel, unknown 99
Shrum, Samuel 99
Shufflin, Edward G. 149, 158
Shuflin, Martha 124, 125, 186
Shultz, John 99
Shump, H.C. (Lieut.) 149, 158
Shupe, Abigail 122, 186
Shupe, Cynthia A. 150, 186
Shute, J.G. 149, 175
Shute, Olive A. 123, 187
Shy, Albrin Brisco 99
Sidner, Samel 99
Sigourney, Lydia H. 99
Sigsby, Christian 99
Sigsby, Christiana 99
Sikes, Sarah 121, 187
Sikes, unknown 99
Sill, Eytge 99
Sill, Joshua W. (Gen.) 99
Sill, Mary 137, 187
Sill, Richard (Esq.) 99

Silliman, Benjamin, Sr. (Prof.) 99
Sillough, William 149, 166
Silver, Stephen W. 99
Simcox, Wm. 149, 174
Simley, Catharine 144, 187
Simmons, Augustus 149, 178
Simmons, Catherine 123, 187
Simmons, Francis 149, 176
Simon, unknown (Capt.) 99
Simonson, Matilda 134, 187
Simonton, unknown 99
Simpson, C.W. 150, 172
Simpson, Mary 99
Simpson, Willie 99
Sims, Mary Jane 99
Sims, Robert 150, 164
Sinton 153, 187
Sinton, Artemisia 153, 187
Skeen, Josiah K. 99
Skelton, Cynthia 135, 187
Skimmer, Mary A. 136, 187
Slack, Mary Ellen 130, 187
Slack, William J. 150, 167
Slagle, David W. 99
Slaney (see Smith, Jane) 100
Slattery, Jane C. 153, 187
Slaughter, Richard C. 150, 174
Slavens, Wm. 99
Sleigh, male 99
Slimp, Alfred 150, 162
Sloan, Geo. W. 150, 175
Sloan, George W. 150, 175
Sloan, Jonathan (Hon.) 99
Sloan, Peter 150, 175
Sloane, Jas. 99
Sloat, John 150, 184
Sloat, Mary E. 123, 187
Sloat_all, Mary E. 123, 187
Slocomb, George L. 99
Slocum, Cyrus 99
Slocum, Sarah Ann 99
Slocumb, Clarissa 130, 187
Slone, P.P. 150, 175
Slusser, J.A 99
Sly, Joseph 150, 180
Sly, M.G. Tully Cicero 150, 186
Sly, Marthy Ann 138, 187
Sly, Samuel 150, 160
Sly, unknown 99
Smallwood, Wm. (Rev.) 150, 166
Smart, William 99
Smedley, Isaac F. 150, 188
Smiley, Polly 99
Smiley, Walter 99
Smith (see Iliffe, Alice) 61
Smith, A.L. (Judge) 99
Smith, Agnes 149, 187
Smith, Allen 99

Sprangler, Isaac (Dr.) 101
Spriggs, Benjamin F. 151, 165
Spring, Wm. O. 101
Springer, Calphurnia M. 149, 188
Sproat, John 101
Sprouse, Elizabeth 142, 188
Spry, Frances 133, 188
Spry, John Henry 101
Spry, John W. 151, 164
Spry, Thomasin H. 146, 188
Spurck (see Berry, Amelia) 20
Squires, Antionette 125, 188
Squires, Elizabeth 131, 188
Squires, John 101, 102
St. Arnaud, Marshal 102
St. Peter, Joseph 102
St. Williams, male 102
Stacey, Byran 102
Stacy, Joseph 102
Stafford, male 102
Stage, Garret 102
Stains, Mary 141, 188
Staley, Stephen 151, 168
Stall, Agnes 102
Stallcup, John 102
Stallman, Frederick 151, 169
Stamford, George 102
Stanbury, unknown (Dr.) 102
Stanley, Abigail 128, 188
Stanly, Susan 154, 188
Stapler, Mary B. 148, 188
Stapleton 145, 188
Stapleton, male 102
Stapleton, Mary 145, 188
Star, E. 102
Starkum, Aaron 151, 190
Starkweather, Ella 102
Starkweather, female 102
Start, William 102
Stedman, Charles J. 102
Steece, M.J. 120, 188
Steele, John 102
Steen, James G. 151, 157
Steen, james G. 151
Steenbergen, Sarah M. 125, 188
Steene, Nancy 153, 188
Stein, male 102
Stemshorn, Harry 102
Stemshorn, Henry 151, 166
Stemshorn, Magdalene 102
Stemshorn, Magdaline 133, 188
Stentemann, Barbara 134, 188
Stentzmann, Barbara 134, 188
Stephens, male 102
Stephenson, Joseph 6, 151, 158
Stephenson, Mary C. 102
Stephenson, Rachel 102
Stepheson, Mary Ann 145, 188

Stepleton, Nancy 146, 188
Stepleton, Wm. 151, 170
Stetson, male 102
Stevens, Calvin J. 151, 184
Stevens, Cyrus Martin 8, 102
Stevens, George H. 151, 160
Stevens, Harrison 102
Stevens, Hon. A. 102
Stevens, John 102
Stevens, male 102
Stevenson, Annie Emeline 135, 188
Stevenson, Canzada 141, 188
Stevenson, Edward O. 102
Stevenson, female 102
Stevenson, Harriet A. 127, 188
Stevenson, Richard (Capt.) 102
Stevenson, Sarah 140, 188
Stewart, Agnes 130, 188
Stewart, Arch V. 151, 177
Stewart, Charles W. 102
Stewart, Elizabeth J. 130, 188
Stewart, female 102
Stewart, Fletcher 102
Stewart, Flora A. 124, 188
Stewart, Hugh D. 151, 160
Stewart, J.H. 102
Stewart, John 151, 193
Stewart, John L. 151, 178
Stewart, Mildred E. 102
Stewart, Walter P. 102
Stewart, William 103
Stickney, male 103
Stigler, Joseph 103
Stillwell, Mattie L. 128, 188
Stillwell, Wm. 103
Stilwell, Adeline Louisa 103
Stimp, Celia 145, 188
Stimpson, Rodney M. 151, 173
Stiner, Peter 151, 157
Stinton, Mary E. 128, 188
Stockham, Aaron 151, 164
Stockham, Samuel 151, 175
Stockwell, D.C. 103
Stockwell, unknown (Ensign) 103
Stoeker, male (Rev.) 4
Stokely, Mary 133, 188
Stone, A.P. (Hon.) 103
Stone, Chloeette 103
Stone, Ethan 103
Stone, John 103
Stone, Lucy 121, 188
Stone, Oliver B. 103
Stone, Sarah C. 143, 188
Stone, Washington 151, 171
Stonebaker, Joseph A. 151, 164
Stonebraker, Joseph A. 151, 164
Stoner, William 151, 177
Stonhill, Sarah 149, 188

Vance, Elizabeth 108
Vance, Jerome B. 153, 186
Vance, John 153, 189
Vance, Miles W. 153, 167
Vance, Nancy 144, 191
Vance, unknown (ex-Gov.) 108
Vanden, Joanna 146, 191
Vanderberg, Jas. 108
Vandwater, female 108
Vandwort, James 153, 167
Vanhorn, Bernard 108
Vanmeter, female 108
Vanmetre, Ann 136, 191
Vann, David (Capt.) 108
Vanscoy, Nelson 153, 186
Varner, C.M. 108
Varner, Charles S. 108
Varner, John 153, 180
Varner, Mary J. 127, 191
Varner, Sarah C. 131, 191
Vasmeter, Joseph 153, 168
Vaughan, male 108
Vaughn, Wm. 153, 192
Vaughters, John A. 153, 160
Vaughters, Wm. 153, 160
Vaustavoren, Wm. 108
Veach, Elizabeth 147, 191
Veach, Mary 138, 191
Veach, Sylvester 108
Veach, Wm. (Esq.) 153, 193
Venn, Aplona 121, 191
Vermillion, Ratliff 153, 157
Vermillion, T.B. 153, 187
Vernon, Salena 143, 191
Verplanck, female 108
Vessall, Nancy 140, 191
Vickers, Margaret I. 130, 191
Vickers, Margaret J. 130, 191
Vickery, male 108
Victor, Orsville J. 153, 168
Vigus, Benjamin F. 108
Vigus, Franklin 108
Vigus, George Oscar 108
Vigus, Hannah C. 129, 191
Vigus, Rachel 108
Vigus, Sylvester Warren 108
Vildabee, female 108
Vildabee, unknown 108, 109
Vincent, Joseph T. 153, 183
Vining, Sarabell 150, 191
Vinton, Romain M. 148, 191
Violet, Sam'l. B. (Esq.) 153, 187
Violet, Samuel B. 153, 187
Violet, Samuel B. (Esq.) 153, 187
Virgin, Kinsey 153, 194
Voglesong, William (Dr.) 109
Voglesong, Wm. (Dr.) 109
Voglesong, Wm. G. (M.D.) 153, 184

Vollanvaider, Augustine 148, 191
Voorhes, Abraham 109
Voorhes, Eliza Ann 109
Voorhies, Mary E. 133, 191
Vorex, Rachael 137, 191
Vorhees, Garrett 109

W

Wade, Jacob F. 154, 184
Wadleigh, male 109
Wado, John W. 109
Wadsworth, Adna A. 109
Wadsworth, unknown (Gen.) 109
Waggaman, Geo. A. (Hon.) 109
Waggener, Chas. P. 109
Waggoner, D. 109
Wainright, unknown (Bishop) 109
Wainsley, John A. 154, 187
Wainwright, (Bishop) 109
Wait (see Llocumb, P.S.) 119, 176
Wait (see Wyeth, Isabella) 116
Wait, Asa 109
Wait, Belle 156, 191
Wait, Melissa 123, 191
Wait, O. 133, 191
Waits, George 154, 177
Wakeman 109
Wakeman, Jennie C. 136, 191
Wakeman, Margaret 109
Walderen, B. 109
Waldo, Jehoil 154, 176
Wales, Jonathan 109
Walke, Anthony (Hon.) 109
Walker, David M. 154, 164
Walker, Elizabeth 121, 147, 191, 192
Walker, Geo. Paul 154, 180
Walker, George P. 154, 180
Walker, Hannah 137, 192
Walker, John W. 109
Walker, Margaret 154, 192
Walker, Old Mother 109
Walker, P. Frances 144, 192
Walker, Perilla F. 144, 192
Walker, Samuel 109
Walker, Thomas 154, 192
Walker, Thomas D. 154, 189
Walker, William 109
Walker, William (Rev.) 109
Wall, Alexander A. 109
Wall, Wm. (Maj.) 109
Wallace (or Wallis), Philip 109
Wallace, J.W. 154, 163
Wallace, John 109
Wallace, Nancy A. 140, 192
Wallbright, Christian 154, 166
Waller (see Cleveland, Margaret) 31
Waller, Robert 154, 173

Withers, Evalne 147, 194
Withers, George 115
Withers, unknown 115
Witherspoon, Alexander S. 115
Wolcott, Henry 156, 184
Wolfard, Mary 128, 194
Wolfe, Adolf (Corporal) 115
Wolfe, Henry F. (Sergeant) 115
Wolfe, Wm. V. 115
Wollom, Margaret 141, 194
Womeldorff, Daniel L. 156, 180
Wonderly, unknown 115
Wood, Benjamin 115
Wood, Emily 115
Wood, F.H. 135, 194
Wood, Fanny A. 145, 194
Wood, French 115
Wood, Gilbert J. 115
Wood, Phineas T. 115
Wood, Phoeba 142, 194
Wood, Robert 156, 182
Wood, William 115
Wood, Wilson 115
Woodall, John R. 115
Woodbridge, Dudley Henry 115
Woodbury, male 115
Woodford, Seth 115
Woodhouse, female 115
Woodruff, Jane Ann 125, 194
Woodruff, Nancy 124, 194
Woods, female 115
Woods, John 115
Woods, unknown 115
Woodside, Wm. J. 156, 174
Woodward, E.W. 156, 179
Woolsey, female 115
Worcester, Joseph 115
Worcester, S.H. 156, 158
Worcester, Samuel H. 156, 158
Work, Charles D. 115
Work, F.C. 115
Work, Felicity C. 115
Work, unknown 115
Workman, Mary A. 115
Worley, Sylvester T. 156, 172
Worley, W.C. 156, 193
Wormster, Sarah 130, 194
Worthington, Augustine (Dr.) 156, 168
Worthington, female 115
Worthington, James 156, 167
Worthington, James Chaytor 115
Worthington, James Chaytor (M.D.) 115
Worthington, James, Jr. 156, 167
Worthington, Nancy 119, 194
Worthington, Thomas 115
Worthington, unknown (Lieut.) 115
Worthington, William D. 115
Woster, Adam 116

Wouge, unknown 116
Wright 137, 194
Wright, Agust J. 116
Wright, Anna Rebecca 122, 194
Wright, Charles H. 156, 193
Wright, Dilla 148, 194
Wright, John C. 156, 185
Wright, male 116
Wright, Mary 141, 194
Wright, Presley 156, 184
Wright, R. Jennings 116
Wright, Salina 137, 194
Wright, unknown 116
Wright, unknown (Dr.) 116
Wroten, Nathan 116
Wyckoff, Cornelius 116
Wyckoff, John 156, 178
Wyeth, Isabella 116
Wyeth, Walter N. 156, 191
Wyeth, Walter N. (Rev.) 156, 191
Wymer, female 116
Wymer, Martha E. 127, 194
Wynn, Isaac C. 156, 190
Wynn, William H. 116

Y

Yale, Benjamin (Dr.) 116
Yates, R.W. 116
Yaunot, Charles 116
Yeager, Cornelius H. 156, 173
Yeager, Fanny L. 135, 194
Yeaman, Samuel Hempstead 116
Yeamons, Elisa Ann 119, 194
Yearning, Sarah 135, 194
Yeates, or Lates, Adelaide 124, 194
Yeates, or Lates, Sarah 129, 194
Yeley, James W. 156, 176
Yellow Wolf 116
Yemens, Susannah 136, 194
Yerger, Peter 116
Yoakem, Catherine 116
Yoakley, Susan R. 116
Yokiam, Caroline 116
Yokiam, Drucilla 116
Yokiam, Harriet R. 116
Yokiam, Nancy Ellen 116
Yokiam, Susanna 116
Yost, unknown 116
Young (see Glidden, female) 51
Young, Alex. (Rev.) 116
Young, Daniel 116
Young, David 116
Young, Eliza 153, 194
Young, Eliza E. 131, 194
Young, Fanny Belle 136, 194
Young, female 116
Young, Henderson (Hon.) 116